Hengest, Gwrtheyrn
and the Chronology
of Post-Roman Britain

ALSO BY FLINT F. JOHNSON

Evidence of Arthur: Fixing the Legendary King in Factual Place and Time (McFarland, 2014)

Origins of Arthurian Romances: Early Sources for the Legends of Tristan, the Grail and the Abduction of the Queen (McFarland, 2012)

Hengest, Gwrtheyrn and the Chronology of Post-Roman Britain

Flint F. Johnson

McFarland & Company, Inc., Publishers
Jefferson, North Carolina

LIBRARY OF CONGRESS CATALOGUING-IN-PUBLICATION DATA

Johnson, Flint.
Hengest, Gwrtheyrn and the chronology of post–Roman Britain / Flint F. Johnson.
  p.   cm.
Includes bibliographical references and index.

ISBN 978-0-7864-7819-4 (softcover : acid free paper) ∞
ISBN 978-1-4766-1338-3 (ebook)

1. Great Britain—History—Anglo-Saxon period, 449–1066.
2. Hengist, King of Kent, –488.   3. Vortigern, active 450.   I. Title.
DA152.J67 2014   942.01'4—dc23   2014001592

BRITISH LIBRARY CATALOGUING DATA ARE AVAILABLE

© 2014 Flint F. Johnson. All rights reserved

No part of this book may be reproduced or transmitted in any form or by any means, electronic or mechanical, including photocopying or recording, or by any information storage and retrieval system, without permission in writing from the publisher.

On the cover: "The Treaty of Peace Between the Saxon Leaders and the British King," *John Cassell's Illustrated History of England Vol. 1* (London: Cassell Petter & Galpin, 1865), 24

Manufactured in the United States of America

McFarland & Company, Inc., Publishers
Box 611, Jefferson, North Carolina 28640
www.mcfarlandpub.com

Table of Contents

Preface 1
Abbreviations 2
Introduction to the Source Material 3

1. The Traditional History of Britain: 350–700 9
2. The Primary Sources 16
3. The Secondary Sources 35
4. Guessing Date Ranges 47
5. Saints and Nobility in the Sources 54
6. Reconstructed British History 59
7. Reconstructed Anglo-Saxon History 66
8. The Kentish Source 74
9. Ansehis, Hengest and the Kentish Line 82
10. Gwrtheyrn, Vortigern and Outigern 86
11. Ambrosius and Guitolin 93
12. The Fifth Century 96
13. A Reevaluation of Key Post-Roman Figures 100
14. Applying Lesser Figures to the New Framework 104
15. Pertinent Facts Drawn from the Primary Sources 106
16. Celtic Genealogies and Date-Guessing 131
17. Germanic Genealogies and Date-Guessing 144
18. Pertinent Facts Drawn from the Secondary Sources 153
19. Chief Interactive Peoples 165
20. The Revised Celtic Genealogies 183

21. The Revised Germanic Genealogies 198
22. The Ecclesiastics 201
23. The Other Figures and a Sequence of Historical Events 202
24. The Heroic Age in Britain 207
25. The Age of Saints 210
26. Conclusion 213

Appendix 215
Chapter Notes 231
Bibliography 243
Index 253

Preface

In researching and writing *Origins of Arthurian Romances* (2012) I came upon some intriguing questions that bore closer scrutiny but were not a direct part of the subject matter.

In examining Gildas' chronological sequence, I realized that there was no place for Gwrtheyrn and, by extension, the Kentish foundation legend that dominates thinking about post–Roman Britain. In fact, eliminating the characters that were a part of that document seemed to open up the entire fifth century for examination.

In my basic readings for my thesis, I had also come upon several of Dr. Molly Miller's writings. It seemed to me that she had a brilliant approach to genealogies, and had come to some well-reasoned conclusions with several dynasties. And it struck me: What if I applied her approach to all of the dynasties? The first part of this book is a response to the former of these revelations; the second, a reaction to the latter.

This volume was originally intended to be two different books, combined at the request of the publisher. It has worked out for the better, however. Putting the two together avoided taking a purely deconstructionist approach to the period in this book, and has instead allowed me to explain the problem and then begin to find a solution. For that I am grateful.

This was the last book I researched between drafts of my thesis. And, while I have never had the benefit of an academic looking over the work, I still find myself in debt to several scholars. Dr. Bromwich's patience and guidance fortunately permeated several lines of thought; I will miss her. Professor Caie's guidance and support encouraged me to continue pursuing the project, despite my many setbacks. Professor Clyde Smith's advice and fascination with academic writing provided a fertile ground for my studies. Marina's inspiration has been refreshing and energizing. Mr. Warren has given the gift of mental discipline. Mr. Schleh's ability to see the world through a child's eyes of wonder made him an excellent role model. Ms. Klein's invaluable editing has helped me to avoid several pitfalls. Of course, any that remain are of my own doing.

I would like to dedicate this book to Jack Mozena, Gloria Boerio, and the crew of the Countyline Goodwill. Thanks for your support as I have written all three Arthurian books.

Abbreviations

Anglo-Saxon England .... ASE
Britannia .... Brit
Bulletin of the Board of Celtic Studies .... BBCS
Cambridge/Cambrian Medieval Celtic Studies .... CMCS
Classical Quarterly .... CQ
English History Review .... EHR
Étude Celtique .... EC
Irish Historical Society .... IHS
Journal of Theological Studies .... JTS
Modern Language Notes .... MLN
Proceedings of the British Academy .... PBA
Studia Celtica .... SC
Transactions of the Cumberland and Westmoreland
   Antiquarian and Archaeological Society .... TCWAAS
Transactions of the Dumfriesshire and Galloway Natural
   History and Antiquarian Society .... TDGNHAS
Transactions of the Honourable Society of the Cymmrodorion ..... THSC
Transactions of the Royal Historical Society .... TRHS
Welsh History Review .... WHR

Introduction to the Source Material

In 1800, the study of modern history accepted all "historians" of the past as honest recorders of the facts, with no personal interest in what they wrote. It was believed that events occurring before the historians' lifetimes were recorded honestly as well, and then passed on to the present day with an equal degree of accuracy. Thus most if not all of recorded history had been written by firsthand witnesses, and because of this it was entirely reliable.

Keeping this in mind, there were only two difficulties in studying British history. The first was the limited knowledge the surviving sources contained. The second was in making a consistent whole of what had survived. As Geoffrey was the only writer to give context to the post–Roman period, his work formed the canvas upon which the details of the other source materials were placed. To a more limited and less obvious degree, he continues to do so. Gildas and *Historia Brittonum* were the core of that history. Gildas laid out a sequence of events from the last century of Roman rule and the first century of independence. *Historia Brittonum* added details to the story and expanded the scope with information about the formation of Gwynedd and British politics after Gildas' lifetime. Other sources were similarly invaluable in the areas and time-frames their interests encompassed.

However, as the twentieth century approached and emerged, studies into the sources of the above historians and their own biases took the fore in the exploration of post–Roman history. Soon it was learned that the earlier extant sources were written by monks but heavily influenced either by their kings or by the political climate they had been a part of. It was discovered, too, that they were based on materials kept in monasteries. Accepting these realizations meant that the ancient historians, whose writings had been counted as sources of the most reliable information, were seen as fallible. Every person who wrote history had specific reasons for collecting and preserving the information he spoke of. Further, those intentions could be deduced by the work that was produced, the timing of the writing, and the treatment of the events and persons that were recorded. What was left out was often equally important. Occasionally, these materials contained information that was entirely false but had no apparent connection with the motivations of the writer. These were probably the biases of the writers' sources.

Geoffrey of Monmouth was a unique historian of his age, making no attempt to be accurate in his work. Piggott's look at Geoffrey revealed his whimsical techniques,[1] and the subsequent work of Tatlock only confirmed it by documenting every instance where the events of his contemporary world had influenced him.[2] Geoffrey had randomly organized historical and pseudo-historical information into a coherent whole, filling in the missing data with events, names, and places from his own time. His *Historia Regum Britanniae* was designed to ingratiate him with the more powerful men of contemporary England and to win himself a position among them. The themes he created were entirely of his own making, designed for the sole purpose of catering to the whims of his would-be benefactors.

In fact, we have learned that all the people under study here had a unique agenda. Without a doubt, we cannot be certain we know all the biases of our earliest sources. This fact is a formidable obstacle in advancing our understanding of the period. A perfect picture of post–Roman life in Britain may never be reconstructed, and we might never know if we had formed one.

The advances and revelations that have occurred over the past thirty-five years have truly opened the eyes of those who study the field, making British history more diverse and multi-dimensional than any scholar of 1800 could have imagined. They have taken the straightforward sources of the period and revealed many different layers of information and bias. The sources upon which historians have traditionally relied do not contain the information they purport to have. More frightening, they have revealed that we may never know everything about any of our sources. Our innocence is shattered, and an age of skepticism and overcaution has naturally followed. Sources have often been entirely discounted because their full background has not been revealed, or because the origin of one passage has been proven entirely untrustworthy. One composite history has been entirely thrown out as a source for the period by some because it was written for political reasons.[3]

However, the same problems of incomplete information are present in the study of any ancient culture. Take, for instance, Egypt, where the only absolute chronology was a calendar based on the 1460-year cycle of the star Sirius. At that interval, the star rises just before the sun in the morning, making it an accurate measurement of time over centuries. Unfortunately, no extant Egyptian source was active for any one full cycle and because of this, none can be considered reliable in dating events to the year.

Instead, any student of ancient Egypt is forced to rely on other historians. The first historical writings come from the Ptolemaic annalist Menethos. He poses four significant problems to the study of early Egyptian history. The first is that he did not make use of Egypt's Sirius calendar, and therefore had no means of accurately placing the events and pharaohs of Egyptian history that were remote in his time. Second, he was active in the third century before the Common Era; he was writing some three millennia after the first events he recorded. Third, it is known that he far preceded those historians who followed him. By the time the next extant historian took to writing about ancient Egypt, so many centuries had passed that Menethos' words were taken as those of a firsthand observer.

Finally, Menethos' work hardly lends itself to credibility. There is no indication in his history that he may have accessed primary historical materials.[4] What we know of his background suggests that whatever historical information he had access to was manipulated; Menethos wrote for a Greek pharaoh whose interests are known to have been political in nature.[5] It should also be noted that the names of several pharaohs are to be found on stellae throughout the region that are not to be found in his "complete" history of Egypt. These are overwhelming difficulties in any study of his work. In fact, any post–Roman British historian with the same issues would be considered entirely unreliable.

On the other hand, Menethos matches up amazingly well with an overwhelming amount of archaeological evidence. His writing spans two full cycles of Sirius, and both are placed accurately in his history.[6] Even in the modern era, his work has been successfully used as the broad canvas of ancient Egyptian history. No British source can make any similar claims.

However, British studies has several advantages over Egyptian. First, the lag between events recorded and the historians who wrote about them is considerably smaller than between the first historical Egyptian events and the lifetime of Menethos. Second, intensive research over the last few decades has revealed much about the authors' biases and sources. Finally, we have at least two entirely independent and relatively early historical (as opposed to Egypt's annalistic) sources from which to construct a history. It has also been seen that there are a rather sizeable number of sources for the period, even if they must be treated more carefully. The unfortunate aspect of British history is that there is no overwhelming amount of obelisks, pyramids, or other archaeological evidence that could be used to support the data given in the written sources of the period. As a result, the early historians of Britain have been largely discounted. This is unfortunate, and with recent advances in our understanding of the sources themselves, the author believes it is no longer a necessary state of affairs.

The situation and solution is something akin to what a scientist studying history would experience. In the twentieth century, such an individual would consider it absolutely necessary to have and make use of only entirely accurate information in order to study his topic, just as he would strive for in science. He would, of course, be disappointed and unable to make any headway.

In the twenty-first century, we have learned there are no absolutes even in the more mathematical fields. For instance, one of the venerable facts of physics was that the speed of light was a constant. Now we know it may be increased or decreased by factors such as gravity. Science is a fluid study, and must remain so for our understanding of the universe to continue developing.

A social scientist is forced to deal with this fact at a more basic level. Whereas a scientist has a reliable guide as to which aspect of each experiment is verifiable, the social scientist does not. The first task of any historian is to sift through the sources and determine where bias, political or financial necessity, or lack of information has rendered information invalid. The more sources that can be studied, the wider the possible range of perspectives and sources. The process is more difficult and, even with a finite amount of materials, more time-consuming. However, it is both practical and worthwhile.[7]

The thrust of any historical topic, then, should necessarily be to derive a method for mining the secondary sources for reliable information as thoroughly and with as much efficiency as possible. In my *Origins of Arthurian Romance*, a method was proposed and its viability demonstrated in reconstructing the probable historical origins for three "Arthurian" stories, devolved as they were into romance form. That methodology was:

1. Determine all pertinent sources on the given topic, regardless of chronological or geographical distance from the location of the event and/or persons involved and the manner in which the information is presented. Even a romance may contain valuable and unique information that can be refined or better understood through more traditional sources.
2. For each extant source, gather as much information as possible. Learn as much about its date and location, the author or editor, and any potential biases it might contain.
3. Determine as much about the sources of the extant record as possible; this includes its date of creation, location, author, biases, and the original state of the information.

4. Determine the amount of time each source spent in an oral state, and how historical the verifiable information is. If the information that can be crosschecked is accurate or may well be truthful based on the available data, that which cannot be checked but would give the author or his patron no foreseeable benefits may be considered potentially accurate information as well.
5. Go through each of its sources, determining where there is and is not a perceivable reason for bending facts. This process must be conducted on an individual basis within each source. An untrustworthy source may still have valid information to give, while even a devoted historian might have allowed his own philosophies to influence his perception of events.

Once this task is accomplished, the usability of the raw data may be determined, laid out, and applied accordingly. Once all sources and their data have been collated on a topic according to their strengths and weaknesses, a reassessment of conflicting sources normally bears out a clear resolution. There is almost always a reason why a source or sources might have had access to more or less accurate materials, or why it might have chosen to portray the pertinent details in an alternate manner. At that point, the most reasonable answer, given the materials at hand, becomes apparent.

The primary question posed in this book is simple: What can be learned of the legendary figures Hengest, Horsa, and Gwrtheyrn and how does our improved understanding of them alter our view of post–Roman Britain? The three figures dominate the early and mid–fifth centuries, so that an understanding of them and the materials behind their legend seems vital to any reconstruction of early British history. In the pages following, the author will begin by going over the accepted and received accounts of late Roman and fifth-century Britain as it was held before the scholarly revolution of the 1970s dismantled it.

The overview is followed by two chapters devoted to all relevant period sources, which examines by the methodology laid out above. The newly scrutinized materials will then be deployed in discussing the nature of the British and Germanic peoples in the fifth century. Focus will be on the state Britain was in during the years around 410 specifically. This will include chronology, continuation of British *romanitas*, local government, and factors involved in the rise of kingship. Conclusions found there will help to determine how the latter three individuals may have interacted.

In the following chapter, attention is on Germanic groups migrating into Britain throughout the Roman period, and their ability to retain their ethnicity. Their chronology and the reasons surrounding the rise of Germanic kingship is discussed as well.

The collective information accumulated in these studies bears out several items contrary to traditional thinking. There were Germanic tribes in Britain before the traditional migration of Hengest and Horsa in 449, and they retained their culture. There is no evidence suggesting that Britain was united during most of the fifth century. Kent was not home to the most powerful Germanic rulers until well into the sixth century. In short, the first few chapters show there is no historical context for the legend of Gwrtheyrn and Hengest. There is no support for the contention that Britain was controlled by a single person after 410. There is no evidence that the Germanic peoples *began* settling in Britain during the fifth century. This does not mean that Gwrtheyrn and Hengest could not have existed and held the same positions as history has assigned them. It also does not mean that the legendary invasion did not occur as Gildas and Bede tell us, only that all these items need to undergo a good deal of scrutiny before such statements may be held as valid again.

The work above shows that a story contained in three of our earliest sources is ahistorical. Such a result suggests that a deeper look into them and their common story is called for. Why would three seemingly independent sources have recorded the same false history? The examination will show that they derived their information from a common source, and that it was created by Kent for the purpose of establishing its political preeminence over the other kingdoms in Britain. More intensive study of the sources which used it determines that it was created at some time just before or after about 600. This realization in turn makes Hengest and Gwrtheryn's contemporaneity unnecessary. This means they may be studied separately, without the chronological and geographical limitations that have traditionally accompanied any study of them together.

A discussion of Hengest demonstrates that he may have been a man of the fourth century, a mythical founder of Kent, or a historical figure transplanted in literature to the Kentish pedigree. Regardless, he has no bearing on the historical Kentish house or any reconstructable history of early Britain, and is of no further use as a historical figure in this study. Gwrtheyrn, on the other hand, is shown through genealogy and associations with other historical individuals to be a man of the mid–sixth century. This work also demonstrates that one and possibly two oral legends produced different variations of his character that also found their way into *Historia Brittonum*, though by different means of transmission. Intriguingly, each character has been given entirely different personalities and historical responsibilities.

With the accepted wisdom about post–Roman Britain thrown on its ear, the window is open for a new approach. First, all the information drawn from the discussions laid out above is used as raw materials in an attempt to construct a new, rough outline of Britain's history and relative chronology from the mid–fifth century to the end of the seventh. If done properly, the process alone should provide a firm foundation for future research in this area.

Second, an attempt is made to determine the relative birth years of as many significant figures from the period as possible. Genealogies, known associations to other historical figures as well as absolute and relative years as they have been verified, are employed in the effort. Note that when dealing with relative (as opposed to specific) chronologies I've used an x to indicate range, e.g., Inabwy (515x565), indicates he was born between 515 and 565, whereas a dash would suggest birth and death years. The results should open new doors for the understanding of post–Roman Britain. The effort also provides some background for the later medieval history of the British Isles. Such, at least, are the aspirations of this author.

It should be noted again that the chapters to follow are purely theoretical, without any attempt made to draw firm conclusions. A deconstructionist historian would have little trouble in pointing out potential flaws in the model proposed above based on holes in our current understanding of the period and the manner by which the sources have been preserved. That said, our current level of knowledge is all we have, and therefore using it and a good deal of legwork provides the best possible means of approaching the problem at this time. Much of the specific knowledge used and determined below may well be inaccurate, but the methodology is sound. Regardless of the means by which future enhancements to our grasp of this era are made, any future scholar wishing to tackle the same problem would do well to approach it in like manner.

1

The Traditional History of Britain: 350–700

Of all the provinces of Rome, the history of late Roman Britain is unique. Unlike their counterparts on the continent, the Picts and free Britons of the border areas had no interest in Romanization, and regularly raided as deeply into Roman territory as possible. Those under imperial authority, though they spoke Latin and thrived under Roman economy and culture, still lived on an island that made them citizens of the most isolated province in the empire. Because of these three factors, the island was the most likely Roman province to produce rebellions and would-be emperors. This had been a problem from the beginning of the Roman occupation, and it was a difficulty that was only exacerbated in the Western Roman Empire's last couple of centuries of existence as its political stability slowly fell apart.

In 350, what can be considered the beginning of the end of Roman Britain was put into motion. In that year a Briton general named Magnentius was proclaimed emperor of the Western Empire by his soldiers and marched on Rome to make good on his claim. Successful in defeating and killing his predecessor, he was eventually killed by the emperor of the Eastern Empire, Constantius. This left Constantius the ruler of a reunited Roman Empire.

One of his first acts was to punish Britain as the home of his late rival. All individuals suspected of collusion with Magnentius were arrested and had their property confiscated. His actions affected a significant number of the wealthiest Romano-Britons. The result was that the aristocracy of Britain was decimated, the economy shaken, and the citizens who were left began to lose faith in the Roman Empire's ability to rule.

This faltering may be seen in the development of religion on the island. By 400, Augustine and those who preceded him believed that each individual bore the crime of original sin, and that it was only through the grace of God that the burden might be overcome. This meant that any good works done of our free will meant nothing; God had already predestined our fates. Arriving in Rome around 400, the Briton Pelagius immediately set about preaching the concept of free will, that the fate of our souls was determined by our actions and thoughts. His philosophy was banned and declared heretical. Pelagians were hunted down throughout the empire. St. Germanus journeyed to Britain as late as the mid–fourth century to stamp it out.[1] And yet, it could not be eliminated. Eventually, Pelagianism became so much a part of the Britons' approach to Christianity that its deviance from the Roman doctrine was forgotten. Gildas' papers contain Pelagian work over a century later,[2] even though Britain's best writer had no direct knowledge of Pelagianism.[3]

Political reality played a large part in the Britons' loss of awe in Rome as well. The role of the government in Britain diminished from 350 on. The region it was able to administer gradually shrunk, and the traditional method of protecting its citizens there proved to be ineffective. In place of political organization, two independent military commands were formed: the Count of the Saxon Shore was set up along the southeast coast, while the Dux Brittanorum was established to strengthen Hadrian's Wall. These measures proved inadequate as well. Though raids on the island tapered off, shipping was pirated as it crossed the English Channel by the Germanic people. Because of raiding successes, communications and long-range trade to the Continent ebbed significantly throughout the fourth century.[4] The resulting isolation made Britain easier to attack than any other province.

In 360, 364, and 367, raids by the Irish, Picts, and Anglo-Saxons caused a panic in Britain, and the province begged Rome for help. In each case, a senior general was assigned to Britain to restore order. The last man called was Theodosius. Legend has it that he successfully restored order and then set up Roman buffer states. These would later become four northern British kingdoms. He also began the process of dividing Britain into smaller provinces for the purpose of easier defense.

His solution did not resolve the problem, however. Another attack occurred in 383, this time a full-scale invasion by Germanic tribes, Irish, and Picts. Another general, Maximus, was ordered to resolve the issue. He was largely successful, and is remembered in British lore as a savior.

Shortly after Maximus had dispatched the foreign raiders and restored order, his troops elected him their emperor. Maximus accepted the imperial purple and left for the Continent to claim his title in Rome. The medieval British believed that he took most of the best remaining troops on the island with him. And when he was assassinated in 388, his Briton troops were assimilated into the victorious Roman army.

In 407, insurrection began again on the island. Over the course of several months, three men were elected emperor by the Roman army there. The first two were deposed and murdered when they refused to march on Rome. The last was Constantine. He took an army to the continent in 409, but was killed by his lieutenant, Gerontius. His troops never returned to Britain either.

Popular history now has it that the Britons overthrew Constantine's government, and again submitted themselves to Rome as a respectful province. But between the time of the rebellion and the overthrow of Constantine's government, Rome had been sacked in 410. Emperor Honorius was more concerned with stabilizing Italy than sending a bureaucracy to faraway and troublesome Britain. In response to their request, he told the British to look to their own defenses. Left alone, Britain did what it could. It came under attack from the north, west, and east, and some of its inhabitants were taken away to be slaves.[5]

Roman culture lasted for some time after 410, though it likely was not the common culture for long. By the middle of the century, those who had been trained in Latin under Rome were elderly by the standards of the day. Their children would have had no idea what life under the Romans had been like, and the teachers would have become scarce after the government had been superseded by the military in the middle of the fourth century. Without the superstructure of Roman government there was no means of perpetuating its culture after 410.

In its place, British forms of government emerged almost immediately. Some local aristocrats such as Ambrosius and Vortigern managed to transfer their land wealth into gold and war bands. In other cases, military leaders quit the army once it was no longer receiving money from the Continent and used their troops to enforce a local rule over the villages. In both cases, income was easily supplemented by raiding villages outside their area of control. In time, the war bands would be employed much as modern mafia bosses use their men to control their territories. Medieval society was beginning to take shape.

With a degree of stability in the new governments, the need to institutionalize what had happened would have been next. In this, the traditional bards became essential. They made for excellent entertainers as they told stories of the hall's heroes and compared them to famous warriors. Just as important, bards began rewriting political history. They exalted whichever king they served and associated him with legendary warriors and kings of the past.

In about 425 a mysterious figure named Vortigern somehow emerged as the head of the island of Britain. In time he was confronted with attacks by the Picts, Irish, and Anglo-Saxons. In response, he hired Anglo-Saxons to protect his eastern coast while he concentrated on the Irish and the Picts. He settled his mercenaries in Thanet at around 449. Their leaders were Hengest and Horsa.

A relatively small number of warriors turned the initial attacks back. Hengest and Horsa convinced Vortigern that more men would do an even better job of defending the island. Vortigern acquiesced. Soon there were many Anglo-Saxon warriors, enough so that the raiders coming from the east posed no threat whatsoever. By this time, Vortigern could no longer feed all of them. He told Hengest so, but the Anglo-Saxon delayed sending any of the warriors home. With excuses and lies, Hengest bought himself enough time to build up his forces. When he was ready, he overran what is now England and established himself as king there.

With Vortigern's power wiped away, Hengest then returned to Kent, and there established his own dynasty. Other chieftains migrated in and claimed the remainder of the decimated lands for themselves. They continued to attack and expand their territories into the British lands wherever and whenever opportunity arose. In all their expansion, the Germanic peoples were as much racially driven in their motives as any nineteenth-century country.

Eventually, the Germanic peoples reached a point where expansion into British territories was no longer as easy as competing against themselves. This change of circumstance initiated the infighting that characterized Germanic politics. During the course of the fifth, sixth, and seventh centuries, the now hundreds of Germanic settlements competed with each other for the finite resources they had access to. Slowly, the many groups eliminated themselves and grew larger until all that was left were the kingdoms of Northumbria, Mercia, Wessex, Essex, Sussex, East Anglia, and Kent. By that time, the question of which culture group would eventually possess all of Britain had been answered. The Germanic people controlled those regions that were the most productive in Britain, and this helped them to develop a denser population. Now that they had formed large, stable kingdoms, the sparsely populated British remnants had no real chance of taking back their land.

In the meantime, when Hengest attacked Vortigern, the former over-king fell back to Wales. There his downward spiral gained momentum. His son successfully fought against further incursions by the Germanic peoples, but his premature death negated all of his successes. St. Germanus officially stripped Vortigern of his lands by excommunicating him. Vortigern's own daughter bore his child. In the end, Ambrosius led an army against him. He pushed Vortigern back to his own castle and burned it down.

The damage Vortigern caused to the British people was accomplished long before he was dead, however. In 453, the Romano-British wrote to Ætius in Gaul and begged for aid against the Germanic incursions. In that year, however, Ætius was too involved with bringing Gaul back under the Roman banner to worry about the even more distant Britain. He was unable to send any aid. Eventually, Ambrosius rose up to national prominence (perhaps as a result of his defeat of Vortigern?). It was he who organized the Britons and fought against the invaders. Finally, at Badon he or possibly Arthur put an end to their advance for over a generation.

Victory over the Anglo-Saxons could not put everything to rights again, though. The Britons had begun to fragment into kingdoms after the demise of Vortigern, and not even the successes of Ambrosius were enough to stop the process. Soon the rulers of these new kingdoms became comfortable with their peace over the invaders; they began to practice infighting, taking part in endless wars that seem to have accomplished nothing. When their true enemy, the Germanic peoples, began to turn their attention back to the Britons during the very late sixth century, the Britons were no match for them. Northumbria conquered all of Scotland at one point, and was able to assimilate Cumberland permanently. Concurrently, the Mercians made strong incursions into Wales, and the West Saxons pushed into Cornwall. At that point, the end of the British culture was a mere formality and the continued existence of their kingdoms was largely dependent on the political landscape of the Germanic peoples.

Our most consistent evidence for all the kingdoms during this period is the genealogies, which provide us not only with family trees but often continuous lines of rulers for the entire period under study here. These begin fortuitously at the end of the fourth century, right when the Romans left the island. The pedigrees are extremely valuable because royal records were considered sacred by ancient peoples; it was widely believed that to alter one in any way was tantamount to sacrilege. Even more useful for the historian, it is well known from Herodotus that each generation lasted a little over three decades, and three generations covered about a century. Because of this fact, we can be fairly certain in dating the figures we hear of in other sources.

Such is a history as could have been written anytime before Professor Alcock wrote his invaluable book *Arthur's Britain* in 1971.[6] However, the history as laid out in the pages above is littered with problems. Alcock can be considered the first to begin the process of pointing out flaws in the received history, but many scholars have followed and expanded upon his efforts. At present, modern scholarship's difficulties with the above views could be better described as overwhelming issues. To point out only the most obvious, more recent archaeology has shown that mercenary Germanic tribes were in Britain long before 449, and were allowed to retain their cultural identity from no later than the end of the fourth century.[7] As Britain was repeatedly left without her regular defenses from that point on, the mercenaries took on the duties of defending the populace throughout Britain. This was especially true in the southeast where the Germanic attacks were most potent.

The established history has it that Hengest existed in the mid–fifth century, spent years undermining the authority of the ruler of the island and opened the way for all of England to be overrun by his people, then quietly settled down in Kent and did nothing but produce an heir. Such seems an odd biography; surely a man willing to do so much to keep himself in Britain and able to organize so many of his continental kinsmen against a common foe would have taken full advantage of the vacuum his efforts had created and at least attempted to create his own empire on the island. On the other hand, Hengest has no context in the fifth century. Most archaeologists have accepted a date earlier than 449 for the Germanic invasion based on the materials they have unearthed. Some have gone as far back as the late fourth century. There is, too, the fact that Hengest and his brother's name both mean "horse," which implies they were either literary creations or mythological beings. Perhaps Hengest was borrowed from a continental tale to be found buried in a manuscript of *Beowulf* known as *The Battle of Finnburg*. There, the nature of the story would have explained that politics was the reason why he came to Britain. Borrowing the name of a continental figure would have given him and by extension the Germanic people in Britain a connection to the mainland. Then again, maybe Hengest is nothing more than a symbol for those first tribal immigrants who came into Britain. As far as the history of Britain is concerned, it does not matter.

Tradition has it that post–Roman Germanic settlement began in Kent, but in reality it was East Anglia.[8] In fact, Hadrian's Wall along with the eastern coast down to Kent and west again were all settled by the Germanic peoples before or shortly after 410. So much of the history that has been passed on to us seems to place Kent in a stronger light than is historically and archaeologically viable. That fact is a point of concern. This is especially so when it is remembered that Kent was the first Germanic kingdom in Britain to be able to write its own history, and that it was for a good fifty years a dominant power on the island after that point. To be candid, it had the means and undoubtedly the motive to rewrite the history of it people to its own advantage while it was the dominant Germanic influence on the island. Kent had the longevity and the papal authority to make its claims stick.

Badon is said by Gildas to have stopped all Germanic incursions for the forty-three years between his birth and the time of his writing. The truth is, there is no such lapse in the historical or archaeological record. No decade seems to have been without its warring. The *Anglo-Saxon Chronicle*, a history written under some of Gildas' influence, states that battles were fought consistently between the newcomers and the Britons throughout the fifth and sixth centuries. Archaeology shows a consistent pattern of expanding Germanic settlements during this period as well. It will be seen in the chapters below that the decades immediately following the most likely time-span for Badon are the most likely period for the formation of many Germanic polities into the first kingships.

The consistent fragmentation of the British kingdoms from the moment Rome abandoned the island also seems contrary to what is known. Our most complete knowledge of any one area comes from Gwynedd, a kingdom traditionally founded by Cunedda and his many sons. His progeny would go on to rule several regions within the kingdom. Detailed studies by Dr. Miller have eliminated most of the original rulers as sons of Cunedda.[9] This means that Gwynedd probably began the period as several kingdoms, and that they were slowly absorbed into one through conquest and marriage. The regional families would have been tied to the ruling family genealogically only later, and for purely political reasons.[10]

It is intriguing that legend claims the one kingdom we know anything about developed the same way as has been claimed for all the British peoples, and yet intensive study has revealed a reality that is entirely contrary to our model for the British kingdoms. Or perhaps it is a suggestion. Given that Gwynedd represents our only reliable information on the development of the British kingdoms, it seems much more likely that most British kingdoms began small and only gradually gained size.

The theory that kingships developed before 410 in both cultures is also not necessary. Certainly, the British and Germanic kingdoms we know of nearly all have pedigrees stretching back into the fourth century. However, the pedigrees themselves are hardly believable. Much of the time, the founders of these royal lines are gods such as Beli or Woden. Occasionally a British lineage will start with the Roman general Maximus, or his daughter. Inevitably, these impossible founders are followed by a number of now unknown or nearly forgotten figures before they arrive at historical persons to be found in Bede and like sources. Of the individuals found between these two points of whom anything can be determined, only a couple might have been a part of the lineage they have been assigned. This suggests that none of the other gray figures were ever members of the pedigrees they are connected to. If the known persons are any indication, they were found in myth and legend, and added to give the lineages more moral and/or political weight.

Even more telling, it is clear from associations of date and contemporary persons made within the pedigrees that they were created by people who worked under the assumption of three generations to a century as stated by Herodotus and contrary to what has been learned of royal families in early medieval Britain and elsewhere. This allowed the British to extend their dynasties to the Roman past, and the Anglo-Saxon families to go back to the post–Hengest era.

Connecting families to the earliest possible time frame allowed the competing kingdoms to jockey for superior claims as their armies fought to rule over all the other kingdoms in Britain. Secondarily, it gave them a primacy no upstart family could hope to claim. However, it must be remembered at all times that for persons named before the historical era these pedigrees are present for nothing but appearance.

There is no credibility before that point, and in fact there are no external records that confirm most British kingdoms until much later on. Gwynedd may have been active as early as the middle of the fifth century, but the records support the last decades of the fifth century for the other British kingdoms. Gildas confirms this in his *historia*, too.[11] Among the Germanic peoples, there is no historical or archaeological record that suggests any kingship before the mid–sixth century.[12]

Examination of Gildas' tirade has also demonstrated that secular Latinity survived well into the sixth century,[13] and he and several continental examples are evidence that there were private schools that provided appropriate education until then.[14] The very manner in which Gildas' letter was constructed shows that the Roman legal system was still functioning in his childhood, if only on a local level.[15] Heroic ideals may have been the *modus operandi* at the highest levels of society, but Christianity would have its Age of Saints, and towns were able to function on an administrative level with some degree of Roman efficiency at this time.[16] Roman culture did not dissipate immediately after 410; instead, it survived in the structure of local governments.

There was no cultural hatred between the four races in Britain, either. The leaders of the developing Germanic and British societies fought their neighbors regardless of their language or historical background. The Irish only invaded Britain because the island was politically weak and was therefore an easier target than any kingdoms in Ireland. The Picts fought all three of the other culture groups with equal tenacity. There is no evidence in the literary record of any specific hatred of other cultures during the fifth or sixth centuries. Enemies were enemies regardless of the gods they worshipped, the weapons they used, or the language they spoke. The entire modern concept of ethnic-based hatred in early Britain is based on the *De Excidio Britanniae* by Gildas, who saw the Germanic, Irish, and Pictish peoples as instruments of God and his righteous destruction.[17] The fact is that Gildas despised those people who made the lives of the British churchmen harder; he did not necessarily care if they were from different culture-groups. It should be noted that Vorteporix, one of the kings he writes against and hopes to reform, was likely Irish.[18] Yet Gildas did not even mention that fact as he listed the flaws in his person. Vorteporix's origins were unimportant to Gildas. One may also recall that the idea of nationalism comes from the nineteenth century, the very period in which the study of British history can truly be said to begin. It seems only proper that the first modern historians would have added their personal biases to a period that has been so influential to the development of English history.

The sources themselves have come under scrutiny since 1970. Historical scholarship in Britain, one might say, has come out of its infancy. No source is now above suspicion, and the biases and limitations of each must be carefully scrutinized before being used. In this, literary as well as pseudo-historical and historical documents are perceived as equally likely to bear the opinions and motivations of their authors. It has often been said that a historical source is more useful for telling about the period and place it was written in than in giving information about the period it was written for. Such is, sadly, an accurate generalization without the proper use of critical studies.

So what is to be done? The answer is so simple one can only believe others have not seen it because it was too obvious. To better understand Britain in this period, the scholar must assimilate all that has been learned about each source in the past forty years; the knowledge cannot be fragmented. That accomplished, we must determine how and in what places each source may be of use. We must examine each episode and relationship of the period only with materials that have no known bias that would interfere with its accuracy on a case-by-case basis.

On a larger scale, to better understand post–Roman Britain we must begin with a new canvas, without any references to our previous assumptions. We must assume that no part of our received perceptions is accurate. This is what has been attempted in the pages below. The worst possible outcome is that the conclusions that are drawn might be flawed, but then again our current view is demonstrably erroneous. With that in mind, there is nothing to be lost in taking a new approach to this most intriguing period in history.

2

The Primary Sources

Traditionally, the primary sources for the history of Britain were Gildas, Bede, and Nennius. This was because they were the only historians on the island before William the Conqueror to dwell on the British in the years after Rome departed, the development of the Anglo-Saxon kingdoms, and the demise of the British successor states.

The above authors were also held up as reliable. Gildas was believed to have been born within about a century of 410, and thus the entire oral history of post–Roman Britain up to the time of his writing was accessible to him. Bede's Latin was so beautiful that it made scholars believe his contents were above suspicion. It was also clear that he had knowledge beyond what he learned from Gildas, as in when he accurately gave the origin point of the Germanic peoples and seemed to realize that Gildas' *superbus tyrannus* was in reality the Briton Vortigern from Kentish legend. Where Gildas' history was nameless and often formless, Bede added detail and historical context.

As to Nennius, he wrote well after the events that followed the evacuation of Roman authority and the establishment of the first kingdoms on the island. However, the author had said of his accomplishment, "I have made a heap of all I have found."[1] As it was believed that the historians of old had not lied in their writings, that meant that he had mindlessly taken all the information he could find and wrote it down into one book under the broad heading of *Historia Brittonum* (The History of the British). All his information was therefore much older than the date of his writing, and probably had been recorded by contemporaries to the events. He, too, could be considered a contemporary source, even if the exact provenance of all his information remained a mystery.

The reality is that the situation and the historical materials are much more complex than was believed in years past. The written materials were recorded for a reason; this is a universal fact. This reason may well have affected what was and was not recorded and the manner in which it was presented. Any and all sources the author may have used were similarly recorded for a reason, and these too must be articulated and accounted for before the extant materials may be used to outline a clear picture of the period. This will be the main purpose of the chapter below. Unfortunately, it is impossible to determine when all the influences on any given source have been revealed. However, the process of learning as much about the background of the materials as possible does provide for a stable beginning to any examination.

Ammianus Marcellinus is the earliest historian who has left us pertinent information about post–Roman Britain. He was born in Antioch around 365. He spent the first part of his adult life as a soldier and retired later in life when he wrote his history in Rome. Recent scholarship has shown that he wrote during the reign of Theodosius the Great, son of the count Theodosius who put down the coordinated attack on Britain in 367. One author has commented that the history is "hagiographical in tone" with regards to him,[2] and instances the author's commentary on the accession of Valentinian and Valens. Here Ammianus states that the most savage nations against Rome are the Picts, Saxons, Scotti, and Attacotti—all groups that were attacking Britain at the time. However, the historian is generally accurate in this era; he is able to tell us that in the year 360 the *Magister equitum* Lupicinus was sent against the Scotti and Picts.

Claudian was a Roman poet in the service of Hadrian around the turn of the fifth century whose extant work has been collected and dated only once.[3] In the corpus of historical materials for the period, Claudian comes across as straightforward. He wrote to exalt Stilicho and his accomplishments in the eyes of his emperor. He was limited in his portrayal of his subject by his contemporaneity; his audience already knew enough about Stilicho so that Claudian could not lie outright in his praises.

As a chronicler of the early fifth century, Prosper of Aquitaine was a contemporary to the Christian philosophers Augustine and Pelagius, and a staunch supporter of the former. His thoughts on the great scholars might prove untrustworthy, but he is of most use in the date he gives for Germanus' trip to Britain, 429. In this, there is no reason to doubt him, and certainly his peers would have ensured that this date and the reasons for Germanus' voyage were accurate.

St. Patrick is the first native source that we possess. He was born and raised in Britain, most likely during the fifth century. Possibly this was along Hadrian's Wall,[4] or in the most romanized regions of Wales, though he may have been from anywhere near western Britain's coast.[5] At around the age of twelve, he was taken prisoner by the Irish and sold into slavery. He escaped from his captors after six years and returned to his home. There he completed his Latin education and took up the priesthood. He eventually returned to Ireland to evangelize his former captors.

At some time after he returned, a pirate/king named Ceredig raided one of his converted villages and took a number of captives. In response, Patrick wrote two letters to him.[6] The second letter is extant. It demands that his people be returned to their homes and threatens Ceredig with excommunication if they are not. An Irish priest that Patrick had trained from earliest youth delivered the letter.

Probably after this, Patrick was called upon to justify an indiscretion before he was a deacon. His reply, the *Confessio*, is an evenhanded account of his childhood and youth. He gives some welcome information about the political structure of the community he was raised in as a by-product, but does not happen to mention any verifiable locations. It is an irony of history that we have no knowledge of the British context for his *Confessio*, nor any idea of how the affair turned out.

In both extant letters, the language and the details validate a fifth-century date; there has never been any doubt that they are authentic.[7] We are fortunate, too, that they were written to people who would have had the most to gain by pointing out any inaccuracies, and would have been the most able to do so. For these reasons, both are likely reliable. It is unfortunate that Patrick provides so few names from fifth-century Britain. He specifies only Ceredig.

The *Gallic Chronicles* are two simple chronicles that continued the history of Eusebius and Jerome. It is for this reason that the first year in both cases begins in August of AD 378[8]

It is generally agreed that both chronicles were written by two holy men of Gallia Narbonensis. The documents have three separate and consistent methods of dating used throughout both. These are the years of Abraham, the Olympiad number, and the year of the ruling emperor.[9] They are differentiated from each other by the year in which they end—the *Gallic Chronicle of 452* and *The Gallic Chronicle of 512*.

Of the two, only the *Gallic Chronicle of 452* speaks of the devastation of Britain around the middle of the fifth century. It is unknown elsewhere. As has been seen above, little is known of fifth-century Britain, and the chronicle is of little help in that regard. The chronicler may have been a contemporary, but he lived on the other side of the English Channel. Because of this, his statement about the widespread destruction of Britain has been an important issue in British studies.

Archaeology has found some sites in eastern Britain that may well have been burned at this time, but many were demonstrably not, and there is almost no evidence whatsoever for a massive and destructive attack as one goes further west. Because of the lack of evidence, attempts have been made to minimize the authority of the source, and the isolation of Britain has often been used for this purpose. This may well be the reason for the inaccuracy, or may not. The dating of the event, if it did actually occur, is most likely 441. Mommsen gave that year, and Miller, Jones and Casey, and Burgess have all agreed with him.[10]

Zosimus was a pagan Byzantine historian from Constantinople who published his *History of the Roman Empire* in 475. The work survives in only one manuscript, *Vaticanus Graecus 156*. Modern scholars have noted that his integrity was superior to that of his Christian contemporaries. However, as an historian for the Western Roman Empire he is problematic. He had no direct contact with the failing government in Britain, and no alternative means of obtaining information about the forgotten province has ever been uncovered or even hinted at in his writings.

We know his only source in the relevant passages was Olympiodorus of Thebes, of whose writings we possess nothing more than fragments. However, Zosimus is often at odds with what does remain of Olympiodorus' works or what are known to have been his writings through other means.[11] Even his absolute chronology is poor, and one often finds his dates at odds with more reliable sources when he does design to give them.[12] However, his relative chronology seems reasonably accurate so that, coupled with his location, it seems likely that any errors he was guilty of were due more to lack of interest or knowledge than to any sinister motive. This is good news, though it seems clear that Zosimus must be used with extreme caution.

The *Vita Germani*, or Life of St. Germanus of Auxerre, is the earliest saint's life pertaining to Britain. It details two visits to what was probably the Londinium area.[13] Constantius of Lyon probably wrote it in 480x490, though definitely in the period before 494.[14] Constantius' sources likely included St. Lupus, who accompanied Germanus on his trip to Britain in 429.[15] Lupus was still alive at the time of the book's creation.

The book had the same motivations of later *vitae*, primarily to exalt the saint. To this end, one might expect to find events bent to the hero's benefit, or glossed over if they were to his detriment. The former is most probably the case with the "Hallelujah" battle, and the lack of information about Germanus' collaboration with Hilary pertaining to Celidon of Besançon in the latter.[16] What is unusual about this source of information is the unevenness of the materials.

As several authors have noted, Constantius is extremely precise in his information about the continent.[17] In contrast, he is vague to an extreme when his hero is in Britain. It starts the moment Germanus arrives. He meets with an Elafius, who is described as the leading citizen of a region. However, that region is never named. In fact, not one British location in the entire *vita* is designated as an *oppidum, urbs, prouinciae,* or *civitas*. On the other hand, as can be seen with the archaeology, there is consistent evidence that local Roman administrative units continued beyond the mid–fifth century,[18] meaning that any place-names he came across would have sounded familiar.

The most likely explanation is that the British information was difficult to come by.[19] By the time Constantius wrote, communications with the entire island had been nearly cut off, and Lupus would have been a very old man. Of all the episodes in Germanus' life, his trip or trips to Britain would have been the most difficult to learn anything about.

Gildas was the author of *De Excidio Britanniae*. During his sixth-century career he was a wandering bishop who appears to have traveled throughout Wales and Ireland. He journeyed to Brittany at the end of his life. Gildas was probably a leading ecclesiastic of his generation. However, what we know of him is almost exclusively to be found in his writings. He was undeniably trained by a *grammaticus* in the basics of Latin.[20] There seems to be little doubt that he was trained by a *rhetor* in advanced linguistic techniques.[21] This fact is interesting because monastic schools were strictly nonsecular.[22] The basics of language were taught to facilitate the understanding and copying of knowledge,[23] while rhetorical skills were only of use within the framework of the long-dead Roman legal system. What this means is largely undetermined yet.[24]

It has also been noted that Gildas shows no linguistic patterns which would indicate he was a native speaker of Latin,[25] yet he seems to use all of the unusual words in his repertoire accurately.[26] Thus he was well trained and well read.[27] The result is that his Latin is much more the polished language of the fifth century than the rough version his sixth-century contemporaries used.[28]

These facts are of interest when examining the historical preface of his famous letter for a number of reasons. His use of the term *iudices* ranges from judge to ruler, corroborating a sixth-century date for his authorship.[29] So, too, his rationalization of the constructions of the two major walls and the Saxon Shore.[30] These are placed broadly between the death of Maximus (388) and either the Honorian Rescript (410), or the request to Ætius (446x453). As Thompson has shown, both creations are given a reasonable historical context even though archaeology and our better historical records show conclusively that all three structures were created well before the date range he gives.[31] Together, they suggest that at some point between 410 and 453 he reached a point where his oral knowledge was no longer accurate. His odd spelling of *Agitius* for Ætius and his lack of any further details in the interregnum suggest that this impasse occurred very near mid-century, and in turn that Gildas could not have written after about 550.[32]

Two other details seem to have escaped much scrutiny, that his origin legend about the Germanic mercenaries probably came from the Germanic peoples,[33] and that he did have accurate knowledge of the Germanic ships; the latter emerges on his pages as Latinized *ciula*.[34] These two details show more than a mere awareness of the presence of the Germanic peoples, and in fact hint at access to their records.

In his forty-fourth year he wrote *De Excidio Britanniae*. It seems to have addressed five kings in particular, and the other British kings in general. One specific section was also devoted to the clergy. The letter is carefully constructed, and seems to bear the same basic outline as a standard Roman prosecutor's argument.[35]

The theme of Gildas' narrative is simple; the British are God's new chosen people and when they obey him, they prosper. When they stray, they suffer. The *historia* section, his preface, lays down this theme by going over British history with his sermon in mind. He lays out at least two full cycles of sin, wrath, repentance, and prosperity leading up to the most recent period of sin. Then he moves on to the five kings, his specific examples of the depths to which the British have fallen. With them, he names indiscretions specifically in order to drive the point home.

In the overall context of the letter, the purpose of the *historia* is clear; it sets the stage for his main point. It has often been noted that he is sparing in the names he gives there, and in light of his motivations it can be seen that he only employed those names and events that helped him further his purpose. All others would have diverted the reader from his intent. For this reason what he has written, and omitted, must be understood as simple tools of his rhetoric.[36]

Gildas is also known to have written a letter to a *Uennianus* about his philosophy on monastic life. A reference to it may be found in a letter by Columbanus to Gregory the Great around 600. Fragments of what may have been this letter have also emerged, but they add little to what we know of Gildas or the period in which he lived. They do, however, confirm legend in demonstrating that he adhered to the less strict monastic rule in opposition to his contemporaries Samson and David. Gildas believed that a life of bread and water was more the product of man's hubris than of God's demands on a person.

Procopius is the second of the Byzantine historians, and the more removed from the fifth century. He was born around 490 in Caesarea, Palestine. Procopius spent most of his career in the company of the great general Belisarius. Because of his position and location, his work focuses on the famous general and Belisarius' fellow military leaders. However, Belisarius is clearly his favorite subject. Procopius is generally accurate despite his favoritism; scholars of eastern European history speak of his consistency and clarity wherever the information has been compared to other sources.

As a source for western Europe, however, he is less than accurate. To be frank, any region outside of the Byzantine Empire's interests cannot have concerned him, and accurate information from those areas must have been difficult to acquire even if they had. It should, therefore, come as little surprise that Procopius has often been accused of chronological and event inaccuracies in the areas more distant and of less interest to Constantinople.

In Gregory of Tours, we have perhaps the first historian of the British peoples. Gregory was bishop of Tours from 573 until his death in 594, and as such was central to the politics of his day. This makes him an invaluable source of information. Gregory recorded the events in his life as an extended chronicle, often including his own involvement in a given event.[37] Naturally enough, he died having never attempted to edit the book to create the overall themes that have always been the mark of true histories. Because he never concerned himself with a specific purpose in writing, he is all the more reliable. His longevity is equally so. As he was a leader in Gaul for so many years, he would have known firsthand what was going on throughout Gaul from 573, and probably from 563 when he was promoted to deacon. His access to the senior members of the Gallic church from the moment he was anointed bishop may well have allowed him to use credible firsthand witnesses for occurrences of several decades before then.[38]

However, Gregory did have his biases. It has been pointed out that he occasionally returns to his earlier chapters and interpolates materials, chiefly ecclesiastical in nature.[39] There is also strong evidence that he occasionally used his history to set the record of his own relationships straight. However, he has never been accused of giving false information intentionally. It is unfortunate that he saw the Bretons as little more than amusement, and seems to have taken great pleasure in pointing out the petty rivalries and childish activities of their kings when they were useful in that regard.

Unlike all the historians and biographers before him, Taliesin wrote from firsthand experience on the subjects of his poems. He claims to have lived in the halls Cynan Garwyn, Urien, and Gwallog, and the details in the poems are too well-conceived to believe otherwise. Taliesin speaks of the personal ends of their enemies and bluntly asks to be rewarded for his words with gold, silver, and other commodities. One can hardly imagine a different context for writing poetry about contemporary heroic-age kings.[40]

The downside to being patronized by the men whose activities he wrote about is that he was compromised in exactly how much of the truth he could tell, and in where he needed to exaggerate in order to ingratiate his patrons. As a result, the historian cannot believe all that is written and must not accept that what was written was the complete truth. As there is no other firsthand information on any of these three men to help sort him out, the historian's task is all the more difficult. With respect to the persons who are listed as his patron's contemporaries, however, there is no opposing evidence. More than likely, Taliesin would have used contemporary men when speaking of his lords' accomplishments. To have done otherwise would have been to create events within a commonly known past. The war band would have known better, so that such work would have weakened his standing in the hall rather than enhancing the aura of the king. Other bards and neighboring kings would have known to. In their eyes, such rewriting would have made the king appear to be more a clumsy oaf than a man to be taken seriously.

Taliesin was probably the greatest poet of his age, and in fact his myth seems to have grown through the Middle Ages. Later writings associated the famed poet with mystical knowledge of the past and future.[41] In some poems, he was placed in Arthur's or Brân's time. This persona knew magic and confounded the Christian missionaries. He was in several respects the forerunner of Merlin. It is fortunate that these developments occurred rather late in the Middle Ages. The language of the poems in which such claims are made lack the antiquity of the sixth century as well as the mindset of the praise poet.[42] Only twelve poems are generally agreed to have been written by Taliesin, and these do possess the proper setting and orthography to have been formed by Taliesin himself. They are the only examples of Taliesin that will be mined for information in the pages below.

Aneirin was probably a contemporary poet whose main patron was one of the Gododdin rulers. Like Taliesin, he wrote to please his benefactor and in hopes of financial reward. As with Taliesin, many of the details in his poem are much too personal in nature to represent anything but an intimate knowledge of his subjects. As with Taliesin, this also means that he has occasionally exaggerated the accomplishments of his subjects. There is no tradition of Aneirin as a mystic, though Aneirin's extant work has suffered corruption and reinterpretation through the centuries.

Apparently, his *Y Gododdin* was a popular work used by later bards to showcase their talents to potential clientele.[43] As a result, a great deal of poetic license may be assumed in its stanzas. Worse yet is the history of the poem, or rather the histories of the two versions which have been collated to represent it in modern editions.[44]

Internal additions in both versions refer to the Battle of Strathcarron. This indicates that their progenitor made his way to Strathclyde before 642,[45] along with any survivors of the Gododdin royal family and its warriors.[46] The two clearly diverged around 700.

The orthography and content of the first poem indicates that it was first written down before the end of the seventh century.⁴⁷ When Strathclyde itself was in danger of losing independence in the ninth century, the poem made its way down to Gwynedd. There it was rewritten in its present form.⁴⁸

The other version remained in an oral environment during this entire time. This is the adaptation that was used in bardic circles as a method for proving oneself, and was because of this subject to endless variations. While a great deal of its stanzas are demonstrably related to portions of the Strathclyde version of *Y Gododdin*, many of them cannot be. The oral version was finally put in written form during the ninth century.⁴⁹

Clearly later than the poems of Taliesin and Aneirin is the collection of poems commonly known by the title of its most prominent elegy, "Pen Urien." It is found in *Canu Llywarch Hen*. There has been a great deal of discussion over the authorship of this collection, and opinions have varied between two options: Llywarch himself or a number of bards who modified them over an extended period of time. However, Dr. Rowland seems to have settled the matter in favor of the latter option.

Rowland's arguments focus on the nature of the poems and the details they give. For one, the theme behind the Llywarch Hen collection is that Llywarch is too old to fight and must enlist his sons to take on his battles for him. However, this is not consistent with all the extant poems. In "Pen Urien," Urien gives Llywarch's youngest son, Gwên, a horn as a gift. Later on, it is made clear that Llywarch was still an active warrior when he decapitated his cousin Urien. These two details make for an awkward chronology in relation to Llywarch's standing as a retired warrior. Nor could it be that the poems are intended to cover the breadth of Llywarch's life. As Dr. Rowland has rightly observed, beginning a cycle with a warrior in his prime and halfway through transitioning him into a helpless old man would go against the philosophy and training of the bards.⁵⁰

There are further indications that the cycle had different authors with access to alternate information. Some of the Llywarch Hen cycle has Latin and religious influences that indicate a later date,⁵² while the "Pen Urien" materials do not. Perhaps most telling of all, Llywarch asks Dunawd and Brân for aid in the poem "Gwahodd," yet in the "Pen Urien" group of poems these two are opposed to Urien and therefore they are Llywarch's enemies.⁵³ As the Middle Ages progressed, the tendency was to make all of Urien's British contemporaries his allies and opposed to the German invaders in accordance with the devices of the Gwynedd House. Llywarch's alliance with known enemies is simply another example of that trend, and evidence of a later date for that poem.

There has been a great deal of controversy surrounding the central point of the collection, the taking of Urien's head after he died. The subject is treated directly in "Pen Urien," "Celain Urien," and "Efrddyl." The matter is entirely unsettled,⁵⁴ but carries no real weight in studying the group from a historical standpoint. Nor should it have any bearing on the date of the cycle; there is a clear conflict of loyalties for the author. In view of the nationalistic interests of the ninth-century Gwynedd that had them preserved, such is a good indication of traditional saga materials. So, too, the fact that there are no explicit links to *Marwnad Cynddylan*. The place-names contained in the "Pen Urien" group of poems are either independent of *Marwnad Cynddylan* or in perfect accord with those in *Canu Taliesin*'s oldest poems. It is only the orthography and language of the extant poems themselves that bring their probable date to a range of the late eighth to the middle of the ninth centuries.⁵⁵

The concern for the treatment of Urien's head is not important in understanding how the groups of poems are related to each other, either. Each poem has a different approach to the scene. The inconsistency has sometimes been seen as demonstrating that different authors contributed to the poems.[56] However, there are strong verbal links between the poems that suggest there was only one poet. They also seem to perform a different function within the cycle. It seems plausible that their different perspectives are nothing more than poetic devices and verbal echoes.[57]

As to the other stanzas of the group, "Unhwch" and "Dunawd and Urien" seem consistent with the three poems named above. They are pro–Unhwch but fit in well with the conflict of interests the collection demonstrates. "Aelwyd Rheged" is a retrospective look long after the heroes have died and was possibly designed much later as a transition to the Llywarch Hen poems. Stanzas 37 through 41 seem to take an ironic viewpoint towards Urien, and therefore do not belong in the collection proper either.[58] Stanzas 32 through 35 most likely refer to a Run other than Urien's son, and are probably later additions as well. The remaining stanzas are largely stray verses.

Although this group of poetry seems to be at odds with the northern materials in *Historia Brittonum*, both sets of material appear to be based on the same viewpoints and derive from a common type of literature. This suggests all the materials may have derived from the *Northern Memoranda* at one stage or another. If they have, then the sources become valuable as an opposing perspective to the information to be found in *Historia Brittonum*.

Supposedly written from the memories of a very old approximate contemporary of Samson and the saint's mother as received by Samson's uncle, the *Vita Samsoni* has been claimed as a writing of the ninth century.[59]

The more popular take on the *vita* has been to accept it as a document written within living memory of the saint. That is, it is believed that it was written no later than the seventh century.[60] In the main, this conclusion is based chiefly on the details, the name-forms in the *vita* itself, and the fact that other Breton hagiographies, written in the ninth century, were concerned with Breton independence. The *Vita Samsoni* makes no indication of this theme and therefore should not be dated to that period.

One interesting wrinkle the present author has come across is the incident where the saint confronts a *theomacha*, a term normally translated as "witch." In the course of Samson's dialogue with her, the woman reveals that she has eight sisters.[61] The entire episode is curious. Females make for poor opponents in hagiographies, nor are nine devil worshippers a theme or motif in the extant Celtic literature. On the other hand, the author has elsewhere shown that such covens did exist in Britain as hidden religious groups in the centuries following the collapse of Rome.[62] It has also been shown that active confrontations between both saints and kings on one hand and these sects on the other did take place between the late fifth and mid–sixth centuries.[63] That the details given in the *vita* tie together so closely with information about Celtic covens from other sources makes it unlikely that the story could have been in an oral environment for long. Reasonably, the entire life may not have been, either.

Possessing no hint of a story in its contents, *The Tribal Hidage* represents the first example of a tribute list in the extant materials. As Dumville has observed, it consists of three recensions, the earliest and most accurate being A, which is written in Anglo-Saxon. It is to be found in one manuscript, dated to the eleventh century.[64]

There has, for some time, been a debate around the origin of the hidage list. For many years, this was dominated by the opinion that Mercia had composed it. The reason for this was that Mercia was the first kingdom on the list and had subjugated Anglo-Saxon England from the late seventh century till the Viking invasions.[65] However, this perspective has recently come under heavy fire. Brooks and Campbell have reminded us that medieval kings did not take tribute from their own kingdoms, nor would the process be a smooth one once they ruled other lands. It would result in the awkward process of them taking a tribute from their original region as a king, then ceremonially giving tribute to themselves as the over-king.[66]

Also of interest is the fact that Northumbria is nowhere listed in the hidage; it is the only major kingdom which is not. Strangely, Elmet, which was a part of Deira from Edwin on, is listed. As Brooks has suggested, both these details point toward a Northumbrian origin of the list.[67] The latter fact suggests that it may have been Edwin himself who had it made,[68] and certainly no one ruling after him would have listed Elmet at all. The heavy tribute levied against Mercia is a further indication of both date and origin.

These realizations mean that the *Tribal Hidage* was in origin a document of the early seventh century, probably composed in Northumbria. It is a good source of information for the kingdoms in that period as well as their relative power and size. It is limited, however, in the context in which the list was made, and by the fact that it represents only a frozen moment in time and not a dynamic picture of the period.

A far cry from the impersonal nature of the *Tribal Hidage*, *Marwnad Cynddylan* is an elegy to the Cyndrwynyn prince Cynddylan. The meter, vocabulary, and content of the poem are consistent with the seventh century.[69] However, determining anything more specific than the location of Cynddylan's battles and a few of his contemporaries has proven highly problematic.[70] For the purposes of the book laid out below, the only relevant information to be taken from the poem is that Penda was alive during his career and that Cynddylan fought at Lichfield.[71]

The "Northern History" chapters of the *Historia Brittonum* and the bulk of the *Annales Cambriae* entries between 613 and 794 are much less straightforward than the information to be found in the earlier history of Gregory. In fact, a study of them requires a rather lengthy discussion. However, such a dialogue is not only pertinent but necessary to the understanding of much of early British and English history, as it provides a number of extremely useful details and contemporary persons for the late sixth century.

There is no question that there was a written document which contained northern information of the sixth and seventh centuries; even the deconstructionists are willing to concede this point.[72] And apart from Dumville, most scholars have accepted that a majority of the history as we have it is synthesized or highly biased, but not beyond some reconstruction. The problem in dealing with chapters 57 through 65 of *Historia Brittonum* and the relevant *Annales Cambriae* entries is, what exactly was the history of the information before it was written down in these two sources?

Several theories have been advanced, and perhaps a review of them in chronological order will put things in clearer perspective. Professor Jackson suggested in his paper that Rhun son of Urien may have recorded the information about his father and his contemporaries, thereby giving all the information contained in the northern history a firsthand authority. As evidence, he noted that the earliest extant version of the *Historia Brittonum*, the Chartres Recension, actually claimed that a son of Urien had written it. Within the text, he noted that Rhun's brother Owain was not recorded while Rhun's activities were, and that Rhun's granddaughter Rieinmellth had married Oswiu. All were indicators that Rhun was more important, in the author's eyes, than his more powerful and more famous brother Owain. Linguistically, Jackson listed the inclusion of *Atbret*, *Neirin*, and *Cunedag* as showing the great age of the source,[73] while the nicknames ascribed to various leaders would be a sign of the contemporaneity of the recorder to those kings.[74]

Jackson then laid out exactly what may have happened to bring the source from Rhun's hand to the attention of the *Historia Brittonum* author. He proposed that whatever Rhun had written and other information regarding the northern kingdoms was reshaped into a document around 750. A second compiler then added the English pedigrees, which end between 787 and 796 with Egfrith.[75]

In 1977, Professor Dumville wrote on the subject, and proceeded to attack the theory as laid out by Jackson. His assessment amounts to the following. First, that *Atbret*'s absence of affection *could* be indicative of a date as late as the tenth century, though the only linguist he appears to have checked with was Jackson, and Jackson remained fairly confident of his dating at no later than the seventh century. Second, that *Cunedag* may well represent the earliest example of the final -Z after back vowels had been lost, and therefore that it cannot be used to date the source of the *Northern History*. Finally, that there is not enough information to even attempt dating the form *Neirin*.[76] These are the strongest elements of Jackson's dating argument, and Dumville appears to have decimated all but one of them. He then goes on to admit of the source of the Northern British Section:

> The likely nature of a source for the North British material can be agreed: a document which could have contained information about northern history in the greater part of the seventh century, and perhaps beginning as early as the mid-sixth. We see this document only through its use in the *Historia Brittonum*, whose author would doubtless have modernised old linguistic forms. The simplest, and most convincing, solution is that we have here evidence for the use of a set of annals which was perhaps *in part* contemporary, or nearly so, with the events it recorded.[77]

Thus in one stroke, Dumville negates the results of his own testimony. He then attempts to make the entire topic moot by offering: "But whether this annalistic source (if that is what it was) was contemporary or retrospective, the author's method—namely synchronization and interpretation—reduces drastically the value of his testimony."[78] Such, as any dedicated scholar knows, is a sign to be wary and of the need for a great deal of background research. However, it is not an indicator of hopelessness towards the work in general or the historical information it may yield. Dumville's last paragraphs are dedicated to pointing out how clearly interrelated the chapters about the northern British kings, the Anglo-Saxon genealogies, and the Northumbrian king list are. Following Jackson, he suggested that the compiler of the *Northern Chronicle* may well have combined the relative chronology, the Anglo-Saxon genealogies, and the Northumbrian regnal list.[79] If so, this must have taken place some time after 787, when Ecgfrith was first associated with the kingship. He is the last man named in the *historia*.

Most recently, Professor Koch's translation and attempted reconstruction of the *Y Gododdin* verse has led that scholar into this rarely walked path. In this endeavor, he seems to have nearly as strong a linguistic background as Professor Jackson, while the translation of the poem itself required a more detailed knowledge of the sixth and seventh century in northern Britain than Professor Dumville's studies into manuscripts and dating have necessitated. The results are encouraging, and more rooted in a strong understanding of *Y Gododdin* and the time period which created it than any previous scholar was capable of.

First, we may reiterate that there was a recorded northern history; of this there seems to be no controversy. We might also note that the British secular information deriving from this source seems to have run dry with the death of Urien at some time before 600. As Jackson has noted, it does not even mention his son Owain. The ecclesiastical interest in the source seems to have stretched a great deal further, pushing into Rhun's conversion of Edwin and his granddaughter Rieinmellth's marriage to Oswiu well into the seventh century.

Koch reevaluated the linguistic evidence upon which his predecessors had based their arguments. He added on *Urbgen* and *Rieinmellth* to Jackson's list of three names. He demonstrated that Cunedag's second vowel and its consistency over the more modernized "a" version of the schwa indicates a written source for the material. The first syllable stems from Celtic *kuno*, whose latest example comes in a *Book of Llandaff* entry named *Cunhearn* and dated to about 738.[80] Finally, he was able to show through solid linguistic means that both the forms *Neirin* and *Atbret* are as of yet undateable.

Of Urbgen and Rieinmellth he was able to make more headway. The former he traced to Celtic *Orbo-genos*, and saw the consistency of the initial *U* to symbolize the pretonic schwa as an indication of a literate origin for the spelling, in Wales. The *llth* of Rieinmellth he suggested as a dialect peculiar to Cumbric based on its form in the proper name Senïlth and the word *eilth* as found in *Y Gododdin*.[81] Thus, the three together indicated the source for the information in which they were found. The *Northern Memorandum* was created by perhaps 750, in Cumbria.

There is also the *Historia Brittonum*'s historical slant in the northern chapters, which is easily seen once one gets beyond the obvious. As Koch pointed out, the two members of the Strathclyde line are only mentioned because of their associations to more important figures. Rhydderch Hen is an unimportant member of Urien's coalition, while Brude is the king of the Picts who defeats the Northumbrian threat Ecgfrith. Therefore, there is little reason to believe the document would have been created in Strathclyde.[82]

Gwynedd fares little better. The Cadwallon who defeated and nearly destroyed Northumbria is not lauded as a hero nor is the episode he is in considered a victory. Instead, the entire campaign is treated more as a Northumbrian disaster. Later on, Catamail is satirized. Both men were allied to Penda, who is treated as an enemy by the materials.

It is only with Urien that full attention is called to a leader's accomplishments. Even there we are only told that he fought against two Germanic kings and was killed through treachery. No battles are associated with him. Finally, there is his son Rhun, who is credited with converting Edwin and Eanflæd. Later we are told that his granddaughter Rieinmellth and that same Eanflæd were wives of Oswiu. The former appears to have been the mother of Alchfrith.[83]

Omissions are also important. Oswiu's third wife, Fina, is nowhere to be found; nor is her son Aldfrith, who ruled Northumbria after the Battle of Nechtanesmere in 685. Fina was the daughter of an Irish king, so she and her son might well have been considered outsiders in Northumbrian history. On the other hand, there seems to be no reason why the British would have decided to exclude them but include so much other information about Northumbria. Last and as Dumville pointed out, Owain son of Urien is not named in the text, though his less famous brother is. Owain is known from the Taliesin poetry to have been a powerful king in his own right, and certainly would have deserved some note in a family history of Urien.

All of these observations led Koch to see that Rheged, and Urien, were the primary interests of the British secular history. After his rule, there was no importance in recording further information on his family. Instead, whoever was writing down a history turned their interests toward Northumbria, and particularly the interactions between the descendants of Urien and that kingdom. The history seems to have faded out at some time before 700, which is approximately when the last genealogical and king list entries were made.

The question now becomes one of who in the last years of the seventh century would have had the motivation to write a history where Urien was the main hero. Certainly not the

British rulers of Rheged, whose kingdom had lost its independence long before then. It could not have been the monks of the region either. Religious men write about religious men, and have little concern for a kingdom unless they are patronized by its rulers. Besides, we have the testament of Eddius Stephanus and the anonymous author of the *Vita Cuthberti* that seventh-century Northumbrian churchmen were being given Rheged church lands within a decade of the Synod of Whitby.[84] After that date, British churchmen could not have created such a document. There is also the curious inclusion, after Urien, of Northumbrian records.

Here Koch turned to Northumbrian history, and Urien's probable great-great-grandson Alchfrith. Bede tells us he revolted from his father, Oswiu,[85] and as both a powerful member of the Northumbrian House and a descendant of Rheged's royal family, it seems reasonable that Rheged was his power base against the Northumbrian homeland. His revolt would have provided the perfect setting for Rheged to produce a *historia*, and Alchfrith's support for it would have entailed the inclusion of the Germanic genealogies and the Northumbrian king list. With this explanation, all the omissions and peculiar interests of the "Northern History" can be accounted for.

If Alchfrith was the patron and his rebellion the motivation for the history, when did the revolt take place? Alchfrith and Oswiu acted together at the Synod of Whitby in 664, and the younger man was dead by about 671, so the revolt was probably between these two dates. Ergo, the *historia* would have been created then as well.

However, the last event mentioned in the *Northern Memoranda* chapters is the Battle of Nechtanesmere, an event that took place over a decade after the proposed date range for the history. Nechtanesmere was unlike most of the other events and individuals found in the *Northern Memoranda* in that it reversed the fortunes of the Celtic kingdoms for many decades after it was fought. In the aftermath, the Picts and Scots recovered all their lands, while some of the British were able to break free from Northumberland for a time. These kingdoms were all still independent at the time Bede wrote.[86] It has been proposed that the *Northern Memoranda* was propagandistic in nature, and specifically propagandistic in favor of the northern British. This means that the free Celtic lands most likely had it in their possession, and they would have had the most to gain from adding the battle to the history during its stay there.

The Letters of Columbanus have an entirely different context than the "Northern History," as they were not written as a family history, nor were they preserved for political reasons. Instead they were written by an outspoken Irish bishop to the pope. Columbanus was an Irish-raised monk of about 600 who, after many years spent as a monk in Bangor, decided to travel to Gaul with some of his followers. There he raised a great deal of controversy with his outspoken views on royal activities and by his use of the Irish formula for dating Easter. The letters are of most interest because of their tone; he treats the pope as an equal and a straying colleague at that. Columbanus points out the pontiff's errors and chastises him. On a larger stage, the attention Columbanus' outrageous letters attracted was one of the key reasons why the papacy took such an interest in dealing with the Easter controversy over the next few decades.

The collection of his letters is important here because it refers to Gildas as both the writer of *De Excidio Britanniae* and a letter to a named Celtic bishop, one Uinniau. This firmly places Gildas, and therefore his writings, in a period well before 600. It also clearly makes this volatile man a younger contemporary of Gildas. More than that, however, Columbanus' letters not only show the vitality of the Celtic spirit of the period but also give a window into the mindset of his culture.

With the *Vita Kentigerni* we return to histories kept for religious reasons. There are in fact two "lives" of Kentigern, both dating to the twelfth century. The first was written between 1147 and 1164 for Bishop Herbert, and the second was penned for Bishop Jocelyn (1175–1199). Their common source dates to no later than 800. As Jackson noted, the Lothian chapters contain traditional British names.[87] His contention was that an eleventh-century Norman ecclesiastic was both willing and able to go to the remote areas of Lothian to get the information on the saint's conception and childhood. MacQueen, Carney, and Koch have argued for a Occam's razor approach to the survival of British place-names. For the authors to know that Kentigern's life was to be found in Lothian there must have been a Strathclyde tradition that Kentigern was born there, and the tradition would well predate the eleventh century.[88] In fact, the origin of such knowledge would make the most sense in the century or so after Kentigern's death—in other words, in the period before the second quarter of the eighth century.

Koch has also seen two additional pieces of evidence that lend themselves to an early date for the *vita*. The first is that Kentigern's maternal grandfather is in all cases the ruler of Dunpelder/Traprain Law. The later British community in Britain would only know of Din Eidyn as the royal residence, but in fact Dunpelder was a major stronghold of the region up through the fifth century and possibly into the sixth or seventh century. The location of the hero's ancestor in Dunpelder is a claim of royalty that eleventh-century Strathclyde would have been unaware of.[89] Second, Kentigern's mother is called *Thaney* in the Herbertian life and *Taneu* in the Jocelyn version. This is from Archaic Welsh *Täneü*, which in written form was obsolete by about 800.[90]

The early origin of the life is, therefore, fairly well established. As to the context of the story, there seems to have been more debate. What is most likely is that the life was originally written in the last few decades of the seventh century. Gododdin would have lost its voice when it was conquered by the Northumbrians in the first few decades of the seventh century. In 664, the Council of Whitby determined that Roman Catholicism was superior to the Celtic church. This would have left those British religious men and kingdoms still extant in an awkward position. So, as often happened with holy men of the past, Kentigern was chosen as a spokesman for the northern British. By writing a life of Kentigern they were able to claim that Gododdin was Celtic Christian and British long before it had been conquered.[91] They were also able to employ the most famous British saint in their cause.

This is the most likely scenario. At the least, the motivation seems to be accurate because of how it was perceived at the time. In both extant lives, Baldred is named as the successor of Kentigern and the writer of his biography. The author's name should put the authenticity of the claim and the *vitae* themselves in doubt. Baldred is an Anglo-Saxon name. It seems extremely unlikely that a Germanic ecclesiastic would have come to a Celtic kingdom in the early seventh century, so unlikely that it would be the only instance known. That such an individual would have been made a bishop there is preposterous. He is nowhere named in the *vitae* either, suggesting that his association was a later one.

The evidence supports this supposition. There is a Baldred to be found in the *History of the Church of Durham* (dated 1104–1108), which marks his death at 757.[92] His existence is confirmed in the *Aberdeen Breviary* and the *Scottichronicon*. His floruit would have covered a good portion of the first half of the eighth century, tying in smoothly with the dating suggested above for an author to the *vita*. Further, as MacQueen made note, an Anglo-Saxon of the middle of the century would have had good reason to write such a life. At that time, Strathclyde was under Northumbrian rule, and by writing of the British saint, Baldred was able to convert the patron of the region into a model Anglo-Saxon saint without losing touch with the saint's British ties. In one unlikely scene, Kentigern goes to Rome, is informed he was created a bishop by the wrong (British) method, and is reconsecrated according to canon. In one deft move, Strathclyde's most revered holy man was made an ally of the Northumbrian church.[93] Similarly, in one deft move a British life of a British saint was changed from a political piece in support of the British to one for the Anglo-Saxons.

Jackson made one point regarding the contents that should also be mentioned here. Chapters twenty-three through thirty-one deal with Kentigern's exile during the reign of Morken. While Kentigern may well have been forced from the kingdom of Strathclyde during a hiatus in the Rhydderch family line, the details regarding that exile are not historical. The spellings *Karleolum, Dewi, Nantcharvan,* and *Elgu* are all twelfth century and Anglo-Norman.[94] There is no mention of St. Asaph's, which the lives claim he founded, before 1143.

By the twelfth century, Strathclyde was once again a free kingdom. Likely, the reason for the twelfth-century additions was to make the claim that the see of St. Asaph's was of a greater antiquity, and to give it a greater sanctity. Those chapters can be nothing but propaganda. Kentigern meets King Cadwallon while he is there. Cadwallon was, according to medieval chronology, dead by 534. Kentigern was said to have lived another eighty years. If they had met, and Kentigern had only just been consecrated at the age of thirty when he was exiled, he would necessarily have lived to an outrageous 110 years. The author was not aware of this chronological stretch, as he does not claim an unusual age for his subject.

It is, then, conceivable that Kentigern's life was used by both Roman and Celtic churches to make claims on their individual views pertaining to Easter, tonsure, and other contemporary issues. Strathclyde no doubt had a tradition that said he came from Gododdin and thus made the region Christian before Northumbria infested it with their brand of the religion. In the eighth century, Baldred would take that raw information and write a life of the saint that accepted this fact but added on his reconsecration in Rome. This confirmed a pre–Northumbrian Christian presence in Gododdin, but added that the saint himself had accepted the Roman version by agreeing that he had been wrongly consecrated in Britain and by allowing himself to be made a bishop in the Roman fashion. The *vita* was designed to make the transition to the Catholic religion a smooth one. In the twelfth century, the men who used Baldred as their source misunderstood that he was intended to be a successor of the saint's traditions and made him Kentigern's immediate heir. It is likely this period that saw the St. Asaph interpolation as well. This sequence of events would account for Baldred's Anglo-Saxon name, the dating of the original source, the linguistic evidence for the eighth century, and the fact that Baldred nowhere holds a significant part in the *vita* yet is credited as his successor there.

Like much of the *Northern Memoranda, The Llandaff Charters* were in origin religious materials. The charters, however, were allowed to remain in their original context because of the contribution they made to Llandaff's aims, and the inability of any other party to make use of them otherwise. *The Llandaff Charters* are a miscellaneous collection of documents that in some way relate to various saints in the Llandaff sphere of influence and the grants made to the bishopric there for several centuries. They consist of 336 columns written in nine hands. The first is datable to the period 1125x1150, while the other eight range from the late twelfth to the early thirteenth centuries. Two hundred forty-two of the columns were written by the original scribe.[95] The names listed in the charters place them as early as the sixth century, and they terminate in the twelfth. The fundamental problem with the received version of the charters is that the implied chronological order is impossible due to a large number of internal inconsistencies.[96]

The motivations behind the collection seem clear, however, thanks to the work of Wendy Davies. Bishop Urban was consecrated to Llandaff in 1107. From 1120 until his death in 1134 he was involved in property disputes against St. David's and Hereford. He seems to have been largely successful until 1133, when most of his gains were negated by an English synod. This event ended the disputes. Since the earliest hand contains Urban's claims and the document itself would have made for ideal evidence in justifying them, it was most likely composed between 1120 and c. 1129.[97] This also means that any materials that would have served Urban's goals must be treated with skepticism, as Davies was well aware.

However, the material is definitely based on earlier manuscripts, and Davies has produced a system by which the original texts might be reconstructed.[98] Those documents which cover the period of interest here have been put in a relative chronology based on the witnesses to be found there.[99] Because of her work, some of the charters have been dated as far back as the last quarter of the sixth century, giving the current scholar over a century's worth of pertinent documents.

The *Ravenna Cosmography* also appears to be an amalgam. It is a compilation of various Roman sources composed during the seventh century. The preface indicates that the author was a cleric in Ravenna, writing for one Odo. This Odo is described as a friend; it would appear that the author's motivation in writing was simply to complete an assignment for him. On the other hand, there is no way to be certain that this was the case and that there was no other agenda.

The compiler gave a source for nearly every region in which he listed sites, but none of them are known to us. Other scholars have seen this fact as evidence that the sources he did give were accurate, but I.A. Richmond and O.G.S. Crawford suggested that here the author may well have been following the late Roman tendency of inventing sources.[100] Regardless of who the scholar may have used directly, the material is easily seen as the result of consulting a Roman itinerary. The date of this itinerary must have preceded the cosmographer by some time because the Saxons are introduced into the preamble as newcomers.[101] Traditional historiography would date this event to no later than 456, suggesting a date no later than about 500 for the source of the British materials.[102]

The Pillar of Eliseg is a rather unique source for Welsh history, and perhaps should be considered a secondary source for only the sixth and seventh centuries. However, its placement in this book does have a specific function, and for that purpose it is a primary source for the period under study here. The pillar is a monument located at Valle Crucis Abbey. It was built by Eliseg, a Powysian king of the ninth century who claimed descent from Gwrtheyrn through his son Brittu. It is important to this study only because it shows the Powysian dynasty's political genealogy frozen in time. At or after the original *Historia Brittonum* was written, the kings of Powys were claiming Gwrtheyrn as their founder. The next two centuries would introduce a host of changes that may be seen in the various Powysian pedigrees left in an assortment of manuscripts, but this is far and away the earliest non–*Historia Brittonum* source to list it.

The *Vita Garmoni* is probably the first of three distinct primary sources to be found inside the *Historia Brittonum*. The compiler of the British history claimed to be using this source when he wrote many of the chapters in the work, though the claim can only have been a result of poor scholarship on his part. Further evidence for such a conclusion can be found in the name of the primary character of his source; Garmon is misnamed Germanus in the text. The proven name confusion and the politically incorrect use of Garmon also argue that the source from which information about him comes was much older than the *Historia Brittonum*.[103] As will be seen, the chapters that pertain to Gwynedd or damage Powys have most probably been altered to suit the needs of the original compiler or the later editor of the *historia*. Caution is recommended here.

The origin-year of the *Vita Garmoni* is not known for certain, and no scholar has been able to develop any significant hypotheses on the subject. This is because no extant version of the *vita* remains outside the *Historia Brittonum*, and thus there is no way of being certain what was or was not altered at some point in the story's history. However, some guesses have been made despite this barrier. Dumville believed it was written during Cadell's reign, which ended in 808.[104] This was because the version we have in the *Historia Brittonum* claims Cadell as the founder of the contemporary line of rulers, and Garmon as the saint responsible for giving him his throne. Dumville's reasoning was that Cadell somehow commissioned one of Garmon's monasteries to write a *vita* in which his ancestor and namesake Cadell was given the throne by its patron saint. With religious support, the stature of the entire lineage was enhanced.

However, such a theory is heavily flawed in its assumptions about *vitae*. For one, they are not written with political agendas. As has been demonstrated at length, they are made to benefit a monastery or group of monasteries. In this case, a saint selecting the founder of a kingdom would have shown the superior authority of the saint over the king's entire lineage. Kings do not request, or have an interest in, patronizing parties whose stories will be motivated by anything but royal interests.

When and by whom could the *vita* have been produced? Contrary to Dumville's testimony,[105] Benlli and Cadell could not have been mere creations of the author. They are, instead, further evidence that the *vita* contains original materials. It would not benefit the monastery that wrote the *vita* to create the names of kings; doing so would cast doubt on the credibility of the story as a whole. Instead, saints' lives often place real persons and contemporary persons in created situations, lending an air of believability to even the most outrageous episodes.

And, as the subject of the dating of the *Vita Garmoni* has been broached, so too should the point at which it was included in the *Historia Brittonum*'s corpus of information. In this line of thought, there are three curious items in the received history. First, the confusion between Garmon and Germanus. Apart from a similarity between the names, they appear to have nothing in common in Britain. Germanus visited the island twice, probably around the London area, and debated with Pelagian heretics. Garmon was a figure of Powys, and was in the business of dealing with kings.

The second item involves the prologue to the chapters on northern history that has been alluded to above. The reader is told that the source for the information was taken from a life of Germanus, that is, Garmon. However, Garmon is in no way connected with the figures of the North in the work, chronologically or geographically.

The final and perhaps most important detail, was brought to light by Nora Chadwick nearly half a century ago. There was a strong intellectual relationship between Gwynedd and Charles the Bald during the latter's reign of 840–877.[106] Their association was so affable that several Celtic ecclesiastics from Gwynedd and regions associated with it came to Charles' court.

The point is of such importance because Charles is known to have had a strong predilection for St. Germanus of Auxerre and to have communicated that fact, and a good deal of information about him, into Gwynedd. Thus, the temptation to associate Garmon with Germanus would have been strongest *after* 840, a full decade following the production of the *Historia Brittonum*. It seems feasible that the chapters including St. Garmon were added in a later recension of the work. Such a sequence of events would also explain the odd location of the acknowledgment to the *Vita Garmoni*; the note was an afterthought. However, such a theory will require more substantial evidence and better placement of a secondary authorship before the above oddities can be made full use of. This information will be forthcoming in the next chapter, when dealing with the history of the *Historia Brittonum* itself.

Eddius Stephanus is chronologically the next writer. His subject was Wilfrid, a personal hero. Of Eddius very little is known apart from the fact that he wrote within about a decade of Wilfrid's death. We also know he accompanied the saint to the Continent on one of his journeys. Two points need be made about this author. First, he was clearly biased in favor of Wilfrid and against all those who opposed him throughout his career. Second, Eddius is much more detailed about Wilfrid's activities than any other writer.

The anonymous author of the *Life of Ceolfrith* is also something of a mystery.[107] He was a monk of Wearmouth and did accompany the saint on his last trip to Rome.[108] Because he was so close to Ceolfrith, this also means he was more partisan than Bede. This anonymous writer produced his biography within a very short time after the saint's death. He was therefore in a much better position to give accurate details, and much more likely to bend events to his saint's favor than Bede. It is fortunate that Ceolfrith was involved in no major religious issues during his career.

Bede is perhaps the most widely used of the historical sources for early Britain, if for no other reason than that he gives a history for the entire period instead of focusing on just one person or event. There is also a long tradition that he was a careful and unbiased scholar who unerringly discovered and recorded the truth.[109] This was because of his polished Latin as well as his access to an impressive library.[110] Modern scholarship has realized that Bede had his biases, and that he was not always able to neutralize the partisanship of his sources. In the pertinent period, these were the works of Gildas, Nothelm, Daniel of the West Saxons, Cyneberht of Lindsey, Abbot Esi, and the Lastingham community.

Gildas was the primary source for most of Bede's early history. As Dr. Miller long ago made note, however, Bede used him carefully and edited what he had to say in three ways, by omission, interpretation, and style.[111] He omitted items that did not fall into his own themes, interpreted him in light of a different perspective of the island's history, and changed words to fit his own personality. This should serve as a warning of how to read him in general.

Nothelm was at the time in London but would eventually become the archbishop of England. This fact suggests that he had performed some important function for the church and possibly for Kent earlier in his career. The facts are that Bede relied on him mainly for information south of the Thames, from Rome, and about the earliest Anglo-Saxon activities on the island.

Bede was much less reliant on Cyneberht, Esi, or the Lastingham communities for information on various areas of early English history. However, they were used, as well as what must have been the basis of his Northumbrian records, some written records and the oral knowledge held in the monasteries with which he was most familiar.[112] No work has been done to determine the specific biases or even the level of credibility of these sources.

In addition to the specific viewpoints of his source materials, there was Bede. As Higham has recently shown beyond any reasonable doubt, Bede was an extremely biased writer who did not compose simply to record history, but to teach and subvert information he found distasteful. First and foremost, he was a Bernician. In his writing, he regularly minimized the status of even the most powerful of Mercian and Deiran kings, as he elevated those of the Bernician kings. At one point, he even went so far as to exaggerate Cædwalla's independence from Mercia so that he could avoid giving Mercia too much power. He omits Deira whenever he can; seventy years after Whitby he was clearly in support of the Bernician-backed Irish church, and opposed to the Deiran Wilfrid.[113] Military defeats by his kings were described in terms of divine anger for the king's actions, and victories as proof of the divine support for Bernician supremacy. The book itself was offered to the contemporary Bernician king, strongly indicating he would have found its contents in line with the interests of his family.[114]

Second, he was a staunch enemy of the British church. At first sight this might sound only reasonable. After all, Bede was raised in an English church. However, as was noted above, he preferred the Irish church over the Roman, and the British and Irish religious organizations were nearly identical. Still, he managed to separate the two. It is the British who are castigated early on, using Gildas' own words. Augustine, as coming from Rome, is used to symbolize the better version of the Christian faith as coming from the old empire. The Council of Whitby is given a chapter and dealt with fairly, but only so as to highlight the misguidance of the British peoples. Despite the fact that the Irish and their students were the opposing debaters, they are carefully spared his judgments.

Along with this bias, it should not seem strange that Bede was of Germanic descent, and saw the British, Picts, and even Irish as lesser beings in the eyes of God. It is unsurprising that for him the introduction of Hengest and Horsa represented the beginnings of British history; in writing of the history of Britain he gives only the briefest of outlines before their arrival and focuses almost exclusively on them once they appear. He is in this respect perhaps the first racist historian on the island after Rome and should be treated as such.[115]

In addition to all the written sources, there will also be occasion to make use of archaeology. Archaeology does not fall into the above pattern. Here nothing that has been left behind was meant for us to find; all of it is present by chance. In that respect, it is without bias. On the other hand, the interpretation of a site is subjective by its nature. Many finds have been misunderstood over the years because they were set against a context of already accepted truths.

The study has other serious drawbacks as well. Archaeologists cannot excavate every site, or even a good portion of any one site. Funding, time constraints, and other factors often limit the resources that can be devoted to any dig. As a result, proportions of structures and the intentions of finds are often misunderstood. And, as the fifth and sixth centuries have given us so few physical remains supplemented with only a small amount of literature, we have only modest guidance in that respect. It is only when a broad range of excavations return similar results that a pattern may be roughly determined and any one object's nature might be understood. Even then, the simplest assumption may prove haphazard.[116]

Dating, too, is notoriously difficult among artifacts. Certainly, a large number of a specific brooch or type of pottery may allow a date range to be assessed. And, on rare occasions, an artifact is found in context with a relatively unused coin and a year may be determined. At other times carbon–14 or tree ring dating (dendrochronology) of a large number of similar items reveal a narrow range of years. However, these situations are not the rule. Expensive or beautiful items often became heirlooms. Good armaments or even plows might be used for some generations after they were made. This can throw off the dating by as much as a century. The reality of archaeology is that it is useless for absolute chronology and often difficult in establishing a relative date. It is of greatest use in understanding the culture of the people, and can only be done safely with the assistance of written sources. Any use of the field beyond that must be speculative.

The above is a fairly complete listing and discussion of the academic state of affairs on the pertinent primary sources for early British history. As with all studies, very little of the conclusions which have been outlined above are without their critics, but the large part of scholars are in agreement with what has been put forward. As has been seen, a good deal of the influences working on the primary sources is known. This is most fortunate, as whatever history of post–Roman Britain is to be constructed must be based on the primary sources for the period no matter how tempting other supplies of information may be. In the next chapter, the same process of individual scrutiny and the detailing of bias, sources used, and chronology will be applied to the secondary sources. They in their turn will be carefully used to help fill in the blanks left by the primary sources—when there is no reason to believe the many influences upon them have not poisoned the information they offer.

3

The Secondary Sources

A secondary source may most simply be defined as literature that was not written by a person or persons with firsthand knowledge of the information they give. This basic definition does not, however, explain the presence of a good deal of the sources listed below and could easily be applied to nearly all the sources listed in the previous chapter. It would be more accurate to say that the sources below do not purport to contain firsthand knowledge of events, even if some of the information they contain does happen to be accurate.

We will begin with the law codes. For the most part, they deal with no incidents or persons in particular. They are in all cases composed of a series of laws anonymously created and often codified under the banner of an unusually powerful king. They are not helpful in better understanding the history of the fifth and sixth centuries. They do, though, provide a valuable resource for recovering much of the background for the history being studied below. Moreover, as all lawyers tend to preserve laws well after they are obsolete, these will occasionally provide a progression of how law, and with it society, progressed through the centuries from the beginnings of their society to the reign of the king who authorized the law code.

Because they were created by a single individual who possessed a unique amount of power and land within, it must be remembered that the law codes which make up most of our resources here are representative of a single kingdom's laws, not of the entire culture-group they represent. It should also be noted that a man possessed of such a large region for the first time in his family's history might be likely to invest some time in establishing a protocol for succession in order to maintain the stability of the kingdom and keep his immediate family in the kingship. This would not necessarily represent the practical application of succession, however. As with all political entities, the greatest power is taken by the person most capable of it, not necessarily by the legal heir.

The Irish Laws were never codified, probably because no one over-king felt as though the powers he had gathered would much survive his death. This failing is fortuitous for the historian; it has left us with a smattering of often conflicting laws from smaller kingdoms throughout the island.

The differences are chronological as well as geographical. It has been suggested that the laws of centuries before the Christian era have been preserved there.[1] Certainly a glimpse into the pan–Celtic culture is visible through them, a view which extends through the post-Roman era. Nowhere is this variety more apparent than in the *Críth Gablach*.

The Law Code of Æthelberht was the first written set of laws developed by the

Germanic peoples in Britain. As has been seen, Æthelberht was a king in Kent, and was an over-king from no later than 596 till his death in 616. This period is when he most likely authorized the document. However, the specific date of composition is irrelevant; the Germanic peoples came to Britain from the Continent, where they had already amassed centuries of history and laws. For this reason, though the specific fines may have been current during his reign, the relative values were ancient.

Æthelberht's code focuses on standardizing payments for personal and property injuries, and touches on matters of trade. From a historical perspective, the chief worth of the code is the values it places on various objects, the contemporary law system (there are no state offenses, only those that directly involve the king and those pertaining to two conflicting kin-groups), and the focus of the laws. In effect, they may very well represent the common laws of the original immigrants. The two codes that followed, that of Hlothere and Eadric first and of Wihtred second, seem to be more supplements to the original than new and independent documents. They focus more on trade, indicating that this aspect of the law was expanding in the seventh century, and therefore that trade was becoming a more important part of everyday life in Kent. The deduction makes good historical sense, as trade within Britain and with the continent would grow as both regions became more politically stable.

The Law of Ine was composed, by details in the code, between 688 and 694.[2] It is much like its Kentish predecessors in the focus of the laws and its manner of justice. By the late seventh century, though, it would appear that Germanic law had developed further. Here there are more laws involving the church. Its power is at times made superior to the king. For instance, being forced to work on a Sunday can result in a slave being freed, while doing so voluntarily may result in being made a slave. To a lesser extent, the code expands on other aspects of life, revealing a development of the culture and the world around them. The killing of foreigners, trade, and theft are among the more important themes stressed.

Thus, the main concerns in the earliest English laws are personal disputes, while they expanded into trade, the church, and robbery as society developed and daily life became more stable. These, then, were the chief concerns of Anglo-Saxon society.

The Laws of Hywel Dda were created at the command of the tenth-century king of Dyfed. Hywel Dda was a powerful figure, who in his lifetime had influence over a majority of Wales. His law code was authorized for the purpose of establishing for all time the breadth of that power, and impressing upon the other major contemporary kingdoms the depth of that power. It simply codified and rationalized the laws to be found throughout his kingdom.

What any law text or texts will do is provide a picture of an idealized society. It will also show what is or is not a concern, how life is structured, what the main economic unit of society is, and how law is applied to real life. In the case of all the cultures represented above, identity was tribal and secondarily based on an extended family. One's inclusion in that family is what gave an individual the ability to protect himself from harm and to receive reparations in the event of injury.

The *Fer n'Alban* present a much different perspective from the law codes, and seem at first glance to be reminiscent of the Kentish Source or the more carefully organized *Historia Brittonum*, both of which will be discussed in detail below. The *Senchus* is a two-dimensional origin legend; it explains the establishment of the kingdom without any awareness of the political atmosphere of the world around Scottish Dalriada. Despite the tenth-century grammar of the text,[3] it was believed by Bannerman to be a revised version of a much earlier history stretching back to the seventh century.[4] The former conclusion seems to have been generally accepted.

The precise date has not been so well received. Bannerman provided a coherent and valid argument for his position. He noted that the last person named in the history was Conall Crandomna, who died around 660.[5] This detail would suggest a date around the middle of the seventh century for the original document. He also pointed out that Cummíne believed the Dalriadic house suffered a decline after the Battle of Mag Rath in 637.[6] This is supported by the fact that both Alcuin and Bede claimed that Edwin, Oswald,[7] and Oswiu all took tribute from Dalriada.[8] Much beyond Mag Rath there would have been little need to develop the national consciousness the *Senchus* seem to be aimed at as there would have been no strong central power that could have made use of it. All of the above points to a mid-century origin date.

What has not really been explored previously is why someone would have had reason to write, or revise, this early Scottish history. Historically, the only suggestion we have is the unity of the Scottish and Pictish peoples in 843, and the natural need to standardize and nationalize a history of the dominant peoples, the Scots, at that time.

Tying up this loose end will be one of the benefits of the intensive study of the royal houses in the second half of the book. For now, it is only necessary to follow a couple of old hands on the subject in order to prepare the reader. Professor Hector Chadwick long ago noted that there is a discrepancy between the floruit and the death of Fergus, founder of the line. The annals say he died in the same year he came over to Scotland with his sons alone, and named them as his heirs. The *Senchus*, on the other hand, state that he and his brothers were the original settlers of medieval Dalriada.[9] It is interesting that in the latter and more recent source Fergus' grandsons Comgall and Gabran took Fergus' share of the inheritance in opposition to the ithagenic or cousinly inheritance traditions in Ireland. These two individuals were credited with being the ancestors of all the later Dalriadic kings.

Bannerman was the first to point out that there is also a discrepancy between the brothers Oengus, Loarn, and Fergus Mór. The latter was the most prominent figure of his time in Scotland and is the only person mentioned in any histories, yet it is his alleged brothers who have the *cenéls* named after them. Fergus gave his name to no region. It has also been noted that only sources after the tenth century name the three as siblings.[10] Bannerman was convinced that Oengus and Loarn were added to the legend of Fergus only later as brothers. He suggested instead that both men had been the leaders of clans that were based in Scotland before Fergus arrived, and were added to the family tree as a means of pacifying the members of those families as their lands were assimilated.[11] Bannerman was able to find some supporting evidence for other and previous Irish groups in Dalriada from *Tochomlad Muscraigi de Maig Bregoin*,[12] *Amra Choluim Chille*,[13] *Tochomlad Dáil Riatai i nAlbain*,[14] and Bede.[15] These all speak of a Cairpre Riata who led a band of Irish into Dalriada at some time before Fergus.

Research at about the same time showed that similar alterations of family lines would not have been unique. A good deal of research into Niall Noígiallach and his descendants has revealed that he was artificially added to the lineages of several distinct families as a result of his widespread power.[16] Miller's work came to a similar conclusion with regards to Gwynedd.[17]

Much more straightforward are the Irish Annals. These are a set of complex and often contradictory records based on the collation of four monasteries—Bangor, Iona, Lismore, and Clonmacnoise. The first three were compiled into the *Chronicle of Ireland*, and disseminated again into the *Annals of Innisfallen*, the *Annals of Ulster*, and the *Annals of Tigernach*. The latter has come down to us in something like its original form.

To begin with, it is necessary to ascertain the dates from which all the primary annals were first recorded. The extant annals have a complete list of abbots from Bangor for the seventh century, and that monastery is known to have had a *scriptorium*.[18] It therefore dates to about 600. We have a complete list of all the abbots of Iona because of Columba's fame and the prominent role of that monastery in the affairs of Scotland and Ireland over the centuries. However, entries regarding it become more frequent in the 670s and more fully developed in the 680s, and the period 686–740 contains several precisely dated entries. This suggests that contemporary recording took place there from the middle of the 680s, and probably began as informal notes before the 670s.[19]

Lismore's entire eighth-century list of abbots is known,[20] and Grosjean has shown that Munster had a *scriptorium*.[21] The records there must be contemporary from 700. Clonmacnoise also has a complete sequence of abbots from around 740. More important, from that period until 790 all the surrounding monasteries are well represented. There are a good many references to the various ruling houses of Connacht as well.[22] All this means that records are contemporary from about 740.

The common exemplar of the *Annals of Ulster* and the *Annals of Tigernach* was compiled around 712.[23] Up to 766, the *Annals of Ulster* and the *Annals of Tigernach* are closely related. They do not diverge until 913.[24] The extant annals provide a continuous though chronologically untrustworthy history of the Uí Néill, suggesting that their precursor the *Chronicle of Ireland* was composed in Ulster some time during the tenth century.[25] The particular interest in the descendants of Aed Sláine, even the relatively unimportant members of the family, further refines this location to County Louth and eastern Meath. It is noteworthy that the last of these, *Annals of Innisfallen*, contains a considerably smaller amount of materials than the other two.[26]

The three annals deriving from the *Chronicle of Ireland* contain very little information about the period immediately before the year when their common source began contemporary recording. Thus, Ó Máille has noted that all of the entries of the late sixth century are suspect. The orthography in the *Annals of Ulster* is late, in some instances dating to the late ninth century.[27]

Another revelation has been that the common core of information between the *Annals of Ulster* and the *Annals of Tigernach* is one-half the total in the period 500–585, against two-thirds between 650 and 700.[28] Even with the common core, the agreement is poor between the two. It has been suggested that their entries between 488 and 585 were the result of notes and marginalia largely added after the 913 divergence, and this seems the most likely possibility given the above information. In contrast, the *Annals of Inisfallen* contained 98 entries between 488 and 585, while only eight were not in both of the other annals. Reasonably, it is the best representation of the *Chronicle of Ireland*.

Much like the Irish Annals, the *Annales Cambriae* is an amalgam of earlier sources.[29] The *Harleian 3859* version is the most complete of the collection, and it ends in 954. This suggests that whoever was working on it stopped writing either in that year or in the year following.[30] The annals are immediately followed by a genealogy of Owain son of Hywel, king of Dyfed from about 950 to 988.

Between that time and 795, the annal appears to have been kept in St. Davids. Its focus of interest is clear for the period; Maredudd and his descendants as well as Hyfaidd and Llywarch dominate the annals and ruled the kingdom during that period. Five of the bishops

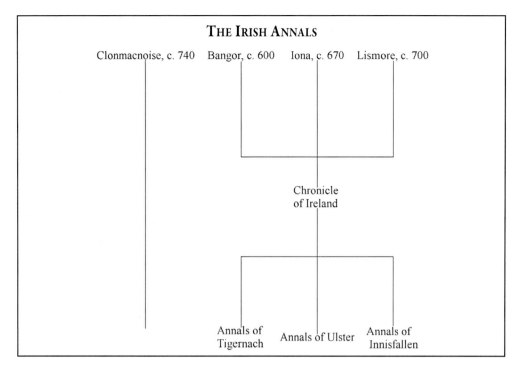

The development of the various Irish annals to illustrate their intertwining history and the unique place of the Clonmacnoise annal.

of St. Davids are also mentioned. Of note is the burning of a city that was near the monastery. The entries are nearly annual during this period as well, and the word forms of the first few entries look to be contemporary to the entries.[31]

The years up to 795 appear to have been written in as an afterthought.[32] The entries up to the Battle of Chester, dated at 613, seem to have been mostly dependent on the Irish Annals.[33] That section names many Irishmen, mostly ecclesiastical. It is also known that the Irish Annals relied heavily on *Isodore's Chronicle*, and that ended in 612.

After 612, the focus of the *Annales Cambriae* changes drastically.[34] Hughes believed this section of the annals had been derived from a *Northern Chronicle* because events from this period seem to focus on Cadwallon and the other Gwynedd kings fighting with Penda and Mercia against Northumbria. Yet there are no Gwynedd abbots mentioned here, nor is it clear from the language that the entries are contemporary.

It is also apparent that this section cannot be derived directly from *Historia Brittonum*. It does not mention Urien, who is the latter's central figure.[35] More convincing, *Historia Brittonum* says that Cerdic was expelled from Elmet during Edwin's reign, while *Annales Cambriae* places it in the year before. *Historia Brittonum* names the restoration of Iddeu, the Battle of Gai, and the death of Penda in that year. The annals name the Battle of Gai, the death of Penda, and the installment of Oswiu in three consecutive years. *Historia Brittonum* says Cadwaladr died in the reign of Oswiu, while the annals say he died fourteen years later. Undoubtedly, a majority of the information in the two sources is similar, even in their biases, indicating an original common source. Most likely, the information for it was found in the *Northern Memoranda*, as it was for the creator of the *Historia Brittonum*. And, as with the *Historia Brittonum*, the information in portions of *Annales Cambriae* may well stretch back to the late sixth century, but records for it were not compiled until about 664x671.[36]

A far cry from the historical documents, the *Canu Heledd* is a cycle of poems revolving around the conquest of a Powysian kingdom by Mercia. According to its contents, the only survivor of the tragedy was the king's daughter, Heledd, who was married to the Mercian king but was abandoned after her family was killed. Heledd acts as the poet's voice throughout the poems. These have traditionally been placed at the middle of the seventh century, the approximate period when the region in question was thought to have been overrun. However, recent study by Jenny Rowland has demonstrated that the poems could not have been written until at least a century later. Her research suggests the poems were most likely written in the last two-thirds of the ninth century.[37] The area was not conquered outright either. It was gradually assimilated.[38]

Nor is the story it tells credible. However, the names seem to fit in well with the extant genealogy of the kingdom. As has been seen, *Marwnad Cynddylan* was contemporary or nearly so to the period in which *Canu Heledd* is placed and it agrees entirely with the names to be found in the latter. Also, the decision to have Heledd as the voice of the poem indicates that some elements of the cycle may be ancient. A woman married off to a potential rival might well have been the only member of the household left alive if the two kingdoms fought a full-scale war. She would naturally have been abandoned once her political value had been mooted.[39] Alternatively, the choice of narrator may well be based on Celtic myth, in which a woman is the personification of the kingdom and is ceremonially married to the new king. As the representative of the Powysian family, Heledd would anguish over the loss of a good mate.[40] Regardless of the origins of the narrator, *Marwnad Cynddylan* has provided a rough idea of the period in which the events laid out here are supposed to have taken place, and any materials which do not comply entirely with that relative chronology must be assumed to be inaccurate.

The most widely used of all the sources for British history is the *Historia Brittonum*. It was likely written by a monk named Ninnius in 829, the fourth year of Merfyn Frych's reign.[41] Merfyn was the first ruler of his dynasty, having married a daughter of the previous king and inherited the throne in default of direct male heirs. Because of his awkward political position, his reign would be marked by attempts to solidify his progeny as Gwynedd's royal family. On this point, Dr. Nora Chadwick and more recently Professor Nicholas Higham have been the sole significant contributors into the nature of the work over the past fifty years, and it is only fitting that their observations dominate the topic.

It was Chadwick who first noted that there was a great deal of antiquarian speculation regarding kingdom foundations in the ninth century.[42] It has been noted above that Dalriada and the Picts wrote down their foundation legends at this time, and Gwynedd's was an important part of the *Historia Brittonum*. The Gwynedd king Rhodri authorized its creation in an atmosphere of growing nationalism and opposition to the Saxons.[43] This sense of kingdom pride, as Higham realized, was only allowed an outlet because of the instability of the Mercian house at the time.[44]

The form it took was mainly genealogical. Chadwick noted that there was a strong intellectual movement in Gwynedd to bridge the gap between themselves and the Romans in this period,[45] and this was most easily accomplished through lineages. It was at this time that the first Gwynedd dynasty was traced back to the Roman-sounding Padarn. His epithet was given as *Peisrud* or "of the red," a phrase that invokes comparison to the uniforms of Roman officers. The oldest set of genealogies may all be seen to converge on Rhodri Mawr, the son of Merfyn Frych and likely the instigator of the movement.[46] However, it seems clear now that the work is indebted to a wider Cambro-Irish community.[47]

Making a connection back to Rome may also be seen in the sole historical work of the time, *Historia Brittonum*. Chapter 62 begins with the legend of Cunedda migrating from Gododdin to Gwynedd to begin the first dynasty, much as Urien's cousin Llywarch Hen was the legendary founder of the second dynasty and a direct ancestor of Rhodri Mawr. Urien is also prominent in the northern chapters. More generally, the most lauded kings in the book are from the North, the same region the kings of Gwynedd migrated from in the ninth century.

What was less obvious from Chadwick's overview of the materials was a second bias. The genealogies which are a part of the *Harleian 3859* collection focus on a later king of the same lineage, Owain. All of his ancestors,[48] apart from those derived from Rhodri's Powysian mother, are named there. Owain son of Hywel Dda was a king in Deheubarth from about 950 to 988. Owain was the most powerful Briton on the island in his lifetime. He even attempted to conquer all of Wales at one point. Powys and Gwynedd resisted, however, and he was never able to bring those two regions under his sway. In an effort at subterfuge, he attacked the latter kingdom by rewriting history. When he authorized a new edition of the *Historia Brittonum,* he used it to characterize some of Powys' most important kings as small-minded fools. Evidence for this updated Dyfed version is to be found in the manuscript history.

The oldest extant copy of *Historia Brittonum* is the "Vatican" Recension.[49] Interestingly, this version contains no information about Gwrtheyrn beyond what is in *Historia Ecclesiastica*. And, as has been seen, he used Gildas but had no compunctions with altering or interpreting him to suit his purposes. It has also been shown that he rarely had positive things to say about British leaders.

It is only with the "Harleian" recension, dated to the tenth century and until recently considered the standard version of the history, that Gwrtheyrn and several other Powysian kings are thrown into a sour light. This suggests *Historia Brittonum* was drastically altered in the tenth century. Such a possibility would account for the new and anti–Powysian information as well as the additional genealogies, which coalesce with Owain son of Hywel.[50]

With the next source, the *Canu Llywarch Hen*, we return to the cyclical poems. This particular group comprises a large number of poems traditionally written by Llywarch Hen, the probable first cousin of Urien and, through his son Dwg, the ancestor of the ninth-century Gwynedd kings. The reality is that probably he created none of the verses; a significant number of them are not even written from his standpoint. Those without the Llywarch persona are the "Pen Urien" group, which have been discussed above.

The purpose behind the "Llywarch Hen" poems has been a topic more hotly debated than any of the sources named above. Patrick Ford has seen the group as created in the ninth century to establish the link claimed by Gwynedd to the North.[51] For this reason, he believes Llywarch to be a political invention. However, Jenny Rowland has pointed out that Dwg is the more likely invention. As she put it, few traditional genealogies went beyond Llywarch, so that it would have been far easier to create a descendant of a prominent figure and add him to an established lineage than to take the most famous person in northern Britain during probably its most famous period and give him a cousin.[52] Rowland also added that the impression of the cycle is wrong for increasing the reputation of the kingdom; the focus is on the sorrow of Llywarch, not the bravery of his sons.[53] Ifor Williams and N.J.A. Williams have gone so far as to say that the character of the poems would have made Llywarch more of an embarrassment than a source of pride for ninth-century Gwynedd.⁵⁴ If these observations are accurate, then there must have been a strong tradition surrounding Llywarch before any of the poems were written, and the possibility of early poems about him exists. Only the poems about his children are of questionable value.

In the latter group, the *englyns* surrounding Gwên show a strong heroic character similar to that found in *Y Gododdin*, and have no romantic qualities. "Pyll" and "Maen Wyn" retain the heroic ethos, but seem to build off the materials in "Gwên."⁵⁵ The primary poem dates from the late eighth century to the middle of the ninth, while "Maen Wynn" and "Pyll" belong to the tenth.⁵⁶ Because of the tenuous nature of their dating, it is fortunate that these three poems offer little more than the names of some of Llywarch's children and a couple of place-names.

An unexpected source of information here is a mnemonic memory device used by the Celtic bards called a triad. Each one associates three individuals with a certain quality, such as generosity or bravery. In practice, triads could be used to help better praise one's patron; they were a means of remembering British history in an oral form with little more than hints, and as such were allowed to survive for centuries. It is to the modern scholar's good fortune that scribes deemed them to be of value before the learning that made them of use was finally lost. The resulting collections have been compiled by Rachel Bromwich in *Trioedd Ynys Prydein, The Triads of the Welsh*.

The triads were recorded in five major manuscripts, and several others contained a few additional triads that were haphazardly added in. Of these, only those forty-six contained in Peniarth 16 and the fragments to be found in the *Black Book of Carmarthen* are of any value here. The other triads tend to add Arthur or another Arthurian character as a fourth member of a triad, or simply to intrude them into the triad. Even here, some alterations have likely been made because of his increasing native popularity, but the other triads have either been influenced by the romances or Geoffrey of Monmouth's pseudo-history.⁵⁷

Peniarth 16 is made up of several fragments whose dates of origin range from the thirteenth to the fifteenth centuries. Their orthography suggests that they all belong to the thirteenth century.⁵⁸ The *Black Book*'s triads are datable to the early thirteenth century as well. The similarities between Peniarth 16 and the *Black Book* suggest they had a common written source, driving back the date the triads were first drafted even further.⁵⁹ The inclusion of significant figures and events from the latter part of the eleventh century and into the early twelfth century seems to match up well with the manuscript evidence and solidly places the original composition to this period.⁶⁰ This is not a dating to inspire faith in their contents. However, as the triads were the foundation from which comparisons were drawn for centuries and because the triads were by design simply made, it seems probable that they contained reasonably accurate information on all the subjects that are extant. This is especially so with the earliest triads, which contain none of the romantic figures or the attributes traditionally associated with them.

The Anglo-Saxon Chronicle was formed during the reign of Alfred and recorded up to the year 891.⁶¹ It has been argued by Stenton that Alfred may not have been the instigator of the work.⁶² However, though the nationalistic undertones and the detailed descriptions of Alfred's activities may not certainly be tied to the king directly, certainly they must connect the final formulation of the document to his time period.

As to the composition of the work, Stenton has noted that there is a duplication in the events of the early history of Wessex in the *Anglo-Saxon Chronicle*. This, he suggested, is evidence of a collation of two versions.⁶³ As one compares the *Anglo-Saxon Chronicle* with the *West Saxon Regnal Table*, one begins to see more of a motive for the double dating. Written in about 891, the chronicle notes the beginning of the kingdom of Wessex in 495, and again in 519, in both cases with Cerdic and his son Cynric. The regnal list, in its extant version copied from an earlier ninth-century manuscript, dates the establishment in the range 525x550. Ceawlin's reign length is extended a great deal in the *Anglo-Saxon Chronicle*, to the point where it is highly suspicious.[64] In the regnal table, it is a reasonable fifteen or sixteen years.

Throughout the centuries between its establishment and the Viking invasion of England, Wessex was a prominent kingdom, and because of this its claim to an early sixth-century establishment was enough to substantiate its position. This changed in the ninth century, when most of the English kingdoms were conquered and Wessex was greatly weakened. Alfred spent most of his early career trying to develop an economic and political base of power from which to mount an effective defense against the Vikings. In this, his most determined opponents would have been the nobles of his kingdom, who could envision a Viking future in which their importance could be maintained and who could see in supporting him only the potential for ruin.

Yet they could read, and Alfred hoped to take advantage of their literacy. In authorizing a chronicle and stretching back the history of the kingdom to the fifth century he was underscoring the length of the kingdom's traditions; no kingdom but venerable Kent had been established in Britain for so long. This, he would have hoped, would be a source of pride for those he hoped to convince.

It is also very possible that the chronicle made one house out of what may have been two or more originally.[65] In this case, the chronicle was a synchronizing history much as we have already seen with Gwynedd and has been suggested with Dalriada. Tying the kingdom founders to Alfred and extending their presence in England back to the fifth century were two innovations introduced by the document, and therefore must be viewed with suspicion. The two changes could only have benefited Alfred or his kindred, thus strongly suggesting that Alfred was, indeed, the person who authorized the writing of the *Anglo-Saxon Chronicle*.

As to the sources the chroniclers used, they were first laid out by Professor Chadwick over a century ago and his list has gone largely unchallenged since then.[66] They are Bede's chronological summary appended to the *Historia Ecclesiastica*, a set of annals extending from Bede's death to Ecgberht of Wessex, king lists of the Northumbrian and Mercian rulers with their respective genealogies, an ecclesiastical history of the world up to the year 1110, a list of the bishops of Winchester down to 754, a series of Wessex annals down to about 688 and contemporary at least from 661,[67] a continuation of those annals up to the middle of the eighth century, and a series of continental annals used for the period 880 to 890.

The genealogies and king lists of Britain were created and edited from the early centuries of the post–Roman era down through the eleventh century. However, they seem accurate on the grounds of their credibility and similar prejudices. Genealogies and king lists are less useful for helping to understand the political situations both within the kingdoms and their interactions without than any previously discussed source. On the other hand, the motivations of each genealogy or king list are clear and consistent. The kingdoms that they represent inevitably created them. There was rarely a reason and opportunity for another kingdom to invent or record a foreign lineage, and the exceptional cases of foreign tampering are easily spotted as they differ so clearly from a majority of the native records.[68] As part of this national propaganda, most kingdoms—Irish, Pictish, Germanic, or British—found it necessary to invent a connection to some deity or widely famed Roman hero of the past. This tie was also intended to give the lineage greater legitimacy. Additional names situated between the founder and the first known king may often be fictitious or not a part of the same lineage. These, too, have been added in order to augment the prestige of the royal family.

Both styles of recording family history have their individual difficulties as well. King lists record no branches of the royal line, and therefore give the impression that each member of the family was a ruler and his father's successor. This is, of course, not true or possible for more than two or three generations (see below). Worse, there have been occasional instances when two or more brothers were placed in a king list as living in consecutive generations. These are the problems encountered in a healthy dynasty. In some if not most cases, there were periods of foreign domination or internal conflict resulting in a change of family rule. Introducing that information into a genealogy designed to show its length and stability is rarely possible without easily seen flaws, as will be seen.

In addition, genealogies are notorious for collating two or more royal families that were at one time rivals but eventually became a single kingdom. In this, the normal technique has been to take contemporary and often competing rulers of an area and form them into a consecutive string of kings. Doing so not only covers up the historical but unpleasant fact of conflict, but it also shows respect to any remaining members of the non-ruling dynasties and extends the age of that kingdom noticeably and thereby gives it greater credibility.

Coming from an entirely different source but used for much the same purpose, the *vitae* make up a substantial portion of the information for the period. It is for this reason that they are important to understand, even if they can rarely be made use of blindly. *Vitae* were motivated by several goals. Most centered on the monasteries who patronized them. Their chief interests were in expanding their holdings, raising their level of religious prestige, and thus in generating revenue from pilgrims.

To this end, beginning in the eleventh century monasteries often hired hagiographers to write a history of their most important predecessor. These mercenary writers were given full access to any oral or written sources which could be found or fabricated,[69] and no doubt were allowed to interact with the local peasantry in order to amass as much folk information as possible on the subject.

The information given to the writer inevitably involved the saint's confrontation with a king or kings, his victory through miracle, the king's apology and promise of territory, and the resulting land grant or grants at the end of the *vita*. A saint and thereby his monastery also gained prestige through his interactions with more popular saints, such as Germanus or David. If a story could be altered slightly to give the saint some special importance in these circumstances, all the better. Miracles, great or small, were certain to give the monastery renown as well. The *vitae* are cluttered with episodes that give such instances, and often the same miracles are repeated from one *vita* to the next.

Other local, oral legends were not ecclesiastical in nature, nor did they involve ancestors of surviving dynasties. Because they managed to survive without containing any of the incentives for preservation the above sources possessed, they have done so without the influences which plague every other written source. On the other hand, in order to do so they have spent upwards of centuries in an uncontrolled oral environment. Extreme caution must be used in extracting any information from them. They are in some ways the basic sources for the romances listed below, and useful information may be plucked from them in much the same way.

Romances are simply the most difficult sources to obtain useful information from.

However, it is possible if one takes into full consideration their limitations. The most useful romances were constructed from the twelfth to the fourteenth centuries. At best, they are six centuries removed from the time they portray. As the author has shown elsewhere, each story has undergone a number of significant transformations in that time. They have likely also survived in an entirely oral environment for an extended amount of time. To review, the generic histories are as follows.

First, a memorable event occurred. This was recorded by a bard for the purpose of extolling his king in return for economic compensation. Later bards would then modify the story for their own personal pleasure or to suit another patron. The longer this process continued, the greater the chance that traditional bardic themes and tools would be integrated into the story, and the greater the chance that characters would be added to it.

The extant romances are mostly to be found in France, though they have been located in a dozen other countries throughout Europe. There is good reason to believe that early forms of the romances were in the hands of *trouvères* and *troubadours* before they made it to the writers.[70] These groups were in the main concerned with taking the Celtic feel of the British tales and "modernizing" them with twelfth-century surroundings and the romantic influences that were popular at the time. Finally, each individual author and the author's patron had very specific reasons for having the Arthurian tales written down.

In order to employ any one story, all variations of that story must be used, and each of the above biases must be accounted for and screened out to hazard a likely original. There is no certainty, however, that the results of this process will be useful. It may well be that a story has been so overwhelmed with bardic themes and the partiality of the romancers that there is nothing of value remaining. It is always possible that what appears to be an Arthurian romance is nothing more than a myth placed into an Arthurian setting. Such was the case with Tristan. To date, the present author has only been able to piece together two tales. One focuses on the abduction of Gwenhwyfar and the other on the anti-pagan campaign of Peredur.[71] There is good evidence that a Gawain tale could be similarly reconstructed, while the details in many of the less popular Arthurian stories may prove entirely unusable.[72] It should be kept in mind that the Arthurian romances were exceptionally fortunate in that they were the first group in this genre; all others came later and after much more time spent in an oral environment.

What can be seen in the above instances is a problematic set of secondary sources. Unquestionably, these sources are more complex than the primary sources; many of the above are the products of compiling, oral memories, strong biases, multiple reincarnations for different purposes, or all four. However, their complexity only makes them more difficult to study and make use of; it does not make them impossible and it does not make it unreasonable to find a utilization for them. In seeing what is the nature of each source and its reason for both creation and preservation, it is not far to understand where each relays accurate information, where that information may have been slanted to suit a purpose, and where it could serve no other function. Once the data has been separated along these divisions and compared to data from other sources, the process of reconstruction is a matter of piecing that information together in the most reasonable manner and with a minimal amount of discrepancy.

Knowing all the above, and having the benefit of at least a century's worth of scholars researching the origins of these sources, we may be confident that a good majority of each source's biases have been identified. The study of each collection of information need only be a matter of making use of the data others have collected on it. We may then employ that information in building a foundation and basic structure created by the primary sources. Such is not an easy task; in fact, it has seemed to the present author to be overwhelming at times. However, the potential rewards of such an undertaking are too substantial to deny, and too obvious to refrain from attempting.

4

Guessing Date Ranges

In 1970, Dr. Molly Miller published a book under the inconspicuous title of *The Sicilian Colony Dates* in which she examined the methods of chronography used by many of the ancient historians to derive specific dates for the distant events they were recording but had no primary materials for. She came to the conclusion that the method used was in all cases a modified version of Herodotus' "three generations to the century" theory. Her conclusions inspired an intricate and extremely useful chapter exploring the lifespans, maximum and minimum generation lengths, childbirth statistics, and methods of succession in the ancient world. The study allowed her to develop a model for how a stable population functioned and was distributed before the Middle Ages. Her conclusions became the foundation for several enlightening discussions on the British and Germanic genealogies.

Miller began with the results of an unusual work of research, *Bones, Bodies, and Disease*.[1] The monolithic work had examined the findings of the skeletal materials of persons from all over the ancient world back to the Neanderthals. Among other things, it discussed the ages at death of several widely separated settlements and how they were distributed. Due to several factors, this approach was not able to provide any useful information on deaths before the age of 30, but it was a sound basis to work from after that age. It was seen that the death rates between 30 and 39 tapered from 61.1 percent in the early second millennium at Tepe Hissar to 57.3 percent at Caister in the Roman period, and between 40 and 49 the numbers went from 96.7 percent to 86.3 percent. That is, typically 60 percent of persons living to 30 would be dead by forty, and 90 percent of forty year-olds would be dead by 50. There were no cases of individuals living beyond 55 in Wells' study.

From these specific calculations it was determined that in the turbulent period between 2000 BCE and 1000 BCE the normal death rates for thirty-year-olds and forty-year-olds was roughly 60 percent and 90 percent, respectively. As an afterthought, she made note that the wake of the Roman Empire's end would have produced similar statistics. She then guessed the death rate between 20 and 29 at 40 percent and, using the above generalizations as well and comparing them to the average life expectancy on various sites in the ancient world,[2] was able to support those numbers.[3] However, she also guessed that the death rate between 10 and 20 would be 30 percent, and provided no support or evidence for this number. It was just a rough guess based on the knowledge that traditionally this was the group with the lowest death rate.

Moving on, she took the numbers above to form a model population from the age of 10. Then she used that model to derive the average number of children born in each year.

All this seemed reasonable, if the 10–20 decade was accurate. However, creating her model she assumed that the age range of mothers was 15 to 49. The reality is that women in ancient society were not considered adult until perhaps 18 because they matured more slowly than in the past few generations of our era. It is also known that, until recently, 40 was considered the limit of a woman's safe childbearing years, and 38 a more likely age. The family history of the Merovingians will point this fact out at the end of the chapter. To conclude, Dr. Miller can be seen to have made two errors in her reasoning: her death rate for the decade 10 to 20 was an unsubstantiated guess and therefore so was the number of persons in that age range in her model. Also, her number for potential mothers included fourteen years during which the chances of childbirth were so low as to be inconsequential. Proceeding, she then used the formula:

$$N = \frac{\textit{maximum age -maximum fertility}}{\textit{maximum fertility-minimum age}}$$
$$\frac{(\text{N-minimum age}) \times (\text{maximum age-N})}{(\text{maximum fertility-minimum age}) \times (\text{maximum age-maximum fertility})}$$

The results were that the demographic maximum fertility of a population would be about two-thirds the number of women in the proper age range in any given year. Fortunately, this number remains basically unchanged even when the range is reduced to 18 to 38.

However, Miller was not done tinkering. She also added that the consequences of child rearing would limit a woman to at most one birth every two years, and stressed that the resulting equation represented the maximum number of reasonable births per year. We come to an equation of (number of fertile women * 2/3 * ½ = births per year). To this estimate she added a fraction of 8/9 to allow for other factors that might limit the number of children a woman might have, such as separation. Her equation formed, she worked out how many children the women between 15 and 49 should have and again estimated the death rate of that group so that it would have the already assigned number of 10-year-olds. She then wrote an entire distribution chart for her model population. This included expectation of life at each Dekaquennium.

Age	Survivors	Survival Rate	Life Expectancy
0	1000	50% (35% 0–5, 15% 6–10)	16.1
10	500	70%	18.1
20	350	60%	13.8
30	210	40%	9.6
40	85	10%	6.3
50	10	0%	2.5

Unfortunately, the chart brings out the flaws in her two estimates. According to her model, life expectancy at birth was 16.1 and at 10 it was 18.1 years. As she herself noted, an earlier work based on archaeology had named the life expectancies as 17–21 and 19–24, respectively.[4] These are not outrageous differences; nevertheless, Miller's specific estimates are lower than the ranges which are factual. The incongruity is all the more noteworthy because these discrepancies are in the very areas where Miller could not provide independent evidence for her estimates, both pre-twenty age groups. Accepting the mean of both archaeological ranges as true, we can derive quite different death rates for them. By raising the survival rate between 0 and 5 up 5 percent and thus raising the 0–10 up to 55 percent, and also raising the 11–20 rate to 75 percent, the following life expectancies emerge.

Age	Survivors	Survival Rate:	Life Expectancy
0	1000	55% (30% 0–5, 15% 6–10)	18.1
10	550	75%	19.8
20	417.5	60%	13.6
30	250.4	40%	9.3
40	100.64	10%	5.8
50	10.064	0%	2.5

The author has no evidence to support these specific modifications. However, it does seem that Miller was right in believing the 0 to 5 quinquennium had a lower survival rate than the 6–10, and the 0–10 dekaquennium had a lower survival rate than 11–20. Also, the changed life expectancies match those to be derived from the archaeological evidence.

An additional improvement is that the modification allows for a more feasible childbearing rate. According to her model listed above, each year 450 persons between 0 and 10 will die, 132.5 between 11 and 20, 167.1 between 21 and 30, 149.76 between 31 and 40, 90.576 between 41 and 50, and 10.064 between 51 and 55. Thus, roughly 1,000 persons would die.

By Miller's estimates, however, there is now a vast discrepancy. In the model population there are 4069.188 women eligible for childbearing, meaning 1356.396 births can be expected per year and that the population will increase by over 356. This is hardly a stable population, and bears out a fourth flaw in her model. It does not take into account sterile couples, widowed women, persons in religious circumstances where procreation is unacceptable, marriages where there is no sex for whatever reason, or the reduced and much more likely childbearing range of 18 to 38. Also, in Miller's model the *average* woman living past 49 would have had 12 children. According to the revised model, there would be 3006.132 women in their prime childbearing years in any given year, and from which a vast majority of the children would come from. The average number of children a woman over 38 would have had would go down to 7, a high but much more practical number.

With the above changes, the materials are mathematically correct and now agree entirely with the archaeological evidence. They retain the fact that a person's maximum life expectancy was 55 years, and that the vast majority of births were by women between 18 and 38. None of the purposes to which this information was used is in any way affected.

Miller then made use of the above numbers to show the chances of a child being an adult at the time of their parents' deaths. From the revised model above, we are in a position to do this as well. Out of a thousand people born in a given year, 483.75 would live to 15. Thus there would be a 48.375 percent chance that a child would live to that age. Of 444 females aged 18, 205.472 would live long enough for their heirs to turn 15, or 46.277 percent. Similarly in the table below:

18	444	205.472	46.277%
19	430.75	190.496	44.224%
20	417.5	175.52	42.041%
21	400.79	160.544	40.057%
22	384.08	145.568	37.9%
23	367.37	130.592	35.548%
24	350.66	115.616	32.971%
25	333.95	100.64	30.136%
26	317.24	91.582	28.868%
27	300.53	82.525	27.46%

28	283.82	73.467	25.885%
29	267.11	64.41	24.114%
30	250.4	55.352	22.105%
31	235.424	46.294	19.664%
32	220.448	37.237	16.892%
33	205.472	28.179	13.714%
34	190.496	19.122	10.038%
35	175.52	10.064	5.734%
36	160.544	8.051	5.015%
37	145.568	6.038	4.148%
38	130.592	4.026	3.083%
Mean survival percentage			24.565%

This would mean the odds of any woman living 15 years after she gave birth would be 24.565 percent. With either parent remaining alive the percentage would rise to 43.1 percent.[5] The chance of a child living 15 years and having one adult parent alive would then be .431 * .484 = .201 or 20.1 percent. As there would in a standard model be 1,000 births per year, there would be 21,000 births in an average woman's childbearing years. And, as there would be 4,069 childbearing women at any one time, each would average out to 5.161 births. Of the average, 1.04 children would live to 15 with at least one parent still alive, and 2.5 children would simply make it to 15. However, in actuality some families would have had several surviving members, while others would have had none. This was not predictable through pure mathematics, and so historical models were employed by Miller.

Of the six dynasties she used from across the world, the average showed only a 59 percent chance of a son surviving his father. However, even this number may be high. The six successions in the Assyrian chronology have often been questioned because the reign lengths seem inordinately long and artificial, making it potentially unhistorical. Also, the Ottoman dynasty had the benefit that its rulers had access to multiple potential royal mothers in the harems, which is not representative of the monogamous pairings in legitimate ancient Greek or British cultures. With these two incompatible examples out of the equation, the odds of a son outliving his father in a royal family were reduced to 56 percent. It might also be added that the four remaining dynasties were quite stable. Returning to the British where dynasties and life were much more haphazard and kings were more at risk in battle, a 50 percent chance of a son inheriting from his father seems reasonable and even optimistic. This means a kingdom would have a 50 percent * 50 percent * 50 percent * 50 percent * 50 percent or 3.125 percent chance of having five consecutive sons on the throne. As Miller noted, there are no runs of more than ten consecutive successions in any dynasty that may be historically verified.

This is an important realization in British and Anglo-Saxon studies. As has been seen, the former have lineages that stretch back to before 400 in unbroken successions of father-to-son and extend forward well into the Middle Ages. The latter have the same strings of father-to-son inheritance back into the pre–Christian centuries. There can be no question about it—the received king lists cannot be accurate.

Miller then proposed an alternative to the unlikely primogeniture scenario of the historical records, an ithagenic or cousinly succession. This is commonly found in Irish records,[6] and there is evidence that it occurred in the historical English and Celtic kingdoms from early on as well.

Of the four cultures to be found in early Britain, the Irish are easily the best documented, and have been the most thoroughly explored. A study conducted by Byrne and used by Miller gave 32 kings and 10 generations of Brega from 604 to 956, 34 kings and 13 generations of Mide from 555 to 1022, and 40 kings and 14 generations of Ailech from 536 to 1061. Averaged out, this gave a 12.75-year reign and a 36.3-year generation over 1344 years and three dynasties.[7]

The raw materials indicate what the Irish annals lay out, that there were nearly three reigns per generation on average. This makes good sense with what has been seen elsewhere. But the necessity of such a ratio is best understood by seeing how royal families could have operated under the most fortunate of circumstances. When reproduction could take place at the earliest convenience, primogeniture was possible in the ancient world.

Year 0: Future founder is born
Year 18: Son is born
Year 30: Founds kingdom
Year 36: Grandson is born
Year 55: Founder dies, is replaced by 37-year-old son and his heir is 19

However, as has been seen, 40 was the longest a man could hope to live, and only three of five of his children could expect to reach adulthood. If a man had five children, he would have a 50 percent chance of producing an adult son, and again odds would be against him living to, let alone beyond, forty. If the father did have a male child who did live to adulthood, that boy could be born anywhere inside his fertile years of 18 to 38. Thus a more probable scenario would be:

Year 0: Founder is born
Year 25: Son is born
Year 30: Founds kingdom
Year 40: Founder dies, son inherits at fifteen
Year 50: Grandson is born
Year 65: Son dies, grandson inherits at fifteen

The precarious nature of such a system need hardly be expounded upon. An early death, a series of female births, fertility problems, and a dozen other unforeseen circumstances could upset such a balance. Even the generation length is optimistic; 27 is the most fertile year, and thus the most likely time in which to impregnate a woman. It is possible that many of the relevant cultures emphasized that the child of a woman married to a crowned king was the most eligible, and so it is very possible that in many instances men waited till much later in life to have children.

The information accumulated above all points in the same direction. While mathematically possible, primogeniture would not have been an effective form of inheritance in the ancient world. That this is so can be seen in the common laws of the Greeks and Celts, which seem to spend an otherwise inordinate amount of time focusing on the raising of orphans.[8]

In practical application, inheritance probably looked something like the roughly contemporary Frankish house of Clovis, whose kings are in the illustration given an asterisk.

Other useful items may be inferred in conjunction with what is known of Celtic and English society. As a layman could not expect to live beyond 55, Celts were given some adult status beginning at 15, and English kings could rule no earlier than 5; contemporary kings among the Celts were born within 40 years and English within 50 years of each other.

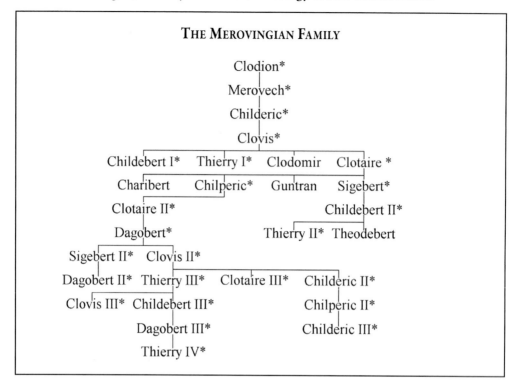

The House of Merovech is provided to demonstrate the necessity of cousinly inheritance during the fifth and sixth centuries.

Bards were generally not fully educated till the age of 20. Priests and monks were at least 18, while it seems to have been tradition that a man could not be an abbot before he was 25 or a bishop before he turned 30. The better records on the Continent show that the maximum lifespan of holy men was as high as 80, probably because of the more balanced diet and the general respite they had from wars and other hardships of a warrior or peasant's life.

For these reasons, a contemporary priest could be born as far apart as 62 years from another contemporary priest, abbot, or bishop. However, he could not be born more than 55 years earlier than an abbot or 50 years earlier than a bishop. Two contemporary abbots could be born no further than 55 years apart and an abbot could be up to 55 years younger than a bishop, but only 50 years older. The maximum difference between two contemporary bishops would have been 50.

An adult Celtic layman could be 65 years younger than any holy man. However, a priest or monk could be no more than 37 years younger than the layman, a bard 35 years younger, an abbot 30 years younger, and a bishop 25 years younger. A Germanic king might be 75 years younger than a holy man, with the same maximum comparisons as the Celts.

Miller and a basic knowledge of the lifespans and minimum ages of the early church have provided us with not only a testing field for the genealogies, but a rough tool with which to work out the chronologies of individuals and events in sub–Roman Britain. With one reasonably accurate date and an acceptable genealogy, it is possible to estimate the birth ranges of all contemporaries to the royal line, as well as the ancestors and prodigy of the entire pedigree. Granted, the inaccuracy will grow steadily larger as the distance from the original person and date progresses, but a second date or some other pertinent information will help narrow such margins once more. More importantly, using the same process on all the available genealogies at one time while using the primary sources as the means of acquiring dates and relationships will allow for not only tighter birth ranges but some strong corroboration that the methods laid out above are valid.

5

Saints and Nobility in the Sources

Dr. Miller's studies in the populations of the ancient world will prove a valuable tool in helping to identify the rough lifespans and family structures of the sub–Roman Britain peoples. They will serve to establish the extremes to which we can push family trees and their chronologies, and by extrapolation they will allow for the development of rough floruits for the individuals of the period.

However, Miller's guidelines, the genealogies, and the primary sources will not provide enough information if British history up to 700 is to be reconstructed in any useable fashion. Secondary sources will provide a necessary supplement, and chief among them will be the *vitae* or the biographies of religious men as composed by professional hagiographers. The origins of the *vitae* have already been discussed above, as have their limits and advantages; they do possess memories of their subject, but these are buried in the designs of the monastery that hired the biographers. One aspect of these religious histories which has not been addressed is the accuracy of the pedigrees their heroes are given. It is, to be sure, a question of some importance. Unfortunately, it is a question without a straight answer.

On one hand, having a saint with a noble or royal background would only have enhanced the prestige of the monastery that claimed him. For this reason, it seems likely that saints would have fabricated connections to royalty. On the other, religion was a precarious institution well into the sixth century, and was not powerful for centuries after that time. The most likely men to have been able to acquire land for monasteries and other establishments, and to deal with kings in general, would have been those who were from the highest sociopolitical echelons, the royal families. The chicken-and-egg conundrum may never be solved absolutely. However, it is hoped that some perspective may be gained here, and from it a useful understanding of how to take the genealogies contained in the *vitae*.

To that end, all the native holy men mentioned in the primary sources have been listed below. All have been labeled with regard to their lineage, their family's status, and the primary source(s) in which they were found.

	Paternity	*Primary Source*
Acca	Germanic	Eddius, Bede
Æbbe	Germanic royal line	*Vita Cuthberti*, Bede, Eddius
Aedan	Irish	Bede
Æthelberht	Germanic royal line	Bede
Æthelred	Germanic royal line	Bede
Æthelwine	Germanic	Bede

5. Saints and Nobility in the Sources

	Paternity	Primary Source
Æthilwald	Germanic	Bede
Agricola	British	Prosper's *Chronicle*
Aldhelm	Germanic	Bede
Ammon	British	*Vita Samsoni*
Asaph	British	*Vita Kentigerni*
Badwini	Germanic	Eddius, Bede
Baithene	Irish Royal line	*Vita Columbae*
Benedict Biscop	Germanic Noble line	Bede
Berhtwald	Germanic	*Vita Wilfridi*
Berthwyn	British	*Llandaff Charters*
Bisi	Germanic	Bede
Biuon	British	*Llandaff Charters*
Boisel	Germanic	Bede
Boniface	Roman	Bede
Bosa	Germanic	Bede
Botulf	Germanic	*Vita Ceolfrith*
Cadwared	British	*Llandaff Charters*
Caelin	Germanic	Bede
Catgen	British	*Llandaff Charters*
Ceadda	Germanic	Bede
Cedd	Germanic	Bede
Ceolfrith	Germanic	*Vita Ceolfrith*
Ceollach	Irish	Bede
Cethig	British	*Llandaff Charters*
Colbrit	British	*Llandaff Charters*
Colman	Irish	Bede, Eddius
Columba	Irish royal line	*Vita Columbae*, Bede
Columbanus	Irish	*Epistolas*
Concen	British	*Llandaff Charters*
Congen	British	*Llandaff Charters*
Conicg	British	*Llandaff Charters*
Cromanus	Germanic	Bede
Cudda	Germanic	Bede
Cuthbert	Germanic	Bede
Cwichelm	Germanic	Bede
Cynebert	Germanic	Bede
Cynebil	Germanic	Bede
Dagan	British	*Llandaff Charters*
Damian	Germanic	Bede
David	British	*Vita Kentigerni*
Deusdedit	Germanic	Bede
Dimanus	Germanic	Bede
Diuma	Irish	Bede
Dubricius	British royal line	*Llandaff Charters*, *Vita Samsoni*
Dunawt	British	Bede
Eadberht	Germanic	Bede
Eadhed	Germanic	Bede
Earconwald	Germanic royal line[1]	Bede
Eata	Germanic	Bede
Ebba	Germanic	*Vita Cuthberti*, Bede, Eddius
Edgar	Germanic	Bede

	Paternity	Primary Source
Eluoid	British	*Llandaff Charters*
Eosterwine	Germanic	*Vita Ceolfrith*
Finan	Irish	Bede
Fomre	Germanic	*Llandaff Charters*
Gebmund	Germanic	Bede
Gildas	British royal line	*De Excidio Britanniae*
Gnouan	British	*Llandaff Charters*
Gurhaual	British	*Llandaff Charters*
Gurthauar	British	*Llandaff Charters*
Hædde	Germanic	Bede
Herefrith	Germanic	Bede
Hilda	Germanic royal line	Bede
Hwætberht	Germanic	Bede
Iacob	British	*Llandaff Charters*
Illtud	British	*Vita Samsoni*
Iudhubr	British	*Llandaff Charters*
Iuniavus	British	*Vita Samsoni*
James	British	Bede
Jarman	?	Bede
Kentigern	British royal line	*Vita Kentigerni*
Maglorius	British	*Vita Samsoni*
Malo	British	*Vita Samsoni*
Maucennus	British	*Vita Samsoni*
Mevennus	British	*Vita Samsoni*
Oftfor	Germanic	Bede
Osryth	Germanic royal line	Bede
Oswald	Germanic royal line	Bede
Oudoceus	British royal line	*Llandaff Charters*
Outigern	British	*Llandaff Charters*
Patrick	British/bureaucrats	*Epistola, Confessio*
Paul	British	*Llandaff Charters*
Petroc	British royal line	*Vita Samsoni*
Piro	British	*Vita Samsoni*
Putta	Germanic	Bede
Rhun	British Royal line	*Northern History*
Samson	British bureaucrats	*Vita Samsoni*
Samson II	British	*Llandaff Charters*
Saranus	British	Bede
Saturn	British	*Llandaff Charters*
Segienus	Irish royal line	Bede
Sexwulf	Germanic	Bede
Sigfrith	Germanic	Bede, *Vita Ceolfrith*
Sona	British	Council of Toledo
Sulgen	British	*Llandaff Charters*
Tatberht	Germanic	Eddius
Terchan	British	*Llandaff Charters*
Tibba	Germanic	*Vita Wilfridi*
Tomianus	Germanic	Bede
Trumhere	Germanic	Bede
Tuda	Germanic	Bede
Tunberht	Germanic	Bede

5. Saints and Nobility in the Sources

	Paternity	Primary Source
Uinniau	Irish	*Epistolae de Gildae*
Umbraphel	British	*Vita Samsoni*
Verca	Germanic	*Vita Cuthberti*
Waldhere	Germanic	Bede
Wilfrid	Germanic	Bede, Eddius
Willibrord	Germanic	Bede, Eddius
Winfrid	Germanic	Bede
Wini	Germanic	Bede
Winnoc	British	Gregory of Tours

There were in total some 115 ecclesiastics active in or coming from Britain during the period in question. Forty-seven of them were Britons, with six and perhaps seven deriving from royal lines. Among the Germanic leaders, there were fifty-eight listed in the sources, with eight persons descended from a king. Of the Irish active in Britain there were ten, with three descended from the royal line of Ulaid for certain. However, the unusual traditions of Iona suggest that most if not all of the ten were related to Columba and therefore were also of royal blood. They are unhelpful in the present context.

We are left, then, with the Britons and Germanic peoples. The ratios of the two culture groups are strangely similar. A little less than one out of every seven British and Germanic saints or major ecclesiastics were royal. This creates a strong sounding board to judge the frequency with which the claim was made for the many British holy men named in later sources, mainly *vitae*. These, too, are catalogued alphabetically by royal ties and any reign, though the number of sources attached to many of the saints below renders listing them impractical here.

	Paternity		Paternity		Paternity
Albinus	Common	Darlugdach	Common	Helanus	Common
Alvandus	Common	Docco	Royal family?	Houardon	Common
Arthmael	Noble family	Domnech	Common	Iacutus	Royal family
Asaph	Common	Domnoc	Royal family?	Ismael	Royal family
Austolus	Common	Eldad	Common	Iwi	Common
Bachan	Common	Elwyn	Common	Justinian	Common
Bernacus	Noble family	Enodoc	Common	Kebi	Royal family
Beuno	Royal family	Ethbin	Common	Ketinlau	Common
Bothmael	Common	Eunius	Common	Leonorus	Common
Brioc	Common	Findbar	Common	Loucher	Common
Cadfan	Royal family	Finnian of Llancarfan	Common	Loveran	Common
Cadoc	Royal family			Madoc	Common
Carantoc	Common	Germochus	Common	Mael	Common
Carincinalis	Common	Gildas	Royal family?	Maeloc	Royal family
Clitauc	Royal family	Gonerus	Common	Maeloc of Anglesey	Common
Coninudrus	Common	Goueznau	Common		
Conoc	Common	Goulven	Common	Maglorius	Common
Conocan	Common	Guiner	Common	Maian	Common
Constantine	Royal family	Guinnius	Common	Mansuetus	Common
Constantine	Royal family	Guistlian	Common	Maucanus	Common
Corentin	Common	Guppir	Common	Maucennus	Common
Curig	Common	Gurgallonus	Common	Melorius	Royal family
Cynidr	Common	Gurval	Common	Meven	Royal family
Daniel	Common	Gwenael	Royal family	Morhed	Common

Paternity		Paternity		Paternity	
Ninnoca	Royal family	Rhun	Royal family	Tangusius	Common
Padarn	Royal family	Rioch	Common	Teilo	Royal family?
Paternus of Llanbadarn	Common	Rochath	Common	Thuriau	Common
		Runon	Common	Titechan	Common
Paternus of Vannes	Common	Sanctanus	Common	Tudwal	Royal family
		Sanctinus	Common	Tudy	Common
Paul Aurelian	Royal family	Sativola	Royal family	Tydecho	Royal family?
Paulinus of Cynwyl	Common	Senacus	Common	Tyssilio	Royal family
		Servanus	Common	Wethenoc	Royal family
Petroc	Royal family	Similianus	Common	Winwaloe	Royal family
Piro	Common	Sulgen	Common	Wulvella	Royal family

The above listing seems a historical possibility as the British sampling is feasible. Of 100 British holies, 29 are listed as having royal connections. This is well over the one of seven standard set above. However, five royals are of questionable lineage, leaving 24. This reduces the margin to less than one of four, and is nearer the mark.

What this means to the current study is that, generally speaking, if a *vita* or other secondary British source makes a claim that a saint had royal parentage and the claim is chronologically and geographically feasible, it is likely to be historical. If either is at all questionable, it will be wisest to avoid that connection.

In a wider perspective, it may also offer some insights into the writing of the *vitae*. There must have been pressure to connect all or at least a majority of the saints to royal families. In nearly all cases, it would have made them more important. That they were never associated with royalty indicates that the biographers were aware of their audience and mindful of keeping their stories believable. A saint might perform a miracle beyond the power of man, but that was feasible as he did it through God's will. Being royalty was not something a saint's faith could guarantee, and such a claim could be disproven. In and of itself, this realization means nothing. However, it does demonstrate that the biographers did have some limits to the assertions they would make for their subjects.

6

Reconstructed British History

The study of Britain after the Roman presence has traditionally been divided into two subject areas, that of the Romano-British who were around before and the Germanic peoples who arrived during the Roman occupation. This approach creates a clear partition along cultural, societal, and philosophical lines and because of this should make the overview below more readily understood.

To begin, the British. Interest in them has often been quite morbid; for any scholar looking to the future they are a culture whose only interest lies in how long their culture survived and in what forms. Because of the perspective, discussion has centered around the period of and immediately after the last series of emperors were crowned in Britain. There has also been some regular debate on the continuation of Roman culture and society as shown in British social organization, education, and political structure. Finally, it has been generally observed that the British would develop heroic age kingships, though when and for what reason have remained somewhat vague. It is these aspects of British post–Roman life which will be examined in the pages below.

A large amount of time and effort has been put into describing how exactly the last years of Roman and the first years of post–Roman Britain progressed. To this end, the matching of dates with events has been attempted time and again. No definitive conclusions have ever been managed. In the main, this has been because Zosimus is our only primary informant for the period and he is uncertain about the affairs of the Western Roman Empire.[1] What the chronology really boils down to is that in 406x407, the Roman army in Britain began to promote men to the office of emperor.[2] The third man raised to the position, Constantine, left for the Continent immediately after his election. He brought with him a good portion of what remained of the Roman troops in Britain in an attempt to conquer the Western Roman Empire.

Probably in 408, but definitely when they realized that Britain was relatively undefended, the Germanic peoples of the Continent launched a full-scale attack.[3] Constantine, strategically involved with campaigning on the Continent, could do nothing to help. His situation would only grow more tenuous. By 409, his lieutenant Gerontius had rebelled from him. Constantine was captured and executed in 411.

According to Zosimus, the barbarian assault coupled with the loss of their protector forced the Britons to rebel from Rome and defend themselves. They did so successfully and beat back their aggressors, though as to how they managed to organize themselves and under what leaders, Zosimus does not speak. No widely accepted theory has ever emerged on that point.

This final rebellion from Rome, however, brings the historian to the crux of the problem, a place where even Thompson faltered in his evaluation of late Roman Britain. He postulated a *bacaudae* revolt of commoners, which spread from possibly all over southern England into Gaul and Italy.[4] If we are to take the other three recorded examples of *bacaudae* revolts on the Continent as a sounding board, the rebellion in Britain was generated to free slaves and weaken the ruling class. Considering the waning economic conditions in Britain, that possibility makes sense, but the admittedly unreliable Zosimus spells out that the revolt in Britain was a means of defending the island from the incoming Germanic aggressors. The aftermath of a *bacaudae* revolt in Britain does not match up with those in Gaul and Italy either. On the Continent, the revolts led to relatively large interregnum kingdoms, yet in Britain, where there was more isolation from Rome, there was no sign of any larger political entities when Germanus traveled there just two decades later. To this glaring flaw in his theory Thompson could only say "The fire had gone out. The spirit of 409 was dead."[5] The present author cannot accept Thompson's explanation and leave the words of Zosimus and Germanus' biographer in such opposition.

Dr. Dark has proposed that the Martinian militant approach to Christianity coupled with the *bacaudae* movement to give the British rebels different motives than the Romans had on the Continent. This idea also has some serious flaws. Most poignantly, the other three *bacaudae* movements were inspired by the one in Britain,[6] yet in those versions the Martinian values did not come into play. It is on the Continent where St. Martin's influence was most strongly felt, so this connection is unlikely in the extreme.

There is a simpler solution to the events leading up to the end of Roman Britain, and one that fits all the evidence. First, there was an invasion by the Germanic peoples in 408 or 409. Second, we know that the British people overthrew the Constantine-formed government of Rome in 409 so that they might better protect themselves. Zosimus specifically tells us that they rid themselves of Roman administration and law and seceded.[7] Third, in 410 Hadrian told the British to look to their own defenses. This suggests two possibilities. Most likely, it means that at some time in the recent past he had received a request for aid. It is also possible that he was simply accepting the changed situation from 409. Regardless of Hadrian's reasons for his response, it would seem the secession of 409 was a reaction to the need to organize themselves against the Germanic peoples.

The revolt of 409, then, was not caused by social unrest. Given the evidence at hand, it can hardly be called a revolt. The people dismantled their own rebel provincial government in order to show Rome that they were willing to be compliant to its authority once again; Hadrian wrote to cities and not kingdoms. When Rome did not send its own governor and bureaucracy in 410, Britain was unable to re-form its island-wide government; all that was left of Roman administration was local by the time Germanus appeared on the scene some twenty years later. In this light, the state of affairs as Germanus saw it was merely a continuation of what can be seen happening in 410.

By this theory, Britain ceased to operate as a Roman state in about 409. However, its loss of political identity does not mean it lost *romanitas*. The British belief that they were still Roman would have persisted for some time after they were no longer associated with Rome. It can be seen in some of the extant native resources, and they are best understood chronologically by the floruits of their subjects.[8] The *Vita Germani* records two visits of St. Germanus to Britain for the purpose of combating Pelagianism.[9] The first took place in 429 according to Prosper of Aquitaine, the second, as we have seen, in either 437, 441, or 448. Three details in the narrative bear observation and commentary here.

First, on his initial visit, a man named Elafius meets Germanus. The name itself is of interest because it is Greek. In the Roman Empire, it was not uncommon for the highest classes of citizen to give their children Greek names. The Greek culture was widely admired by the Romans, who modeled their pantheon of gods after them and hired Greek teachers to educate their children in philosophy and history. The presence of this name indicates that the aristocracy of Roman Britain was not dead, and shows that the Roman culture was still well respected in Britain twenty years after its government had been disbanded.

This Elafius is named as a leading citizen in the region, and he guides the hero through the community. Germanus participates in a debate with the leading ecclesiastics and accompanies a ragged army of Britons as they set out to combat a band of raiders, in the process acting at the highest levels of Briton society. But during his stay, he meets no king. Nor does he on his second visit, when he meets a man with powers Constantius can only describe as like a tribune.[10] Three and perhaps four decades after Hadrian had told the Britons to fend for themselves, it would appear that at least one region in Britain was not controlled by a king.[11] In the place of kingship, it seems that a more constitutional, local, government was in place.

The second point is language. During both visits, Germanus has no trouble speaking to everyone he comes across. This seems perfectly appropriate for 429. If the government of Rome was still in place until 409, a significant portion of the population should have been able to speak Latin twenty years later. But around 440, only those who were forty-five or older would have had a formal Latin education before Rome had been excised. And, as the maximum lifespan in the ancient world was about fifty-five years, only a very small percentage of the population would have been able to speak with Germanus if the schools had closed with the watershed of 410. That Germanus still had no difficulties with language indicates that those schools continued for a decade or two after that date.

Third, a religious philosophy called Pelagianism was the main reason for Germanus' journeys to Britain.[12] When it was declared illegal in 417, the holies of the empire took steps to stamp out the heresy. That it could still be found in Britain over a decade later seems reasonable, and even predictable. What is noteworthy is that Roman-supported Christianity held such a comfortable position in at least one area of Britain that there was a bishop, Agricola, and a good number of wealthy citizens who followed Pelagianism and were interested in debating some of the details of their faith with another Christian bishop. His presence speaks of the deep level of *romanitas* still present on the island.

The next subject is that of Patrick, who died in either the 460s or 490s.[13] His two extant letters offer some valuable information for the current discussion. For one, he clearly tells the reader that he learned Latin from a *grammaticus*, and therefore does not need to haphazardly use vocabulary lists to make use of impressive words in his writings. He apologetically informs his audience that he was taken captive at about twelve, interrupting his advanced lessons with a rhetorician. This statement cannot be verified historically, but does seem perfectly reasonable given the fact that he shows evidence of living in a culture that used Latin, and none of having learned the proper Latin a *rhetor* would have taught him.[14]

Second, Patrick lists his father and grandfather, and informs his audience that they were both religious men.[15] Such a persistence of office, and especially the continuance of such a passive occupation, demonstrates stability in the area Patrick was raised in over the course of at least fifty years. More poignant, it is good evidence of another area with a strong *romanitas* from at least the beginning of the fifth century.

In addition, Patrick's father, Calpornius, held a minor political position that is recognizable as an office in the late Roman Empire. This detail shows a continuation of political structure well into the fifth century as well. Patrick may well have lived in a kingdom, or at least in a village that paid tribute to a king, but the local community appears to have functioned in much the same way as it had during the Roman Empire.

There was kingship in Patrick's Britain, in the person of Coroticus or Ceredig. Patrick seems to know something about Ceredig, and this comes out in his letter to the man. Patrick addresses him as from "Aloo," most probably Alclud.[16] As Ceredig was presumably raiding in Ireland when he kidnapped several of Patrick's converts, he must have been on an extended foray when Patrick contacted him. The way the extant *Epistola* reads, Ceredig had spent several days in the area at a camp. From there, he had raided nearby settlements. He was still in his raiding camp when Patrick wrote his initial letter, though perhaps he was home by the time the extant, second letter was brought into his presence.

This Ceredig seems to have had a permanent residence, but appears to have spent a good deal of time away. His energetic lifestyle is at odds with the raids that we have seen in the oldest poetry, which seem to have lasted just long enough to steal cattle or other items. Aloo may be a permanent residence, but all of his raiding did not need to be within easy distance of it. In this respect, he seems more like a pirate than a king.

Nothing in Patrick's writing indicates a bureaucracy around Ceredig; the letter is addressed solely to Ceredig, not to any potential Christian member of his party. One will note, too, that Ceredig is labeled as a king of a single fortification, Aloo, and not of a region such as Strathclyde. Both clues are indications that Ceredig was a king at a time when kingship was still developing, when rulers controlled very small parcels of land and had not established any form of administration that required them to stay in one place. Ceredig was a king when kingship was just emerging.

Gildas provides the timing when these newly formed kingships may have expanded into kingdoms. As has been seen, he wrote somewhere in the range 522x534.[17] He speaks of Maelgwn as the "Dragon of the Island," presumably Anglesey. Constantine is king of Damnonia, medieval Dumnonia or Cornwall. In both cases, he associates his kings with regions, not cities, and in so doing tells us that at some time before 534 the Britons had developed kingship that far.

At the other end of the spectrum, Gildas plainly tells us that after the appeal to Ætius in 433x439,[18] the British fought off the Germanic peoples through guerrilla warfare.[19] His phrasing implies that bands of people had been brought together for war under a strong leadership; prerequisites to any primitive form of monarchy. Speaking in his present at least five decades after the first British resistance fighting, Gildas bluntly tells the reader that the kings he is speaking of are the sons and, in at least one instance, the grandson of a king. That is, from no later than the turn of the fifth century British kingships were in place which were stable enough to allow a single family to continue ruling.

Gildas also contributes verifiable evidence that the Romans would have recognized the nature of their government at least as late as 522. Gildas' Latin is not only excellent but demonstrates that he was trained in the same manner as the best and brightest had been during the Roman Empire.[20] He would have been fully able to argue his own case in a court of law in Rome.

The enduring Roman-style government that Gildas' writing represents on one hand and the rise of kingships he speaks of on the other seem to be mutually exclusive properties. However, Gildas was a contemporary to the world he spoke of, so that the state of affairs as he presents it made sense to him. If he had any hope of reaching his audience, we must conclude that it was reasonable to them as well. Therefore, there must be some balance to be found between what he tells us and what his words say of his world.

A closer look at the indications of Roman government offers a possible solution to the perceived quandary. With the exception of "Elafius" around 440, no official named or implied in all of the above source material would be considered more than a local official, suggesting that Roman-style governments may have continued at the town and village level, but there is no indication of any kind of regional government.

On the other hand, kingship by its very nature might well have been ruling over several such communities. British kingship is to be understood best in the poetry of the period and in the references Gildas makes to it in *De Excidio Britanniae*. Once accomplished, it may be used to help better explain the culture it was a part of. Of the two poets who lived contemporary to early kingship and whose works are extent, Taliesin is the better preserved, and provides a more useful standard from which to begin. A few lines from the fifth authentic Taliesin poem will make for a strong foundation to the discussion.

> Through a single year,
> one has poured out
> wine, and malt, and mead
> with unrestrained vigour,
>
> for a troop of singers
> and for a swarm around spits,
> with their neck rings
> and fine resting places,
>
> and all of them for their food
> went to the battle.
>
> With his horse under him,
> set to raid Manaw,
> seeking spoils
> and plentiful plunder,
>
> 160 of one colour
> of both cows and calves,
>
> milch cows and oxen,
> and all sorts of fair luxuries.
> I would not be happy
> if Uryen were slain.[21]

In the above stanzas may be seen all the basic components of the ideal king, and much of the society in which he lives. First and foremost, the perfect king is generous; the first three stanzas are clear that Urien feeds both his warriors and the bards, and gives them the jewelry with which they decorate themselves. Second, he is successful and voluminous raider; the last three stanzas focus on cows and oxen taken as booty, with a vague mention of precious goods.

Other items must be inferred from the poem. It refers to only two groups of people that Urien interacts with, warriors and bards. As with Ceredig, there is no sign of an administration, and in fact none of the poems show any indications that Urien may have been at the head of any sort of political engine. On the contrary, from Taliesin's standpoint the king's only concerns appear to be for his warriors. This is a view that is reflected in all the other Taliesin poems, and one to be found in Aneirin's *Y Gododdin* as well.

What may be drawn from the poem about his rule is that the king maintained a relatively small number of men as his personal warriors. These men followed him into battle and on the hunt, and developed a strong bond with their king, much as the men of a small military unit will bond after living through battle together. Our hostile source, Gildas, approaches kingship from a different angle, but gives us much the same information.

> Britain has kings, but they are tyrants; she has judges, but they are wicked. They often plunder and terrorize—the innocent; they defend and protect—the guilty and thieving; they have many wives—whores and adulteresses; they constantly swear—false oaths; they make vows—but almost at once tell lies; they wage wars—civil and unjust; they chase thieves energetically throughout the country—but love and even reward the thieves who sit with them at table; they distribute alms profusely—but pile up an immense mountain of crime for all to see; they take their seats as judges—but rarely seek out the rules of right judgment; they despise the harmless and humble, but exalt to the stars, so far as they can, their military companions, bloody, proud and murderous men, adulterers and enemies of God—if chance, as they say, so allows: men who should have been rooted out vigorously, name and all; they keep many prisoners in their jails, who are more often loaded with chafing chains because of intrigue than because they deserve punishment. They hang around the altars swearing oaths—then shortly afterwards scorn them as though they were dirty stones.[22]

Gildas corroborates Taliesin here. He complains of kings exalting their warriors and treating the meek as inferior. As has been seen, part of British kingship was the paying of bards to write poems about the king and his men. As for treating the meek as inferior, this is so in any kingship. This disparity is only more apparent in heroic age society, where the paying of tribute is little more than a formal arrangement of protection money.

Other items become clear as the pieces of evidence are studied more thoroughly. The British king depended on a strong sense of loyalty between himself and his men to create and maintain his position in society; else there would be no need for the gift-giving to men which is so common in the poems. Good, loyal men who were familiar and respected by a king were rare, then as now. That meant that the king had to accept whichever good warriors offered themselves to him, despite their shortcomings. To hold such men to the same laws as others would have been to compromise a king's position politically, to strain his bonds of allegiance to his other warriors, and often to lose a good friend. As a holy man, Gildas may not have recognized the necessary compromise, which he despises as a lack of integrity. He may not have realized that intrigue is far more dangerous to a king and his kingdom than his lack of morality. This fact was especially so in the period in which Gildas was writing.

As to the bards, Gildas is even more accurate than may, at first, be apparent. When British kingship reemerged and funded a flowering bardic order again, the bards in turn reinvested the kingship with something more than a political platform. Ancient Irish and British lore speaks of kings symbolically marrying their kingdoms. These were personified in the form of a woman. She was a beautiful maiden when matched with the rightful king and acted the part of a dutiful wife; when the rules of kingship were properly respected she was fruitful. If the king acted improperly, she would become barren, and would transform into an ugly old hag.[23] As the land's husband, the king was the mediator between the people and the land that supported him. Because of the symbolism, he took on a significance much greater than simply the ruler of a kingdom.[24]

What the above also shows is that kingship concerned itself with a relatively small number of persons. It had no direct interaction with villages or towns beyond the acquisition of tribute, and no interest in individuals who lived in those areas. A king had no reason to care.

He was in many ways of the same mindset as a mob boss, taking no interest in how those under his protection conducted their daily lives as long as he received his percentage of the food and goods they produced.

With this in mind, it does not seem unreasonable that local governments were able to maintain the same form of organization they had enjoyed under Rome for at least a century after 410 and in the face of developing kingships. In fact, already established, local Roman-style governments might have been encouraged to continue; they provided an organization and law that kings were not able or willing to give in this period. Kings could appreciate such local government because they gave individual communities a centrality that made intercourse easier and more efficient while not threatening to reduce the king's position of control.

The above sources, made use of around their biases and weaknesses and placed in order chronologically, give a clear explanation of the way in which the old Roman government and the developing British kingships coexisted. However, the chronology and reason why kingship was reintroduced into British culture has hardly been touched upon so far. At this point, perhaps a loose relative chronology may be tentatively laid out. The events surrounding 407 left little or no military presence on the island, and the overthrow of Constantine's government had obliterated the provincial governments of Britain. Replacing the island-wide government were hundreds of communities and *civitates* scattered throughout Britain that were in most cases local in their awareness. From this state of affairs would emerge dynastic kingships by the turn of the fifth century. Some of the stages for this change may be seen, but the catalyst for such a drastically different government is unknown. We may only be fairly certain that the process took place at roughly the same time throughout the island.

One problem immediately arises from the above postulation: it concludes that there were no kingships immediately after 411, and that when kingship did emerge it was not focused on a single authority or dynasty, but sprouted haphazardly throughout the island. Such is completely against traditional wisdom, though it is not unknown in scholarly circles.[25]

Some of the less ambiguous pieces of evidence for this conclusion include the Hadrianic rescript. In it, Hadrian addressed the cities, the *civitates*. He told them to look to their own defenses. Had the island remained centrally controlled until this time, Hadrian would properly have written to the governors of the various provinces, or at least to the citizens in those provinces. Had there been a centralized authority, he would have addressed a king or emperor; they were clearly not so far beneath him that they could not be addressed, as he was writing to the rebel island of Britain to begin with. Instead, he addressed the cities, as though they were the largest political organizations remaining in Britain at that time. It is safe to say he had a better feel for fifth-century Britain than we do, and therefore that he had a better idea of who to address and how to address them than we could. The largest political units in Britain by 410 were, then, the *civitates*.[26]

In addition to the evidence for the breakdown of the larger political units, there are problems with believing that Britain was ruled mainly as one kingdom in the years following 410. One man ruling in fifth-century Britain would have had a great deal to do; organizing military units, strengthening the defenses or perhaps erecting new ones, and so on. Instead of seeing some evidence for any of that, there are no signs of renewed energy in the archaeology. The defenses from this period remained untouched.

Finally, there is no mention of a single ruler in Britain by an Irish, Gallic, Byzantine, or Roman scholar. Nor are there any legends about such men even in Britain until Bede three hundred years later, and as we shall see his source had some very specific motives for naming such a ruler.

The primary sources discussed above are in no way complete on their own, and in several places it is clear the memory of their authors or their sources has faltered. However, together they form a clear picture of the fifth century. The wording of Hadrian's letter and the *Vita Germani* show that there was no kingship in the first few decades of the fifth century. Gildas tells us that bands of men were forced together in order to conduct guerrilla warfare against the Germanic peoples in the years following the great mercenary revolt, which probably took place in the 440s. These guerrillas necessarily formed under a charismatic military leader. Such groups would have had a strong appeal to the Britons of the period Gildas describes, and might well have been the initial foundations of kingship.

Patrick gives us our first named British king at some time before about 493, and he appears to be using a primitive form of kingship. His Coroticus seems to have a capital but to control very little additional land. Gildas complains in his own generation of kings killing off their family members to usurp the throne, conducting civil wars, hiring poets to sing their praises, and using those weaker than themselves to make themselves more powerful. These activities are good indicators of established dynasties, of raiding to gain money and prestige, of dynasties looking to establish credibility, and forcing villages to pay them tribute, respectively. The immorality of his time is no more than a series of indications that kingships are developing.

Our primary sources present a clear and consistent picture of the transition from late Roman to post-Roman culture. Dealing with the native sources chronologically shows a consistent decline in *romanitas*, and outlines the rise of local kingships. Yet in all this, there are some strong indications of a continuance of the Roman way of life in local government and the development and later flourishing of Christianity in the sixth century. It is left, then, to see what light Anglo-Saxon studies may throw on the subject, and how British studies might help us to better understand the Germanic presence on the island.

7

Reconstructed Anglo-Saxon History

The British had continuously occupied Britain from well before the Romans first came to the island. Because of their longstanding habitation, they associated themselves with the land, the communities they and their ancestors had been a part of, and their common heritage. In this respect, the continuity of the Roman structure of local government even after the reintroduction of kingship is understandable. It was by then a part of that heritage.

The Germanic peoples did not have the same traditions to stabilize them; they were a conglomerate of many different tribes from widely ranging areas who had been migrating for generations. They had been brought into Britain during the late Roman period haphazardly, and only in force after 410. Because of their recent settlement, the influences on them and their development during the fifth and sixth centuries are more difficult to understand. Perhaps the easiest beginning to Anglo-Saxon studies is to be found in a discussion on the nature and origins of the Germanic peoples in Britain up to 410.

During the late Roman period, the decaying empire was allowed to survive in large part because of its cultural standing; even the barbarians that surrounded its borders looked up to it. Rome made use of its prestige. Many tribes were offered a simple bargain; in return for becoming citizens of the empire, most of their warriors would be assimilated into already functioning military units and stationed throughout the empire. Assimilation made for quicker Romanization of the soldiers, while their families could serve as guarantees of their loyalty to Rome in the meantime. Retired soldiers were offered land near where they had served. This ensured that they would marry local Roman women and their offspring would consider themselves Roman.

To this practice, Britain was no exception. Tacitus tells us that eight Batavian cohorts came with the original invasion force in AD 43[1] Marcus Aurelius brought some Marcomanni to the island after defeating them in the second century.[2] Vandals and Burgundians were transferred to Britain by Carausius after their defeat in the third century.[3] Around 300, Allectus had a substantial force of Germanic tribesmen with him in Britain. There were Batavians at Carrawburgh and Tungrians at Castleheads and Birrens during the third and fourth centuries. It is known that Pannonians and Rhaetians were stationed at Great Chesters, and Lusitanians at High Rochester. There was a *cuneus* of Frisians around Housesteads, and another at Brough-by-Sands early in the third century. The latter was last named moved to Papcastle.[4]

At the height of the empire, the barbarian units were given Roman officers, uniforms, and armaments and posted to Roman fortifications. People who spoke Latin surrounded them as soldiers, officers, and townspeople. Because of their immersion into the culture, Romanization occurred rapidly.

However, by the fourth century the strength of Rome was declining. Its cultural as well as military weakness had a detrimental effect on how newly conscripted tribesmen were indoctrinated into Roman culture. In the years around 300, King Crocus of the Alemanni kept his title in Britain even as he served the empire and supported Constantine in his bid to be an emperor.[5] Crocus' title and evident power as an independent leader within the empire demonstrates that tribal warriors were no longer being absorbed into military units. Instead, tribes were being transplanted *en masse* and under their tribal leaders to regions of conflict.

The evidence suggests that this would quickly become official Roman policy. The *foederati* Fraomar was sent to Britain with the title of tribune in 372.[6] The Ravenna Cosmographer tells us an Ansehis was given the same title at about the same time. In the late Roman Empire, a *foederati* was a tribal group that had agreed to settle in disputed border territory and defend it in return for food and a payment.[7] Like Crocus, it would appear that Fraomar and Ansehis were brought to Britain as independent chiefs of their respective tribes. By this time, however, an attempt was being made to include them in the Roman superstructure. Notfried, Germanic commander of a *numerus* at Housesteads, may well have been an earlier incarnation of the same development.

The failing strength of the Roman Empire may be seen elsewhere, in various names that have to be found in the archaeological record. A girl named Ahtete was buried near the Roman station of Corbridge. The diminutive form on her tombstone shows a knowledge of living German, and it has been suggested that her family may have spoken the language at home.[8] Dagualdus was a soldier of the First Cohort of Pannonians who was buried near Cawfield[9] who did not Romanize his name. Virilis of RIB 1102 and Mahudas of Ebchester both openly declared their German heritage. The Latin name of the former means he was at the least a second-generation Germanic soldier in Britain, while their declarations suggest a decline in Rome's cultural stature.

What may be reconstructed from the above evidence is that by around 300, the integration of Germanic soldiery into the Roman culture was becoming less and less effective. As a result, by this stage the *foederati* who were being transferred into Britain were thinking of themselves more as Germans living inside the borders of the Roman Empire than as newly made Roman citizens. In Britain, this change of perspective would have dire consequences when the Roman government began to crumble at the end of the fourth century, and was finally undermined by British rebellions at the beginning of the fifth century.

Before getting into the part played by the Germanic peoples after 410, however, it is perhaps a good idea to lay out exactly where these later immigrants were being stationed. In this period, the development of the Saxon Shore was foremost.

The Saxons especially among the Germanic peoples had become master sailors since their invasion of western Europe, and as the legions became more focused on protecting the Roman borders and the internal wars that marked the last days of the empire, they put their newfound skills to use as pirates. In the third and fourth centuries, they ravaged the shipping lanes between Gaul and Britain. On occasion, they invaded Britain and plundered as far inland as they could. And, as Britain was less well defended than the Continent, the island made for convenient landfalls during raiding season.

The Romans did what they could to counter the new threat. Probably early on, the stations at Dover and Lympne were converted for military use. Brancaster, Reculver, and Richborough were first constructed in the early third century.[10] Bradwell and Burgh Castle were built decades later. Anderida was constructed in the second third of the fourth century,[11] with Portchester and Bitterne probably not too far behind. At some time during the fourth century, this series of forts was labeled the *Litus Saxonicum*, the Saxon Shore. As the title implies, they were occupied by Saxon warriors who policed the sea near their stations.

In the beginning, these settlements were strictly military in character. However, it appears they did not remain as such. Nearly four decades ago, Professor Myres noted a type of pottery that he called "Romano-Saxon."[12] It has since been associated by motif and form with Frankish and Jutish wares of the late fourth century. It is not Roman, as only one find has been made outside the rough delineation of the earliest Germanic settlements in Britain,[13] and that a hundred miles away from any similar pottery.

This type of pottery is most commonly found near the forts which were earliest settled by the *foederati* of the Saxon Shore command, and especially in the areas with the best access to trade with the Continent. However, eight kiln sites have been identified within Britain.[14] This number and Germanic disposition of the pottery indicates that there were Germanic potters all along the eastern coast of England in the fifth century. Potters are not warriors, which in turn suggests that entire tribes were settling the Saxon Shore from the late fourth century, at the latest.

Such conclusions seem to fly in the face of most historians' assumptions about the period. Traditionally, they have followed Bede and the *Anglo-Saxon Chronicle*. The former ranged the year of the invasion from 449 to 456.[15] The latter based much of its information on Bede, but specified the date at 449.

Bede himself wrote nearly three hundred years after the event he recorded and, as has been seen, did not have access to records that could have given him an accurate date for a fifth-century event. This puts his testimony in doubt and renders 449 at best a guess based on false information. There is also the data furnished by the *Gallic Chronicles*, which gives the year of the legendary Germanic rebellion as earlier in the decade of 440. This implies that there had been Germanic peoples in Britain for some time before 449 and argues against a first or even last *foederati* arrangement being set up in the mid–fifth century. Finally, it has been seen that the Saxon settlements of the eastern coast were not isolated incidents—they were a part of a continuous pattern to be found in Britain and throughout the Roman Empire. Apart from the late and poorly sourced Bede and the *Anglo-Saxon Chronicle*, all the historical sources are consistent with the archaeological evidence in placing full Germanic tribes in Britain decades before 449.

So let us return to the Germanic peoples. What has been seen indicates that there were many groups of ethnically independent Germanic people present in Britain by 410. We might next ask how they reacted to the events of 406x407. More importantly, we might gain some insights as to how they responded to Constantine's death in 411, an event that effectively ended Rome's influence on the island. To that end the historical records on the continent will be of some help.

Zosimus tells us that the British revolted from the Roman Empire to combat the incursions of the Saxons. The context of the passage and the generally healthy relationship between all *foederati* and Romans suggests that what Zosimus *meant* was that non-*foederati* Saxon groups were raiding. Most likely, the malcontents were the same Saxons that had made the Saxon Shore command necessary in the first place. It seems reasonable that a rebelling Britain might have broken off contact with Rome in order to deal with the immediate problem more directly. Rome had proven itself to be impotent in dealing with Britain's problems, and frankly had more immediate concerns at this time.

Constantius, writing at the end of the fifth century, did not have any secular interests. However, he does speak of a "halleluiah" victory during Germanus' first trip in 429, some two decades after the revolt Zosimus mentions. During the battle, Germanus allegedly led a group of untried soldiers to victory simply by having them yell a praise to God during their attack.

The Gallic Chronicle of 452, as has been noted, gives one important piece of information—that in the year 441 the Germanic peoples decimated Britain. Clearly, the precise statement is an exaggeration, as no evidence has been found in the archaeological record to confirm the widespread devastation the entry claims. However, in later times the Franks would have contact with Kent, and during the Roman period trade had centered around London. It has also been seen that Kent and Essex were at the heart of the Saxon Shore fortifications. Most likely, either or both of these regions were what the chronicler was speaking of. If that is the case, it is as likely as not that it was raided by the Saxons who had lately been *foederati* in the region.

The suggestion that *foederati* revolted at this time makes sense for a couple of reasons. First, the limited source material provides for a clear progression of foederati/British relations after 409—of mercenaries as protectors, of untried Romano-British soldiers combating Saxons (suggesting laxness on the *foederati's* part), and finally of Saxons overrunning part of Britain. Second, it has been seen that Britain fractured after 410, and money would not be minted in Britain for centuries after 410; which means that the foederati would have had no consistent means of payment. At that point, it would only have been a matter of time before they were not satisfied with whatever compensation they were being given and turned on their employers.

Lastly is Gildas. As has been seen, his knowledge of British events is sketchy before Ambrosius, with scattered but clearly historical information all the way back to Ætius. He says that from then up to his own childhood the Germanic peoples were not only independent, they were waging war on the British.

From what little there is in the record, we can determine first that there were Germanic people with their own culture living peacefully in Britain by 410, and that these same people did not cause a problem before 429, possibly as late as Ætius was contacted between 433 and 439. It seems reasonable that they grew increasingly lax in their official duties with the inevitable reduction in pay and supplies after 410. There may well have been isolated incidents of *foederati* going on raids or pirating with the weakening of power and authority on the island. It is even possible that some revolted from their Briton employers and took over the land. However, the big shake-up did not occur before 439, and at that time the British areas in closest contact with Gaul fell under the control of the Germanic peoples.

All the above may now be put in context with Gildas' broad history. The newly emancipated Germanic tribes began to raid into the less defended territories. They stole livestock, foodstuffs, and probably women. Metaphorically, they razed the areas they assaulted. They would continue to do so until Ambrosius, and probably others like him, organized the Britons to resist at some time in the last half of the fifth century.

In the meantime, we must also assume that with the disintegration of Roman authority after 410, independent Germanic groups from the Continent had been settling haphazardly along the coast. As each area reached a point where the soil could not support any more, the settled groups would have forced newcoming Germanic peoples further and further west in search of easily taken lands. In this, the British must have been much more the victims than the Germanic peoples, whose unbroken culture for as far back as we can trace was built upon the warrior philosophy and raiding.

It is an unfortunate fact that no one really knows when the migrations ceased. The *Anglo-Saxon Chronicle* claims dynastic founders well into the sixth century, but this is unnecessary. They were certainly no longer coming by about 550, for the Northumbrian foundation legend makes no claims to its first king having crossed over from the Continent. Presumably, he was born in Britain.

Of the culture of the immigrants, however, something more can be learned. The excavated cemeteries from the period have yielded complex results. The archaeological record shows that each individual was identified by his place in well-defined family and tribal groups. The decorations a person wore were determined by his or her position in the group, as were the weapons with which males were buried.[16] In the case of women, they might well take their symbols of status with them after marriage into another community, such as what may have happened with a woman buried near Chessell Down. She had grave goods similar to those found at Sarre.[17]

Artifacts of what may be considered high-status persons have been found in several cemeteries. The number of like individuals found buried at each site may be an indication of a small family surviving over an extended period of time, or of two or more families coexisting over a shorter interval.[18] In each case, they clearly held some sort of dominant position over the "low-status" persons, though the exact nature of this relationship is unknown.

Several cemeteries have also revealed groups of persons who were shorter than the immigrants. It seems likely that each cemetery contained them. Individuals from these families may have been slaves, but certainly there are a number of other factors that may have caused the phenomenon.[19] However, that they held a lower social position seems highly likely. For this reason, they have little to offer the current study.

Throughout England in the second half of the sixth century, a small number of wealthy male burials emerge. These grow smaller in number and more wealthy in content as the seventh century progresses. The initial change has been seen as indicating the rise of regional kingships,[20] while the progression into the seventh century corresponds historically with the emergence of the major kingdoms. Interestingly, the only true genealogical scholar to study the Germanic pedigrees gave the mid–sixth century as the historical horizon for written information on the Germanic peoples, and Dumville, through comparative study, came to much the same conclusion about the royal Germanic families.[21]

Kingship is an interesting phenomenon among the Germanic peoples. As has been seen with the British kingships, the need to validate a line most often inspired the creation of a lineage back to a god, normally Woden, but occasionally Tiw.[22] Unspoken in the myth of other Indo-European cultures but present here was the idea of the royal family's *mana*. This quality has been equated to "divine luck." In a king, it meant that success in battle, the fruitfulness of his people's crops, and anything of importance for the kingdom had been guaranteed by the gods through him.

It was believed that *mana* was possessed in excess by the royal families, and for this reason their dynasties took on a religious quality; those families with *mana* had been given the right to rule by the gods. The religious aspect of their being supported the political reality; as divinely blessed *mana* was what made a ruler successful, no member of an outside family could have any legitimate claim on the throne. A man with royal aspirations could hope for no political support in wishing to contend with a family whose very luck derived from the gods.

The previous two chapters have noted three developments in the early maturation of Britain for which no scholar has put forth any explanation—the emergence of stable British kingdoms towards the end of the fifth century, the ending of Germanic migrations well before the middle of the sixth century, and the formation of regional kingships among the Germanic peoples from the middle of the sixth century. It is not difficult to see these three separate developments as interdependent, and from there to formulate a reasonable explanation.

We know that the Germanic migrations must have come to Britain, as they did to the rest of the crumbling empire, from about 400 on. And reasonably, the newly arrived tribesmen can be seen moving further and further inland and overwhelming the local Romano-British communities of the lowlands as they did so. Just as on the Continent, it seems only reasonable that it was not until the natives were able to restructure themselves into independent governments with standing armies that such migrations into their territory would have ceased. On the Continent, small Roman pockets managed to survive in kingdoms. With so many different tribal groups and political factors to contend with, however, they could not survive for long. In Britain, where the natives were isolated both from Rome and from a majority of the migrations, they were able to hold out longer.

As we have seen, just such a development can be perceived in the emergence of British kingship, which by its very nature would have provided a military force equipped to deal with the loosely organized tribes that were still coming into Britain and able to stabilize its borders against other developing *teulu*. This latter is exactly the evolution that Gildas complains about, one that had engendered the ills of his present.[23] Ironically, without the kingship that had brought about the immoral and unethical kings and men who praised others for money, there would have been no British people toward whom Gildas could direct his complaints.

As a result of British kingship, from the last few decades of the fifth century there would have been no more unprotected land for the Germanic settlers to spread to. Once Britain was no longer an easy target for land, the immigrations would have ceased. There would have been no point in risking a sea voyage if the chance to acquire property was no greater there than was to be had on the Continent. Instead, the small and isolated Germanic communities of two or three extended and dominant families would have been forced to compete amongst themselves for the limited resources they had at their disposal.

In time, the competition for resources forced the Germanic settlers to adopt a more militarily oriented culture; this way of life would have been better equipped for surviving the changed conditions. With the fighting would have come the development of strong leadership, and eventually of primitive kingship. Necessity is why the Germanic peoples developed monarchies, and more importantly why they formed them over a half-century after British kingships. The British developed kingship as a response to invaders who were moving in and taking over their land. It was a defense mechanism to protect themselves against a culture that lived off the warrior ethos. The Germanic peoples developed kingship on the island to help them better compete for the land they already had once there was only a finite amount at their disposal.

Other Germanic peoples were in Britain from the first century, and may have retained their ethnic individuality from the third century. They came as military units, and later as tribal groups. They were isolated from one another by geography and tribal backgrounds, and only united by a common culture and language. When Rome no longer controlled the island, they most probably turned to the Britons as their new employers. When the British were no longer able to pay them, the Germanic peoples joined their cousins in dominating their former employers. They would collect what they needed by force from that point on.

One fortune of fate was that the most Romanized parts of Britain also happened to be the best farmland. This fact meant first that lowland England was the easiest to conquer, and in fact much of what had been late Roman Britain was in Germanic hands by 500. It also meant that the immigrants could support a much denser population, despite occupying a smaller area than the Celts on the island. This would mean more fighting men and, in time, larger armies. Even with the emergence of several dominant kings, such as Arthur, the Celtic peoples would be unable to drive them from the island. It was only a matter of time before the Germanic people began to form their own kingdoms. When this happened, the historical record in Germanic Britain began, and the oral histories of every kingdom's respective pedigrees were first recorded for posterity. In the next chapter, one of their earliest, the Kentish Source, will be studied.

8

The Kentish Source[1]

The previous two chapters have correlated a great deal of information, most of which will be touched upon throughout the rest of this book. However, it is necessary here to restate a couple of key facts. First, that while there is good evidence that *romanitas* continued in language and local government through the end of the fifth century, there is no evidence that one man had control over any significant portion of the island during that time. In fact, the information presented above suggests that tiny kingdoms slowly amalgamated into larger ones. This gives the legendary and powerful Vortigern no context in the fifth century, nor as a person wealthy enough to hire Germanic warriors from across the channel during that time.

Second, it has been seen that there were whole Germanic tribes in Britain from perhaps the third century, but certainly by the fourth. Specifically, the first named *foederati* on the island arrived in the latter half of the fourth century. There is every reason to believe that most, if not all, of these groups preserved their ethnicity as Britain passed out of Roman control. It has also been seen that they did not generally revolt until about 439, some thirty years after the events of 406x411. Knowing this, there would have been plenty of Germanic warriors to use as *foederati* in Britain after 410 or at any time in the next three decades. Because of Rome's legacy, there would have been no need to hire any. After the revolt of 439, it hardly seems likely that a British leader would have hired more Germanic warriors from the continent. This leaves Hengest and Horsa with no historical context either, and no *raison d'être*.

These new realizations about Vortigern, Hengest, and Horsa leave the scholar with a serious dilemma in understanding early medieval British history; the accounts of these three individuals in *Historia Brittonum* and Bede are derived from opposing perspectives. Their conflicting perceptions, agreement on the key points of early post–Roman history, and the fact that all later historical works were derived from them have led to these two sources being used as primary materials for reconstructing the period in question. However, it has been seen that neither of them had access to primary materials for the period. In fact, there is good evidence to show that in the matter of the settlement of Britain their materials ultimately derive from a shared source.

It is known that there was a body of information stored in Canterbury when Bede was writing his *Historia Ecclesiastica*, because he tells us he has come to most of his data on pre–Christian England from Albinus, abbot of the monastery of St. Peter and St. Paul.[2] Albinus accessed all the written material from Canterbury and other, oral information, apparently edited what Bede should and should not have, and then handed it on to Nothelm. Nothelm brought the documents to Bede, and also went to Rome for corroborating information. It is interesting to note that, while Albinus died a year after Bede's last book was published, Nothelm went on to become the archbishop of Canterbury.[3] Perhaps this is just coincidence; perhaps his promotion was due to his historical contributions to Canterbury. We may never know.

The main point, however, is that our earliest true historian claims to have used information from a storehouse in Canterbury. This is a useful revelation; any information that seems to carry with it a Kentish or Canterbury bias and is in contrast to our primary sources for the period may well have been influenced by Kent.

The reader is not disappointed in anticipating such an influence. As is well known, Bede's account contains a plethora of Kentish influences. Britain's history is a broad one, almost Roman in its outlook, until the introduction of Hengest and Horsa at the beginning of the post–Roman period. Their entire careers focus around Kent. For Bede, the two chieftains were the first Germanic chiefs on the island, and Hengest happens to be the founder of the Kentish line.[4] Their dimwitted benefactor is once called *Uurtigernus*, a name form doubtless deriving from Kent but no doubt intended as Gwrtheyrn.[5] Horsa is said to be buried in eastern Kent.[6]

All this flies in the face of what the primary sources for the fifth century can tell us. As Chapter 6 has demonstrated, there were independent Germanic chiefs in Britain well before 410 and they were stationed all across the eastern seaboard and Hadrian's Wall. It has also been seen that many if not all of these locations were still populated by people who considered themselves more Germanic than Roman in 410. The fact that Kent figures so prominently in the initial migration cannot be right, either. Historically, Kent was not the focus of the Saxon Shore defenses, Essex and especially London were.

Nor can this focus on Kent be Bede's contrivance. It may be recalled that his priorities were religion, Northumbria, and the Germanic peoples. In fact, the Kentish information must have put him in a quandary. On the one hand, the records were coming from Canterbury and his fellow churchmen, so that he either had to or felt compelled to accept the information being provided. On the other, he must have understood that the data Nothelm was giving him made his home kingdom of Northumbria entirely irrelevant in the fifth century.

The problem must have done more than irk the scholar, and one can see him waging the war between integrity and blind loyalty to the church in his book. The verb *perhibentur* tells us that the story of Horsa's burial in eastern Kent is something not as believable as the rest of his narrative. When it is mentioned that Hengest and Horsa settled in Britain, Bede is uncharacteristically vague in saying only that they are along the eastern coast. Naming Kent there would have strengthened its royal family's position as the rightful rulers of the island. Bede could not do that even if the rest of the narrative makes clear he could only have meant Kent.

The clearest example of Bede's dislike for the Kentish information is to be found in an intimation he makes. In Book I, Chapter 15, the Germanic invaders are introduced generally as Angles. It only makes sense to see the leaders of this group as Angles as well, though this is nowhere stated. And, when Bede tells us that the Angles are the ancestors of all the people north of the Humber while the Saxons and Jutes were the ancestors for the South, the reader can see why he has done this. He has implied that Hengest was the father of the Northumbrian line. Using the only interpretation left open to him, he has attempted to turn the tables on the Kentish claim of precedence. It is noteworthy that he did not give Hengest's connection to Kent there, presumably because Bede wanted to leave the impression of Hengest's ties to Northumbria strong in his readers' minds. Still, he stayed true to his sources, and did not blatantly state the point either.

He was also capable of using other sources to inveigle the question of Hengest and Horsa's location. Gildas' mistaken conclusion that the Picts were the main threat during the mid–fifth century was strategically placed in Bede's history, using it to hint that Hengest and Horsa had originally settled in Northumbria. But he never actually said that either. As much as the evidence suggests he wanted to bluntly state that the co-founders of the Germanic peoples in Britain lived in Northumbria, he did not, showing that he could not find such information in his Kentish source, and there were no corresponding sources from Northumbria.

That he could find no early information on Northumbria seems clear. He recorded the origin legend for neither Bernicia nor Deira, the two kingdoms from which Bede's Northumbria emerged. Nor did he have one for Northumbria itself. In fact, Bede does not even mention his home kingdom in his history until after the conversion of Kent in 616. It is solely Kent's legend up through the sixth century that is recorded. This is odd because Bernicia and Deira emerged as important kingdoms at about the same time as Kent, but makes perfect sense if Bede's only information up to that point was from Kent; Kent had no reason to remember anything of Northumbria in the sixth and early seventh centuries.

The Kentish pedigree in Bede, the only one he gives, also could have been made in no other place but Kent. Hengest's great-grandfather is named as *Uecta*. Uecta is obviously an eponym for the Isle of Wight, suggesting what Dumville noted as a politically motivated manipulation of the royal line.[7] It has been suggested that the genealogy may reflect sixth- or seventh-century conditions,[8] and would therefore have been of use in confirming the legality of what was already a political reality. Wight was at the time a part of Kent's kingdom, and the pedigree's inclusion of an eponymous ancestor of Wight was intended as an indicator that the island had been a part of Kent from the start. The historical and archaeological truth is that Hampshire had a much stronger claim to a common ancestry with Wight's rulers than Kent did.[9]

A second noteworthy piece of information, and one that will be developed below, is that Æthelberht reigned for fifty-six years.[10] Remembering that no king ever ruled at younger than five in this period, that number would imply he lived at least sixty-one years, and probably a good deal longer; the evidence as pointed out in Chapter 5 would argue that such a lifespan was mathematically highly improbable. In sixth-century Britain, this claim strains the limits of credibility.[11]

Historia Brittonum also clearly made use of a source from Kent, though this is nowhere stated in the history and on first look the Kentish information actually appears to come from a British source. However, closer inspection reveals an undeniable use of a Kentish source. In the main, the editor retains the story of Hengest and Horsa as it is seen in Bede, suggesting direct borrowing. However, *Historia Brittonum* is specific in placing the brothers' landing in Kent, unlike Bede. In addition, there is an episode where Gwrtheyrn meets and falls in love with Hengest's daughter. In return for marriage to her, Vortigern gives Kent to Hengest. Neither of these Kent-oriented details are to be found in Bede.

The development of our understanding of the *Historia Brittonum* over the last forty years has seen the additional materials as first the result of access to native sources and then as a product of tenth-century Dyfed political machinations.[12] However, when one looks at them as a whole, the consistent theme of Kent suggests that the inspiration for the added details likely came from that region. In fact, short of arguing for the editor's personal predilection toward Kent (which makes no sense coming from a British scholar working for a Gwynedd king), no other point of origin for the material is identifiable.

Additional evidence lies in the Kentish origin legend as given there. Only three origin legends are given in *Historia Brittonum*. Kent is the first, Deira the second, and Gwynedd the third. Chapter 3 laid out the history of the *Northern Memorandum*, and in the process demonstrated a strong motivation for stressing Deiran history. Chapter 4 showed that Gwynedd had nationalistic motives for constructing the original *Historia Brittonum*, and that the presence of its origin legend there played a key role in its theme. Kent's origins would only have been of interest for Dyfed because it was of use in undermining Powys by humiliating its greatest king, Gwrtheyrn. However, they could not have received such information from British sources, which are all consistent and quite positive about Gwrtheyrn. They must have received this information from another source, and a Kentish point of origin seems the most likely.

The two sources discussed above, the *Historia Ecclesiastica* of Bede and the *Historia Brittonum*, are the earliest sources that discuss the beginnings of Kent in their respective cultures. However, there is a third source, the *Anglo-Saxon Chronicle*, which makes mention of Kent's early history. As has been seen, it is largely based on the data from Bede. Where Bede gave dates, it normally follows them. Where Bede did not, the editor tried to derive them based on what Bede wrote. When the chronicle has additional information on a topic Bede wrote about, history has shown that the information was a natural progression of what Bede had written and not evidence of better source material.

However, it has now been established that there was a Kentish Source. In addition, one may see in the above-named sources three writers who are progressively less concerned about tempering the original themes which we already know were prominent in it. Where Bede put Hengest somewhere along the eastern seaboard and *Historia Brittonum* placed Hengest's landing in Kent, the *Anglo-Saxon Chronicle* named his landing site specifically at Ebbsfleet in Kent. Where Bede said Hengest generally devastated the island and *Historia Brittonum* named several battles all across southern England, the editor of the chronicle placed all of Hengest and Horsa's activities inside Kent. A closer examination of the *Anglo-Saxon Chronicle* would appear to be in order.

The political environment that produced the *Anglo-Saxon Chronicle* was entirely different from Bede's time. For the editor of the chronicle, Kent was no longer of any political value and had not been one for as long as anyone could remember. Its ancient claim to have been the first dynasty was irrelevant. Because of this reduced state, attacking Kent's position in Germanic history would have been pointless. More importantly, it would have been counterproductive to Wessex's nationalistic designs.[13] Realizing this, the editor retained the established history. This allowed him to present the new materials into an already accepted history so that Wessex's origins appeared as accurate as was possible.

One of the earliest Wessex entries involved Æthelberht and a battle he lost to Ceawlin and Cutha in 568. It has been claimed by some that this may have been a contemporary record kept in Kent, in which case it would have been the first historical record of that kingdom.[14] However, it has been often noted that when battles in the chronicle were lost to the British, the victor was not named. It seems likely that when Kent's history was originally being composed, all defeats were similarly treated. This reasoning suggests that Kent did not create the entire entry. The pages above have also demonstrated how careful the Kentish historians were to only write pro–Kentish history, so that mention of this battle at all makes little sense. Whether or not there was any Wessex/Kentish battle is another matter, best saved until more evidence has been presented and a more thorough picture of the sixth century has been laid out.

As to the names that are associated with the event, they were most likely generated by Wessex while the chronicle was being put in a final form. Likely they were not the product of a contemporary notice.[15]

A second entry is one very odd battle contained in the records under 577, that of Dyrham in what was Dubonnia and would become Wessex. In the notice, three recognizably Welsh names are listed—Coinmail, Condidan, and Farinmail. Assuming the first *i* in Coinmail is intrusive, it was Welsh Cynfael, Old Welsh Conmail. Farinmail may well stand for Welsh Ffernfael, Old Welsh Fernmael. Condidan is probably Welsh Cynddylan, Old Welsh Condilan with oral or scribal confusion of *l* to *d*. These names are all possibly derived from a contemporary source, though there is not enough evidence to assume that this conclusion is correct.[16] The most likely name to have been contemporary is that of Farinmail, which as it stands must have been recorded before 700,[17] though Sims-Williams has expressed some hesitation on the matter.

The possible age of this listing brings up the subject of British names during the period. Certain of them tended to be regional. The genealogical framework for Dubonnia is sketchy at best, however Ffernfael is a common Glywising name, while Cynddylan is to be found in the Wroxeter region. They are found nowhere else. The names are British, found in the same region they are associated with in the entry, and possibly contemporary on linguistic grounds. The second of these observations is extremely important. It is highly unlikely that a Germanic person could have used credible names without contemporary records, or a good deal of familiarity with the Welsh genealogies. And while the former possibility suggests a date not much later than 600, no other English scholar ever demonstrated a knowledge of Welsh pedigrees.

One omission is also significant here. It is curious that the chronicle never makes the claim that Æthelberht was a descendant of Hengest. It names Æsc as son to Hengest as king of Kent,[18] and Æthelberht as son to Iurminric, but makes no connection between Æsc and Iurminric. This curiosity will be returned to in the next chapter. For now, it is enough to note that in the chronicle, Hengest is strongly associated with Kent and his son is named its king. Æthelberht was also a king of Kent, thus implying a relationship with Æthelberht and Hengest.

In Sims-Williams' paper, he is very clear that he does not believe that the *Anglo-Saxon Chronicle* may be of any use.[19] To this, the present author must disagree vehemently. The above information, in conjunction with what has been seen of the sources for *Historia Ecclesiastica* and *Historia Brittonum*, makes it clear that all three histories made use of a common source deriving ultimately from Kent. It is in better understanding that common source that the chronicle is most valuable.

There must have been some motivation for writing the "Kentish Source." Some reasons have been seen above, and others may be deduced. The clearest theme is the supremacy of the Kentish royal house over all other families on the island. This was probably initiated with the creation of a pedigree descended from Woden and the assimilation of the legendary or mythical heroes Æsc/Oisc and Hengest.[20]

In writing a history, it was necessary to show that Kent was the first kingdom. Undoubtedly, the Kentish Source would have preferred to place the landing of Hengest and Horsa within the Roman period, but a host of other problems arose from trying to mesh a Roman immigration with the established information that was already in Gildas.[21] In compromise, it maintained and expanded on the *historia* of Gildas, setting the *adventus* in or after 446 as Gildas had implied.

A second aspect of Kent's claim was legitimacy. In this, the existence of a ready-made villain in Gildas must have been a fortunate and extremely useful tool. Gildas had said that his *superbus tyrannus* was the ruler of the island. This gave him the authority to sanction the migration of the Germanic people to Britain.[22] Once this was spelled out in the Kentish Source, there could no question of the Germanic people's right to be there. By extension, Hengst's contract with Vortigern and the fact that no other kingdom could make such a claim with a British leader implied that all other kingdoms were illegitimate.

The Vortigern character in Gildas was also handy when it came to providing a righteous explanation for why the British were no longer in control of Britain. His inability to control his own employees demonstrated his people's incompetence to rule Britain. His status therefore brought them to the island, while his incompetence had forfeited the Briton claim to the island.

The Kentish Source had one more motivation, much less apparent than the others but nevertheless key to understanding its nature; it served to enhance the reputation of Canterbury as a holy site. One must not forget that in this period writing was done by the clergy, and it was their responsibility to record their own history in order to document their accomplishments. One will note that in all three sources that used the Kentish Source, Canterbury was credited with converting every Germanic kingdom but Northumbria.[23]

Such alterations to history were not at all uncommon during the Middle Ages. A recent book by Abrams and Carley has documented Glastonbury's extreme approach to the craft and its competition with Canterbury as the most holy site in Britain.[24] It has been seen that saints' lives had the same objective if on a smaller scale. Such claims, if they could be validated by generated physical evidence, helped to improve the standing of the religious site that claimed them. In turn, their improved status would generate more pilgrims and with them more donations.

It was, then, a combination of Kentish political designs and Canterbury's religious priorities that provided a large portion of the information to be found in the Kentish Source. From there, the information found its way into Bede, *Historia Brittonum*, and the *Anglo-Saxon Chronicle*. But what of the nature of this source? When was it first written down, and under what circumstances? These are important questions as the answers may contain more useful information.

The first question is the simplest to answer. No good historian would simply invent history, and so it is probable that whoever wrote the Kentish Source did so with a combination of historical sources and the patronage of the Kentish royal family. Specifically, the "historian" Gildas was used as a guideline. In the post–Ætius chapters, the British author had created the setting that was needed to introduce Hengst as a legitimate ruler in Britain and created a villain, Vortigern. With Gildas as the broad canvasser of the period and Kentish and Canterbury interests in mind, it does not require a great deal of imagination to see how the Kentish Source might have been constructed from that point.

The chronology of the source is much more problematic. To begin with, it could not have been written before about 580, the earliest time that Bertha and her Christian entourage could have landed in Kent prior to her marriage to Æthelberht.[25] Gregory tells us she could write, and her father, Charibert, was praised for his Latin by Venantius Fortunatus. It seems unlikely that the chaplain and other religious persons sent over with her would not have been able to as well. These would have been the most likely authors of the Kentish History. Before Bertha, there was no significant Christian presence in Kent, and therefore no one with the ability to write the history.

At the other extreme, the history must have been composed before 731 when Bede published his work based largely upon it. It is possible that the Kentish Source was only created in response to Bede's inquiries for early historical information. That the history was written well before then is more probable, but certainly 731 is a perfectly safe outside date.

Looking at similar histories of the period, it is seen that they were generally written while a kingdom or people were dominant. Such was the case with Rome and the *Aeneid* and Jordanes' history of the Ostrogoths. In fact, it was two of their most powerful rulers at the peaks of their respective careers that allowed history to be rewritten as they saw fit. Both men took advantage of their influence to improve their pedigrees in order to sanctify the foundations of their rule. Drawing from this information, Æthelberht's *Bretwaldaship* is the most likely candidate for a period when the Kentish Source could have been written. He had attained the position at some time after 593 and held it nearly to his death in 616.

More important, though, was the context the new technology would have been put in. As Wallace-Hadrill put it: "In no family was hereditary descent more strictly observed and buttressed than in the Merovingian.... If he took little else from his formidable connexions, Æthelbert would surely have learned how to make the most of his blood."[26] Or, as Nicholas Brooks recently put it:

> It may have been at that time too that the Kentish origin legends and the Kentish royal genealogy were first formulated for the gratification of the itinerant king and his *leode*. The court of an ambitious and initially pagan overlord is exactly the place where we would expect there to be cultivated stories of his heroic and divine ancestors, claims of his descent from the first Anglo-Saxon leaders, and accounts of their glorious activities in the most recently acquired part of his kingdom. In the English origin legend in its various forms may we not detect some of the political cement of the kingdom of Æthelberht?[27]

More generally, Kent was a major force in Britain until about 686. In that year, Bede tells us that a number of warlords began to squabble over sovereignty and Kent permanently lost the prestige of being one of the most powerful kingdoms in Britain.[28] Most likely, there was no reason for Kent's royal family to compose such a history after that time.

Given the information above, the range of Æthelberht's *Bretwalda* makes the most sense. Further evidence for this conclusion may be found in the previously mentioned name forms of Coinmail, Condidan, and Farinmail. They indicate a potential contemporary record. If the battle was a historical event that was written down somewhere, then the event took place at some point within a decade of 577, let us say no later than 590. From what has been learned about date guessing, any adult in that year would have been dead by 630 (15 years of age + 40 years = 55). This means that by that year the British names would surely have been forgotten. If the names came from Kent, then its sources must have been developing by then.[29] If they did not, then we must posit another and unknown source developing at that period.

Finally, there is Æthelberht himself. He is the first Germanic ruler in Kent of whom there is external evidence. He was the most powerful man in Britain during well over a decade of his reign. It makes good sense that, if there were records kept in Kent during his lifetime, they would have recorded both his father and grandfather.[30] We are certain of his father's name, and may know that of his grandfather.[31]

8. The Kentish Source

The Kentish Source was created definitely between 580 and 731 and possibly in the more narrow range of 593 to 616 while Kent was in the ascendancy. It was designed specifically to enhance Kent's reputation among the other kingdoms in Britain, and to place Canterbury above the other holy places. This was accomplished by creating a history antedating that of other kingdoms, and by writing about a religious institution which founded those of other regions. To manage both tasks effectively, the creators of the source made use of Gildas and his relative chronology.[32] The decision to do so made the Kentish Source the most believable of fictions, a lie lodged between two accepted truths. Because it seemed to be the same account as Gildas only with more information, it was believed to be a good supplement in better understanding the fifth century. Because it was so easy to believe, it was used by the three main later sources for fifth-century Britain in the Middle Ages.

Unfortunately, even the foundation history in Gildas was not necessarily an accurate one. As has been seen, the British ecclesiastic may well have added to the history he could find as well, and he was influenced by his own priorities. Because of these two points, and the overwhelming authority Gildas has had over later historians, the stories *De Excidio Britanniae* tells of the century after 410 have dominated thought in British and Anglo-Saxon studies, and undermined our understanding of other sources which had better access to accurate fifth-century materials. Nowhere is this more visible than in the figures of Hengest, Horsa, and Vortigern, interwoven biographies that were the very foundation of Kent's history and credibility. While it is true he did not name them, it is with Gildas that the story line and characters were first set in place. It is without Gildas that we will understand the true nature of fifth-century Britain.

9

Ansehis, Hengest and the Kentish Line

The last chapter has established that there was a Kentish Source created possibly between 593 and 616, probably between 593 and 630, and certainly in the range of 580 to 731. Its main purpose was to demonstrate that the Kentish house was the sole legitimate royal family in Britain, and secondly to confirm Canterbury's singular religious status on the island. This first objective was achieved best of all in the story of Hengest and Horsa, and their invitation by and consequent dealings with Vortigern. This Kentish source was later used, either directly or indirectly, for the creation of Bede's *Historia Ecclesiastica*, the *Historia Brittonum*, and the *Anglo-Saxon Chronicle*.

It follows that, as all three sources obtained their information on the *adventus* from the same source and this source had a known motivation for writing its particular version of the *adventus*, the migration it portrays is not necessarily historical. Accepting that, the connection between Hengest and Vortigern must be proven independently of the legend before it might be believed. The same may be said of Hengest's genealogical relationship with Æthelberht and Kent's royal house.

The intention of this chapter is to discuss the last of these now-unsupported assumptions—the viability of the extant Kentish genealogy. This will involve the development of a historical context in which the prehistorical persons of that genealogy might originally have lived in. As no Insular sources name either Hengest or Oisc outside the context of the Kentish Source, this will entail the use of the continental works *Ravenna Cosmography* and Jordanes' *Getica*. Limiting the source material will prove a blessing, as the sources to be used will be much nearer in time and more credible as witnesses than those derived from the Kentish Source.

To begin, however, a more detailed examination of the extant genealogy and what Bede says about the activities of Hengest, Horsa, and Oisc is in order. Most clearly, Hengest could not have migrated over to Britain as the first *foederati* in the mid–fifth century, as Gildas implied and later historians have followed. Nor was he probably the last immigrant as Myres has suggested and others have accepted[1]; he was not the last *foederati* because the last person to have the power to make such an arrangement had left the island in 407. He could not have been the leader of the last group of Germanic migrants, either. The Germanic settlements of lowland Britain continued well past 450 and nearly into the sixth century. If we are to accept Hengest was a *foederati*, we must place him forty years earlier than his traditional date of 449. If we are to make him the last settler, we must move him forward about forty years. And, while either option is possible without further information, such an alteration of his floruit does have one significant drawback; either option alters the lengths of each of the three generations between Hengest and Æthelberht to such an extent as to make them infeasible.

Second, there is a discrepancy in the *adventus* as Bede gives it. When Bede first announces the arrival of Hengest in Book 1, Chapter 15, it is with his brother Horsa. However, in Book 2, Chapter 5, he tells us that Hengest had arrived with his son Oisc. As Turville-Petre long ago noted, this indicates the existence and use of a second invasion legend that had been not entirely meshed with the first before it was put in written form by Bede.[2] It was fully refined by the late ninth century, where the *Anglo-Saxon Chronicle* has Hengest and Horsa land together. There Oisc, now Æsc, emerges only after the death of his uncle.

Oisc son of Hengest is a curious figure, and is also the source of another line of questions. In Bede and elsewhere, Hengest is the man who first comes over to Britain, who manipulates events to get Kent, and who comes to settle his people in Kent as their ruler—yet his son is the one who is credited with founding the dynasty. Oisc is first named Orric and, alone among the early Germanic peoples, he seems to have an alternate appellation, Oisc, that is used exclusively after it is first introduced. This switch seems to have no purpose as it stands, and again suggests genealogical tampering such that there has been an attempt to forge two individuals into one. The fact that Bede names the Kentish lineage the *Oiscingas* only supports such an assumption.

Finally, there are Hengest and Horsa, whose names mean "gelding" and "pack-horse," respectively. Even without deeper examination, they are the English equivalents of Romulus and Remus or a dozen other legendary brothers/royal co-founders whose names translate as something symbolic of kingship in their respective cultures.[3] To believe they actually existed as legend has laid their story out is to be without critical faculties.

What the above information leads to is that, first of all, the Kentish Source was not accurate in its earliest sections. Nor could it have been correct, as anything dated to before about 530 would have been beyond the limitations of any oral knowledge by the time the Kentish Source was written no matter how early that may have been. In fact, there may well have been no contemporary records before about 616 by the most generous estimate, and therefore no historically viable materials before well after 550. With this in mind, we must conclude that any of the details presented in the Kentish origin legend cannot be based on any historical materials.

More important, the mythical founders and the indecision about Hengest's son's activities and name suggests tampering with the genealogies. Specifically, it seems likely that two foundation legends were being forged into one history. With this in mind, Turville-Petre believed the point of determining the historical placement of Hengest, Horsa, and Hengest's son was moot:

> The personage Oisc represents the divine ancestor, and he is appropriately styled "the divine." On the other hand, Hengest and Horsa owe their names to the cult-image venerated by the warriors of early Kent. Of course they were military adventurers who answered the British call for federates, just as Aeþelberht of Kent had a human great-grandfather. But they were not known to their contemporaries as Hengest, Horsa and Oisc. When their deeds attained a retrospective importance, they were dignified by obsolete titles, in accordance with their historic functions.

However, his conclusion is not necessarily accurate. Addressing ancestors with symbolic appellations is not a tendency of oral records. Instead, they find legendary or mythical characters from a broader heritage or from a time nearly unremembered and infuse them into their royal families.[4] Knowing this, the historical horizon of the Kentish genealogy begins to come together.

The Ravenna Cosmographer tells us that a group of Saxons came to Britain under an *Ansehis* in the latter half of the fourth century. His name is normally emended to *Anschis*, which is a title that translates as "semi-divine." It derives from Old Germanic *Anski*, equivalent to Old English *Oski*. This latter form gave rise to *Oisc*, the same name as the man who founded the Kentish royal family of the Oiscingas.[5] As only two chieftains migrating to Britain in the fourth century are known, it seems the cosmographer's Saxon chieftain was probably a notable person, and if so it would explain his place in a Germanic genealogy.

Hengest is a much trickier figure, and here the author thinks it wise to follow the course of action set by Sims-Williams. He has lain out three possible ways of interpreting the figure. First, Hengest and Horsa could be mythical figures. Second, Hengest could originally have been an independent figure of literature superimposed on the genealogy. Last, it is possible that Hengest is a corruption of Anschis.

The possible ties to mythology are in line with the thinking of Turville-Petre and other scholars of epic and heroic literature.[6] This covers a barrage of possibilities. It is always a possibility that Hengest and Horsa were local gods who were later euhemerized, like Woden and Belatacudros, when the historical migration was forgotten.

The idea that Hengest could have been independent and Horsa a later add-on seems plausible as well. As Sims-Williams pointed out, the extant fragments pertaining to the Battle of Finnsburgh end with the Jutish hero, Hengest, likely being forced into exile. Any historian who had read Gildas and was aware of the story would have seen the potential to take the hero from the traditional legend and make him the unnamed *foederati* whom Gildas had introduced. One can see a similar borrowing, if indeed it was intended, with the founder of the Mercian royal house.[7]

The final option, and probably the least likely, is the oft-proposed theory that Hengest is the result of some scribal corruption or intentional attempt to make linguistic sense of Anschis. This requires a great deal of linguistic creativity, and is unnecessary in light of the first two options. One must keep in mind, too, that it would make Oisc and Hengest doublets of one original person. Granted, their careers seem to complement each other in the Kentish Source in that one lands in Britain and takes Kent while the other founds a dynasty there, but it has been seen that Kentish history is entirely fallacious. Our mysterious Kentish historian took Gildas' outline of events and built characters, relationships, and themes based on it. It hardly seems likely that the original creator of the story would have had the difficulties necessary to insert a doublet to the story.

The above has shown that Anschis was the most likely inspiration for Oisc. This would mean he was a figure of the late fourth century and could not possibly have been the great-grandfather of Æthelberht. His genealogical connections to Kent, if he had any, are now irretrievable. Hengest is likely the product of the euhemerization of a god or the borrowing of a continental hero. In either case, there is no historical evidence that he was connected to Kent.

We are left, then, with a curious situation. It is known that Æthelberht existed; his name appears both in the native Kentish Source and also in a letter written by the pope to him and his archbishop. It is reasonable to believe that his father, Iurminric, existed as well. Even if Æthelberht's children or grandchildren were the ones who commissioned the Kentish Source, they would have known their ancestors' name back that far. In fact, they might have known the paternal lineage back another generation to Oisc, who would have lived roughly in the middle of the sixth century. This, as we have seen, was the period when the Germanic kingdoms first emerged.

On the other hand, the inception year of Æthelberht's reign is not known. Bede does not deem him worth mentioning before he invites the Roman representatives of the church in 596. Neither is there a record anywhere of his father or grandfather's activities. There is also the matter of Æthelberht's unrealistic reign of fifty-six years. If this length were historical, it would not only mean he lived at least an unreasonable sixty-one years, but that his son lived at least into his late forties. The odds against even two generations approaching fifty in the early seventh century are high, that one of them could have reached sixty is astronomical.

Together, these two unusual groups of information mean that the Kentish Source was written no later than the 690s, about a century after records become internally consistent and just within the established limits of oral knowledge for churchmen. They could have been written no earlier than the period of Æthelberht's *Bretwaldaship*, when Kent would first have had the power and ability to create a national history. If the Kentish Source was written during the former end of this range, then Oisc may have been an ancestor of the line. However, his chronology must be considered totally unreliable. Because of his Frankish name, Iurminric was likely Æthelberht's father, but nothing more can be guessed at about him. If the date is closer to 616, then these two generations were within living memory until that time, and the relative chronology may be considered historical as they have been remembered, excepting of course the bias of the Kentish Source's historian.

The uncertainty as to the source's year of publication means that in Kent nothing before 596 may be considered absolute chronology, and little can be of use in relative chronology. Æthelberht was probably born before 591. It is possible that Iurminric was not his father, nor Oisc his grandfather. It is feasible that both were early and now unremembered chieftains who were placed where they are in the Kentish pedigree in order to enhance the Kentish lineage. And, unless another reason can be found to believe the earlier evidence in Bede, Æthelberht will have to be considered the first historical member of the family, while Iurminric and Oisc will have to be looked on as nothing more than possible members of the family line. An analysis of the early Kentish family and a better understanding of the Kentish Source's date of composition are two of the goals of the next chapter, which will involve a fresh look at an old topic.

10

Gwrtheyrn, Vortigern and Outigern

The previous chapter has provided conclusive evidence that the received Kentish Source is unhistorical in the fifth century. If the connection between Vortigern and Hengest is to be sustained, another means of doing so must be determined. We are left, then, with an evidently powerful British figure who has no historical context. This is an unsatisfying state of affairs that must, if possible, be tidied up.

To begin with, it should be stated bluntly that English Vortigern of *Historia Ecclesiastica* and the *Anglo-Saxon Chronicle* is the British Gwrtheyrn of *Historia Brittonum*. This is known for a number of reasons. The first is that all three histories seem to rely on the Kentish Source with regards to his career. Second, all three figures play identical roles in inviting the brothers Hengest and Horsa; they are all duped by their employees. More important, Vortigern/Gwrtheyrn is an extremely powerful individual who at one time dominates Kent as well as the Germanic mercenaries. Specifically, *Historia Brittonum* credits him with control of an area from Gwynedd to Kent.[1] Add in the obvious similarities of the two names and there can be no question that *Vortigern* is simply the Anglicized adaptation of British *Gwrtheyrn*.[2]

To the heart of the matter, then. Gwrtheyrn has been associated with Saint Germanus, a figure belonging to the first half of the fifth century. However, this connection is even more tenuous than the link to Hengest. As was seen in the critical examination of *Historia Brittonum*, Germanus was not added to the work until the second editor of the *Historia Brittonum* in the tenth century. It was also demonstrated that Germanus was conflated with Garmon, a local saint in Powys.[3] The name similarity and the negative influence of the Kentish Source with regards to Vortigern probably led to the confusion.

Despite its lateness and lack of historical content, the Germanus chronology has been central to dating Gwrtheyrn to the middle of the fifth century.[4] Germanus of Auxerre is known to have been in Britain in 429, and may have returned around 440. So when he is credited with excommunicating Gwrtheyrn, it is assumed that the Powysian king was active during the same period as well. This reasoning is also flawed.

Primary sources also fail to place him in the mid–fifth century, either. It has often been assumed that when Gildas mentioned a *superbus tyrannus*, he meant Gwrtheyrn. And the fact is that his villain's name is the Latin equivalent to British Gwrtheyrn and Anglo-Saxon Vortigern. However, Gildas did not say Gwrtheyrn's name. The connection between the historical figure and the man Gildas speaks of was forged largely by Bede or his Kentish Source. It was these two who first gave the incompetent king an actual name, Vortigern, instead of a title. Bede was followed by later recensions of *De Excidio Britanniae*, and these have given rise to the modern connection there. But the fact remains that neither of them could have known any better than we do of whom Gildas wrote. At 729 and no earlier than 580, respectively (Bede and the earliest possible year for his source), both were too far away from the mid–fifth century to have direct access to the information.[5] It is best, then, to proceed without assumptions in trying to learn more about Gildas' infamous king.

As powerful as he is supposed to have been in Insular lore, no Roman, Gallic, Byzantine, Germanic, or Irish writer mentioned Gwrtheyrn. Another Insular figure of the same period and with the same legend of power was Niall of Ireland. Despite the fact that he was further removed from the continent than Vortigern was, he is mentioned in Roman and Gallic as well as Irish records. This is only negative evidence, but the simple fact that someone of Vortigern's supposed standing was never named by anyone on the Continent or Ireland is cause for concern, and again casts doubt on his traditional place in the fifth century.

In Britain, where he is mentioned, he appears to have undergone a complex process of development. Dr. Nora Chadwick noted that the anti–Gwrtheyrn chapters were added to *Historia Brittonum* in Dyfed at about the time the last rulers of Powys were naming him as their progenitor and most prestigious ruler on the Pillar of Eliseg.[6] It would seem on this evidence that the rulers of Powys looked on him with reverence. It was, however, the traditions of Dyfed that were put into the dominant history, and its passages came to overwhelm any native traditions that may have existed about him. There remains next to nothing that can directly counter any of the accusations the *Historia Brittonum* makes about him.

We are left with evidence of a less decisive sort with which to verify his chronology— the extant genealogies and very little archaeological evidence. The former vary a great deal because of the turmoil of the tenth century and the resulting interests in undermining the family that ruled Powys. However, when adjusted to resolve these issues, one Powys line does place Gwrtheyrn in the sixth century, not in the fifth.[7] As will be seen, the other Powysian dynasty, that derived from Cadell, also puts its founder in the mid–sixth century. This means that Gwrythern and Cadell's mutual contemporary, Garmon, was probably from that era as well.

Some of the archeological evidence we have seen already. It indicates there were *foederati* in Britain from well before the Romans left, and what evidence we have suggests that the migrations did not end until the middle of the sixth century. Again, this also fails to put Gwrtheyrn in a mid–fifth century context. In short, of what little evidence we have, nothing points to an over-king named Gwrtheyrn living in the middle of the fifth century.

Without a history, genealogy, or even archaeological evidence for a fifth-century Gwrtheyrn, the scholar is left with evidence of a more questionable nature. The Irish high-king Laogaire (428–462) had a grandson named Foirtchernn through his daughter and a British father. As the name is unfamiliar in Ireland, it most probably came from Britain. Either he or another Fortchern were also said to be contemporary to Finnian, Abban, and Columba (mid to late-sixth century). A third Fortchern was son to Tigernach of Airgalla and brother to Catchern (mid to late-sixth century). Catchern, according to tradition, was the name of a son of Gwrtheyrn.

Whether anything can truly be made out of the loose affiliations listed above is uncertain. However, it is worthy of mention that apart from Loegaire's grandson the other persons all seem to have been active into and beyond the mid–sixth century. That would make no sense if their namesake had been dead for nearly a century before they were born, and still less if he had been the cowardly fool history has made him.

Geography may also offer a clue as to his floruit. There are three independent verifications that Gwrtheyrn was a king in Powys—the genealogies, the Powysian region of Gwrtheyrnion, and his interactions with the Powysian saint Garmon. However, none of these evidences are all that sound on closer examination.

A good deal of work has been done by Miller, Kirby, and Rowland regarding Powysian lineages. Kirby was the first to realize that there were in fact two dominant families in medieval Powys,[8] while Rowland's study into the *Canu Heledd* poems has suggested that there were several lesser houses in the region as well.[9] The most prominent was Gwrtheyrn's family, while the second was founded by Cadell. The Pillar of Eliseg represents an attempt at blending the history of the two dynasties after their kingdoms had been made into one political unit.[10]

However, the earliest genealogy dates to the ninth century, some four centuries after Gwrtheyrn's assumed floruit. It was also funded by a king who was attempting to add prestige to his lineage. These facts about their background do not make for a credible source.

The second piece of evidence that Gwrtheyrn was active in Powys is that Gwrtheyrnion was named after him. This is hardly testimony. Regions named after people, eponyms, do not prove that their namesake ruled the area, or even that they founded the line which did. Witness the four and seven Pictish kingdoms,[11] or the Gwynedd provinces named after the sons of Cunedda.[12] And unlike the above examples, there is no origin legend associated with Gwrtheyrnion, suggesting that the region had not intended to claim it had been ruled by him. As Kirby long ago suggested, the eponym suggests only that his descendants lived there.[13]

Finally, there is the matter of Saint Garmon. He is undeniably a Powysian saint. However, saints' lives are notorious for associating their hero with as many powerful kings as possible. And, where a king's fame was overwhelming, the facts of chronology and geography could be overlooked on occasion. By all accounts, Gwrtheyrn was a powerful king. He was so powerful, in fact, that it would appear the kingdom of Powys adopted him into its official dynasty.

With the obvious connection of Gwrtheyrn and Powys out of the way, a more scrutinizing examination of the materials proves illuminating. The pedigree stretching behind Gwrtheyrn is consistent in all the sources, and gives him a great-grandfather named Gloiu and a grandfather Guidolin. Whether or not these might have been his historical ancestors is unimportant for the time being. What is of note is the geographical context they both provide. Gloiu is often found in British sources and relates to Gloucester, a city of modern Hampshire. Guidolin has often been regarded as the Welsh equivalent of Vitalinus. This figure is noted as fighting Ambrosius in the Battle of Gueleph, probably modern Wallop in the same region. These two points would argue that Gwrtheyrn's family was based in Hampshire, ancient Dubonnia. It is feasible that Gloucester was his chief residence.

This reasoning allows for a few puzzle pieces to fall in place. We know of no Dubonnian holy men. From what the archaeological records tell us, that region was under Germanic control by the latter part of the sixth century, well before the writing of *vitae* became common among the Britons. Its early conquest not only explains why no Dubonnian ecclesiastics have been preserved, but also serves to elucidate one lingering question: Why does Gwrtheyrn's career seem to be more the product of historical fancy than the poetic license of biased historians?

On the other hand, Gwrtheyrn's relations with Garmon may be historical. The Gwrtheyrn of the sixth century was a king with widespread influence, and Powys was nearby. The likelihood that he dealt with Powys from Dubonnia is high, and that he interacted with

Garmon reasonable. This is especially so because of the Pillar of Eliseg's prejudice—it is opposed to *Historia Brittonum*'s Gwrtheyrn story. Instead of having the saint curse him, Garmon blesses Gwrtheyrn's son. The duality of viewpoints suggests that the common facts are accurate; he controlled some of Powys during at least part of his career, and was able to found a dynasty there.

The various pieces of usable information regarding Gwrtheyrn have yielded that he was a powerful figure. He could not have controlled the island, but he was memorable. The narrow geography of place-names in any material related to him suggests that his power extended to only a part of Dubonnia; however, he could have collected tribute from regions as far away as Kent and Gwynedd during his career. It has also been seen that he belongs more in the mid–sixth century than in the mid–fifth century.

This seems to be all that may be learned of Gwrtheyrn given our present state of knowledge. However, here the author would like to speculate on what has been discussed in the pages above. Namely, the fact that Gwrtheyrn was likely a person of the sixth century whose name seems to appear nowhere apart from genealogy and in conjunction with the Kentish foundation legend is a fact worth exploring. His limited exposure given his power and the period he was active seems entirely unlikely.

Outigern is the name of an otherwise unknown chieftain who is found in *Historia Brittonum* associated with five poets in the "Northern History" section.[14] It is possible he was the patron of Talhaearn, the first named bard in the list. The passage he is mentioned in has been sandwiched between a chapter focusing on Maelgwn and another which mentions the conquest of Bamborough by Ida. For this reason, Outigern has normally been placed in the middle of the sixth century.[15]

What has bothered scholars, and this one in particular, is that by about 550 we know a fair percentage of the British kings, and the more powerful rulers are generally mentioned in a couple sources, such as Rhydderch, Morgan, Urien, and Rhun. In all cases, they are associated with both a region and a genealogy. The *Historia Brittonum* editor thought Outigern was important enough that he needed no introduction, and yet is to be found nowhere else.

Perhaps some sense can be found in the name, however. Let us for the moment pass over the nonsensical "Ou" and focus on the second syllable, "tigern." It is the Latin version of "theyrn," prince. Tigern is an unusual syllable even among the British, and only Vortigern and Kentigern share that root word with him in all of British studies. Tigern's uniqueness makes the first syllable, "Ou," that much more interesting. A little dyslexia in a tired scribe might have produced Outigern from Votigern, a reasonably close form of Vortigern's name.[16] Such a suggestion makes all the more sense now that it has been shown that Gwrtheyrn/Vortigern was active in the same era.

Given that Outigern and Gwrtheyrn were the same individual, why might the ninth-century scholar of *Historia Brittonum* have missed the connection between the reference point of his passage and the famed king? Simple. It has been shown that Gwrtheyrn was based in Dubonnia and had power into Powys. However, by the ninth century Dubonnia was gone and Powys' borders had shrunk from a kingdom that may well have stretched up to Reged down to its late medieval borders within modern Wales. At that point, any mention of Gwrtheyrn as a figure associated with areas long ago conquered by the Germanic invaders would have made no sense with what was known of the famous and virile king of Powys. A minor spelling variation on the name, and the fact that the *Historia Brittonum*'s chapters were compiled from several independent sources, and one can see why the author never realized they were the same person. Even with hundreds of scholars looking over the materials in the modern era, this is the first time the association has ever been suggested to this writer's knowledge.

One other figure should be mentioned in conjunction with the Gwrtheyrn figure, his "son" Gwrthefyr. The character is given several unusual quirks that seem to beg further exploration. One may note first of all that he shares a first syllable with Gwrtheyrn, and that their common *Gwr* means "over." One might also note that the last syllable "thefyr," translates as king. While it is not at all uncommon for members of a dynasty to share the same first syllable of a personal name, it is unusual that the second should mean so much the same in both cases. This is especially noteworthy as both names look like titles. Gwrthefyr and Gwrtheyrn translate as "great-prince" and "over-king," respectively.

There is more to the similarity than just their names, however. Gwrthefyr's story is oddly placed in the history, and intimately related to his father's legend. In *Historia Brittonum*, Gwrtheyrn is in control of the island, invites Hengest and Horsa, marries Ronnwen and gives Hengest Kent, and allows his father-in-law to first manipulate and then revolt from him. At this point Gwrthefyr appears. In chapters forty-two and forty-three of *Historia Brittonum* he is mentioned and fights four battles against the Germanic warriors. He then dies, with no fanfare. Gwrtheyrn's story resumes with his excommunication and death. When Gwrtheyrn is involved in the storyline, Gwrthefyr is absent. When Gwrthefyr is involved, Gwrtheyrn disappears. The *Historia Brittonum* editor apparently noticed this discrepancy and attempted to explain it by excusing Gwrtheyrn from the fighting because of his age. But this statement is merely a bad excuse. Medieval historiographers believed that several contemporary kings lived up to eighty, and were active in battles until nearly the end of their careers. If Gwrthefyr was his son, he would logically have reached adulthood only recently when he began helping with kingdom affairs, making Gwrtheyrn considerably younger.

The mystery deepens when one compares Gwrthefyr's career with the English sources. In the *Anglo-Saxon Chronicle*, Gwrtheyrn is specifically named as the opponent for the first battle that Gwrthefyr is connected to. He is implied in the other three. Clearly the Germanic side remembered Gwrtheyrn as the only Briton they fought in this period.

One more curious fact emerges when the scholar goes over the British records; Gwrthefyr is not to be found in the pedigrees. As has been demonstrated in British studies and elsewhere, significant figures of history were regularly added to the catalogue of family names in every kingdom lineage. Yet somehow, Gwrthefyr is different. We are to believe that the genealogists managed to forget this individual, who temporarily stemmed the tide against the Germanic figures and heroically attempted to undo his father's mistakes?

We are left, then, with two men whose etymologies are nearly interchangeable. In the case of the battles, they overlap. In the rest of the history, they exactly complement each other in their appearances. In the Welsh history, it has been seen that one was powerful, while the other was successful in battle. In the English versions, Gwrtheyrn was powerful and lost all the battles associated with Gwrthefyr, while his son does not exist at all. It has been seen that the man whom modern historians have known as Gwrtheyrn was in large part the creation of the Kentish Source, while Gwrthefyr seems more the remembrance of British oral history. It seems to the present scholar more than possible that Gwrthefyr's battles are the independently recorded memories of Gwrtheyrn's successes, added to the *Historia Brittonum* by an individual who did not know that he and Gwrtheyrn were the same person and that Gwrthefyr's battles better represented the historical truth of Gwrtheyrn's reign than anything he had found in the Kentish Source. In short, the character of Gwrthefyr was created by the *Historia Brittonum* author.[17]

These battles bear closer scrutiny. They were all fought in Kent, and if Gwrtheyrn was a figure of the mid–sixth century, the period around 550 is probably the time around which the battles were fought as well. It is now impossible to tell which army emerged ahead in the conflicts, or even the order in which they were fought. However, the fact that the place-names from the opposing sources do not match up well guarantees that they are independent remembrances. Apart from that, all that we may be fairly certain of is that the four battles were decided between Gwrtheyrn and Kent at some point around the middle of the sixth century.

However, even this rough timing and geography is of great use. It has already been seen that the period before 593 is quite gray in Kent, and noted that Æthelberht was assigned a fifty-six-year reign ending in 616. This has normally been taken as his lifespan.[18] In the present context, however, it might be suggested that Æthelberht's reign had been artificially extended for another reason. He represented the golden age of Kent, when Christianity had been introduced through him. It was also the period when his kingdom collected tribute from most of the Germanic kingdoms below the Thames, and from a few north of that line.

The author would like to suggest here that, though his reign might have been the high point in Kent's history, the years immediately preceding him might have been humiliating for his people on the same scale. During that time, a British king, Gwrtheyrn, may have collected tribute from Kent. It seems reasonable that the creators of the Kentish Source, having developed a foundation legend and set up a strong genealogy designed to establish Kent as the most significant kingdom in Britain, would not have wanted such an era remembered. Recording their kingdom's subservience would have relegated Kent to the political stature of every other kingdom. To avoid this, they extended the reign of Æthelberht to include that of his predecessor, possibly his father Iurminric. This was done much as Bede tells us he has extended the reign of Oswald to smother the genocidal year of Cadwallon. On the English side of things, this tells us the historical horizon may well go back beyond 593, and thus that the Kentish Source could have included accurate materials before then. On the British side, it gives us a firm range of dates from which to learn more about Vortigern's floruit. He was active at some point between 560 and 593.

If Vortigern were as powerful as we have been led to believe, and he did take tribute from Kent, this would have been extra incentive for the writers of the Kentish Source to equate the *superbus tyrannus* fool of Gildas with Vortigern. It insulted their nemesis on a subtle level. It turned him from a great warrior to a weak-minded man while using him to show why Kent was the only legitimate house to rule Britain. Gwrtheyrn was, after all, a powerful British king. By outwitting him and undermining his authority, Kent's royal house had proven beyond a doubt their own validity as his heirs.

Gwrtheyrn and Vortigern are essentially the same character. Vortigern was an attempt by Kent's historians to enhance Kent's kings' statures and undermine the legacy of their worst enemy. The British Gwrtheyrn was the inheritor of this hostility in *Historia Brittonum*, and had more insults heaped upon him when Dyfed edited it in the tenth century. The final revision left a character known only in literature who at one time possessed the dual qualities of uniting Britain and defending her on one hand while personally being a weak man with little ability in warfare. He protected his kingdom with a unique strength of will during a period of turmoil, yet was willing to give away an entire province to marry the daughter of a pagan underling.

What Outigern and possibly Gwrthefyr represent are alternative memories of Vortigern that were uncorrupted by the Kentish Source and Dyfed's influence. Knowing this, the Pillar of Eliseg is noteworthy as well. It shows Gwrtheyrn as a strong and successful man who left descendants strong enough to persevere and remember him, notwithstanding the strong influence of the above written sources. If we are to learn anything at all of this historical character, it must be through information that has not been influenced by Kent or Dyfed.

That the Kentish Source may contain information for the period between 560 and 593 is also of interest to Kentish history. If it does contain something of value from 560, what was the significance of that year?

Three options come to mind. First, that Iurminric may have begun ruling at that time; this is chronologically possible if not likely. The second is that Oisc may have begun ruling at that time, and thus the dynasty itself may have first formed.

The third option is slightly more complex, but agrees best with the materials that can be brought to bear on the question. It is that in about 560, Gwrtheyrn conquered the area and formed it into a basic political unit for administrative simplicity. This option would explain why Kent seems to have had a kingship considerably sooner than the other Germanic kingdoms; it inherited the government of Gwrtheyrn's province. The year 560 might well have been the year of the inception of the Kentish kingship, begun under the aegis of Gwrtheyrn.

11

Ambrosius and Guitolin

Ambrosius is one of the more tantalizing figures of post–Roman Britain, dancing as he does on the border between history and prehistory. He is one of only two British leaders who are named by primary fifth-century sources, the other being Ceredig. He is also the hero that Gildas credited with beginning the movement against the Germanic invaders. Despite his noteworthy accomplishment, however, Ambrosius is associated with no dynasty. Because of this, we cannot be certain he was active in any place, nor any range of dates outside of what may be deduced about him.

Which is why a 437 entry in *Annales Cambriae* associated with him is such an enigma. That notice states that Ambrosius fought a Vitalinus at Gueleph, certainly a feasible activity for a British war-leader. However, it is the date which is the curiosity; 437 is some eighty years before Badon. That would make it some sixty to eighty years before the traditional date of Badon. As has been seen, it would make him active and fighting another British leader decades before any native British kingships could have developed. If Gildas' testimony is any indication, the battle would have taken place long before any reasonable form of record-keeping might have been attempted. It is, to any objective scholar, an unreasonable date to associate with Gildas' hero.

And yet the information is to be found in the records, and there is so little else to be found regarding the fifth century; the temptation for generations of scholars has been to simply accept what little information we have about him and attempt to assimilate it into our knowledge of the period. Inevitably, that decision has proven to be a trap.

The simplest way of integrating it has been to accept the data as is. However, simplicity in this period rarely makes for a lasting solution. In this case, associating Ambrosius with 437, assuming he did not have the reputation and authority to command an army until his mid-twenties, and using the normal dating for the great revolt at the late 460s or early 470s, we arrive at a feasible but extended lifespan for the hero. But of course that is not taking into account how many years he would have fought.

Others have subscribed to a theory that there were two Ambrosii, probably related to each other.[1] According to that argument, one fought Vitalinus in 437. The other, perhaps his son or grandson, was at Badon or was active in the generation just before Arthur.

Another scholar noted the linguistic connection between Vitalinus and the Guitolin who is named as an ancestor of Vortigern. In conjunction with the *Historia Brittonum* episode devoted to Ambrosius' revenge upon Gwrtheyrn, he saw two instances of kings from rival houses fighting. He hypothesized a family rivalry between Ambrosius and Gwrtheyrn.

Through all the conjecture about these two figures, however, it must be remembered that even the basic facts upon which all these theories are based is hearsay. As has been seen, 573 is probably the historical horizon of the *Annales Cambriae*, meaning any dates listed a century earlier than that could only have been developed through the roughest of chronological estimates; there is just as good a chance that Gueleph occurred in 500 as 437.[2] As to Ambrosius' appearance in the Gwrtheyrn saga, it has already been seen that he was only inserted there because of the damage his historical successes could do to Vortigern's reputation, and thereby to Powys' standing. His character was probably first introduced in the tenth century, when Dyfed was busy trying to make a claim over Powys and was using a revision of *Historia Brittonum* to do so. For that reason, no part of his story there is to be believed.

On the other hand, we do have some assurance that there was an Ambrosius at Badon. It has been generally agreed that this battle took place in the decades surrounding 500,[3] and in the region around the river Wye.[4] Judging by the small areas of influence British and Germanic rulers of this period had, the rough location of the battle is probably a good indicator of where Ambrosius was active.

The preceding chapter has also demonstrated that Gwrtheyrn was Guitolin's grandson, and that his ancestral home was probably Dubonnia, an area to the west of the Wye. It has shown, too, that Gwrtheyrn was active somewhere in the late sixth century, making it very likely his grandfather was a figure of the late fifth or early sixth century and a possible contemporary of Ambrosius.

What does this new take on Ambrosius mean for British studies? It points to nothing for certain, though it does corroborate some of the theories formulated above. With an understanding of the developing British political structure in the fifth century, it would have been unlikely that Ambrosius could have led men into battle without being a king. That he is nowhere directly associated with any kingdom suggests that his dynasty was taken over by another through conquest or simple expansion at some time after his historical accomplishments. As Ambrosius' father is unknown to us, and Guitolin's ancestors are questionable from the generation prior to him, what has been laid out above also suggests that the end of the fifth century saw the development of petty kingdoms that were slowly absorbed into much larger kingdoms. This has already been demonstrated above through different means.

The above also offers some details and points toward a few broader conclusions. First, by accepting the evidence for what it is there is no need to posit the existence of two Ambrosii; knowing that there is no set date for Gueleph apart from the fifth or early sixth century, one man could have been at both legendary battles without assuming an extended life for him.

It is also clear from the above arguments that Guitolin was active in roughly the same period as Ambrosius, and that the *Annales Cambriae* note for 437 was based on some traditional memory. This in turn makes it ever more likely that his grandson Gwrtheyrn would have been active in the last third of the sixth century.

As to the historical order of the engagements Gueleph and Badon, it is easier to see Ambrosius fighting with a rival Guitolin at Gueleph prior to Badon rather than later. The rationale is straightforward; he would have been uniting the Britons against the Germanic peoples. However, it is also possible the two fought afterward, when the barbarian threat had lessened and dissension was more practical. Such activity would have been precisely the infighting that Gildas complained of.[5]

As to political development, the possible range of locations for Badon, Gueleph, and Guidolin's family must focus around the area to the west and southwest of the Wye river. This in turn reinforces the limited sphere of influence that was predicted for both men in the chapter above. The size of their control reinforces the period in which they were active, in the early stages of kingship during the mid- to late fifth century and during the early stages of kingship.

12

The Fifth Century

A good deal of ground has been covered since the traditional history of post–Roman and sub–Roman Britain was laid out in the second chapter of this work. It has been seen that much of what has been accepted as historical fact was based on faulty data or sources with questionable backgrounds. Other aspects of the traditional history have been shown to be wholly wrong. One thing has proven certain through all the revelations, however: the received history of post–Roman Britain is not built upon sturdy foundations.

What exactly has emerged from this study? The last century or so of Roman rule was marked by a gradually decreasing Roman presence in Britain, followed by a diminished Roman influence. This started a pattern that would continue till 410. Beginning with Magentius in 350, a series of would-be emperors were crowned in Britain, and most of them invaded the Continent in order to establish themselves at Rome. Each claimant failed. The Britons would then sue Rome for protection and government, and Rome would return. But Rome had other problems and not enough troops to go around. Each time Rome reasserted itself, it provided the island with fewer of its precious soldiers. As a result, the Roman garrisons became smaller each time Rome returned. This meant they were less effective at defending the frontier and less capable of Romanizing the *foederati*.

It was in 406 that a series of three emperors were elected in quick succession, ending with Constantine. He went to the Continent to claim his imperial crown, and must have taken most of what little remained of the Roman army as well as the British auxiliaries with him. He never returned to Britain. In 410, Hadrian wrote a letter to Britain telling its cities that they could expect no help from him, suggesting that Constantine had abandoned them and that they were under immediate threat. Constantine died in 411, his army absorbed by the emperor. With those two events, Roman Britain came to an end.

However, the other aspects of the Roman way of life were falling apart long before Constantine was ever elected. Increased raids by the Germans, Picts, and Irish all contributed to a decline in long-range trade. At first, this only destabilized the supply of wine and other high-status goods coming from the Continent. This must have been inconvenient to the wealthy, but probably had no serious effect on the economy. As the pirating continued, however, it began to affect pay, supplies, and food meant for the soldiers and Germanic auxiliaries. If this did not end the standing military in Britain and wean the Germanic peoples of dependence, it certainly localized both and undermined their ability to coexist peacefully with the natives.

In the meantime, we have good evidence that a Roman education continued into the sixth century. Roman goods remained highly prized through the period, with wine and olive oil remaining symbols of high status. Roman culture in all its forms was retained. Christianity continued to make headway on the island.

However, the Germanic people's culture properly dominated the period. As *foederati*, they had been coming to Britain for centuries. At first they were simply tribesmen that were absorbed into the regular army. As the Roman presence declined and its legions became focused more on the internal conflicts of emperor-making, however, the Germanic warriors who entered into service were no longer indoctrinated as thoroughly as they had been at the beginning. This was not as dramatic a change as it might seem, though. What little we know of the Germanic peoples and the history of the early Middle Ages makes clear that they had a deep respect for everything Roman, and sought only to be a part of the civilization, not to end it.

However, the situation became more complex. The British dependence on these auxiliaries to protect them only grew with time, which led to greater and greater numbers of Germanic tribesmen being brought to the island. By the late fourth century, entire tribes were being transferred to Britain under their chieftains. As with the rest of the empire, there were no longer enough Roman troops stationed there to ensure that they were fully Romanized. It has also been seen that there was one issue the Continent did not face—the strangulation of supply lines including food and money. Because of this fact, the British auxiliaries, possibly more than any other Roman garrisons, became strained in their relationship with the local population.

However, their respect for the Roman Empire continued, and there is no record that the mercenaries revolted as soon as they had the opportunity. In 408 or 409, the continental Germanic tribes attacked. As has been seen, the British ousted Constantine's government and defended themselves. Along with removing all of his administration, they probably also took direct responsibility for the *foederati*'s food and supplies. This would have the effect of permanently severing the island's ties to Rome, and with it terminating any long-term solution to their problems. More immediately, overthrowing Constantine's government and severing its connection to Rome, Britain may have lost the respect of the Germanic tribesman.

There was an additional problem. In disbanding the Roman government of Constantine and requesting new administrators from the emperor, Britain put itself in an untenable position. When Hadrian refused to send them officials, the Britons found themselves without any administration at the regional and provincial levels. Only the local government was maintained as it was made up simply of the wealthiest landowners in the region. In short, the employers of the Germanic peoples overnight transformed from citizens of the Roman Empire to hundreds of individually governed local villages along the southern and eastern coasts of England.

These two fundamental modifications must have made it apparent to the *foederati* that their employers were nearly helpless without them. The transparent dependence would have altered their relationship. The loss of an island-wide government would also have put the burden of feeding and supplying the mercenaries on the local population, the people most benefited by them. Eventually, they would have buckled under the strain, resulting in inconsistent payments. It would not have taken long for even the most loyal of soldiers to realize the situation would not improve in the foreseeable future. Probably in 441, the Germanic *foederati* in Britain finally revolted. This may well not have been an organized rebellion, and certainly isolated tribes had probably revolted before then. But in 441, the movement was widespread. This is when the Gallic chroniclers took notice. Most likely, all the regions which had been held by the *foederati*, from Wight to Northumbria along the coast, fell into Germanic hands at this time.

The British people did not have the organization, training from birth, or culture of the warrior. What was more, they were a sedentary people, comfortable only in the isolated villages they spent their lives in and too far apart to render immediate mutual aid. Each was too small to contain enough men to defend against a determined assault. The Germanic peoples, by contrast, were comfortable with their mobility. Their culture was based in fighting, as was their philosophy of life. What was more, they had numbers. All these points gave the Germanic warriors a massive advantage in battle.

As a result, they continued to spread. More Germanic tribes undoubtedly migrated into Britain in search of easily taken property throughout the fifth century. Most were unable to settle where they came to shore because their cousins drove them away. So they moved inland. There they met with independent and isolated British settlements, and these they overcame easily. By all appearances, they must have continued to encroach on British land for some time into the fifth century.

In the meantime, the British had appealed to Ætius, to no avail. They must have thought the world was burning and the barbarians were carrying the torches. But eventually kingships emerged in the closing decades of the fifth century. These were not the kind we see in the seventh century. Instead, they were haphazard affairs. One man might be able to take control of a few local villages during his lifetime, only to have his life's work swallowed up by another king or dissolve on his death. The size and the stability of the kingships did not matter, though. The development of militarily based governments had the effect of holding back the encroaching Germanic peoples. Kingships meant a military leader and professional warriors, and the end of easy pickings for Germanic settlers.

Nevertheless, impromptu kingships are innately unstable, and cannot transform back to a democracy once the immediate threat is over. When the Germanic threat subsided, the primitive kingships began to compete with each other. It was not long before old traditions returned; the war bands, bards, cattle raids, and mythical pedigrees of the pre–Roman Celtic peoples soon became a part of everyday life once again. Over the course of time, death without heirs, failure of crops, or a general inability to retain power weeded out many of the earliest rulers, allowing the remaining kings to expand their control and begin dynasties. By perhaps 500, what we could consider kingdoms were born. These would continue to develop throughout the Middle Ages, coalescing to an ever-shrinking number of growing kingdoms.

In the meantime, the Germanic peoples may well have reduced the number of migrants to the island, but there was most definitely a problem with the land, too many tribes and too few settlements to leach food and supplies from. The result was a great deal of internal conflict. This competition over land in turn resulted in the development of kingship among the Germanic peoples on much the same lines as had already occurred with the British kings. This process would have begun as soon as the rise of British kingdoms began to curtail their spread west and north. The process was probably initiated shortly into the sixth century, with regional rule emerging in the middle of the century and the first of the medieval kingdoms towards 600.

The Irish and Picts had also been affected by the Roman presence and absence. It is likely that the Picts were a loosely coordinated culture group when the Romans arrived in the first century. By the time they left, kingships were forming. They would follow much the same course as their British counterparts. When the Roman presence weakened, it was they who were on the boundaries to test the British defenses.

The Irish may have formed larger kingships as a result of their secondhand contact with Rome. Certainly they took the opportunity of the Roman withdrawal to migrate into Britain. As history records almost no Irish royal claims to British territories, outlaws probably led these migrations, with perhaps a few disinherited royals on occasion.

The fifth century in Britain was not a clean break from the old life; it was a rough transition into another society. As with all social and political changes, it was a natural evolution resulting from the easiest way to deal with newly developing circumstances. The British, now thoroughly Romanized, tried to preserve the culture they had been raised with, even as their economic and political decisions forced them out of the sphere of Roman influence. At first, the Germanic peoples were more than willing to follow any culture that had been a part of the Roman tradition, but when their stomachs grew empty, they were forced to become more practical. The Irish and Picts were pragmatic as well. With the departure of the Roman legions, they saw the opportunity to claim more or better land. They pounced on the opportunity in a half-dozen areas. Such was the end of Roman Britain.

13

A Reevaluation of Key Post-Roman Figures

With the essays laid out above, the history of fifth-century Britain is made largely devoid of named figures, much as Gildas handed the information over to his peers in his *historia* 1,500 years ago. What has remained was not by design; certainly any century is more interesting with people. Nor will the first century after Rome remain nameless. The next section of this book will set about date-guessing the figures of the fifth, sixth, and seventh centuries. Probably very few individuals from the period 410 to 470 will ever be known, however. In recompense, this book should have gone a long way in explaining why this is so, and should be. There were no kingships in Britain for some time after the Roman government was disbanded. And, when there were and the requisite bards/skops had asserted themselves into the culture again, the native leaders who had lived before them were either forgotten or could not be put to practical use by the new and politically insecure kings and their emerging pedigrees.

More broadly, this book has so far covered a great deal of ground, and the foundations have been laid to learn even more. A careful review of Bede, *Historia Brittonum*, and the *Anglo-Saxon Chronicle* has revealed that their versions of Kent's foundation were all derived from the same source, and that source was the clergy through the royal house. Kent could only have written such a history between the last years of the sixth century and the first half of the seventh, and in this we can see both a reason for its creation and a potential bias in the information it gives. The Kentish Source could only have been written to demonstrate the strength and antiquity of the Kentish pedigree over other Germanic kingdoms and Kent's right to land on the island by way of the incompetence of the British over-king. This legend established that Kent alone had the right to rule Britain by way of strength, guile, and marriage. In such a history, the pedigree, chronology, and contemporaries of the story must be considered suspect, for obvious reasons.

Individual study of Hengest has shown that he may have been a legendary name from the migrants' homeland, a symbol of kingship, or a botched misspelling of *Ansehis*. Regardless of the eventuality, the first *foederati* were in Britain from the mid–fourth century, not the mid–fifth century. If Hengest has any historical context, it is a hundred years before the period he has been assigned. Similar study of Gwrtheyrn has shown that the pedigrees, the floruit of his grandfather Guitolin, and the breadth of his power place him more in the middle or later part of the sixth century. In conjunction with the study on Hengest, this revelation has served to show that the Kentish Source was not only created to develop a national history for Kent, but that whomever wrote it had no qualms in displacing historical figures in order to do the job more convincingly.

What we are left with is a much different set of sources than was presented at the beginning of the book. Gildas remains an elusive character. It is unclear when exactly he wrote, but his *historia* section undoubtedly had some notion of Ætius' career, so that from 446x453 on he becomes a strong witness. On the other hand, his post–388 introduction of the northern walls and the Saxon Shore cannot have happened in anything like the circumstances he describes.

As has been seen, the Kentish Origin legend did contain some historical materials, and these occasionally emerge in the *Anglo-Saxon Chronicle*, or perhaps in some of the unique data that comes to light in the Wessex traditions. The continuing difficulty with this source is to determine what was influenced by the biased portion of the Kentish Origin legend, what was a part of Wessex's origin legend, and where did the Wessex royal interest in unifying the history of at least two of her houses influence the entries which are extant.

Dalriadic history is a result of several factors. The *Senchus* is the only complete history, but it is not a primary material. Instead, it represents the efforts of ninth-century Scottish historians to create a history in which two or more royal Dalriadic families were forged into one. This historical editing covered up the historical fact of internal conflicts within early Scotland, and by taking contemporary and opposing rulers and presenting them as consecutive kings it extended back the foundations of that kingdom several decades. The Irish Annals are less biased on British history, but as has been seen they are only accurate from the late sixth century. Even then, they are limited to what was important in Iona and to Irish Bangor. The *Vita Columbae* is generally reliable except for when Columba's participation in secular affairs or holy miracles is concerned. However, its purview is a small and fragmented part of the political arena, and is only interested in a relatively short span of time.

Among the Britons, there is a strong body of evidence showing that a *Northern Memorandum* existed, and that both *Annales Cambriae* and *Historia Brittonum* took much of their information from it. However, the editor responsible for that information probably lived in the last quarter of the seventh century, and was more concerned with holding up Urien's family as a pillar of strength for the northern kingdoms than in writing a true history.

The original patron of the *Historia Brittonum*, the Gwynedd king Rhodri Mawr, wanted to highlight Urien's career as well. Rhodri had made a claim on Gwynedd and needed to bolster it by showing that his ancestors had been great kings. He also wanted to demonstrate his family's superior right to lead the other Welsh kingdoms. The entire history was designed to generate a sense of nationalism among the Welsh and against the English kingdoms, with him at the center of the movement. This history was written in 829. It was edited in the tenth century under Dyfed influence, when the chapters involving Gwrtheyrn were subject to the most change. The purpose of the alterations was to weaken the moral foundation of Powys' dynasty. Doing so would have allowed its conquest to be rationalized as an act of purification.

The *Annales Cambriae* would have nothing to do with Urien's fame. Its bias was entirely in favor of the Dyfed kings, who wanted no part in praising the kingdom of Gwynedd or its rulers. Instead, Urien and his family were omitted from the annals. Unfortunately, as St. David's had very little native historical materials, they could not provide much Dyfed history to supplement what its scribes must have deleted. Instead, the annalists took what seemed to be neutral materials from the Irish Annals and the *Northern Memorandum* and placed them in the earliest historical British entries, then supplemented the rest of the work with more recent Dyfed events, both political and ecclesiastical.

Unlike the sources above, we know who Bede was, where and when he wrote, and precisely what his predispositions were. He has proven an excellent historian with regards to secular affairs. From the time when he first begins to report the activities of his native kings, he is clearly making use of materials that were stored in Northumbria. Most significantly, he has made no effort to hide the fact that there had, until fairly recently, been more than one royal family in Northumbria competing against one another. As a nationalist, Bede should have been hidden this fact as part of the theme of any history he wrote, yet he resisted the temptation. This choice has made his work invaluable to us, both in direct study of Northumbria and in comparison with the development of other kingdoms in the period.

The *Llandaff Charters* are largely historical, that is when not serving the purpose of Bishop Urban during the 1120s. They give the names of kings, chiefs, and holy men beginning in the sixth century and offer a good sounding board for any political, genealogical, or ecclesiastical study of the period. The fact that so many persons are named as signatories to each document has also allowed for a good deal of cross-checking involving the more important individuals to be found there. The result has been more securely dated individuals.

In addition to these traditional sources, others have emerged. The *Life of Kentigern*, in both of the extant versions, is helpful when the interests of the original biographer and those of the two surviving *vitae* can be accounted for. So, too, with the *Vita Garmoni* which is embedded in *Historia Brittonum*. It has proven useful in both showing the historical precursors to the "Vortigern/Hengest and Horsa" myth, and in helping to establish a relative chronology for the two major Powysian dynasties.

To a lesser extent, the other *vitae* have demonstrated their value as well. The specific places and activities of the saints must remain highly suspect, but when they claim a noble or royal tie, they may well contain historical fact. When saints are connected to lesser kings, the relationship is probably an accurate one. Moreover, when both historical chronology and region agree with the association to a significant king, there is no reason to doubt that either. Under similarly limited conditions, the romances have also proven their worth, though the effort has proven to be something like squeezing juice out of a raisin, by hand.[1]

What can be seen developing in the pages above as an extension of the criticisms of the primary and secondary materials is not necessarily a cynicism about the usefulness of the primary sources in understanding British and Anglo-Saxon history. On the contrary, it has created a better awareness of all the pertinent sources. Each is no longer being looked at as a whole, but more as a body of sources grouped together under a common theme. Each of them has been influenced by a different writer or group of writers whose perspectives may or may not have been compatible with others to be found in the same work. In the case of the primary historical sources, this has often limited the extent to which they may be employed even while it has vindicated their use in other areas. In the case of the secondary or literary sources, the effort has consistently shown that there are segments where they may provide information more accurately than any extant primary historical source. This lesson is invaluable in an arena where there are so few sources of any sort, and these have often been found to be both internally inconsistent and at odds with each other.

More specifically, what has been created here is a rough format of the fifth century—the political and economic state during and after the Roman presence and the development of the Irish, British, and Germanic kingdoms in the centuries following that period. Using the sources within the parameters set by the specialists over the past fifty years, they may easily be used to form a single and consistent model. Time and further efforts in the field might show that many things about it are in error, but any future model will necessarily have to point out its flaws before a better one may be built.

Also, the studies above have provided a good context for where the chronological sources may or may not be useful. The dates when each was first set out is in all cases well established. The pages above have reiterated most of this information, and for the first time have set them all out in one location. In order to use that datum, we must simply apply what we have learned. If a chronological source was first created in 600, then it cannot contain relative chronology before 500, it is questionable within decades of 600, and it can only have been specifically accurate a few years before the recorder was first born.

All of the above has allowed the historian to produce a reasonable picture of the broad chronological development on the island as well as helping to pin down the dates for certain key events. The next logical step is to attempt the same approach on a kingdom-by-kingdom basis, and for this task one more tool will be necessary. This is where Dr. Miller's work on date-guessing will prove invaluable. In collusion with the dates and date ranges provided by the chronological sources, the traditional and modified genealogies laid out over the past few decades may be checked and, where necessary and feasible, refined. This done, those same dates may be used to limit the birth ranges of an entire dynasty and, in many cases, may help to tighten the birth ranges of its members' contemporaries.

The process will be intricate, and the results can never be fully accurate. However, together the relative chronology developed from these studies will allow for a better understanding of the events of the period, a better understanding of the sequence of events, and as a result a clearer perspective on the period and the people who lived it. And if the model or even the approach be shown partially or wholly inaccurate in the future, then the discussion which points out its flaws will only bring a more educated attempt closer to the mark. As such, there is no downside to the study undertaken below.

14

Applying Lesser Figures to the New Framework

In my *Origins of Arthurian Romances*, a radical and innovative idea was laid out, that carefully researched and appropriately pruned secondary and literary sources could be used to provide valuable, if limited, supplements to historical knowledge. This revelation was borne out most visibly in the less well-recorded portions of history. Since *Origins of Arthurian Romances* was published, the focus of the author's interests has remained sub–Roman Britain. The developments have been regular. The historical basis for the abduction of Arthur's queen has been seen, the mystery of the Holy Grail solved, Tristan's place in post–Roman history determined, and the question of Arthur's historicity, location, and floruit answered. The first half of this book then approached the period from a broader perspective and tried to reevaluate the sequence of events, political and economic transformations, and chronology of early Britain from the withdrawal of Roman troops after 410. In the process, the method I've developed was employed to develop topic specific tools. These instruments, and the conclusions which the author's previous works came to, make what comes next a natural sequel. I attempt to improve our understanding of the relative and absolute chronology of the period. This is done in the pages below, mainly by using the genealogies of as many dynasties as possible, but also through information about the saints and their contacts, and isolated references in the oldest poetry to lesser known historical figures. It is hoped the effort will lead to a better understanding of the period and the individuals who lived it.

The pages below follow a simple and occasionally tedious pattern, making use of the ideas developed in the first portion of this book. First, all of the information determined to be from primary sources is listed and their contents catalogued. Second, the traditional genealogies and any scholarly suggestion are noted and, using Miller's date-guessing method, tested. The process should serve to make apparent any potential flaws in the lineages, and point out the more likely of any variations.

The method above should give the most likely genealogies of the major kingdoms of the period. The goal then is to refine the dates of the members of the major dynasties, and from there to develop the chronologies of the minor dynasties as well as ecclesiastics and other significant figures of the period. To begin with, the dates and relationships provided by the secondary sources are laid out. This provides the raw data to be used. Second, the major interactive figures of the period are listed along with any and all materials relating to their contemporaries and their rough chronologies. Using elements of Miller's techniques, each of the persons listed are assigned a range of birth years. This is followed by another examination of the genealogies using the secondary information and the information derived about the most interactive people of the period. This should further refine the birth years of many of the above persons.

This done, and the major kingdoms set fairly well in their chronologies, the information developed there is used to help determine a stronger chronology for the lesser kingdoms of the period through any provided dates, contemporaneity to members of the major dynasties or ecclesiastics, and possible marriages they might have been involved with. This research is followed by a chapter devoted to those figures who are not known to have been attached to any kingdoms, and that will make use of all of the above acquired information. The results of these workings is more tersely and readably summarized in the appendix.

It is to be remembered that the date ranges determined below are not useful in themselves. However, they do lead to other and more valuable information and, hopefully, may allow for a more thorough understanding of the period. Finding patterns in the periods when the British and Germanic dynasties first began has already suggested something of the development of fifth-century Britain. Expanding and detailing such a study undoubtedly allows for more broad-ranging conclusions. A few questions come to mind immediately. What exactly did Ambrosius lead when he began the resistance, a national army or a very local militia? What is the sequential chronology of the key British events of the late sixth century—Catraeth, Ardferydd, and Urien's death? What is the pre–Æthelfrith Northumbrian chronology? Why is it that the political Dalriada we find in Adamnan and the Irish Annals seems to be fundamentally different from the one we find in the *Senchus*?

What of the heroic age, and how exactly did war bands controlling a few villages and developing into medieval states interact with each other? How were the raids noted in heroic poetry differentiated from the conquests that led to the development of larger kingdoms and, occasionally, to over-kings in the sixth century?

There is question, too, about the Age of Saints, and the migration of so many ecclesiastics to Brittany. What were the events that led up to such an event, and why did it end so abruptly? Why did several of the most significant ecclesiastical figures of the period migrate?

The above are intriguing queries, and various authors have broached most of them. However, it is impossible to fully answer any of them without working out the relative chronology of the relevant kingdoms. That cannot be done thoroughly without better understanding the chronology of every other kingdom on the island. This is, indeed, a massive task to set, but not an impossible one. The author's thesis has served both to show that literary sources may be used to better understand the period and has offered a means to cultivate the materials each might have to offer. The first portion of this book helped to form a treatment of all the relevant sources, showing the reader which sources to rely on and where. It is left only to employ the known dates and relationships and make the most reasonable deductions from the above information in order to come to the relative chronology of the persons living in Britain during this period.

15

Pertinent Facts Drawn from the Primary Sources

As has been seen, all the sources listed below have already been thoroughly treated. Those following were either written by contemporaries or within oral memory of their particular subject. Their point of origin has also been determined, the biased information pruned and the specific information separated from the sources in which they were found. It remains to go source by source and list whatever data remains. In this, the reader should readily see many absolute as well as relative dates emerging. A combination of the years found below and the resulting deductions will form the foundation for the rest of this book.

Patrick's Epistola *and* Confessions

- Taken captive at about twelve, a slave for six years, escaped, trained to be a missionary, returned to Ireland
- Wrote *Epistola* twenty or more years after returning to Ireland
- Wrote his *Confessions* about a sin committed thirty years ago, before he was a deacon
- There is no note of exception in Patrick's letters that would suggest a deviation from the norm of bishops being elected at or after thirty
- Coroticus was an active king twenty or more years after Patrick left for Ireland as a bishop

From the information given by Patrick, he was taken captive to Ireland at about twelve and escaped at eighteen. This means his Latin training would have been incomplete; he could not have been a deacon at the time of his abduction. With the six years of training he missed, he must have been no younger than about twenty when he had finished his Latin and would have been made a deacon some time after that. He was made a bishop at thirty or older. His *Epistola* to Coroticus was written at some time after he was fifty but before his death at no later than eighty, and his *Confession* was written when he was sixty or more. In this, Coroticus must have been active at some point between when Patrick was fifty and eighty. All that is needed is a death notice to take these abstract deductions and exchange them for reliable date ranges.

Gildas' De Excidio Britanniae *and* Epistulam

- Badon fought in the year of his birth
- Maelgwn, Vortipor, Cuneglasus, Constantine, and Aurelius Caninus alive in his forty-fourth year (at 43)
- Uinniau at least a priest while Gildas a bishop
- Ambrosius was active before Badon and his grandchildren were alive when *De Excidio Britanniae* written.

The information from Gildas may be organized as follows. Gildas was born in the year of Badon. As Ambrosius was active before then and his grandchildren were still living forty-three years after Badon, Ambrosius was born 61x98 years before *De Excidio Britanniae*. The kings Gildas mentions were clearly active when he published *De Excidio Britanniae*, meaning they were all born 15x55 years before it was written. Uinniau was at least a priest and Gildas clearly a well-known man by the time of his letters, so that Uinniau must have been born in the range of fifty years before Gildas to sixty-two years after. He may have been born anywhere from ninety-three years before *De Excidio* to nineteen years after.

Garmon

- Active with Gwrtheyrn, Benlli, and Cadell
- Cadell has children who act as servants when Garmon visits his home

Cadell must have been at least twenty-three to have a child old enough to act as a servant, and could have been no older than fifty-five when he met Garmon. Garmon must have been between thirty and eighty at the time he met the three secular men, and Benlli and Gwrtheyrn were between 15 and 55 when Garmon interacted with them. It has been shown above that Gwrtheyrn was active between 560 and 593, suggesting he was born in the range 505x578, so that Garmon was born in 440x577, with Benlli and Cadell in 465x618.

Llandaff Charters

As was mentioned above, Wendy Davies has made use of internal details as well as historically known events and characters in order to generate a rough dating scheme for all the individual charters. The following chronology makes use of her results, giving the date she computed for each charter and naming all those individuals credited with signing it.

c. 575   King Peibio, Bishop Dubricius, cousin Inabwy, and Condiuill father of Cynog
c. 575   King Peibio and Bishop Dubricius
c. 595   King Cinuin and brother Gwyddgi, Bishop Arwystl, King Iddon, Gwyddi, Aergol, Collfyw
c. 600   King Iddon and Teilo
c. 605   King Circuin, Bishop Aidan, Collfyw, Aergol
c. 610   King Gwrfoddw, Bishop Ufelfyw, Gurdauau
c. 615   King Gwrfoddw, Bishop Ufelfyw
c. 620   King Meurig, Bishop Ufelfyw, King Gwrgan, Bishop Inabwy, Gurdauau, Cynog

c. 650	Athrwys and father King Meurig, Bishop Euddogwy, Canuetu, Gindag, Gwyddien, Guallonir son of Gwyddnerth
c. 655	King Meurig and Onbrawst, Bishop Euddogwy
c. 660	King Meurig and Bishop Euddogwy, Briafæl
c. 665	King Meurig, Bishop Euddogwy, Canuetu father of King Cynan, Gindog, Gwyddien, Briafael, Gwengarth
c. 670	King Morgan and uncle Ffriog, Gindog, Conuil son of Gyrceniu, Gwyddien, Iunet
c. 675	King Morgan, Bishop Euddogwy, Gindog, Conuil son of Gyrceniu, Briafæl, Gwyddien, Iunet, Samuel
c. 680	Athrwys and father King Meurig, Bishop Euddogwy, Briafæl, Iunet, Gindog, Gwyddien, Guallonir son of Gwyddnerth
c. 685	King Ithel son of Athrwys, Bishop Euddogwy, Brochfael son of Gwyddien
c. 688	King Meurig, Bishop Euddogwy, Iunet, Guallonir son of Gwyddnerth, Brochfael son of Gwyddien, Gwengarth
c. 693	King Meurig (Morgan?), Iddig son of Nudd, Bishop Euddogwy
c. 695	Athrwys and father King Meurig, Bishop Euddogwy, Briafæl, Iunet, Gindog, Gwyddien, Guallonir son of Gwyddnerth
c. 698	King Morgan, Bishop Euddogwy, King Ithel son of Athrwys, Gwengarth, Iunet, Samuel
c. 700	King Morgan, Bishop Berthwyn, Bishop Grecielis, Bishop Cerentir, Clodri, Eliog, Oleu, Gwyddnerth son of Guallonir, Fau
c. 703	King Morgan, Bishop Berthwyn, Ithel son of Morgan, Biuhearn
c. 705	King Conuil son of Gurceniu and sons Conuint and Gwyddgi, Bishop Berthwyn, King Idwallon, Idnerth, Biuhearn, Gwyddnerth son of Guallonir, murdered Eliog, King Morgan and son Ithel and wife Ricceneth, Iunet, Samuel
c. 710	Elffin son of Gwyddien, Bishop Berthwyn
c. 720	King Awst and sons Eiludd and Rhiwallon, Bishop Euddogwy, King Ithel, King Morgan, Gwrfoddw, Gurdoc, Idnerth, Elffin son of Gwyddien, Cynfor, Cerio
c. 722	King Ithel son of Morgan and sons Ffernfæl and Meurig; Bishop Berthwyn, Gwrfoddw, Elffin son of Gafran, Gwyddien, Idnerth, Deunerth son of Iddig
c. 725	King Ithel, Canhæ, Idnerth son of Idwallon, Cerio, Gwrfoddw, Gafran
c. 728	King Ithel and son Meurig, Bishop Berthwyn
c. 730	King Ithel and sons Ffernfæl, Meurig, and Rhodri, Bishop Berthwyn, Iddon son of Cerio
c. 733	King Ithel and sons Ffernfæl and Meurig, Elias, Bishop Berthwyn, Idnerth, Cerio, Deunerth son of Iddig, Elffin son of Gwyddien, Gwrfoddw, Canhæ
c. 735	King Ithel, Bishop Berthwyn, Gurdoc, Biuhearn, Athrwys son of Ithel dead, Gwrgan married daughter of Elffin, Gafran
c. 738	Bishop Berthwyn, Mabsu, Gurdoc, Rhiadaf, Idnerth
c. 740	King Ithel and sons Ffernfael and Meurig, Bishop Berthwyn, Pasgen, Cynfor, Rhiadaf, Clodri's sons Conuin and Gwyddgi, martyr Clydog, Elffin son of Gwyddien, Cynug son of Conuil
c. 743	Conblus, Bishop Berthwyn

c. 745   Erbic son of Elffin, Bishop Tyrchan, Cynwg son of Conuil, King Ithel, Eliog, Dewi, Freudur, Gellan

c. 748   Erbic son of Elffin, Bishop Tyrchan, Elias brother of murdered Catgen, Cynfar, Bishop Berthwyn, Cors, King Meurig, King Rhys

c. 750   Brii, Bishop Tyrchan, Ceredig and Iddig sons of Rhydderch, Cynfor, King Ffernfael

There is a great deal of information to take from this source, and it will be explored briefly here using the parameters Miller laid out.

Peibio was king when he signed two documents dated to about 575. Judging by the other entries there is a five-year margin of error, so that he was ruling at some time between 570 and 580. He was then born 515x565. Similarly, the others can be gauged as follows, separated as lay and religious men:

Inabwy: 515x565
Cinuin: 535x585
Gwyddgi: 535x585
Iddon: 540x590
Circuin: 545x595
Gwrfoddw: 550x605
Gwrgan: 575x610
Meurig: 605x610
Caneutu father of Cynan: 605x655
Morgan: 615x660
Ffriog: 610x660
Athrwys: 635x670
Meurig: 635x670
Ithel son of Athrwys: 640x675
Morgan: 660x685
Clodri: 640x690

Ithel son of Morgan: 680x690
Conuil: 650x695
Conuint: 650x695
Idwallon: 645x695
Gwyddgi: 650x695
Awst: 670x700
Idnerth son of Idwallon: 675x710
Eiludd: 670x700
Rhiwallon: 670x700
Ffernfael: 690x710
Meurig: 690x710
Rhodri: 680x710
Rhys: 695x730
Conuin son of Clodri: 680x730
Gwyddgi son of Clodri: 680x730
Cynwg son of Conuil: 685x730

Dubricius: 490x550
Arwystl: 510x570
Teilo: 515x575
Aidan: 520x580
Ufelfyw: 530x585
Inabwy: 515x585

Euddogwy: 615x665
Berthwyn: 665x675
Grecielis: 615x675
Cerentir: 615x675
Tyrchan: 665x720

In addition to those named above, the extant documents contain a good many laypersons that may well have been significant in the kingdom, but none of them or their families are mentioned anywhere else. They are, therefore, of no value to the present study.

Samson

- The son of Ammon and Anna, nephew of Umbraphel, cousin of Maglorius
- He was a child when Maucennus was active
- He was taught by Illtud and ordained deacon, priest, and bishop by Dubricius

- He was a priest when Piro died, and contemporary to Iuniavus, Docco, comes Guedianus of Trigg, Comedianus, Petroc, Mevennus, Jonas, Iudwal, Cunomorus, Childebert, Kentigern
- He and Piro were abbots of a monastery founded by Germanus
- He left Britain after Illtud and Dubricius died
- He was present at the Third Council of Paris, 554x560

The information given as things stand is relatively small. It may only be assumed that if Samson was at the Council of Paris around 557, he was at least a bishop at that time and therefore was born in the range 474x530. His contemporaneity to Childebert shows that he was active in Brittany at some time between the years 511 and 558 and further limits his birth range to 474x528. This is little to go on; however, Samson dealt with a good number of persons who themselves interacted with many other people, so that he will not be too difficult to date. It can also be assumed that the laymen he knew before he migrated to the Continent were born in the range 444x543, and those he knew after the migration were born 444x593, while the named holy men would range 419x583.

In addition, it is noteworthy that there is no direct record or evidence that Germanus visited Wales. Therefore, Garmon or one of the people from his monasteries probably founded the monastery attributed to him, so that Garmon can be assumed to be earlier than Samson, and may or may not have been his contemporary.

Columba

- Was born in 521, went to Scotland in 563, and died in 598
- Trained by Uinniau who was elderly but alive when Columba departed for Iona
- Domnall and Forcus son of Erc were alive before and Columba's transfer to Iona
- Conall son of Comgall, Eochaid son of Domnall, Eoganan son of Gabran, Domangart son of Aedan, and Eocho Bude son of Aedan were active after Columba moved to Iona
- Artbranan king of Geona was active during one of Columba's visits to Bridei
- Columba converted Bridei
- Columba appointed Aedan king
- Columba attended the Convention of Druim Cett with Aed son of Ainmire King of the Uí Néill and Aedán son of Gabrán in 575
- Constantine son of Rhydderch was alive before he died in 598
- Baithene succeeded Columba

From the above information, it may be learned that Baithene could not have been born before 517, nor after 567. The tone of the *vita* is that Columba visited Bridei shortly after the arrival of the former to Scotland in 563, so that Bridei must have been ruling then. This puts his birth year at 508x548. Aedan was appointed king in 563x575, but was active in 575, so that he was born in 520x560. If both Constantine was very young and Rhydderch was alive before Columba died in 598, then Constantine must have been born 585x598 and Rhydderch 547x580.

The dating schema for Uinniau is most helpful. Adamnan tells us he was active in training Columba, and thus was at least seven years Columba's senior. The biographer also tells us that he helped Columba's cause when others sought to excommunicate him in 563. He was thus born between 483 and 514. The high end of this estimate gives an age of forty-nine for him when he watched Columba depart for Scotland. Forty-nine is hardly the age of an elderly man, but is feasible for old in the sixth century at which time laymen did not live beyond fifty-five.

The information pertaining to Erc and his sons is most interesting. Erc, one might recall, is the name of the legendary founder of the Dalriadic royal house. There is much to call attention to the name and to the names of his descendants Fergus, Domnall, and Eochaid. For now, however, it is sufficient to note that he appears to be a significant figure during the lifetime of Columba, even though Adamnan simply refers to him as a thief.[1]

Kentigern

- Son of Thaney daughter of Leudun
- Morken was a king of Strathclyde after he was made bishop
- Attended the Councils of Orleans (549) and Paris (554x560)
- Returned to Strathclyde upon the accession of Rhydderch
- Contemporary of Columba, Languoreth wife of Rhydderch, and Constantine

Kentigern's associations with his contemporaries will prove invaluable as the study progresses. However, with the information as it stands, his attendance at two continental councils is the only means of dating him, and they range his birth from 474 to 519. He was a bishop before he was banished from Strathclyde, and we might assume this took place between 504 and 549. This seems an innocent enough date range, for now. It also means that Morken, likely Morgan of the Gododdin region, was born 449x534. If we are to give Rhydderch the standard maximum of fifty-five years, then he was born no later than 580, and Constantine no later than 598.

Gregory of Tours

- 544x551, Chanao kills three of his brothers, his fourth Macliau escapes; Cunomorus is a contemporary
- 560, Chanao killed
- 568x577, Macliau and Budic contemporaries, Budic dies first; Waroc and Jacob are the sons of Macliau, Theuderic is the son of Budic. Theuderic kills Macliau
- 568x577, Macliau dies
- 568x578, Winnoc in Brittany
- 578x579, Waroc is a king; Eunius is a Bishop of Vannes
- 579, Eunius taken from office
- 585, Winnoc dies
- 587x588, Waroc and Vidimael alive
- 589, Ingoberg dies at 69; her daughter had already married a prince of Kent
- 590, Waroc and his son Canao adults

The information provided above is quite informative. Chanao was born between 505 and 536, and died in 560. His siblings would range from 485 to 551. His contemporary Cunomorus was born between 489 and 536.

Macliau and Budic are at the core of the next group of individuals. The former was a sibling of Chanao and a father of two, so that his range may be narrowed to 513x551 and that of his siblings to between 493 and 551. His children were born between 531 and 577. Budic was born in the range 513 to 559. However, as Theuderic killed Macliau in or before 577, he could not have been born after 562. With this in mind, Budic's birth range can be narrowed to 513x544, and Theuderic's to 531x562.

Waroc was both son to Macliau (513x551), and a king in his own right in 578x579. He was still alive in 590. Together, these facts indicate a birth range of 535x557 for Waroc, 553x575 for Canao, and one of 513x539 for Macliau.

As Winnoc arrived in Brittany between 568 and 578, and died in 585, he was born in 505x548. Ingoberg died in 589 at 69, meaning she was born in 519 or 520, and she could not have had a child before 537 or after 558. Her husband was Charibert who died in 567, so their daughter could not have been marriageable before 548 or able to produce heirs after 596. She was most likely Bertha, who married Æthelberht before he was a king.[2] Her name makes clear she was not English or British, and Kent is well known to have had warm relations with the Franks during this period. With this in mind, all sons of Æthelberht were born between 555 and 596.

Eunius was a bishop in 578/9 and was removed from office in 579. He was therefore born in 498x549. Vidimael was active in 587/588, meaning he was born 532x573.

Rhun[3]

- Converted Edwin during his banishment
- Urien was his father and Owain his brother
- Urien was contemporary to Taliesin, Gwallog, Rhydderch, and Hussa. He and his sons were contemporary to Theodric, against whom Urien died
- Taliesin was the bard of Urien, Gwallawg, and Cynan kin to Cyngen contemporary of Aercol
- Rieinmellth was Urien's great-granddaughter, she married Oswiu
- Cerdic son of Gwallawg was evicted from Elmet by Edwin

Although Rhun was likely the reason that much of the information here was retained, the history was first recorded in Urien's honor, and for that reason Urien is central to the materials which are provided. It is only fitting, then, that his birth year is x. His sons Rhun and Owain were born in x+18 to x+38. His great-granddaughter Rieinmellth was born in the range x+54 to x+114. Urien's allies were then born x−40 to x+40 and Cerdic x−22 to x+78. Taliesin was born in x−65 to x+35, while the information on Cynan Garwyn gives him a range of x−102 to x+100. The Edwin data will be more helpful in context with the other information below, where more specific dates can be added.

Aneirin's Y Gododdin

- Yrfai son of Wolstan rules in Gododdin
- Gorthen son of Yrfai lives after the Battle of Catraeth
- Tudfwlch son of Madian rules in Gododdin
- Pobddelw fights at Catraeth

- Cynon son of Clydno fights at Catraeth
- Geraint of the South fights at Catraeth
- Dwywei daughter of Lleenog is the mother of Aneirin
- Madawg Elmet fights at Catraeth
- Grugyn of Lleu fights at Catraeth
- Gwanar of Pennawc fights at Catraeth

The most useful pieces of information from *Y Gododdin* center on Elmet. Madawg Elmet most likely refers to a king of that region, much as Maelgwn Gwynedd and Urien Rheged are inseparably linked with their respective kingdoms. Second and more tangible, Aneirin is named as a son of Dwywei who is the daughter of Lleenog. This Lleenog is to be found in the genealogies as the father of Gwallawg, whom we have already met in the Rhun orbit, and who is there named as the King of Elmet. Probably, Madawg was another member of this royal house and, judging by the nature of the period and Aneirin's bias to the battle, it seems most likely that Madawg was a son or grandson of Lleenog, though there is the possibility that he was descended from one of his siblings.

Also of note are the three generations of Gododdin rulers at Din Eidyn who are given. One with patronymic is placed at Catraeth, while the third is clearly stated as having lived after the battle. Once it is better established when Catraeth occurred, this information may well provide for a solid relative chronology for the house.

There are also many persons listed in the poem's stanzas who are not associated with Gododdin. Pobddelw has often been linked to the Gwynedd house, and may well fit into that lineage. As to the other figures, little can be done with them until Catraeth may be relatively dated because they are not associated with any known dynasties or outside individuals.

Bede's Primary historia

- Ælle a *Bretwalda*
- Ceawlin a *Bretwalda*
- 565, Columba arrives in Bridei's ninth year, dies at 77 after 32 years in Britain
- 592/3, Æthelfrith succeeds to Northumbrian kingship
- Æthelfrith marries Acha
- 596, Augustine is sent to Britain
- 597, Augustine arrives and is welcomed by Æthelberht
- 601, Mellitus is made Bishop of London
- Peter is made abbot of St. Peter the Apostle
- Before Gregory becomes a pope, he sees slaves from Ælle's kingdom
- 603, Dinoot goes to the Conference at Augustine's Oak; the Battle of Degsastan
- 603x616, Æthelfrith and Brocmail fight at Chester[4]
- 604, Mellitus and Justus are made bishops, Sæbert is the nephew of Æthelberht through Ricula; Augustine dies
- Cerdic alive to poison Hereric while Hilda is an infant
- Rædwald is ruling during Edwin's banishment by Æthelfrith; Acha marries Æthelfrith
- 616, Laurentius is appointed the new archbishop; it is the twenty-first year after Augustine sent, Æthelberht son of Irminric father of Eadbald dies; Sæbert dies; Æthelfrith dies

- Osfrid and Eadfrid are the sons of Edwin, born of Cœnberta during his exile; Æthelhun, Æthelthryth, and Wuscfrea were born to Edwin and Æthelberga during his kingship
- 619, Laurentius dies, Mellitus succeeds him
- 624, Mellitus dies, Justus succeeds him; Romanus is made bishop of Rochester
- 625, Edwin ruling, Paulinus and James are present; Edwin married Æthelberga or Tata; Eadbald is ruling Kent
- 626, Cwichelm and Cearl are ruling; Eanflæd is born; Edwin makes a campaign into Wessex
- 627, Edwin baptized in the eleventh year of his reign, rules for another six years; Eorpwald son of Rædwald is alive but is killed shortly
- Sigbert brother of Eorpwald rules for three years, Bishop Felix is active for seventeen years
- 633, Edwin dies at Heathfield; Cadwallon, Penda, Osric, and Eanfrid are alive; Penda rules for twenty-two years; Iffi is alive but not an adult. Romanus and James are active
- 634, Bishops Tomianus, Columbanus, Cromanus, Dimanus, and Baithene are active; Saranus is an abbot
- Eorpwald dies. Sigbert's reign includes 633 and 635, he retires in favor of Ecgric, but both are killed by Penda; Osric dies, Oswald kills Cadwallon and succeeds to Northumbrian throne
- 635, Aedan is given a bishopric; Cynegils is ruling Wessex with Birinus as his new bishop, Segienus is ruling Iona
- Eadfrid dies during Oswald's reign
- Cynegils dies, his son Cenwalh rules, then is driven into a three-year exile in East Anglia where Anna is ruling
- Agilbert is the bishop on Cenwalh's return, then Wini. Wini abandons his post and flees to London, leaving it vacant until Leutherius assumes the office
- 640, Eadbald dies; his son Earconbert succeeds and reigns for twenty-four years
- 642, Oswald rules for eight years and dies at thirty-eight; he falls at Maserfelth and is succeeded by Oswy
- c. 642, Oswy marries Eanflæd
- 643/4, Oswine succeeds to Deiran throne
- 644, Paulinus dies after nineteen years in office and during Oswy's second year in Bernicia; Oswy began his rule at 30, Ithamar replaces Paulinus
- 646, Hereswith is alive
- 651, Oswine dies in his ninth year, he is succeeded by Oswy; Aedan dies
- 653, Alhflæd marries Peada; Felix rules for seventeen years, Thomas succeeds and rules for five years, Bertgils/Boniface succeeds him in 658
- 655, Honorius dies, Deusdedit succeeds him and rules for nine years; Deusdedit is consecrated by bishop Ithamar, Damian succeeds Deusdedit in his old post; Diuma made Bishop by Finan, he rules shortly and is followed by Ceollach who in turn rules shortly and is followed by Trumhere in the reign of Wulfhere; the Battle of Winwæd occurs in the thirteenth year of Oswy, his sons Alchfrid, Egfrid, and Æthelwald are all old enough to fight; Penda is ruling; Æthelhere the brother of Anna die; Ælfflæd is one year old and dies at sixty; Peada gets South Mercia, three years later Wulfhere claims the Mercian throne and rules

for seventeen years; the Mercian bishops under Wulfhere are Jarman, Ceadda, and Winfrid
- 660/1, Ælfwine succeeds to Northumbria
- Another Sigbert ruling East Anglia, he was baptized by Finan; Cedd is made bishop, Suidhelm son of Sexbald succeeds Sigbert
- Cedd, Cælin, Cynebil, and Ceadda are brothers
- Bishops of Northumbria are Aidan, Finan for 10 years, and then Colman
- Synod of Whitby in twenty-second year of Oswy with Colman, Wilfrid, Alchfrid, Agilbert, Hilda, Ceadda, James, and Romanus
- 664, Tuda succeeds Colman and dies. Eata of Lindisfarne, Wilfrid, and Ceadda made bishops there; Eadhed is a priest
- Sighere and Sæbbi succeed Suidhelm in the time of Wulfhere and Jarman
- 665, Wini is a bishop of the West Saxons
- 668, Theodore dies after twenty-one years in office at 64 years old; Earconbert dies and is succeeded by Egbert for nine years; Hadrian is made the Abbot of St. Peter the Apostle, and Putta the Bishop of Rochester
- Ceadda is Bishop of Mercia for two and one-half years
- 669, James the deacon is active; he lives until at least 690
- 670, Oswy dies at 58; he is succeeded by his son Egfrid
- 673, A council with Bisi Bishop of East Anglia, Wilfrid, Putta, Eleutherius, and Winfrid; Egbert dies and is succeeded by Lothere for twelve years
- 673/4, Cenwalh dies, Seaxburh rules for one year
- 674, Benedict Biscop founds Monkwearmouth
- Winfrid is deposed and replaced by Sexwulf, Earconwald is a bishop under Sæbbi and Sighere; Sæbbi rules about thirty years
- Waldhere succeeds Earconwald, rules when Sæbbi dies, succeeded by Sigehard and Suefred
- Wessex goes ten years without a king after Cenwalh dies; Eleutherius dies during this period and is succeeded by Hedda
- Cædwalla rules for 2 years
- 676, Æthelred King of Mercia, Putta retires, succeeded for short time by Cuichelm, then Gebmund
- 678, Eighth year of Egfrid, Bosa and Eata bishops, Eadhed Bishop of Lindsey followed by Æthelwin, Edgar, and Cynebert; Wilfrid expelled. Eanfrid father of Eanher and Ebba; Ebba married Æthelwalh King of Sussex when Bosa and Eata made bishops
- Cædwalla kills Æthelwalh, conquers Wight from Atwald
- 679, Battle of Trent, Egfrid's ninth year, brother Ælfwine killed at about 18; Æthelred of Mercia alive, married Osthryth sister of Egfrid and Ælfwine
- 680, The Synod of Heathfield is held on October 17, the tenth year of Egfrid, sixth of Æthelfrith, seventeenth of Aldwulf, seventh of Lothair; Benedict is an abbot, Ceolfrid is a priest; Hilda dies aged 66l, the monk Caedmon is active, Abbot John the Archcantor arrives and dies
- Eanflæd dies before Trumwine
- 680x685, Tatfrid dies before he can be consecrated bishop
- 681, Tunbert made Bishop of Bernicia, Trumwine of the Picts, Benedict Biscop founds Jarrow

- Ætheldreda (Æthelthryth) daughter of Anna marries Tonbert for a short time, then Egfrid for twelve years; Sæxburga daughter of Anna married Earconbert, lived seventeen years beyond Ætheldreda
- Osric is King of Wessex; Bosel is his first bishop and Oftfor his second
- Benedict Biscop dies
- 685, Egfrid dies at thirty-nine in his fifteenth year of reign, succeeded by his brother Alfrid; Lothere dies after twelve years, succeeded by his brother Egbert for one year, followed by Wictred son of Egbert; Merewalh dies; Cuthbert, Bosel, and Trumwine are bishops
- 687, Cuthbert dies; he is succeeded by Æthelwald for twelve years during Alfrid's reign
- 688, Eata dies when Alfrid begins his rule, succeeded by John for thirty-three years
- Cædwalla rules for two years, abdicates in Alfrid's third year
- 689, Cædwalla dies at about 30 years old, succeeded by Ine who rules for thirty-seven years
- 690, Archbishop Theodoric dies after thirty-two years in office at eighty-eight, succeeded by Berhtwald in 692; Berhtwald comes to his office while Wictred and Swæbherd are kings
- 698, Eadbert dies
- Wilfrid returns to Britain under Alfrid, he is about 30 when made bishop; expelled by Egfrid, he is given back his see after five years
- 705, Alfrid dies after almost twenty years, succeeded by Eadwulf for two months, then Osred who is 8 and rules for eleven years; Hedda dies, Aldhelm and Daniel succeed him. Aldhelm rules for four years
- Coinred of Mercia resigns in Osred's fourth year, Wilfrid dies
- 725, Ine dies after thirty-seven years of rule

In keeping with the conclusion reached pertaining to Bede's materials, only the religious history of Britain has been used as far back as Bede gives it, and the political to just before 600, or a century before the latest possible time the Kentish Source could have been written. Even with this conservative use of the source, there seems to be one serious discrepancy, the date surrounding Columba's move from Ireland to Scotland. In Adamnan's biography, he arrives in Britain in 563 and dies in 598, while in Bede he arrives in 565 and dies in 597. Clearly 563 and 598 are the more accurate dates; they align well with the other events that led to Columba's exile and are recorded in the Irish annals but were apparently unknown to Bede. So why is Bede so far off? Perhaps a little historical background is in order.

The first holy men in Northumbria were selected from Iona, Columba's home for thirty years. At first glance, this would suggest that the monks of Lindisfarne had access to accurate information about Columba. However, the Iona monks would hardly have been forthcoming about data surrounding the banishment of their founder. When the Easter controversy reached a peak after the Synod of Whitby in 664, the Columban abbots returned to Iona, which means that from that time forward any English historian would only have had access to knowledge derived from native Northumbrian or Kentish sources; information pertaining to Iona and Ireland would have been more difficult to acquire. The Northumbrians had only accepted Christianity from about 625, while the people of Kent did not concern themselves with the Britons until early into the seventh century, and never dealt with Columba. Bede here only guessed based on what he knew or could derive, as he has been shown to do.[5] Such is why he came very near to the correct years but was not exactly right.

Other than this one anomaly, Bede's chronology seems to be fairly reliable, and perfectly so with regards to events and relative chronology within living memory of the Kentish Source. When he has direct access to information, he is unhesitant. When he hears things at one or more removes, he tells us with indications of uncertainty such as "said to be." While it is true that he had biases to the Roman Catholics first, his native kingdom second, and the Germanic peoples third, there is absolutely no evidence that he has anywhere created the events he records or even misdated those he uses. He is therefore an excellent source of information for this author's purposes and within the guidelines previously laid out.

The depth and breadth of information he gives is also invaluable for the purposes of the author. A closer look at the raw information he provides is of great use. This is especially so with regards to Northumbria. Ælle was ruling between 586 and 590. If Oswald was thirty-eight when he died in 642, he was born in 603 or 604. If Oswy died at fifty-eight in 670, he was born in 611 or 612. Osfrid and Eadfrid were born to Edwin while he was in exile, and therefore at or before 616/617. Æthelhun, Æthelthryth, and Wuscfrea were born after 625, the year he married Aethleburga. Eanflæd was born in 626, and her siblings at or before 633 when Edwin died.

If 655 was Oswy's thirteenth year and 664 his twenty-second, then he began his reign in 643. The Battle of Trent took place in 678x679, in Egfrid's ninth year. This makes perfect sense if his rule began in 670.

Bede says that Cerdic poisoned Hereric while Hild was an infant. As Hild died in 680 at the age of sixty-six, she must have been born in 613 or 614, meaning she was an infant between the years 613x617. Sighere and Sæbbi began their rule between 658 and 664 if they had power during the tenure of Wulfhere and Jarman. The Synod of Heathfield took place on October 17, 680, when Æthelfrith was in his sixth year and Aldwulf his seventeenth. This means that Æthelfrith was a king from 674x675 and Aldwulf was crowned in 663x664. Bede tells us that there was no king for ten years after Cenwalh died in 673x674. Assuming he counted his wife a ruler if not a king, this would bring the date at which Cædwalla took the throne to 684x685, which fits in exactly with a two-year reign, a resignation in 687x688, and his death in 689 just as Bede tells us. In digestable form, what Bede gives us is:

	Born	*Ruling*		*Born*	*Ruling*
Acha:	554x580	592x596	Anna:	580x635	635x640
Ælhflæd:	615x641	653	Cadwallon:	578x619	633–634
Ælfflæd:	654	d. 714	Cædwalla:	656x662	686–688
Ælfwine	660x661	679	Cearl	571x621	626
Ælle:	531x585	586x590	Cenwalh:	618x635	635/40–673/4
Æthelberht:	561x578	+596–616	Cerdic:	558x602	613x617
Æthelfrith:	561x588	592/3–616	Coinred:	656x704	709
Æthelfrith:	625x669	674/5–680	Cwichelm:	571x621	626
Æthelhere:	600x650	d. 655	Cynegils:	580x630	635
Æthelhun	625x633		Eadbald	585x620	625–640
Æthelred:	621x674	676–679	Eadfrid	604x616	d. 634x642
Æthelthryth	625x633		Eadwulf	650x700	705
Æthelwald:	600x640	fl. 655	Eanflæd	626	
Æthelwalh:	623x662	-678	Eanfrid:	578x627	
Aldwulf:	625x658	663/4–680	Earconbert:	609x635	640–664
Alfrid:	650	685–705	Ecgric:	580x631	635x636

	Born	Ruling		Born	Ruling
Edwin	585x597	616–633	Oswy:	611x612	642–670
Egbert	631x680	685–686	Peada:	600x641	653–655
Egfrid:	645/6	670–685	Penda:	578x628	633–655
Eorpwald	572x622		Rædwald	572x611	617–627
Hereric	558x597		Sæbbi:	619x663	664/8–674/6
Hereswith	591x646		Sæberht:	561x599	604–616
Hilda	613/4	680	Selyf:	548x601	603x616
Iffi	628x633	633	Sigbert	605x659	660x664
Ine:	670x683	688–725	Sigbert:	580x628	633–635
Lothere:	630x668	673–685	Sigeheard:	619x671	674/6
Merewalh:	630x680	685	Sighere:	619x663	664/8–674/6
Osfrid	604x616		Suefred:	619x671	674/6
Osred:	696/7	705–716	Suidhelm:	609x659	660/4–664/8
Osric	626x680	681x685	Swæbherd:	637x687	692
Osric:	578x629	d. 634	Wictred	631x681	686+
Osthryth:	624x667	679	Wulfhere:	630x653	658–685
Oswald	603x604	634–642	Wuscfrea	625x633	
Oswine	596x637	642–651			

	Born	Ruling		Born	Ruling
Aedan:	571x605	635–651	Earconwald:	594x646	674/6
Æthelwald	619x657	687–699	Eata	608x634	664–688
Agilbert:	584x610	635/40–664	Egbert:	618x659	664x673
Aldhelm	650x675[6]	705–709	Felix:	567x600	630–647
Augustine:	524x561	596–604	Finan:	581x621	651–661
Baithene:	554x604	634	Gebmund:	598x647	677–678/80
Benedict	601x649	674–681/5	Hadrian:	588x643	668
Berhtwald	612x662	692	Hedda	594x653	674/83
Birinus	555x605	635	Hilda	613/4	680
Bisi	593x643	673	Honorius:	575x583	601–655
Boniface:	573x623	653	Ithamar	575x614	644–655
Bosa	600x650	680	James	590x607	625–690
Bosel	605x655	685	Jarman:	584x634	664
Ceadda:	587x634	664–667	John Beverl	641x658	688–721
Caedmon	600x662	680	John Arch	600x655	680
Cedd:	584x634	664–667	Justus:	544x574	604–624
Ceolfrid	600x662	680	Laurentius:	539x581	616–619
Ceollach:	576x629	656x659	Leutherius	593x640	670–674/83
Colman:	584x631	661–664	Mellitus:	544x571	601–624
Columba:	519/20	d. 597	Paulinus:	564x595	625–644
Columbanus:	554x604	634	Peter:	523x576	601x603
Cromanus:	554x604	634	Putta:	596x638	668–676
Cuichelm:	597x646	676–677/9	Romanus:	553x594	624–633
Cuthbert	607x655	685–687	Saranus:	554x609	634
Damian:	584x629	664+	Segienus:	555x635	635
Daniel	651x675	705–731	Sexwulf	594x646	674/6
Deusdedit	584x620	655–664	Tatfrid	600x655	680x685
Dimanus:	554x604	634	Theodore	603/4	647–668
Diuma:	575x627	655x657	Theodoric	601/2	658–690
Dunawd:	523x573	603	Thomas:	573x617	647–653
Eadhed:	598x648	678	Tomianus:	554x604	634

	Born	Ruling		Born	Ruling
Trumhere:	578x631	658x661	Waldhere:	594x646	674/6
Trumwine	605x651	681–685	Wilfrid	633/4	664–705
Tuda:	584x634	664-	Winfrid	594x643	673–674/6
Tunbert	601x651	681	Wini	585x635	665

Event	Date Range	Event	Date Range
Chester:	603x616	Trent:	679
Winwæd:	655	Heathfield:	680
Whitby:	664		

Cuthbert

- Aidan dies, Boisil and Eata are priests, and Sigfrith is a youth when Cuthbert is seven
- Ripon founded, Boisil made bishop, and Alhfrith a king when 9x18
- Boisil is alive when taken from Ripon
- Ecgfrith is a king, Æbbe a nun
- Cuthbert is made bishop; Bishop Trumwine, Theodore, and Ælflæd are contemporaries
- One year after Cuthbert becomes bishop Ecgfrith dies and is succeeded by his bastard brother Aldfrith; the priest Herefrith, Abbot Cudda, and Abbess Verca are alive
- Hereberht dies
- One year after Hereberht dies, Eadberht is made bishop
- Eleven years after Hereberht dies, his body is still uncorrupted
- Hermit Felgild is cured of a disease after Cuthbert dies

The information given here will be of more use when employed along with Bede and other chronologically oriented sources. However, relative dating is of some use. To put the above in more digestible form: Aidan died, Boisil and Eata were priests, and Sigfrith a youth when Cuthbert was seven. In a single year between then and the year Cuthbert was made bishop, Ripon was founded, Boisil made a bishop, and Alhfrith was made a king aged somewhere between nine and eighteen. Boisil was still alive when the followers of the older Easter dating were evicted from Ripon in 664. Ecgfrith was a king and Æbbe a nun in the same year at one point.

In the year Cuthbert became a bishop, Trumwine, Theodore, and Ælfflæd were alive. A year later Ecgfrith died and was succeeded by Aldfrith. A year after that, Eadberht was made a bishop. He was still alive eleven years later.

Wilfrid

- At 14 he was a contemporary of Eanflæd and Oswiu
- One or two years later Earconberht was King of Kent; Alhfrith, Oswiu, and Cœnwalh were also kings
- Ripon was given to him by Alhfrith and Oswiu

- During the Council of Whitby, Colman, Oswiu, Alhfrith, Hilda, and Agilbert were in office
- Wilfrid made a bishop at thirty
- Chad made a bishop while Wilfrid was in Gaul being consecrated
- Two or three years after that, Wulfhere was ruling and Putta made a bishop
- Theodore brought Wilfrid to York and Chad to Mercia
- Ripon rebuilt under Ecgfrith, his wife Æthilthryth, and Ælfwine
- Ecgfrith won a battle over the Picts with his subking Beorhæth
- Iurminburh was the queen of Ecgfrith, Archbishop Theodore and Bishop Winfrid were active when Wilfrid was taken from his see.
- One year later Ælfwine died
- Wilfrid returned; at that time he was a contemporary to Æthilred and his nephew Berhtwald, Centwine of Wessex, and Æthelwalh of Sussex; Cædwalla was a noble
- Theodore, Bishop Erconwald, the kings Aldfrith and Æthilred, and abbess Ælfflæd were Wilfrid's contemporaries
- In the second year Aldfrith ruled alone, Wilfrid returned for five years
- Wilfrid exiled again while Aldfrith and Æthilred were alive
- Council of Austerfield with Aldfrith and Archbishop Berhtwald; twenty-two years after Iurminburh helped take the see, forty years since he was made a bishop
- Bishops Bosa, John of Beverley, and Badwini, Archbishop Berhtwald, a retired Æthilred, the priest Acca, and King Coenred still alive when Wilfrid returned
- Aldfrith died, succeeded by Eadwulf for two months; Osred ruled after him, and abbesses Ælfflæd and Æthilberg were active during this time
- Wilfrid died while Ceolred of Mercia, abbots Tibba and Ebba, and abbess Cynithryth were active; Acca made an abbot

The Life of Wilfrid contains nearly as much information as Bede, crammed into a period of perhaps fifty years. Because of its compact nature, a proper handling of the material makes it a good supplement to the first English historian. Most of the data centers around Wilfrid, who for the purposes of this study has the birth year x. At the age of fourteen, Oswiu and Eanflæd were alive ($x+14$). In $x+15$ or 16, Oswiu, Earconberht, Alhfrith, and Coenwalh were all kings. Wilfrid was made bishop just before the council of Whitby. He was prominent at the Council, which Colman, Oswiu, Alhfrith, Hilda, and Agilbert attended. The reign dates that can be derived for the rulers named here are in perfect agreement with Bede. Wilfrid was ejected from his bishopric shortly after it was over.

Wilfrid's abandoned bishopric of Northumbria was given to Chad almost immediately thereafter, in $x+30$. In $x+32$ or 33, Wulfhere was ruling Mercia, with Putta as his bishop. At that time, Wilfrid was given the bishopric of York, and Mercia was taken from Putta and given to Chad. Before a major victory by Ecgfrith over the Picts, he, his wife Æthilthryth, and Ælfwine all took part in the rebuilding of Ripon. After the battle, in $x+48$, Wilfrid was stripped of his see. Ecgfrith, his new queen Iurminburh, Archbishop Theodore, and Bishop Winfrid were all active at this time. A year later, Ælfwine died. Once again, Wilfrid was allowed back into Northumbria, and this return was contemporary to Æthilred and his nephew Berhtwald, Centwine of Wessex, and Æthelwalh of Sussex. Cædwalla was a noble at this time.

The source then gives another series of contemporaries—Theodore, Bishop Erconwald, kings Aldfrith and Æthilred, and abbess Ælfflæd. In the second year of Aldfrith ruling alone (y+2) Wilfrid returned from a trip to the Continent of several years. In Aldfrith's seventh year, y+7, Wilfrid was exiled; Æthilred was still alive as well. At the Council of Austerfield in x+70, Aldfrith and Berhtwald were present. The rest of the *vita* offers little material that is of use in constructing a broad canvas of post–Roman history, apart from the note that Eadwulf ruled for two months after Aldfrith had died.

Ceolfrith

- Becomes a monk at 18, goes to Billing where his brother Cynefrith was lately abbot and now his cousin Tunbert rules
- priest at 27
- Abbot Botulf alive
- Wearmouth builds in Ecgfrith's fourth year
- Eosterwine dies after four years as abbot, Sigfrith after three years
- Ceolfrith rules eight years before Benedict Biscop dies, twenty-seven years after

The Life of Ceolfrith provides very little useful information outside that given about the saint himself. It is learned that Botulf was alive between when Ceolfrith turned twenty-seven and Ecgfrith's fourth year, that Eosterwine ruled for four years, and Sigfrith for three. Ceolfrith was abbot for eight years before Benedict died and twenty-seven after. It is also learned that when Ceolfrith was eighteen, his brother Cynefrith had already been an abbot. This suggests that Cynefrith was at least twenty-five.

Abbots of Jarrow and Monkwearmouth

- Benedict enters a monastery at 25
- Benedict begins his rule in Ecgfrith's fourth year; it lasts for sixteen years
- Alchfrid, Oswiu, Egbert of Kent, and Theodore ruling
- Two or more years later Coenwalh is in Wessex and Ecgfrid is in Northumbria
- One or more years later Ecgfrid, Ceolfrith, Eosterwine are in their ninth years of rule Eosterwine dies in his thirteenth
- Eosterwine enters a monastery at twenty-four; serves seven years as a priest, four as an abbot, and twelve years total
- Ecgfrid dies and Aldfrid succeeds
- Three years later Sigfrith and Benedict die
- Ceolfrith ruled one year before Sigfrith and Benedict dies, twenty-seven after, thirty-five years total; he lives forty-seven years from entering the priesthood and dies at seventy-four
- Hwætbert followed him, he spends twelve years as a priest; Bishop Acca confirmed him

This ecclesiastical material contains one clear discrepancy. It says that Ceolfrith ruled for one year before and twenty-seven years after Benedict died, and that the total number of years he served as abbot was thirty-five. Fortunately, the *Life of Ceolfrith* corrects this to eight years before and twenty-seven, giving the correct total of thirty-five years. Ceolfrith was a monk at eighteen, a priest at twenty-seven, an abbot at thirty-nine, and died at seventy-four. Other noteworthy items are that Eosterwine dies in Egfrid's thirteenth year, Egfrid in his own seventeenth year, and Sigfrith and Benedict died three years later. The rest of the information is of more use to cross-check whatever conclusions the above information may lead toward than in providing useful information in and of itself.

Annals of Innisfallen

446	Nath I dies
448	Secundinus dies
464	Aillil Molt reigns
470	Aillil Molt loses at the Battle of Duma Aichir
499	Ibar dies
500	MacErc wins the Battle of Inne Mór
502	MacErc wins the Battle of Segais
503	Domangart of Cenn Tire dies
528	Ailbe of Imlech Ibuir dies
541	Comgall son of Domangart dies
542	MacErc dies
552	Colum of Terryglass dies
560	Gabran son of Domangart dies
561	Ainmire son of Sétna dies
565	Domnall son of MacErc dies
567	Gildas dies
569	Ainmire son of Sétna dies
571	Baetán son of MacErc and Eochaid son of Domnall son of MacErc die
574	Conall son of Comgall dies after ruling sixteen years
581	Colgu son of Domnall son of MacErc dies, Aed son of Ainmire wins a battle
583	Aedan wins Manu
584	Bruide son of Maelchu dies
601	Aed son of Ainmire dies
605	Comgall of Bangor dies
607	Aed Slaine dies
609	Aedan dies
611	Aengus son of Aed Slaine dies
613	Mael Coba son of Aed rules
614	Battle of Chester fought
615	Fintan of Bangor dies
616	Mæl Coba dies
622	Aillil son of Cellach dies
631	Eochaid Buide son of Aedan, Aed son of Cuimíne son of Colgu dies
633	Cinaed of the Picts and Edwin die
636	Aillil son of Aed dies

643 Domnall son of Aed and Domnall Brecc die
644 Oswald dies
649 Diarmit son of Aed alive, Dunchad and Conall sons of Blathmac die
653 Cenn Faelad son of Colgu dies
659 Conall Crandomna dies
664 Cú-cen-máthair, Diarmit son of Aed Slaine dies
666 Diarmit and Blathmac sons of Aed Slaine
670 Blathmac son of Mæl Coba and Oswy die
679 Colmán of Bangor dies
685 Great Pictish battle
691 Bruide son of Bile king of Picts dies
699 Bishop Colmán dies
705 Flann Fina son of Oswy dies

Annals of Ulster

445 Nath I dies
447 Secundinus dies
467 Feast of Temair held by Aillil Molt
475 Aillil Molt wins Brí Éile
485 MacErca wins Granairet
499 MacErca wins a battle
500 Muirchertach wins a battle, Ibar dies
502 Muirchertach wins a battle
507 Domangart son of Nisse retires in his thirty-fifth year
513 Aed Bishop of Slane dies
520 Colgu Moo Cluethi king of Airthir and Muirchetach MacErca win the Battle of Detnae
527 Ailbe dies
528 Muirchertach wins Cenn Eich and Áth Sige
533 Muirchertach wins Éblenn
534 Deaths of Muirchertach MacErca and Ailbe of Imlech Ibuir
538 and 542 Comgall son of Domangart dies in thirty-fifth year
542 Ailbe dies
543 and 547 MacErca son of Ailill Molt dies; Forgus and Domnall sons of Erca Ainmire and Ninnid sons of Sétna win a battle
550 Forgus and Domnall win Cúil Conaire
558 and 560 Gabran son of Comgall dies
566 Domnall son of Muirchertach dies, succeeded by Ainmire son of Sétna; Forgus still alive
568 Conall son of Comgall dies
570 Gildas died

572	Baetán son of Muirchertach and Echaid son of Domnall son of Muirchertach die in the third year of their reign
574	Conall son of Comgall dies in sixteenth year
575	Druim Ceat, at which Columba and Aed son of Ainmire are present
576 and 577	Dondchad son of Conall died; all sons of Gabran fought at the Battle of Telocho
580	Galam and Colgu son of Domnall son of Muirchertach die, Aed son of Ainmire wins the Battle of Druim Meic Erce
582 and 583	Aedan son of Gabran wins the Battle of Manu
584	Bruide son of Maelchu dies
587	Colman Bec son of Diarmit dies; Aed son of Ainmire wins the Battle of Doaethe
588	Constantine converted
595	Columba and Eóganan son of Gabrán dies
596	Bran and Domangart die
598	Aed son of Ainmire dies at Dún Bolg
599	Gartnait dies
600	Cainnech dies, Aedan beaten by Saxons
602	Colmán Rímid king of Cenel nEogain wins and Conall Cú son of Aed son of Ainmire loses Slemain, Fiachna son of Báetán wins Cúil Caíl
604	Colmán Rímid (son of Bætan son of Muirchertach), Aed Sláine, Conall Cú son of Aed son of Ainmire, and Cú-cen-máthair son of Eocho Bude son of Aedan die
606	Aedan son of Gabran dies
608	Fiachna son of Bætan dies
620	Aillil son of Baetan and Mael Dúin son of Fergus son of Bætan, Fiachra son of Ciarán son of Ainmire son of Sétna die
622	Conaing son of Aedan dies
623	Fiachna son of Bætan takes Ráith Guala
628	Domnall son of Aed son of Ainmire (?) alive
629	Connid Cerr king of Dalriada, Echaid Buide, Failbe and Rigullon grandsons of Aedan die, Domnall son of Aed wins battle
631	Cinaed son of Lugthréine king of Picts dies
632	Cadwallon and Ainfrith fight, Rónán son of Baetan dies
633	Iudris of the Britons fights
635	Gartnait dies
637	Conall Cael son of Mael Cobo of the nEogain wins the Battle of Sailtír
639	Oswald fights a battle
641	Bridei dies
642	Domnall Brecc dies at the Battle of Strath Carron fighting Hoan after fifteen years; Oswy fights against the Britons
643	Conall Cael and Cellach sons of Mæl Cobo begin rule, Diarmit and Blathmac sons of Aed Sláine begin rule
649	Diarmit son of Aed Sláine wins Carn Conaill

650	Cellach and Conmall Cæl wins Dún Cremthainn, Cathusach son of Domnall Brecc alive
651	Aedan dies, Dúnchad and Conall sons of Blathmac son of Aed Slaine die
652	Death of Ségéne abbot of Iona
653	Death of Tolarg son of Foth
654	Conall son of Mæl Cobo, Fergus son of Domnall (?) dies; Aed Rón son of Mæl Cobo, and Dondchad son of Conaing dies at Strath Ethairt
656	Penda and Oswy fight
657	Tolorgan son of Ainfrith king of the Picts and Guret of Strathclyde die
658	Cellach son of Mael Cobo dies
659	Dúndchad son of Aed Slaine dies
660	Echaid son of Blathmac and Conall Crandomna die
663	Gartnait son of Domnall dies
664	Battle of Luith Feirn in Foirtrenn; Cernach son of Diarmit son of Aed Slaine dies
665	Diarmait son of Aed Slaine dies
666	Ailill Flann Esa son of Domnall son of Aed son of Ainmire dies
670	Blamac son of Mael Cobo dies
671	Oswy dies, Sechnusach son of Blamac begins to rule
672	Cenn Faelad son of Blamac son of Aed Slaine begins to rule; expulsion of Drost and the burning of Bangor
673	Domangart son of Domnall Brecc dies
675	Cenn Faelad, and Penda's son dies
676	Maelduin son of Rigullan son of Conaing alive
678	Domnall Brecc loses at Caladros
680	Aelfwine son of Oswy, Dunchad son of Eoganan dies
681	Conall Cael son of Dunchad dies in Cenn Tire
686	Egfrid son of Oswy dies after ruling fifteen years; Domnall Brecc son of Eochu dies
688	Cano son of Gartnait dies
689	Cathusach grandson of Domnall Brecc, Mælduin son of Conall Crandomna dies
693	Bruide son of Bile king of Foirtrui is active, Penda fights a battle, Alphin son of Nechtan and Dumngual dies
694	Ferchar son of Connad Cerr dies
696	Domnall son of Conall Crandomna, Congalach son of Conaing son of Congal son of Aed Slaine dies
698	Brectrid son of Bernith dies, Ainfellach son of Ferchar taken captive
700	Fiannamail grandson of Dúndchad king of Dalriada dies
701	Conaing son of Dúndchad dies
704	Aldfrid son of Oswy dies
706	Bruide son of Derile dies

Annals of Tigernach

490	Muirchetach MacErc wins the Battle of Coll-osnad
493	Patrick dies
494	Cairbre son of Níall wins Tailtu
495	Eochaid son of Cairbre wins second battle of Grone
499	Cairbre son of Níall wins Slemaine; Mochoe and Bishop Cormac die
501	Cairbre wins the Battle of Cenn Ailbe
502	Muirchertach MacErc wins the Battle of Segais over Duach; Simacus active
503	Fergus Mor MacErc goes to Dalriada and dies
504	Iubar dies
505	Aedan son of Gabran wins the Battle of Mano
506	Brude son of Maelchu dies, Domangart son of Nisse dies
507	Fiachra son of Níall loses the Battle of Fremainn
508	Lugaid son of Loegaire and Eochaid MacMuiredaigh die, Cairell son of Muiredach ruler of Ulaid
509	Muirchertach MacErc high-king
511	Simacus dies
512	Fiachra son of Níall wins the Battle of Druim Dergaige
514	Cainnech of Aghaboe dies
521	Muirchertach MacErc wins the Battle of Detna, Ardgal son of Conall son of Níall dies, Columba born
524	Cairbre wins the Battle of Luachar
525	Felix rules four years
527	Muirchertach MacErc wins the Battle of Cenneich and Áth Sige
529	Muirchertach MacErc wins the Battle of Ebliu
530	Muirchertach MacErc, Ailbe of Imlech and Ibar die
537	Comgall son of Domangart, reigned thirty-two years
542	Fergus and Domnall sons of Muirchertach MacErc and Ainmire son of Setna win the Battle of Slicech
543	Tuatha son of Cormac son of Cairbre son of Níall dies
545	Fergus and Domnall win the Battle of Cúil Conairi
550	Duach dies
556	Diarmit son of Cerball calls a Tara assembly; Gabran son of Domangart dies; Bruide son of Mælchon active
	Fergus and Domnall and Ainmire son of Setna win Cúil the Battle of Dremne
565	Pict Aed Brecc dies; kindreds of Eogan and Conall fight
568	Fergus and Domnall win Gabra Life; Colcu, his father, and Domnall die; Ainmire son of Setna succeeds
571	Ainmire dies
572	Aed son of Ainmire active
576	Baetán son of Muredach and Eochaid son of Domnall killed
577	Brendan of Birr dies

15. Pertinent Facts Drawn from the Primary Sources

578 Galam dies; Fiachna son of Baetán wins the battles of Tola and Fortola
579 Conall son of Comgall dies after twelve years
581 Bridei dies
583 Brendan of Clonfert dies
585 Uinniau nephew of Fiatach dies
586 Colgu son of Domnall son of Muirchertach dies and Aed son of Ainmire is active
587 Aedan wins the Battle of Mano
589 Aedan wins battle
590 Bruide son of Maelchu dies
596 Augustine heads for Kent
599 Colman Becc active, Aed son of Ainmire takes high-kingship
603 Aedan wins the Battle of Leithri
606 Fiachna son of Bætán wins the Battle of Eudunn Mór
607 Columba dies
608 Battle of Circenn, Aed son of Ainmire active
609 Aed dies in nineteenth year of his rule at sixty-five
610 Gartnait of the Picts dies
611 Aed Slane active
614 Comgall abbot of Bangor and Conall son of Aed son of Ainmire active
615 Aed Slane dies
618 Beughna abbot of Bangor dies
619 Fiachra killed by Picts
621 Sillan son of Cumaine abbot of Bangor dies
623 Conall son of Aed Slaine dies
624 Fintan of Bangor dies; Battle of Caerleon, Solon son of Conan, and Cetula, lose to Etalfraydh
629 Cinaed dies
632 Aillil son of Baetán son of Muirchertach, Maelduin son of Fergus son of Baetán dies
637 Bridei dies
653 Talorc dies
657 Talorcan dies
663 Gartnait dies

Annals of Clonmacnoise

449 Drust son of Erb dies
457 Aillil Molt begins reign
457x482 Docus dies
478 Sons of Erc go to Scotland
Fergus, Domangart, Enos, Comgall, and Gabran rule, Comgall and Gabran are sons of Domangart

487	Aillil Molt dies, Mortagh MacEarck wins the battle of Oicke
501	Moriertagh MacEarck alive; Fergus More MacEarke goes to Scotland
504	Moriertagh MacEarck wins Inne; Iber dies
509	Brude son of Maelcon and Domangart MacNisse die; Moriertagh succeeds to high-kingship
518	Comgall of Bangor born
519	Moriertagh wins the Battle of Delna; Columba son of Felym son of Fergus Ceannada son of Conall Culban son of Neill of the Nine Hostages is born
529	Moriertagh dies
535	Twahal son of Cormac Keigh son of Carbry son of Neill of the Nine Hostages begins reign, rules eleven years, Mocteus dies
539	Comgall son of Domangart dies in thirty-fifth year
547	MacEarck son of Aillil Molt dies at Tortan, Fergus and Donall sons of MacEarck win Slygeagh
547x583	Ainmire and Eoganan rule Ireland, Conall son of Comgall and Eoganan son of Gabran rule
550	Fergus and Donall sons of MacEarck win the Battle of Cowle Conery in Keara; Aillil Molt of Invanna dies
561	Bangor of Ulster founded
563	Brendan founds Clonfert, Brendan Birr dies, Gabran son of Domangart dies, Columba to Scotland
569	Colman Becc son of Fergus Kervel son of Conall Criowhan son of Niall son of Nine Hostages is alive; Donall, Fergus, and others are joint kings for seven years from 569; Fergus and Donall wins Gawra Liffee, Brendan Birr Ainmire and Eoganan sons of Setna, and Conall son of Comgall die
577	Brendan of Confert dies
580	Eoganan son of Ainmire wins the Battle of Drom McEircke over Colga son of Donall son of Murtough; Aidan wins the Battle of Man; Uinniau and Pictish kings Galam and Kenneth die
584	Brude son of Mailcun dies
587	Ainmire son of Setna begins three-year rule; Eoganan begins twenty-five year rule; Eoganan, Aidan, Columban and St Bohyn meet at Drumceat; Colman Becc dies
589	Aidan fights the Battle of Leihrye
590	Columba dies at seventy-six; Aedan loses Circenn; Aedan's sons Brian, Domangart (?), Eahagh ffinn, and Arthur die; Gartnait dies
598	Gartnait dies
599	Cainnech of Achad Bo dies at eighty-three
603	Aidan beats Saxons; Comgall of Bangor dies at eighty-nine in the fiftieth year of his abbacy; Conall Chowe son of Eoganan put to flight
604	Aedan son of Gabran dies at seventy-seven in the thirty-fourth year of reign; Sillan abbot of Bangor dies
613	Æthelfrith kills Folinn son of Conan at the Battle of Cærleon, then dies
614	Enos son of Colman More dies

617	Sillan of Moville dies
629	Cinaed dies
630	Ælle dies, Edwin defeats Acathlon king of the Britons
632	Cenay son of Lachtren king of the Picts dies
634	Oswald wins a battle; Idris fights another battle and wins
638	Penda defeats Oswald
642	Lochyne son of Finnie king of the Picts; Maclaisre abbot of Bangor dies; Oswy defeats and kills Penda
648	Aidan dies
649	Talorc and Segene die
651	Colman of Clonard dies
652	Penda loses to Oswy and dies
653	Talorcan son of Eanfrith dies
654	Ceallach son of Moyle Cova and Ceallach son of Sarayne abbot of Othna dies
658	Conall Crandomma dies
659	Gartnait son of Domnall dies
662	Moyle Keith son of Scanalt and Eochie Jarlaly kings of the Picts die
664	Colman Casse dies
667	Oswy son of Æthelfrith dies
669	Domangart son of Donall Brick of Dalriada dies
671	son of Penda dies
675	Colman of Bangor, Almon son of Oswy, Conall son of Donough die
677	Cahasagh son of Moyledoyn king of Picts dies
677	Cahasagh son of Moyledoyn
678	Colman of Clonmacnoise dies
681	Domnall Brecc killed by Henery of the Britons
683	Segene bishop of Armagh dies
685	Ailleall son of Dongall king of Picts dies
686	Theodorus of Britain dies
693	Bregghtra son of Bernith dies
713	Osfrith son of Alhfrith dies

The four Irish annals give a great deal of self-apparent information when collated. The data, however, is not all pertinent, and perhaps it will be better to make use of it only when they and the contained items become relevant.

So far as accuracy, the only trouble seems to be that they are not in perfect agreement with each other. Generally, however, the anomalous materials are in opposition with earlier primary sources, and therefore may be safely discounted.

Ionic Records

- Baitan, Abbot of Iona (598–601), born in 537
- Lasrian, Abbot of Iona (601–608), born in 528x576

- Fergna Brit, Abbot of Iona (609–624), born in 544x584
- Segene, Abbot of Iona (624–652), born in 572x599
- Suibne, Abbot of Iona (652–655), born in 575x627
- Cuimine, Abbot of Iona (657–669), born in 589x632
- Failbe, Abbot of Iona (669–678), born in 598x644

This simple list, compiled by Adamnan, is of little use as the Ionan abbots listed above were not active in British affairs.

All the sources listed above, the information they give, and what may be derived from them, offer data on a diversity of subjects, kingdoms, and individuals. Together, they may also be used to verify or balance each other and reveal possible new biases in their counterpart sources. Surprisingly, the exercise above has shown that they generally concur where they speak of the same persons and events. In the few exceptions found, the most likely alternative has been determined without much effort.

The conversion of Edwin is described in different contexts as we find them in *Historia Brittonum* and *Historia Ecclesiastica*. However, Edwin did spend some time in the British kingdoms before his accession, and it is highly likely that he would have taken up the religion of his saviors as a gesture of respect. It is also likely that, as a ruler, he followed many of the Germanic leaders in realizing the benefits that following the Romans' religion had to offer. Once he was the king of Northumbria, public baptism would no doubt have won him the church favor he desired. Both claims might well be true, being accomplished under different circumstances, by alternative versions of Christianity, and for different purposes.

It is also curious that, though Adamnan's work names all of the earliest members of the Dalriadic dynasty as we have it, he does not include the paternities for the generation before Comgall and Gabran. Thus he provides no primary source corroboration for the received Dalriadan genealogy. It is possible that the mention of people who were in Adamnan's time the dead grandparents of prominent individuals was unneeded or incongruous with his interests. However, Adamnan came from a culture in which family going back several generations was the basis for personal identity in society; he would have been unlikely to give false information about a dynasty his monastery was so closely linked to. This is especially so if the new data would have weakened Dalriada's political position.

A more likely explanation is also possible—that all the individuals he named and that are to be found in the official genealogy were not a part of the same family. What little Adamnan does provide about their families is fundamentally different from that found in the official history.

It has often been noted that the Irish annals are closely related, and suggested both that Ulster provides the most accurate version of the original and that it is consistently one year off in certain places. This suggestion seems undeniable given the information collected above. However, to avoid any dissatisfaction about the dates used here, those of Ulster and the other Irish annals will only be assumed to be accurate within three years at all times.

With the above listing and individual date derivations of the primary sources, it is left only to apply the above results to the pedigrees as given by the various genealogists of the British, Scottish, Pictish, and Germanic kingdoms and those of modern scholars. In order to make cross-checking between the dynasties easier for the reader, they have been divided into Celtic and Anglo-Saxon families, and then each of the divisions has been order alphabetically.

16

Celtic Genealogies and Date-Guessing[1]

Brycheiniog

Meuric: 377x402
Erbic: 415x420
Erb: 453x538
Nynnyaw: 491x556

Llywarch: 529x574
Thewdric: 567x592
Meuric: 605x610
Adroes: 623x648

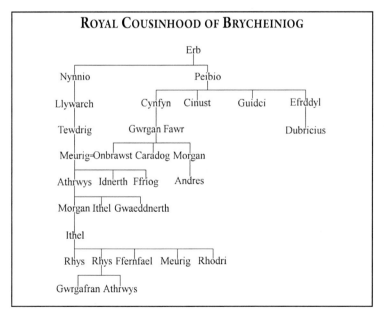

The royal family of Brycheiniog as represented in the source materials

The traditional pedigree of the Brycheiniog royal house

Erb: 473x496
Nynnio: 491x534
Peibio: 515x514
Llywarch: 529x572

Cynfyn: 533x552
Cinust: 533x552
Guidci: 533x552
Efrddyl: 533x532

Tewdrig: 567x592
Gwrgan Fawr: 575x590
St. Dyfrig: 551x550[2]
Meurig: 597x610

Onbrawst: 597x624
Morgan: 615x628
Caradog: 593x628
Athrwys: 635x648
Idnerth: 623x648
Ffriog: 623x648

Andres: 633x666
Morgan: 660x672
Ithel: 653x675
Gwaednerth: 653x686
Ithel: 680x690
Rhys: 698x728

Ffernfael: 698x710
Meurig: 698x710
Rhodri: 698x710
Gwrgafran: 716x748
Athrwys: 716x748

Cornouailles

Cybr Daniel: 475x526
Budic: 513x544
Mauricus: 531x582
Oudoceus: 531x582

Theuderic: 531x562
Meliau: 531x582
Ismael: 531x582
Melorius: 549x620

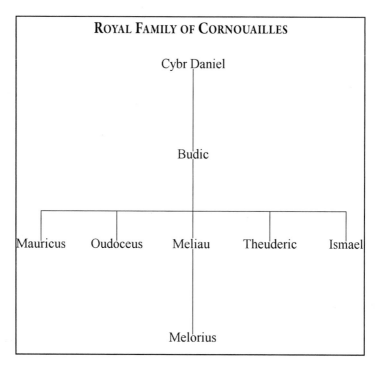

A historical construction of the Cornouailles royal family

Dalriada

Erc: 475x496
Fergus: 513x514
Loarn: 493x534
Domangart: **535x530**
Comgall: **553x535**
Gabrán: **553x548**
Conall: **567x553**
Eoganán: 571x588

Aedán: **571x566**
Connad Cerr: **598x591**
Dúncath: 589x626
Eochaid Buide: 589x604
Artur: 564x606
Conaing: 564x606
Gartnait: 564x584
Ferchar: **636x629**

Domnall Brecc: 589x630
Conall Crandomna: 607x642
Dunchad: 596x642
Cano: 582x622
Domangart: 627x661
Maelduin: 631x677
Domnall: 638x680

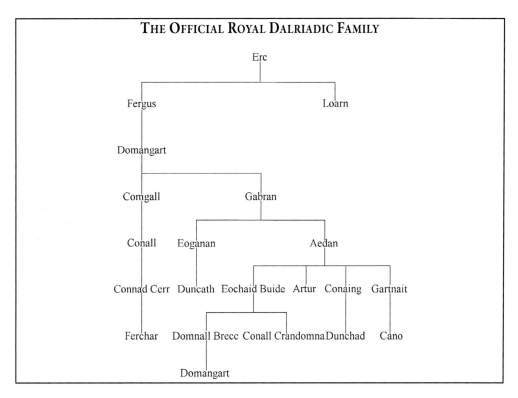

Dalriada's lineage as found in the *Senchus*

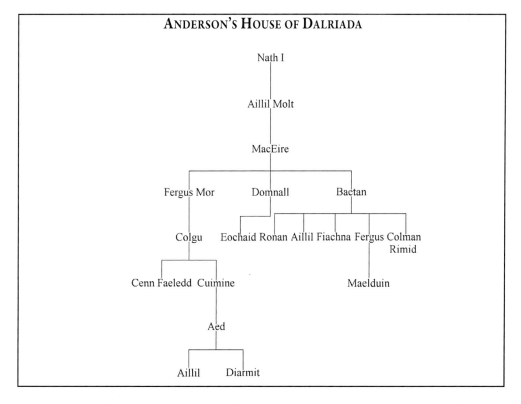

Dalriada's royal families as reconstructed from the primary sources; the descendants of Nath I

As can be seen above, the information given in the primary sources is incompatible with the official Dalriadic genealogies; clearly, the former or the latter are wrong. As the former derive from independent sources and the latter are all variations of what is found in the *Senchus*, most likely the genealogies are false. As was explained in passing above, the *Senchus* are a product of the nationalizing process of ninth-century Dalriada, which had recently acquired all of Scotland and whose interests would have been best served in creating a synchronizing history.

The genealogies have seemed the more suspicious to other scholars as well. Bannerman suggested another clan may well have inhabited Kintyre before Fergus Mór settled there, and that the reign or personality of his son Gabrán may have caused that clan to adopt one or more of his family into their lineage.³ Whether or not his suggestion is the most likely one, his theory implies that multiple houses may have occupied different areas of Dalriada at the same time. This seems to be what the primary sources imply as well. Looking at them from this perspective, one arrives at three separate families. Allowing for the fact that Donnchad cannot be both the son of Connad Cerr and have an obit of 694, these are:

Nath I: 445x478
Aillil Molt: 463x496
MacEire: 501x512
Fergus Mór: 519x530
Domnall: 519x546

Baetán: 539x550
Colgu: 555x567
Eochaid: 537x564
Rónán: 576x588
Aillil: 557x588

Fiachna: 557x588
Colman Rímid: 557x574
Fergus: 557x588
Mael Duin: 575x620

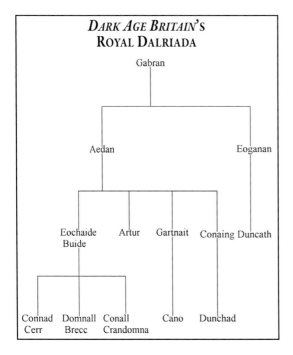

Dalriada's royal families as reconstructed from the primary sources; the descendants of Gabrán

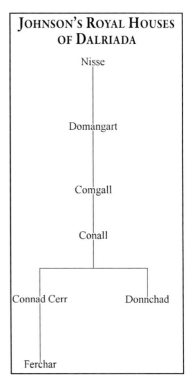

Dalriada's royal families as reconstructed from the primary sources; the descendants of Nisse

16. Celtic Genealogies and Date-Guessing

Gabrán: 508x548
Áedán: 551x566
Eóganán: 526x586
Eochaid Buide: 589x604
Artúr: 564x604
Gartnait: 564x584

Conaing: 564x604
Duncath: 544x624
Connad Cerr: 607x642
Domnall Brecc: 607x630
Conall Crandomna: 607x642

Cano: 582x622
Dunchad: 596x642
Domangart: 628x661
Ferchar: 636x680

Nisse: 419x483
Domangart: 457x501
Comgall: 495x519μ

Conall: 533x537
Connad Cerr: 571x575
Donnchad: 551x555

Ferchar: 589x613

Dumnonie

Father: 429x502
Iudoc: 447x540
Iudicael: 467x530
Winnoc: 505x548

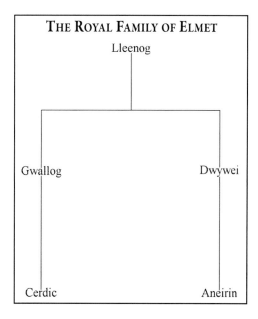

A historical construction of the Dumnonie royal family

Elmet

Lleenog: 482x566
Gwallog: 520x580
Dwywei: 500x604
Cerdic: 558x602
Aneirin: 518x642

A construction of Elmet's royal family using the possible connection of Aneirin

Gwynedd

Cunedda: 374x493
Einion Yrth: 412x511
Dunawd: 392x531
Owain: 430x529
Cadwallon: 450x536
Dingad: 410x569
Isaac: 410x569
Eifion: 410x569
Einion: 448x547
Cynlas: 448x567

Maelgwn: 488x554
Meurig: 428x607
Pobien: 428x607
Brochwel: 428x607
Cynlas: 466x565
Rhun: 506x592
Eurgain: 506x592
Bridei (Pictish king): 526x572
Pobddelw: 446x645

Eigion: 446x645
Iago: 502x583
Ieuanaul: 464x683
Cadfan: 540x601
Caradog: 482x721
Eueilian: 558x639
Cadwallon: 578x619
Bleiddud: 500x759
Cadwaladr: 596x657
Cuhelyn: 518x797

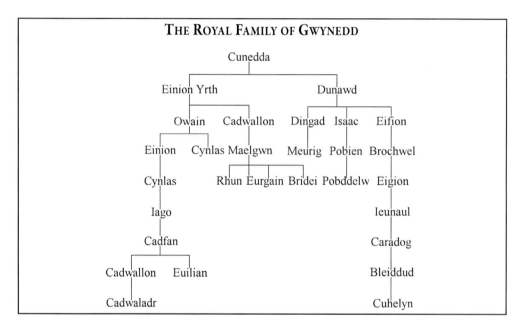

Gwynedd's pedigree as modified by Molly Miller's work

Lleuddinyawn

Lleudun: 398x483
Teneu: 436x501
Cynan Colledauc: 416x521
Kentigern: 474x519

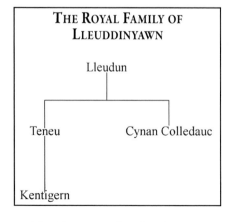

Lleuddinyawn as found in the *vitae*

A Pictish Range

Maelgwn[4]: 467x558
Female: 487x538
Bridei: 525x571
Female: 505x556
Domelch: 485x576
Gwyddno: 504x607
Female: 524x587
Gartnait: 539x574
Uerb: 534x582

Lutrin: 514x602
Nectu: 562x605
Cinioch: 572x618
Female: 556x600
Uiud: 536x620
Garnard: 582x618
Breidei: 582x622
Talorc: 594x628
Female: 578x608

Eanfrith: 587x627
Male: 576x646
Female: 596x626
Donuel: 576x646
Talorcen: 598x640
Bile: 594x690
Female: 614x670
Gartnait: 614x644

Drest: 613x650

Female: 593x646

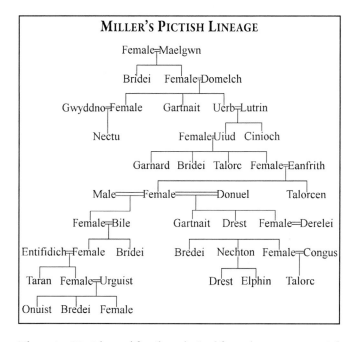

The major Pictish royal family as derived from the source material

A possible partial royal family

Powys

The Powysian dynasty is clearly achronological as things stand. Examining it more carefully, the problem is centered on the mutually exclusive testimony of Bede, who places Brochmael at Chester, and *Annales Cambriae*, which names Selyf as the participant. The two men stood two generations apart. Bede is the earlier source, but his knowledge of British affairs is sketchy, so that that of *Annales Cambriae*, though more distant in time, is more likely the historically accurate. This realization also fits in much more comfortably with the supplementary primary and secondary information pertaining to the house.

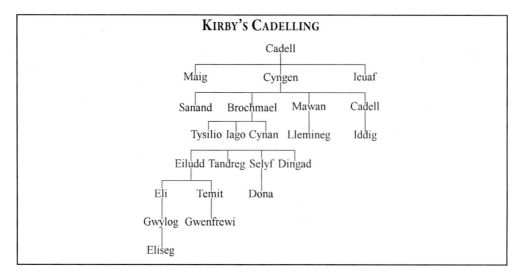

The less extended and more likely lineage of the Powysian Dynasty

Cadell: 465x529
Maig: 483x567
Cyngen: 483x547
Ieuaf: 483x567
Sanand: 501x605
Brochmael: 501x565
Mawan: 501x585
Cadell: 501x585

Tysilio: 519x603
Iago: 519x603
Cynan: 519x583
Llemineg: 519x623
Iddig: 519x623
Selyf: 537x601
Eiludd: 537x621
Tandreg: 537x621

Dingad: 537x621
Eli: 555x659
Temit: 555x659
Dona: 555x659
Gwylog: 573x697
Gwenfrewi: 573x697
Eliseg: 591x735

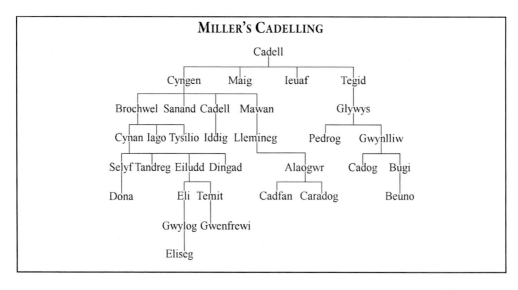

The extended lineage of the Powysian dynasty, including the saintly lineage of Glywising

16. Celtic Genealogies and Date-Guessing

Cadell Ddyrnllug: 465x529
Cyngen: 483x547
Maig: 483x567
Ieuaf: 483x567
Tegid: 483x567
Sanand: 501x567
Brochwel: 501x565
Cadell: 501x585
Mawan: 501x585
Glywys: 501x605
Cynan Garwyn: 519x583
Iago: 519x603

Tysilio: 519x603
Iddig: 519x623
Llemineg: 519x623
Pedrog: 519x643
Gwynlliw: 519x643
Selyf: 548x601
Eiludd: 528x621
Tandreg: 528x621
Dingad: 528x621
Eiludd: 528x621
Alaogwr: 488x661
Cadog: 468x681

Bugi: 468x681
Dona: 566x639
Eli: 546x659
Temit: 546x659
Cadfan: 506x699
Caradog: 506x699
Beuno: 486x719
Gwylog: 564x697
Gwenfrewi: 564x697
Cowryd: 524x737
Elise: 582x735

Even using the broad strokes employed for the Tegid of the second Powysian family tree, the above lineage is still unlikely as it has been received; it makes Cadoc most likely a younger contemporary of his junior Gildas despite a strong hagiographic tradition to the contrary. There is also a simply geographical problem. Cyngen and his progeny inhabited northern Powys, while Tegid's descendants ruled Glywising well south and west of Cadelling Powys. Supplementary studies in the next few chapters will confirm that the family of Tegid and that of Cadell were not descended through the same male line.

Rheged

Meirchion: 410x529
Cynfarch: 448x547
Elidyr: 428x567
Efrddyl: 566x585

Urien: 486x565[5]
Llywarch: 446x605
Rhun: 524x583
Owain: 504x603

Pasgen: 504x603
Gwên: 464x643
Royth: 553x632
Rieinmellth: 591x650

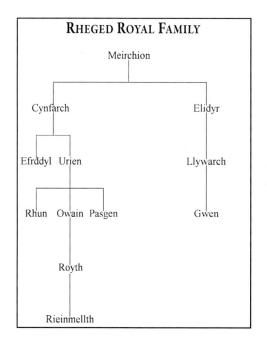

The royal line of Rheged as reconstructed by primary sources

Strathclyde

Ceretic Guletic: 357x490
Cinuit: 395x508
Dumnagual: 433x526
Guithno: 451x544
Clinoch: 471x544
Neithon (Pictish king): 569x562

Tutagual: 509x562
Bili: 597x600
Alpín: 597x600
Gwid: 597x580
Rhydderch Hen: 547x580
Owen: 615x627
Bruide: 635x638

Gartnait: 615x598
Bruide: 615x618
Talorg: 615x618
Constantine: 585x598
Dumnagual: 635x645
Elphin: 618x665
Beli: 636x703

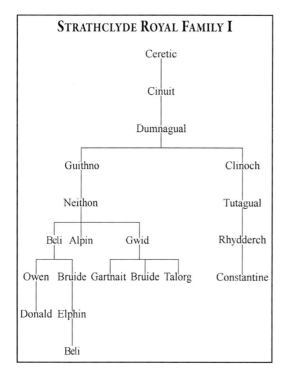

Left: The royal dynasty of Strathclyde with its Pictish connections. **Right:** The royal dynasty of Strathclyde without the Pictish connections

As can be seen, the branch involving Gwid and his descendants renders the entire genealogy inaccurate. He cannot have been a part of the family line as his relationship has been received.

Cynllwb: 369x472
Ceredig: 407x490
Cynwyd: 445x508
Dyfnwal: 483x526
Gwyddno: 521x564
Clynog: 501x544

Cynfelyn: 501x564
Neithon: 559x591
Tudwal: 519x562
Clydno: 519x629
Beli: 597x609
Rhydderch: 547x580

Cynon: 537x667
Bruide: 635x645
Owain: 615x627
Constantine: 585x598
Elffin: 633x665
Beli: 651x703

16. Celtic Genealogies and Date-Guessing

Cyndrwynyn

Egryn: 473x573
Gwyn: 491x611
Ermid: 511x591
Cerennior: 491x611
Cyndrwyn: 549x609
Caranfael: 509x649
Cynddylan: 587x627
Heledd: 567x647
Boddug: 527x687

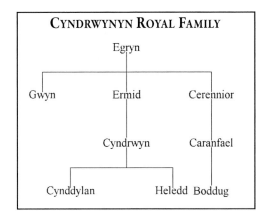

The Cyndrwynyn dynasty as reconstructed from the Heledd poems

Vannes

Father: 475x518
Chanao: 505x536
Macliau: 513x539
Waroc: 535x557
Jacob: 531x577
Canao: 553x575
Trifina: 553x575

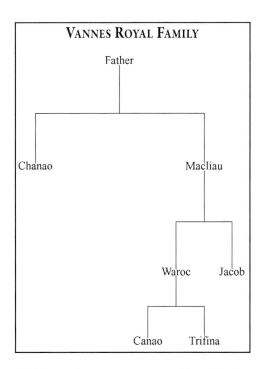

The Vannes dynasty as constructed from the *vitae* tradition

Caneutu: 605x655   Cynan: 623x693

Caneutu and his son's birth range as independently reconstructable

Gurceniu: 612x659
Conuil: 650x677
Conuint: 668x695
Gwyddgi: 668x695
Cynwg: 685x715

Gurceniu's descendants' birth ranges as independently reconstructable

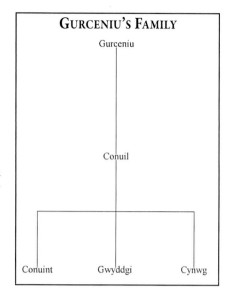

Coel: 345x493
Garbonion: 363x537
Gwrwst: 362x511
Ceneu: 383x522
Dyfnwal Moilmut: 381x575
Meirchion: 400x529
Maeswig: 421x540
Pabo: 401x560
Gwrwst: 401x560
Cyngar: 399x613

Bran Hen: 399x613
Cynfarch: 438x547
Lleenog: 459x558
Sawyl: 419x598
Dunawd: 419x598
Eliffer: 419x598
Morgan Bulc: 417x605
Urien: 476x565
Gwallog: 497x576
Guitcun: 437x632

David: 437x632
Gwrgi: 437x632
Peredur: 437x632
Coleddog: 435x643
Owain: 494x603
Rhun: 524x583
Pasgen: 494x603
Cadwallon: 475x670
Morgan: 453x681

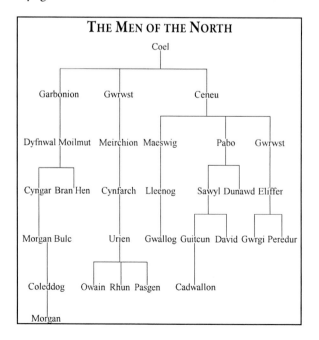

The traditional pedigree as reconstructed from the genealogies

While the genealogy as presented above is remotely feasible, the mathematical improbability of a single individual becoming the sole progenitor of all the major royal families between Hadrian's and Antonine's Wall must be kept in mind—this especially in the period as described in the first half of this book, where there had been no central authority to begin with. Any kingship that had developed would have emerged in the late fifth century, and would have functioned only at a local level. The above genealogy would have Coel becoming one of the first kings, and his ruling areas all along the Borders area.

A clue that the medieval genealogist/s responsible for this family tree realized it was inaccurate may be found by the appearance of David. This individual, intended to be the Dyfed saint, is otherwise exclusively located in Dyfed and so does not belong here. More evidence for the genealogy's inauthenticity will be forthcoming in the next chapters.

17

Germanic Genealogies and Date-Guessing

Berneich

Before looking at the various genealogies of Berneich, it is necessary to point out that the earliest version, to be found in the *Historia Brittonum*, appears to be flawed for several reasons. One sees a problem with the first king, Ida. He is credited with eleven male children who lived to adulthood. According to the laws of probability, this would suggest he had at least twenty male children, and forty in all. Forty is a highly unlikely number, especially when it is noted that the Germanic peoples are not known to have practiced extensive polygamy.

Second, it should be remembered that this section of the history may be dated to only 796, while Ida is placed some 250 years before that; well outside the credible limits of oral history. Bede did not handle early Berneich history, suggesting that there may not have been a written record either.

The third problem appears to be a discrepancy with the Germanic genealogies. An earlier chapter, dateable to perhaps the 680s and deriving from a British source, notes that Urien fought against Hussa, but died in siege against Theodric. The Germanic king lists clearly state that Theodric ruled first, and was later followed by Hussa.

The confusion is only compounded with Frithuwald. He is put into the list between the Hussa and Theodric and, given the internal data, ruled 579–585. In contrast, Bede's *Historia Maiora* says that he was alive in 597 when Augustine arrived in Britain.

Add to this the problem of Æthelfrith, who appears to have been the most important Bernician of the late sixth/early seventh centuries. As has been seen above, he is credited with a reign beginning in 592/3, and to have ruled for twenty-four years, through the reigns of Hussa, Theodric, and Frithuwald. Clearly, the king list as it has been preserved details an entirely different chronology for its kings than is possible given the extant source material.

Together, the above problems suggest that the kings recorded in Berneich before the rise of Æthelfrith did not rule sequentially. It seems likely that they represent several different kingdoms all active in what would become Berneich, and living approximately contemporary to each other. These rulers were taken out of historical context and put into one consecutive lineage for the purpose of giving the sense of a united and long history to Berneich, at one stroke nationalizing the diverse histories of its kingdoms into a single, distinguished lineage.

17. Germanic Genealogies and Date-Guessing

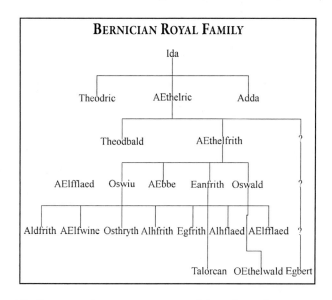

The Bernician dynasty as constructed from the early sources

Ida: 497x550
Æthelric: 535x568
Theodric: 515x585
Adda: 515x585
Æthelfrith: 573x586
Theodbald: 553x606
Second Generation:
  553x605
Oswiu: 611x612

Oswald: 603x604
Eanfrith: 591x604
Æbbe: 591x624
Third Generation: 571x623
Aldfrith: 648x650
Ælfwine: 660x661
Ælfflæd: 654
Osthryth: 629x650
Alhfrith: 629x650

Egfrith: 645x646
Alhflæd: 629x641
Œthelwald: 621x642
Talorcan: 609x640
Fourth Generation:
  589x641
Egbert: 618x659

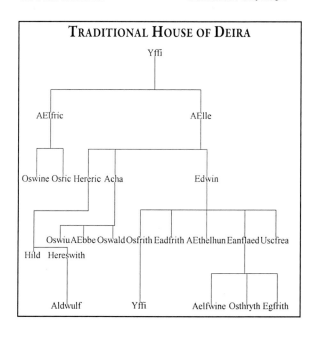

One interpretation of the Deiran lineage, without Æbbe as the daughter of Acha

Deira

Yffi: 521x548
Ælfric: 558x586
Ælle: 559x566
Osric: 578x624
Oswine: 596x624
Hereric: 575x596
Edwin: 587x598
Acha: 573x580

Hild: 613x614
Hereswith: 591x640
Oswiu: 611x612
Æbbe: 591x622
Oswald: 603x604
Osfrith: 615x616
Eadfrith: 615x616
Æthelhun: 625x631

Uscfrea: 617x631
Eanflæd: 622x628
Aldwulf: 625x658
Yffi: 624x654
Ælfwine: 660x661
Osthryth: 640x650
Egfrith: 645x646

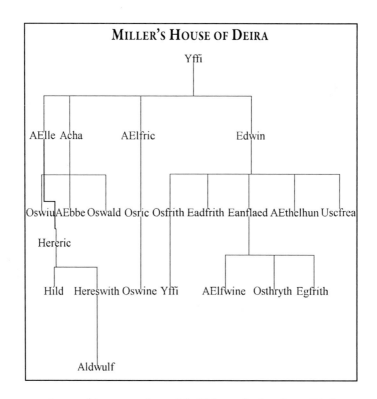

A second interpretation, with Æbbe as the daughter of Acha

Yffi: 549x560
Ælfric: 567x583
Ælle: 537x578
Acha: 573x584
Edwin: 587x598
Osric: 578x601
Hereric: 558x597
Oswiu: 611x612

Ælle: 537x560
Æthelric: 555x578

Æbbe: 591x622
Oswald: 603x604
Osfrith: 606x616
Eadfrith: 605x616
Æthelhun: 625x633
Uscfrea: 605x636
Eanflæd: 622x628
Hereswith: 591x635

Hereric: 575x596
Hereswith: 593x635

Hild: 613x614
Oswine: 596x619
Yffi: 624x654
Ælfwine: 660x661
Osthryth: 640x650
Egfrith: 645x646
Aldwulf: 625x658

Hild: 613x614
Aldwulf: 625x658

17. Germanic Genealogies and Date-Guessing

Ælfric: 558x586
Osric: 578x616
Oswine: 596x637

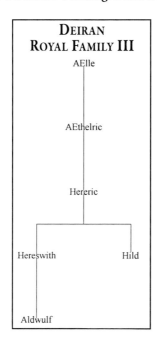

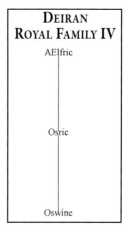

Above: A fourth interpretation, focusing on the descent of Oswine.
Left: A third and more limited interpretation, focusing on Ælle's descendants

Yorke's East Anglia

Tyttla: 534x579
Rædwald: 572x604
Eni: 562x597
Ræganhere: 590x642
Eorpwald: 590x622
Sigbert: 590x628
Anna: 587x615

Æthelhere: 600x640
Æthelwald: 600x640
Æthelric: 587x620
Ricbert: 608x660
Seaxburh: 605x650
Æthelthryth: 625x633
Æthelburh: 605x653

Aldwulf: 625x658
Egbert: 631x680
Hlothere: 630x680
Eorcengota: 623x688
Eormenhild: 623x688

The East Anglian dynasty as consistently shown in the source material

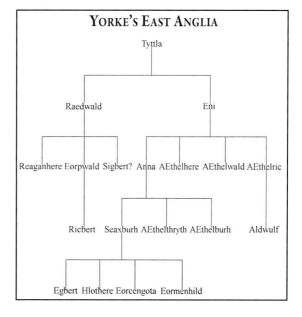

Yorke's Early Essex

Sledd: 523x581
Sæberht: 561x599
Seaxa: 541x619
Sæward: 579x627
Seaxred: 581x635
Seaxbald: 579x637
Sigeferth: 559x657
Sigeberht: 605x645
Sæbbi: 619x653
Swithelm: 609x659
Swithfrith: 597x675
Seleferth: 577x695
Sigehere: 623x663
Swæfheard: 637x687
Sigeheard: 637x671
Swæfred: 637x671
Sigebald: 595x733
Offa: 641x701
Sigemund: 655x709
Selered: 613x771

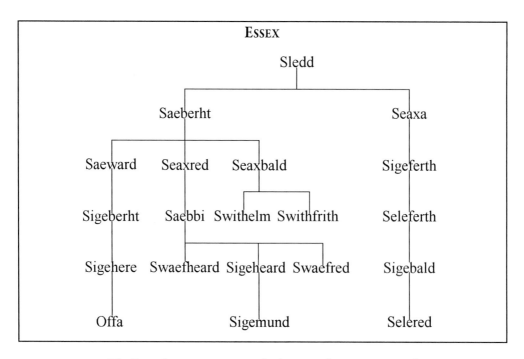

The Essex dynasty as consistently shown in the source material

17. Germanic Genealogies and Date-Guessing

Kent

Eormenric: 523x560
Æthelberht: 561x578
Ricula: 541x581
Eadbald: 585x596
Æthelwald: 579x596
Æthelburh: 587x596
Sæberht: 561x599
Eormenred: 603x634
Eanswith: 579x634
Eorcenberht: 597x634

Æthelthryth: 625x633
Æthelhun: 605x653
Uscfrea: 605x633
Eanswith: 597x658
Æthelred: 621x672
St. Æthelberht: 621x672
Æbbe: 621x672
Eormenburh: 621x672
Hlothere: 630x680
Egbert: 631x663

Eorcengota: 615x672
Eormenhild: 615x672
Mildfrith: 639x710
Merchelm: 639x710
Mildfrith: 639x710
Mildburh: 639x710
Eadric: 649x701
Wihtred: 649x701
Werburh: 633x721

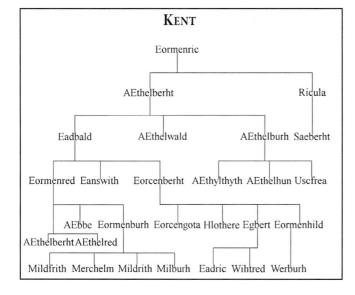

The Kentish dynasty as consistently shown in the source material

Mercia

Cearl: 571x580
Cwoenburh: 589x598
Osfrith: 607x616
Eadfrith: 607x616

The descent of the family through intermarriage

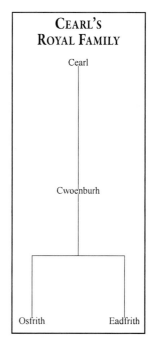

Pybba: 580x605
Penda: 598x623
Eowa: 598x643
Cenwalh: 618x635
Wulfhere: 630x653
Cyneburh: 616x661
Osyth: 621x661
Æthelred: 621x641

Merewalh: 630x661
Peada: 616x641
Alweo: 616x681
Osmod: 616x681
Cundwalh: 654x691
Cenred: 656x691
Ceolred: 648x691
Ceolwald: 648x691

Mildrith: 639x699
Mildburh: 639x699
Aethelbald: 634x719
Headbert: 634x719
Eanulf: 634x719
Centwine: 672x729

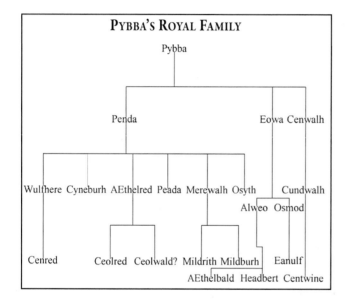

The descent of the primary Mercian family as reconstructed with the earliest sources

Wessex

Cerdic: 397x513
Creoda: 435x531
Cynric: 473x549
Ceawlin: 506x587
Cuthulf: 511x567
Ceolwulf: 491x587
Cutha/Cuthwine: 544x605
Ceol(ric): 549x585
Ceolwulf: 549x565
Cuthgils: 509x625
Ceadda: 582x623

Cynebald: 562x643
(Cuthwulf): 575x643
Cynegils: 587x603
Cenferth: 527x663
Cenbert: 620x641
Æthelbald: 580x681
Ceolwold: 593x675
Cenwalh: 618x635
Cwichelm: 598x621
Centwine: 625x655
Æscwine: 598x655

Cenfus: 545x701
Cædwalla: 658x659
Oswald: 598x719
Cenred: 633x665
Cuthred: 616x659
Cwoenburh: 651x703
Cuthburh: 651x703
Ine: 670x683
Ingild: 651x703

Ceawlin: 542x584
Cutha: 560x605
Cynegils: 580x602
Cuthwine: 560x611
Ceadda: 582x623
Cwichelm: 598x620
Cuthwulf: 578x629

Cynebald: 588x662
Cenberht: 620x641
Cuthred: 616x658
Ceolwold: 618x647
Osric: 560x637
Oswald: 560x637
Oshere: 560x637

Mul: 638x679
Cædwalla: 658x659
Cœnred: 632x665
Cwoenburh: 651x703
Cuthburh: 651x703
Ine: 671x683
Ingild: 651x703

17. Germanic Genealogies and Date-Guessing 151

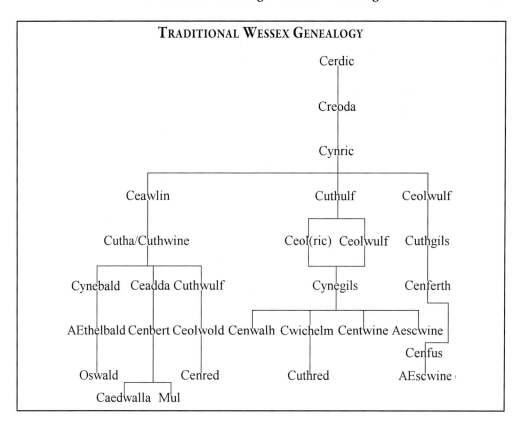

The family tree of the Wessex royal house as received

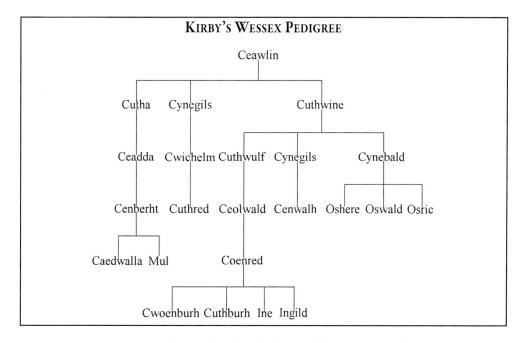

An interpretive lineage based on the theory of dual, competing houses

Between work on the Celtic and Germanic genealogies, one common theme emerges. Among the kingdoms that later patronized histories, there was a tendency to alter their history. Instead of the historical fact of early internecine conflict eventually resulting in a single kingdom, the most renowned rulers of all kingdoms were fictitiously combined into a single dominant lineage that had been stable throughout its recorded history. As has been demonstrated from several perspectives, neither continuity nor stability throughout Britain makes any sense with the political landscape of the fourth and early fifth centuries. It has been seen that there is strong historical reason to doubt the extant Dalriadic genealogy, and support for this opinion was to be had in the date guessing. Gwynedd and Powys have long been seen as composed of several smaller kingdoms throughout the sixth century, while Professor Kirby pointed out the same possibility with Wessex, and a simple examination of Brycheiniog has forced the same conclusion there as well. Bede's own testimony is evidence of the process of amalgamation to medieval kingdoms still ongoing in the seventh century. He began his history of Northumbria with events around 600, and even at that late date he described two kingdoms competing for Northumbria. He implied several others. A closer look at the region with additional materials has shown that there must have been at least three and possibly four kingdoms in the region at the time. At this point, it may safely be concluded that multiple kingdoms within a region were the norm and not the exception up to at least 600. Incidentally, the opposing Wessex genealogy is:

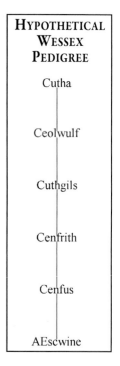

A second interpretive lineage based on the theory of dual, competing houses

Cutha: 529x569

Ceolwulf: 552x592

Cuthgils: 570x615

Cenfrith: 588x633

Cenfus: 606x651

Æscwine: 624x669

This process of amalgamating history served to give the regions a sense of unity and no doubt helped to bond former opponents together under one leadership. Unifying histories was a good technique that served a conqueror well in the early Middle Ages. To the modern historian, that approach has led to many problems of interpretation and chronology. As was suggested in the first half of this book, there were in fifth and much of sixth century Britain literally hundreds of kingdoms playing a deadly game of conquer and survive. At this point in the study, date guessing mainly serves to support that conclusion.

In the next chapter, the relevant raw information from the secondary sources is listed and categorized by kingdom. This information is then plugged into Miller's formula to gain a better grasp on the chronologies of both the major and minor kingdoms as well as the churchmen of this era.

18

Pertinent Facts Drawn from the Secondary Sources

The following is a summary of information to be derived from the secondary sources. They have been divided by kingdom.

Aeron

- Clydno was contemporary to Rhun son of Maelgwn, Elidyr Mwynfawr, Nudd Hael, Mordaf Hael, and Rhydderch

Aran

- Scanlan was contemporary to Ailbe
- Corbanus was contemporary to Enda

Brecon

- Clydog was the son of Clydwyn and brother of Dedyw
- Gwledyr married Aed son of Corath
- Rhain was contemporary to Cadoc of Llancarfan
- Maucennus was contemporary to Maelgwn, Cadoc, David, Enda, and Tigernach grandson of Eocho

Brennych

- Ida was the father of Adda, Æthelric, Theodric, Edric, Theodohare, and Osmera. By the concubine Occa he was father to Ealric, Ecca, Oswald, Sogor, and Sogethere (*Historia Brittonum*)
- Adda ruled eight years, Æthelric ruled four years, Theodric ruled seven years, Freod-

wald ruled six years, Hussa ruled seven years, Æthelfrith ruled twelve years and an additional twelve years over Northumbria (*Historia Brittonum*)
- Ida was the father of Æthelric father of Ecgulf father of Leodwald father of Eata Glin Mawr father of Edbert and Egbert the bishop (*Historia Brittonum*)
- Æthelric was the father of Æthelferth (*Historia Brittonum*)
- Æthelferth was the father of Eanfrid, Oswald, Oswy, Osguid, Osgudu, Oslaph, and Offa (*Historia Brittonum*)
- Oswy was the father of Aldfrith, Ælfwine, and Egferth (*Historia Brittonum*)
- Egferth was the cousin of Bridei (*Historia Brittonum*)
- Theodric fought against Urien, Rhydderch, Gwallog, and Morken (*Historia Brittonum*)
- Hussa fought Urien and Morken and was alive when Urien died (*Historia Brittonum*)
- Gall was a contemporary of Gwenddolau; Diffydell killed Gwrgi
- Oswy ruled for twenty-eight years, six months. Cadwaladr died during his rule (*Historia Brittonum*)
- Ælfflæd Abbess of Whitby was the daughter of Oswy and Eanflæd (*Historia Brittonum*)
- Egferth was the father of Oslac father of Aldhun father of Æthelsige father of Ecca father of Oslaph (*Historia Brittonum*)
- Egferth son of Oswy ruled for nine years (*Historia Brittonum*)
- Æthelfrith succeeded to kingship in 593 (*Anglo-Saxon Chronicle*)
- Theobald died at Degsastan in 603 (*Anglo-Saxon Chronicle*)
- Æthelfrith won Chester in 605 (*Anglo-Saxon Chronicle*)
- Æthelfrith died and was succeeded by Edwin in 617 (*Anglo-Saxon Chronicle*)
- Oswald ruled for nine years and killed Cadwallon. He fought Penda at Gaius' Field (*Historia Brittonum*)
- Eanfrith succeeded and died, then Oswald became king for eight years in 634 (*Anglo-Saxon Chronicle*)
- Oswy succeeded to Deira in 641 (*Anglo-Saxon Chronicle*)
- Oswald fought at Maserfelth and died, succeeded by Oswy who reigned twenty-eight years (*Anglo-Saxon Chronicle*)
- Battle of Cogwy, Oswald and Eowa died in 644 (*Annales Cambriae*)
- Ælfwine died in 679 (*Anglo-Saxon Chronicle*)

Ceredigion

- Paternus was contemporary to Teilo and Cadfan of Bardsey
- Ceredig died in 616 (*Annales Cambriae*)

Cornouailles

- Ismael was a son of Budic and brother of Tyfei
- Ismael was contemporary to Teilo
- Corentin Bishop of Quimper was a contemporary of Gradlon, Winwaloe, Tudy, Paternus, and Malo

- Winwaloe was a son of King Fracanus of the Catovii and brother of Wethenoc, Iacobus, and Chreirbia. He was a contemporary of Riwal, Gwenael son of Romelius, Conomaglus, and Maglos son of Conomaglus
- Cunomorus and Trifina of Weroc were contemporaries of Columba (floruit 563–598), Cadoc, and Gradlon's death.
- Conocan of Quimper was a bishop after Corentin; he was contemporary to Winwaloe and Childebert
- Ismael was a contemporary of Teilo, he was a bishop after the death of David
- Gwenael son of Romelius of Quimper and descendant of Conan Meriaduc succeeded Winwaloe; he was a contemporary of Riwal and Waroc.

Cornwall

- Cunomorus died in the sixth century
- Enodoc was a bishop in the mid-sixth century
- Cynan Colledauc was a son of Lleudun and a contemporary to Theodoric
- Fingar and Breaca were contemporaries of Theodoric
- Petroc son of Glywys was a contemporary to Wethonoc, Samson, King Theodoric, Petrus, Dator, and Dagan; he baptized Constantine
- Docco son of Constantine was a contemporary to Kebi, Peibio, and Enda
- Kebi son of Saloman taught Docco; he was a contemporary of Ailbe, Enda, Ethelic, Maelgwn, and David
- David was a contemporary to King Constantine
- Gerennius was a contemporary to Teilo and was living after Maelgwn died
- Finnian of Clonnard was a contemporary to Enda, David, and Gildas
- Constantius was a monk in Ireland and was contemporary to Kentigern and Columba
- Constantine succeeded Carthacus as Abbot of Rahan

Dalriada

- Brendan of Birr was alive when Columba transferred to Iona
- Cairnech was a brother of Luirig King of Alba; he was active when MacErca was exiled
- Gabran son of Domangart died in 558 (*Annales Cambriae*)
- Morgant and Rhiwallon were grandsons of Aedan

Deira

- Soemil was the father of Swærta father of Westerfalca father of Wilgsil father of Wyscfrea father of Yffe father of Ælle father of Edwin father of Osfrid and Eadfrid (*Historia Brittonum*)
- Ælle died and was succeeded by Æthelric in 588 (*Anglo-Saxon Chronicle*)
- Edwin succeeded in 617 (*Annales Cambriæ*)

- Edwin defeated five Wessex kings and his daughter Eanflæd was born in 626 (*Anglo-Saxon Chronicle*)
- Edwin was baptized in 627 (*Anglo-Saxon Chronicle*)
- Edwin ruled for seventeen years (*Historia Brittonum*)
- Edwin and two sons died against Cadwallon at Meigen in 630 (*Annales Cambriæ*)
- Edwin fought at Hatfield Chase, he and Osfrid died later in 633 (*Anglo-Saxon Chronicle*)
- Osric succeeded to the throne and died within the year of 634. Osric was followed by Oswald, who ruled for eight years (*Anglo-Saxon Chronicle*)
- Oswald died at Maserfelth, Oswy succeeded to Northumbria in 641 (*Anglo-Saxon Chronicle*)
- Oswine son of Osric succeeded to Deira and ruled for seven years beginning in 643 (*Anglo-Saxon Chronicle*)
- Aedan and Oswine died in 650/1 (*Anglo-Saxon Chronicle*)
- Oswy died and was succeeded by Ecgfrith in 670 (*Anglo-Saxon Chronicle*)
- Ecgfrith died and was succeeded by Aldfrith in 685 (*Anglo-Saxon Chronicle*)
- Osthryth was killed in 697 (*Anglo-Saxon Chronicle*)
- Aldfrith died and Osred eventually succeeded him in 705 (*Anglo-Saxon Chronicle*)
- Osred died after ruling seven years, Cœnred succeeded him in 716 (*Ango-Saxon Chronicle*)
- Osred died after ruling for eleven years in 717 (*Annales Cambriae*)
- Cœnred died and was succeeded by Osric in 718 (*Anglo-Saxon Chronicle*)
- Osric died in 729 (*Anglo-Saxon Chronicle*)

Domnonie

- Riwal was a contemporary of Winwaloe, Illtud, and Gwenael
- Winwaloe was a son of King Fracanus of the Catovii; he was a brother of Wethonoc, Iacob, Chreirbia. He was a contemporary of Riwal, Conomaglus, Maglos son of Conomaglos, and Gradlon
- Leonorus was a pupil of Illtud, and contemporary of Riwal, Iudwal, and Childebert; he died just after the defeat of Cunomorus and the restoration of Iudwal at the age of 51
- Brioc of St. Breock was a contemporary of Tudwal, Riwal, Conan of Trigg, and Illtud
- Tudwal was a son of Pompa, a brother of Riwal, a cousin of Deroch, and a contemporary of Cunomorus and Ruilmus
- Deroch was a contemporary of Childebert
- Cunomorus was a contemporary of Leonorus, Albinus, Malo, Samson, Tudwal, and Childebert
- Paul Aurelian son of Perphirius was a subking. He was a brother of Notolius, Potolius, and Sitofolla. Paul Aurelian was a contemporary of Iudwal as was Iaoua, son of an Irish prince and a sister of Paul Aurelian. Iaoua succeeded Paul Aurelian. Paul Aurelian was taught by Illtud with Gildas
- Jonas son of Iudwal was exiled to Childebert
- Iudicael was a father of Winnoc, a brother of Iudoc, and ruled from about 640 to about 650. He was a contemporary to Meven son of Gerascenus

- Malo was a cousin of Samson. He was a contemporary of Iudicael, Meliau, Hailoc, Corentin, and Cunomorus

Dubonnia

- Eldad was a bishop of Dyrham during Battle of Dyrham in 577 (*Annales Cambraie*)

Dunawding

- Sanctanus was a son of Pabo Post Prydein and a contemporary of Cadoc; he was a half-brother of Matoc son of Deichter who was a daughter of Muiredach Muinderg and Canton
- David was a son of Sanctanus and Nonnita daughter of Cynyr.[1] He was contemporary to Ailbe, Teilo, Paternus, Gildas, Cadoc, Padarn, and King Constantine
- Dunawd fought at Arfderydd, fought Owain and Pasgen later, and died in 595 (*Annales Cambriae*)

Dyfed

- Aed son of Corath married Gwledyr
- Aircol was a contemporary to Cynan Garwyn
- Tydecho was a brother to Tegfan. He was a contemporary of Dogfael, Maelgwn, Cadfan of Bardsey, Maelgwn, Cynan Garwyn, and Cynan
- Drutwas and Erduduyl children of Tryffin were contemporaries of Arthur
- Samson was baptized by Ailbe. He was a pupil of Illtud with Gildas. He was present at the Council of Paris. He was a contemporary of Teilo, Tysilio, Malo, Dubricius, Petroc, Cunomorus, Meven son of Gerascenus, and comes Guedianus. He was succeeded by Maglorius
- Guadam was a king near Llandeilo Fychan. He was a contemporary of Teilo and died before David
- David was baptized by Ailbe and taught by Paulinus of Cynwyl. Gwistlian was a bishop during his youth. He was a contemporary to Kentigern, Illtud, Finnian of Llancarfan, Maucanus, Teilo, and Kebi son of Saloman; he died after Guadam.
- Finnian of Llancarfan was a contemporary of Cadoc, Gildas, David, Gwynlliw, and Bitheus
- Maredudd died in 796 (*Annales Cambriae*)
- Owain died (*Annales Cambriae*)

East Anglia

- Wilhelm Guechan was the father of Wuffa father of Tytill father of Eni father of Æthelhere father of Aldwulf father of Æthelric (*Historia Brittonum*)
- Rædwald defeated Æthelfrith in 617 (*Anglo-Saxon Chronicle*)

- Eorpwald was baptized in 632 (*Anglo-Saxon Chronicle*)
- Anna was a contemporary of Penda (*Historia Brittonum*)
- Anna died in 653/4 (*Anglo-Saxon Chronicle*)
- Wihtburga was a daughter of Anna
- Æthelhere died at Winwæd in 654 (*Anglo-Saxon Chronicle*)

Elmet

- Gwallog was contemporary to Elphin

Ergyng

- Pebiau was contemporary to Docco
- Dubricius taught Illtud, Samson, and Leonorus

Essex

- Sæberht son of Ricula and Sledd began ruling when he was converted in 604 (*Anglo-Saxon Chronicle*)

Eteliciaun

- Etelic a contemporary of Kebi

Fracani

- Fracan was the father of Winwaloe, Iacutus, Idunet, and Wethenec; he was a contemporary of Riwal

Glywising

- Cadoc was a son of Gwynlliw and a nephew of Paul Penychen; he was educated by Tatheus, Cainnech of Achad Bo, and Bachan; he was contemporary to Arthmail, Findbar, Run, Rhain of Brecon, Gildas, David, Caradoc son of Ynyr, Sawyl, Maelgwn, Petroc, Etelic, Mouric son of Enhinti, Elli, Machan, and Sanctanus.
- Tatheus was contemporary to Caradoc son of Ynyr, and Gwynlliw; he taught Cadoc
- Finnian of Llancarfan was contemporary to Cadoc, Gildas, David, Gwynlliw, and Bitheus
- Illtud and Brioc were taught by Dubricius. Illtud taught Paul Aurelian, Samson, and Leonorus; he was contemporary to Cadoc, Merchiaun of Glywising, and Riwal
- Dubricius died in 612 (*Annales Cambriae*)[2]

18. Pertinent Facts Drawn from the Secondary Sources

Gododdin

- Cynan Colledauc son of Lleudun was a contemporary of Theodoric of the South
- Cadrod and Clydno fought at Arfderydd
- Bran son of Ymellyrn was a contemporary of Urien

Gwlad

- Digwc married Maelgwn
- Beuno was a contemporary to Idon and Ynyr Gwent in his old age
- Bugi was father to Beuno and contemporary to Ynyr Gwent
- Idon was a contemporary of Beuno and Owain

Gwynedd

- Bwyn was a son of Cunedda
- Maucanus was contemporary to Maelgwn, Cadoc, and David
- Maelgwn married Digwc; he was contemporary to Maucanus, Paternus, Tydecho, and Kebi son of Saloman
- Eurgain daughter of Maelgwn married Elidyr Mwynfawr
- Daniel was a bishop before Comgall founded Irish Bangor
- Rhun son of Maelgwn was a contemporary of Elidyr Mwynfawr, Clydno Eidyn, Nudd Hael son of Senyllt, Mordaf Hael son of Serwan, and Rhydderch Hael
- Cadfan of Bardsey was a son of Eneas Ledwic; he was contemporary to Hewyn, Paternus, Tydecho, and Mael
- Eueilian daughter of Cadfan married Gwydyr Drwm
- Cadfan and Cadwallon son of Cadfan were contemporaries of Beuno
- Cadwallon son of Cadfan had a bard Afan Ferddig
- Cadafael ruled between Cadwallon and Cadwaladr
- Cadwaladr was contemporary to Einiaun son of Aed

Kent

- Hengest was the father of Octha father of Ossa father of Eormenric father of Æthelberht father of Eadbald father of Earconbert father of Egbert (*Historia Brittonum*)[3]
- Eanswith was the daughter of Eadbald
- Earcongota was the daughter of Earconbert and Sæxburg
- Archbishop Paulinus was contemporary to Edwin, Hild, James, and Romanus (*Anglo-Saxon Chronicle*)
- Eadbald died after reigning twenty-five years and was succeeded by Eorcenberht in 640 (*Anglo-Saxon Chronicle*)
- Eorcenberht died and was succeeded by Egbert in 664 (*Anglo-Saxon Chronicle*)
- Egbert died and was succeeded by Hlothere in 673 (*Anglo-Saxon Chronicle*)

- Hlothere died in 685 (*Anglo-Saxon Chronicle*)
- Wihtred succeeded in 694 and ruled for twenty-three years (*Anglo-Saxon Chronicle*)

Leon

- King Godian was contemporary to Goulven and lived after Paul Aurelian
- King Withur was contemporary to Paul Aurelian and Childebert

Lleu

- Lleudun father of Cynan Colledauc was contemporary to Theodoric of the South

Lleyn

- Melyn died at Chester
- Tegid married Ceridwen

Llydaw

- Cadfan of Bardsey son of Eneas Ledwic of Llydaw was contemporary to Hewyn, Paternus, Tydecho, Corentin, David, and Mael

Magonsæte

- Milburga daughter of Herewald was a sister of Mildred and Milgitha

Manau

- Conindrus was a bishop during Patrick's life

Manaw

- Penarwan daughter of Culfanawyd married Owain son of Urien
- Yseult daughter of Culfanawyd married Drust son of Tallwch
- Bun daughter of Culfanawyd married Fflamdwyn

Mercia

- Offa was the father of Angengeot father of Eomer father of Icel father of Cnebba father of Cynewald father of Creoda father of Pybba father of Penda and Eobba (*Historia Brittonum*)
- Penda succeeded in 626 and ruled for thirty years (*Anglo-Saxon Chronicle*)

- Penda father of Æthelred ruled for ten years and separated Mercia, he was contemporary to Anna and Oswald (*Historia Brittonum*)
- Eowa died at Cogwy in 644 (*Annales Cambriae*)
- Eobba was the father of Osmond father of Eanwulf father of Thingfrith father of Offa father of Egferth; he was also the father of Alweo father of Æthelbald (*Historia Brittonum*)
- Peada was baptized in 652/3 (*Anglo-Saxon Chronicle*)
- Penda died at Winwæd and was succeeded by Peada in 654/5 (*Anglo-Saxon Chronicle*)
- Eormingilda was the wife of Wulfhere and mother of Werburga
- Peada was killed and Wulfhere succeeded him. Æthelred, Cyneburh, and Cyneswith were alive in 656/7 (*Anglo-Saxon Chronicle*)
- Wulfhere fought at Biedanheafod and later died. He was succeeded by Æthelred in 675 (*Anglo-Saxon Chronicle*)
- Osthryth was killed in 697 (*Anglo-Saxon Chronicle*)
- Æthelred abdicated and was succeeded by Cœnred in 704 (*Anglo-Saxon Chronicle*)
- Cœnred abdicated and was succeeded by Ceolred in 709 (*Anglo-Saxon Chronicle*)
- Ceolred fought at Adam's Grave and died later. He was succeeded by Æthelbald in 716 (*Anglo-Saxon Chronicle*)

Middle Anglia

- Osgytha daughter of Frithewald of Surrey was the wife of Sigehere of Essex. She was contemporary to Modwena and Earconwald

Nouoant

- Elphin son of Gwyddno was contemporary to Maelgwn

Picts

- Drest I reigned one hundred years, Patrick arrived in his 19th year (SL, SB)
- Talorc II reigned four (SL) or two (SB) years
- Nechtan I reigned twenty-four (SL) or ten (SB) years and founded Abernethy in his fourth year
- Drest II reigned thirty years (SL)
- Galam I reigned twelve (SL1), fifteen (SL2, SB), and twenty-five (SB) years
- Drest III and Drest IV reigned five (SL1, SB) and twelve (SL2) years
- Drest III reigned eight years (SB), and Drest IV five or six of those and four alone (SB)
- Drest IV reigned five years (SL)
- Gartnait III reigned seven (SL) or six (SB) years
- Cailtram reigned one (SL) or six (SB) years
- Talorc III reigned eleven (SL) or twelve (SB) years

- Drest V reigned one year (SL)
- Galam II reigned one (SL1) and four or seven (SL2) years
- Bridei I reigned thirty (SL) or nineteen (SB) years
- Gartnait IV reigned eleven (SL) or twenty (SB) years
- Nechtan II reigned twenty (SL) and eleven or twenty-one (SB) years
- Ciniod I reigned nineteen (SL) and fourteen or twenty-four (SB) years
- Gartnait V reigned four (SL) or five (SB) years
- Bridei II reigned five years (SL)
- Talorc IV reigned twelve (SL) or eleven (SB) years
- Talorcan I reigned four (SL) or five (SB) years
- Gartnait VI reigned six and one-half (SL), six or five (SB) years
- Drusticc daughter of King Drust was contemporary to Finian of Moville and Abbot Ninnian

Powys

- Beuno was a contemporary of Cadfan and his son Cadwallon, Mawan, Cynan Garwyn, Tysilio, Brochmael, Selyf and his sons
- Cynan Garwyn was a contemporary of Beuno, Aircol, and Tydecho
- Dingad son of Cynan Garwyn was present at Arfderydd
- Llemineg son of Mawan and brother of Brochmael was a contemporary of Cynddylan
- Brochmael was a brother of Llemineg and the father of Tysilio; present at the Battle of Chester; Meic was the father of Avan
- Iago was husband to Haiarme and ruled for two years after Brochmael; Haiarme succeeded him
- Teilo was contemporary to Samson, Ismael, and Budic
- Cynddylan was a son of Cyndrwyn and was contemporary to Llemineg and Eluan

Rheged

- Ciaran of Saigir preached before Patrick
- Arthur was the son of Uthr father of Madog father of Eliwlod and the father of Amr and Llacheu; a contemporary of Drutwas and Gildas
- Urien was the son of Cynfarch, brother of Efrddyl, cousin of Llywarch, and father of Owain, Pasgen, and Elphin; he was the paternal uncle of Gwên and Pyll through Llywarch and the contemporary of Rhydderch, Morgant, Gwallog, Theodric, Hussa, Elgno Hen, Unhwch, Dunawd, Brân, and the bard Tristfadd; Dunawd and Brân outlived him
- Owain and Pasgen were contemporaries to Dunawd son of Pabo
- Owain married Penarwan and had a bard Dygynnelw
- Elphin was contemporary to Gwallog

Rheinwg

- Dwg a king

Selgouia

- Dreon was a son of Nudd. He fought at Arfderydd
- Nudd Hael was a son of Senyllt; he was contemporary to Rhun son of Maelgwn, Elidyr Mwynfawr, Clydno, Mordaf Hael, and Rhydderch

Strathclyde

- Enda was contemporary to Kebi son of Saloman, Maucanus, Pope Hilary, Docco, Finian of Clonard, and King Corbanus
- Ethni Wyddeles was the daughter of King Eochu and wife to Tudwal
- Uinniau moved to Whithorn and interacted with Tudwal
- Finian of Moville was a fellow pupil of Ninnian with Drusticc daughter of King Drust; he was contemporary to Pope Pelasgius, Columba, and Gildas
- Rhydderch Hael was father to Angharat Ton Velen. He was contemporary to Aedan, Kentigern, Constantine, Rhun son of Maelgwn, Elidyr Mwynfawr, Clydno, Nudd Hael, Mordaf Hael, and Theodric

Sussex

- Æthelwald a ruler in 660 (*Anglo-Saxon Chronicle*)

Tegeingl

- Wenefred was the daughter of Teuyth; she was contemporary to Beuno, King Cadfan, and Caradoc son of Alauc

Vannetais

- Waroc was the father of Trifina and contemporary of Gwenael and Ninnoca
- Ninnoca was a contemporary of Waroc, Morhed, Gurgallonus, and Ilfin
- Budic was contemporary to Teilo
- Cunomorus married Trifina and was a contemporary of Melorius and Goueznau the successor of Houardon
- Melorius was the son of Meliau son of Budic, a nephew of Rivoldius and a contemporary of Cunomorus and Malo
- Oudoceus was contemporary to Gildas; he, Mauricus, and Theodoric were the sons of Budic son of Cybr Daniel
- Meven son of Gerascenus was taught by Samson and was contemporary to King Cadvenus of Gueroc and Iudicael

Wessex

- Cuthwine and Ceawlin fought at Durham in 577 (*Anglo-Saxon Chronicle*)
- Ceawlin and Cutha fought at Fethanleag and Cutha died in 584 (*Anglo-Saxon Chronicle*)

- Ceol(ric) reigned four or five years from 591 (*Anglo-Saxon Chronicle*)
- Ceawlin was expelled in 592 (*Anglo-Saxon Chronicle*)
- Ceawlin, Cwichelm, and Crida died in 593 (*Anglo-Saxon Chronicle*)
- Ceolwulf son of Cutha succeeded in 597 (*Anglo-Saxon Chronicle*)
- Ceolwulf fought the South Saxons in 607 (*Anglo-Saxon Chronicle*)
- Cynegils son of Ceol son of Cutha succeeded in 611 and ruled for 31 years (*Anglo-Saxon Chronicle*)
- Cynegils and Cwichelm fought at Beandun in 614 (*Anglo-Saxon Chronicle*)
- Cynegils and Cwichelm fought at Cirencester in 628 (*Anglo-Saxon Chronicle*)
- Cynegils was baptized and Oswald was the sponsor in 635 (*Anglo-Saxon Chronicle*)
- Cwichelm was baptized and died in 636 (*Anglo-Saxon Chronicle*)
- Cuthred son of Cwichelm son of Cynegils was baptized in 639 (*Anglo-Saxon Chronicle*)
- Cenwalh succeeded and ruled for twenty-one years from 641 or thirty from 643 (*Anglo-Saxon Chronicle*)
- Cenwalh gave Cuthred or Eadred land in 648 (*Anglo-Saxon Chronicle*)
- Cenwalh fought at Posentesburh, Cuthred son of Cwichelm and Coenberht died in 660 (*Anglo-Saxon Chronicle*)
- Cenwalh died in 672, his wife Seaxburh ruled for one year (*Anglo-Saxon Chronicle*)
- Æscwine son of Cenfus son of Cenfrith succeeded in 674 (*Anglo-Saxon Chronicle*)
- Æscwine died and was succeeded by Centwine son of Cynegils son of Ceolwulf in 676 (*Anglo-Saxon Chronicle*)
- Centwine drove the Welsh into the sea in 682 (*Anglo-Saxon Chronicle*)
- Cædwalla son of Coenberht son of Cadda son of Cutha son of Ceawlin contended for the kingdom in 685 (*Anglo-Saxon Chronicle*)
- Cædwalla and Mul attacked Kent and Wight in 686 (*Anglo-Saxon Chronicle*)
- Cædwalla abdicated and Ine son of Cenred son of Ceolwald son of Cuthwine succeeded and ruled for thirty-seven years in 688 (*Anglo-Saxon Chronicle*)
- Ingeld and Cuthburh died (*Anglo-Saxon Chronicle*)

Et Cetera

- Hueil and Gildas sons of Caw were contemporary to Oudoceus, Gradlon, and Childeric; Gildas was taught by Illtud and was a pupil with Samson and Paul Aurelian; Brendan of Clonfert was alive when Gildas died
- Childebert was contemporary to Conocan, Leonorus, Deroch, Samson, Cunomorus, and Jonas
- Gwalchmei was a son of Gwyar
- Ailbe baptized both David and Samson, he was contemporary to Scanlan
- Eliffer was the father of Peredur, Gwrgi, and Ardun
- Elgno Hen was contemporary to Urien
- Mordaf Hael son of Serwan was contemporary to Rhun son of Maelgwn, Elidyr Mwynfawr, Clydno, Nudd Hael, and Rhydderch Hael
- Senacus of Anelog, an ecclesiastic, has a tombstone dating 500–570; he was born 420x552

19

Chief Interactive Peoples

The previous chapters have exhaustively listed nearly all of the individuals named in the most reliable source material for the period. However, they are of little use independently, providing only scattered dates and unusably wide birth ranges. What follows is a list of those individuals who interacted with the largest quantity of people. The results should produce more narrow birth ranges. The author has begun with those individuals who make the largest impact on the study, and has employed their results in the rest of the study.

First Group

Abbot David[1]: He was a contemporary of Constantine (466x520), Maucennus, Illtud, Cadoc, Uinniau (483x514, died 579x586), Teilo (515x575), and Kebi. Ailbe (died 527x542) baptized him, Gwistlian was a bishop in his youth, and David was taught by Paulinus of Cynwyl. Guadam died before he did. Thus David was born 465x512. Guadam was dead by the end of 592, and possibly as early as 465; his birth range is thus 410x577. Cadoc, Maucennus, and Illtud must have been born 415x567. Kebi's birth range is established at 415x562, Gwistlian to 415x500, and Ailbe to 447x512. Teilo is altered to 515x562, Paulinus at 415x500, and Uinniau and Constantine are unaffected.

Abbot Illtud: He was a contemporary of Dubricius (490x550), Cadoc, Riwal, Merchiaun of Glywising. Illtud was the teacher of Samson (474x530), Leonorus (507x508–561), Paul Aurelian, and Gildas (478x491). To be teacher to his three relatively dated pupils, he must have been born in the range 450x477. Samson is then reduced to 474x525, and Paul Aurelian must have been born in the range 457x525. Riwal and Merchiaun would have been born 425x552 and Cadoc and Brioc in 400x527. As Dubricius always appears as a bishop, he would be limited to 490x496.

King Childebert (ruling 511–558): He was contemporary to Conocan, Leonorus (507x508–561), Deroch, Samson (474x530), Cunomorus (489x536), Withur, and Jonas (444x593). Conocan was born in the range 431x528, while Jonas, Deroch, and Withur were born 456x543. Subsequently, Iudwal father of Jonas dates to 438x505.

Bishop Gildas (478x491, died in 569x572): Maelgwn (488x554), Vortipor, Constantine, Aurelius Caninus, and Cuneglasus were kings when he was forty-three. He was contemporary to Uinniau (483x514, died 579x586), Paul Aurelian, Oudoceus (531x582), and Arthur (420x510) as a bishop and Illtud as a student. He interacted with Cunomorus (489x536) and Trifina (553x575) in his later years. Vortipor, Constantine, Aurelius, and Cuneglasus were then ruling in 521x535, and were thus born 466x520. Maelgwn would be modified to 488x520 and Arthur to 453x510. Paul Aurelian would have been born 458x542. Oudoceus is modified to 531x542 and Trifina to 553x557. Uinniau and Illtud are unchanged.

Abbot Leonorus: He died in 561, aged 53, thus born 507/8. Leonorus was a pupil of Illtud, and contemporary to Riwal and Childebert (ruling 511–558). He died just after the defeat of Cunomorus (489x536) and the restoration of Iudwal. With these notes in mind and assuming that the relative chronology here is not perfectly accurate, Riwal was born in the range could not have been born in 482x546. For Iudwal, the limits are 482x505, while Cunomorus is unaltered.

Second Group

Bishop Aedan: Died in 651, the same year Boisil (605x655) and Eata (608x634) were priests, Sigfrith was a youth, and Cuthbert (607x655) was seven. He ruled 635–651. Thus Boisil and Eata were born 605x633 and 608x633 on this information, Sigfrith in the range 634x646, and Cuthbert in 643x644. Aedan was born 571x605.

Bishop Æthelwine: Bishop of Lindsey (680–692), and was therefore born in 612x650. He was brother to Æthelhild, Æthelhun, and Ealdwine. Æthelhild was contemporary to Osyth (621x661), and Ealdwine was Abbot of Partney. This information ranges Æthelwine's siblings to 592x670.

Bishop Agricola: He was the son of Severianus and a bishop during Germanus' visit in 429x448. This means he must have been born in 349x418, and his father in 311x400.

King Aldfrith (650): His succession took place in 685, and the priest Herefrith, the Abbot Cudda, and Abbess Verca were all active in that year. His death was contemporary to Æthelberg and Ælfflaed's abbacy. Thus Herefrith was born 605x667, and Cudda and Verca in 605x655. Hereberht died within a year of his accession to a bishopric, thus 685x686. Therefore Hereberht was born in 605x656. Eadberht was made bishop in 686 and ruled till 697. He was thus born 617x656.

Dux Ambrosius: He was active before Badon (478x491)[2] and was contemporary to Guitolin. Ambrosius would have been born in 423x476, and Guitolin in 383x516.

Bishop Arthmael: He was a student of Carincinalis and contemporary to Childebert (ruled 511–558), Cunomorus (489x536), Samson (474x525), Jonas (456x543), and his father Iudwal (482x505). Arthmael was then born 431x528 and Carincinalis 356x521.

King Arthur (453x510): He was a contemporary to Drutwas, Hueil, Gildas (478x491), Medrawt, Gwynlliw (450x643), Tallwch, and his son Drust. Arthur's date range is unchanged, while Hueil would be 458x511, and Medrawt and Drutwas 413x550, Tallwch would be 413x532, Gwynlliw 450x550, and Drust 431x550.

Abbot Benedict (601x649, ruled 674–681/5): He began his rule in Ecgfrith's (670–685) fourth year, so 673/4, ruled sixteen years and died three years after Ecgfrith (688/9) at the same time as Sigfrith. Thus Benedict died in 689 and his abbacy was from 674 to 689. He was born 609x649. It is also known that Sigfrith ruled for three years and Eosterwine was an abbot at some point between Ecgfrith's fourth year and Benedict's death, and died at 36. Thus Sigfrith ruled from 685/686 to 689 and was born in 605x661, while Eosterwine was an abbot 673x689–677x693 and was born 636x653.

Bishop Beuno: He was contemporary to King Cadfan (540x601) and Cadwallon

(578x619, died 634) of Gwynedd, Tysilio (519x603), Cynan Garwyn (510x583), Selyf (548x601) and Dona (555x659), Brochmael (501x565), Ynyr Gwent, Idon, Mawan (501x585), Wenefred, and Caradoc son of Alauc. The above would date Beuno to 513x604. In turn, this would limit Caradoc to 506x669. It would establish a birth range of 488x669 for Ynyr Gwent, Idon, and Wenefred. Cadfan, Cadwallon, Selyf, Mawan, and Dona's birth ranges would remain unchanged.

Abbot Brioc (400x527): He was the son of Alclud and Cerpus, and was contemporary to Illtud (450x477), Conan of Padstow, and Riwal (482x546). He died at the age of ninety and in the same year as Riwal. He was thus born in 417x517, whereas Conan would range 375x582.

Abbot Cadoc (415x527): He was educated by Tatheus, Cainnech of Achad Bo (born 513x520, died 597x603), and Bachan. He was contemporary to Maelgwn (488x520), Maucennus (415x567), Illtud (450x477), Rhun son of Maelgwn (506x592), Gildas (478x491, dies 569x572), Uinniau (483x514, dies 579x586), Cunomorus (489x536), Petroc, David, (465x512), Enda, Etelic, Elli, Caradoc son of Ynyr, Sawyl, Rhain, Arthmail, Trifina (553x557), Machan, Mouric son of Enhinti, and Sanctanus. He taught Findbar of Llancarfan. The above contemporaries would limit Cadoc's birth range at 520x527, while his birth range places Tatheus and Bachan to 445x525 and the ecclesiastics Maucennus to 465x567, Enda and Petroc to 465x592. Illtud is limited to 465x477. Among the laymen Etelic, Elli, Caradoc son of Ynyr, Sawyl, Rhain, Arthmail, Machan, Mouric son of Enhinti, and Sanctanus could be assigned the rough birth range of 490x607. Findbar would date to 527x607. Trifina's birth range would remain unchanged at 553x557 and Maelgwn's at 488x520.

Abbot Ceolfrith (Jarrow and Wearmouth in 680, born 600x662): He was a monk at 18, a priest at 27, and ruled as an abbot for 8 years before Benedict died (689) and 27 years after. He died at the age of 74. Ceolfrith was also the brother of Cynefrith (died 669/670), who was already an abbot when he became a monk. Ceolfrith was thus an abbot from 680 to 716 and was born in 641x642. His brother was therefore born in 621x634. Ceolfrith was taught by Botulf, Abbot of Gilling, who was active at least until Ceolfrith was 27. Botulf would have been born in the range 588x635. Hwætberht was abbot for twelve years following Ceolfrith, meaning he was born 648x691.

Abbot Columba: (512, 521–563, came to Iona in 563, died in 598): In Iona he was contemporary to Brude (525x571), Macarius, and Baithene (554x604). Macarius was born 483x545. He would have been born in the range 466x568, and Baithene and Brude are unchanged.

King Cunomorus (489x536): He was contemporary to Samson (474x525), Columba at Iona (563–598), Gildas (478x91, dies 569x572), Childebert (ruled 511–558), Leonorus (507x508–561), Chanao (505x536–560), Macliau (513x539), Trifina (553x557), Cadoc (400x527), Iudwal (482x505), Albinus, Tudwal son of Pompa, Malo, Melorius (549x620), Goueznau, Hennin, and Gradlon's death. These modify Cunomorus to 513x536 and give Hennin, Melorius, and Gradlon a date range of 549x576, and Albinus, Malo, Tudwal, and Goueznau one of 448x561. Cunomorus also establishes Cadoc at 448x527 and modifies Trifina to 553x556.

Abbot Cuthbert: (643x644, abbot from 685 to 687). He taught Iwi son of Brano and Ægidia, meaning Iwi was born in 667x682.

King Cynan Garwyn (510x583): He was a contemporary of Beuno, Agricola, and Tydecho. Beuno and Tydecho would then date to 445x608 and Agricola to 470x623.

King Cynddylan (587x627): He was a contemporary of Penda (598x623–655), Llemineg (519x623), and Eluan and was present at Maserfelth (642). Llemineg is then modified to 547x623, and Eluan established at 547x667.

Abbot Docco: He was a contemporary to Peibio (514x515) and Enda, and was taught by Kebi (415x562). This would place him at 464x545 and Enda at 414x595. Kebi would date to 415x538.

King Ecgfrith ruled 670–685: His rule was contemporary of Beorhæth, who would date to 615x670.

King Edwin (587x598, ruled 616–633): Married to Cwœnburh (589x598) during his exile, which means her birth range must be limited to 589x596 in order to have two children before 616. He married Æthelburh (587x596) after 616. Edwin was converted by Rhun (524x583) before 616. He was a contemporary to Bishop Paulinus (born 564x595, ruled 625–644), Bishop Felix (born 567x600, ruled 630–647), King Eadbald (born 585x596, ruling 625–640), King Cadwallon (born 578x619, ruling 633–634), an uncrowned Penda (598x623, ruling 633–655), King Cwichelm (571x621, ruling 626), King Cearl (571x580, ruling 626), King Eorpwald (590x622), Osric (578x624, died 634), and King Sigbert (590x628, ruling 633–635). Nothing may be gained from his contemporaries.

Abbot Enda: He was contemporary to Kebi son of Saloman (415x562), Docco, Uinniau (483x514, died 579x586), and King Corbanus. He was a student of Maucennus (412x536). He was born in the range 433x561. This means Corbanus was born in the range 408x626, Docco in 383x611. Uinniau and Kebi's date range are unaffected.

King Gradlon: He was a contemporary of Corentin, Winwaloe, and Gildas (478x491, died 569x572). Cunomorus (489x536) and Trifina (553x557) were alive on his death. Therefore he was active at some time after 517 and was dead by 591. He was therefore born 528x576, meaning Corentin and Winwaloe were born 463x591.

King Gwallog (520x580): He was a contemporary of Taliesin, Urien (486x565), Elphin, Morgan, and Rhydderch (537x580). This has no effect on his birth range. However, Taliesin, Elphin, and Morgan were born in 480x620.

King Gwrtheyrn (505x578, active 560x593): As has been shown above, his birth range of 505x578 provides Garmon with one of 440x577, and Benlli and Cadell with 465x618. The latter is modified with the genealogical data to 465x529.

Bishop Kentigern (474x519): He was present at the councils in 549 and 554x560. Kentigern was also contemporary to Rhydderch (547x580), Columba (563–598), and Morken. Together these tighten Kentigern's birth range to 483x519 and give Morken a range of 458x584.

King Maelgwn (488x520): He married Digwc, and was contemporary to Vortipor (466x520), Cuneglasus (466x520), Constantine (466x520), and Aurelius Caninus (466x520), Curig, Kebi (415x562), Maucennus (415x567), Paternus, Tydecho, Cadoc (415x527), Gerennius, and Gildas (478x491). Maelgwn's date range is unaffected. He modifies Maucennus to 415x550. Kebi, Paternus, and Tydecho are limited to 423x545. It gives Curig and Gerennius a range of 448x560. Cadoc is limited to 423x527. Vortipor, Cuneglasus, Constantine, and Aurelius Caninus are unchanged. His wife would range 468x540.

Bishop Malo: He was a cousin of Samson (474x525), and contemporary to Cunomorus (489x536), Iudicael (467x530), Meliau (531x582), Bishop Corentin, Melorius son of Meliau as a young boy (549x620), Hailoc son of Iudicael (485x568), and the hermits Domnech and Areon. He was the successor of Gurval. Thus Malo was born 470x561. His predecessor Gurval was born in 420x611, Corentin in 420x611, and the monks Domnech and Areon in 420x623. Iudicael, Maliau, Hailoc, and Meliau are unchanged.

Abbot Maucennus (415x567): He was Abbot of Rosnat and contemporary of Maelgwn (488x520), Cadoc (415x527), David (465x512), Tydecho, Elphin son of Gwyddno, Gwistlian (415x500), and Darerca. This reduces his birth range to 423x550. It establishes Elphin's birth year at 393x615, and Tydecho to 368x600, and Darerca to 368x605. Gwistlian, Cadoc, and David are unaffected.

Abbot Maudetus: He was contemporary to Childebert (ruling 511–558) and Deroch of Leon, and his disciples were Bothmael and Tudy. Maudetus was therefore born 431x528, Deroch in 401x593, and Bothmael and Tudy in 376x590.

Abbot Meven: He was the son of Gerascenus and contemporary of Iudicael (467x530), Samson (474x525), King Cadvennus, and Austolus. Meven then dates to 424x560, his father Gerascenus to 386x542, Cadvennus and Austolus to 394x625, and Samson is unchanged.

Abbess Modwenna: She was contemporary to Aldfrith (650, ruled 685–705), Osyth (621x661, active 691–709), and Ronan. Modwenna was then born 611x680, and Ronan 556x730. If Osyth did not live beyond eighty her range is reduced to 629x661.

King Morken/Morgant: He was contemporary to Urien (486x565), Rhydderch (547x580), Gwallog (520x580), Theodric (515x585), Kentigern (474x519), and Hussa. This places Morgant's birth year in 497x605, and Hussa's in 447x650.

Abbess Ninnoca: She was contemporary to Waroc (535x557), Morhed, Bishop of Vannes, Gurgallonus, Bishop of Vannes, and Elfin, Bishop of Vannes. She is also listed as the daughter of Brychan, sent from Ireland by Patrick, baptized by Columba, and taught by Garmon (440x577). This would make her the most distinguished ecclesiastic of her generation, and is therefore highly unlikely. The dates of those named make that a certainty. Patrick was born 413x443 and died in 493. Columba was active 563–598. Garmon belongs between the two. Clearly she cannot have been of importance in Britain for over half a century, so that her association with these churchmen can be discounted. We are left with her association to Waroc. This gives a range of 470x587 for her birth year. Morhed, Gurgallonus, and Elfin would have been born 415x637.

King Owain: (504x603) He was a son of Urien (486x565) and contemporary of Theodric (515x585), Dunawd, and Brân. He had a poet named Dygynnelw, and his wife Penarwan was the daughter of Culfanwyd. Dunawd and Brân would then range 464x643, Dygynnelw 467x640, and Penarwan 484x623.

Abbot Paternus: He ruled over Llanbadarn Fawr, son of Petronius and Guean, and contemporary to Samson (474x525), Maelgwn (488x520), David (465x512), Teilo (515x562), Caradoc son of Ynyr, Malo, Hewyn, and Bishop Cadfan of Bardsey. This puts him at 465x545, Malo and Cadfan at 415x595, and the disciple Hewyn at 415x607. Caradoc son of Ynyr was born in 440x610.

Bishop Paternus: His see included Cynwyl Gaeo, where he has a tombstone dated 500x550. He was a pupil of Kebi (415x562), and the teacher of David (465x512) and Teilo (515x562). Paternus would have been born between 420 and 520, Kebi in the range 415x520, and Teilo to 515x520. David is unaffected.

Bishop Paternus: His see was Avranches. He was present at the Council of Paris (556x573), and died at 83. He was thus born 472x543.

Bishop Patrick (413x443, died 493): He was contemporary to Ceredig (407x490), Macarius, Conindrus, Rumilius, and MacCuil. Ceredig is modified to 407x478, while Conindrus, Rumilius, and MacCuil would range from 367x475. Macarius falls in the range of 367x488.

Bishop Paul Aurelian (458x525): He was a son of Perphirius, contemporary of Childebert (ruling 511–558), Iudwal (482x505), Samson (474x525), Gildas (478x491), Cunomorus (489x536), Godian, and Withur (456x543). He was a pupil of Illtud (450x477). Paul Aurelian, Samson, and Withur are unchanged. Godian is made at 433x590.

Abbot Petroc: He was the son of Glywys, contemporary of King Theodoric, Cadoc (415x527), Samson (474x525), Wethonoc, Petrus, Dator, Dagan, and the hermit Guron. He baptized Constantine (466x520). Petroc was therefore born in 424x545, which establishes Theodoric at 399x610. Wethonoc, Petrus, Dator, Dagan, and Guron would have been born in the range 374x607.

Rhun: He was the son of Urien (486x565), baptized Edwin (587x598, dies 633), and was the grandfather of Rieinmellth (591x650) who married Oswiu (611x612, ruled 642–670). Rieinmellth would then be modified to 591x632.

King Rhydderch (547x580): He was the son of Tudwal and father of Angharat and Constantine. He was contemporary to Aedan (551x560, ruling 566x583–601x612), Kentigern (474x519), Theodric of Northumbria (515x585), Rhun son of Maelgwn (506x592), Elidyr Mwynfawr, Clydno, Nudd Hael, and Mordaf Hael. Elidyr, Clydno, Nudd, and Mordaf would then range 497x620.

King Riwal (482x546): He was a contemporary of Leonorus (507x508–561), Illtud (450x477), Winwaloe, Cunomorus (489x536), Cunomaglos, Ruilmus, Gwenael, and Fracan. He died in the same year as Brioc (400x527). This means he was born 482x542. Gwenael and Winwaloe would then date to 417x571, and Cunomaglos, Ruilmus, and Fracan to 442x586.

Abbot Samson (474x525): He was the son of Ammon and Anna, the nephew of Umbraphel, and cousin of Maglorius. He was present at the Council of Paris (554x560), and was a pupil of Illtud (450x477). He was a contemporary of Childebert (ruling 511–558), Maucennus (415x567), Iuniavus, Jonas (500x543), Iudwal (482x505), Kentigern (474x519), Petroc, Cunomorus (489x536), Teilo (515x562), Tysilio (519x603), Malo, Docco, comes Guedianus of Trigg, Comedianus, and Meven son of Gerascenus. Ailbe (died 527x542) baptized him and elderly Piro died when Samson was an adult in Britain. David was succeeded by Maglorius. From the above information, Samson's birth range is unaffected. It can also be determined that Maucennus was born 419x567, Petroc and Malo 419x575, and Docco 419x580. Iuniavus, Guedianus, Comedianus, and Meven have a birth range of 444x590. Piro must have died between 492 and 558, by which time Samson was dealing with Childebert. He was born 412x528. Samson's parents' birth range was 436x507x and his cousin one of 372x568.

Bishop Sona: He was present at the Seventh Council of Toledo (646). He was then born in 566x616.

Bishop Sosanus: He was active during the Eighth Council of Toledo (653), and was thus born in 573x623. His priest Matericus was born in the range 523x685.

Bard Taliesin: He was the father of Afaon, and contemporary to Cynan Garwyn (510x583), Urien as a white hair (486x565), and Gwallog (520x580). Together and assuming Urien would not have had white hair before thirty, these limit Taliesin's birth year to 480x575, and do not affect the other individuals.

Bishop Teilo (515x562): He was a contemporary of Budic (513x544), Ismael (531x582), Paternus of Llanbadarn Fawr, Samson (474x525), David (465x512), Guadam (410x577), and Gerennius. Teilo, Budic, David, Samson, and Ismael's birth year are unaffected by this information, but Paternus' would run 465x612, Guadam at 490x577, and Gerennius at 490x627.

King Theodoric of the South: He was contemporary to Teilo (515x562), Petroc (412x536), Cynan Colledauc (416x521), Fingar, Breaca, and King Germochus. Theodoric was born 530x586. Theodoric's range limits Petroc to 465x536 and Cynan Colledauc to 465x521, and gives Fingar and Breaca one of 465x636. Germochus was born 490x651.

Bishop Tydecho: He was the brother of Tegfedd, and contemporary of Dogfael, Cadfan of Bardsey, Maelgwn (488x520), and Cynan Garwyn (510x583). This means that Tydecho would date to 445x495, Tegfedd to 425x515 and Dogfael to 420x560. Cadfan was then born 395x545.

Abbot Tysilio (519x603): He was the son of Brochmael (501x565), and contemporary of Samson (474x525), Beuno, and Guimarchus. He was present at Maserfelth/Cocboy in 642. The above limits him to 562x575, Samson to 512x525, and gives Beuno a birth range of 512x625 and 557x640 for Guimarchus.

Abbot Uinniau (483x514, died 579x586): He was contemporary to Cadoc (415x527), David (465x512), Enda, Gildas (478x491, died 569x572), Gwynlliw (450x643), Bitheus, and Tudwal (519x562). He was the teacher of Drusticc son of Drust, and an old man when Columba went over to Iona in 563. Gwynlliw can be limited to 469x579 and Bitheus to 483x568, while Tudwal's birth range is unchanged. Cadoc is limited to 444x527 Enda is established at 444x556, and Drusticc at 506x579. Her father, possibly a Pictish king, would then date to 468x561. David's birth range is unaffected.

King Urien (486x565): He was the son of Cynfarch and father of Owain, Pasgen, Elfin, and Rhun, grandfather of Royth, and great-grandfather of Rieinmellth (591x650). He was contemporary to Hussa, Theodric (515x585), Rhydderch (547x580), Brân, Morgan, Gwallog (520x580), Elno Hen, Unhwch, and Dunawd. The above would date Urien to 497x565, and Hussa, Brân, Morgan, Elno Hen, Unhwch, and Dunawd would all range 457x605. Theodric, Rhydderch, and Gwallog are unaffected.

King Waroc (535x557): He was contemporary to Eunius Bishop of Vannes (498x549), Vidimael (532x573), Gwenael, and Ninnoca. This means that Ninnoca dates to 470x587 and Gwenael to 495x597. No one else is affected.

Abbess Wenefred: She was the daughter of Teuyth. She was contemporary to Beuno, King Cadfan (540x601), and was married to Caradoc son of Alauc. Wenefred must have been born 475x631, her husband in 455x651, and Beuno 475x626.

Bishop Wilfrid (633x634–709): He was fifteen or sixteen when Coenwalh was king, so that Coenwalh was ruling in the range 648x651. On one of his returns from the continent, Æthelred (621x641, r. 676–679) was ruling and his nephew Berhtwald was an adult. Centwine of Wessex (625x655) and Æthelwalh of Sussex (623x662, r. +678) were also ruling at that time. This means first that Wilfrid returned at or prior to 678. Æthelwalh was then born 624x671, Berhtwald in 622x673. Æthelwalh and Centwine are unaffected.

Forty years after he was made bishop in 664, Archbishop Berhtwald (612x662) was alive and active, thus limiting his birth range to 612x634. Wilfrid's return in 704x705 was contemporary to Bosa (+680+), John of Beverley (688–721), Badwini, Acca's priesthood, Coenred's rule (+709+), and Æthelred's retirement. His death was contemporary to abbots Tibba and Æbba and abbess Cynithryth, Ceolred of Mercia (648x691), and occurred at the same time Acca was made an abbot. This means that Bosa was ruling at least in the range of 680–704 and was therefore born in 624x654, while Badwini was born in 624x675. John of Beverley was born at or prior to 658 and at or after 641. This means Coenred's rule extended from at least 705 to 709 and his birth range was 654x700. Acca was born in 624x684. Tibba, Ebba, and Cynithryth belong in the range 624x680. Ceolred was ruling in 709, he was thus born 654x704.

Finally there are the Picts, perhaps the most enigmatic peoples of the British Isles. As has been seen, Pictland's kingdom had several versions of a king list, all with very much the same people in the same order. However, it is also clear that the list is a rather late one. An older version of Pictish history is to be found in *Historia Brittonum*, though it does not possess any of the interest in their kings that the native histories have. Leaving the mythological elements aside for a moment, one is left with a memory of seven independent Pictish kingdoms. This is in direct contrast to the official history, but does serve to explain information to be found in other sources. The Irish Annals list five men as Pictish kings who do not show up on the Pictish king lists. *Y Gododdin* names a Pictish king Gwyngwn who seems to have been independent as well. Both Caw and his son Hueil are stated in secondary sources as kings "above Bannawc," and seem to act without either supervision or protection. This gives us eight independent Pictish kings who are not to be found in the king lists.

Other clues are also present, if less obvious. When Adamnan speaks of Bridei, he never calls him *the* king of the Picts, only a king. The Irish Annals treat him in the same manner, even though he was by far the strongest Pictish king during the period under study. As with the Dalriadic kings, it appears that the oldest sources did not explicitly state that there were several independent kingdoms which were all Pictish. Later, when the process of nationalization became necessary with the unification of the kingdom some time before 843, a king list was drawn up. The official historian who did it likely made contemporary kings of the various regions appear to rule sequentially, though he was wise enough to make use of the Irish Annals as far back as they extended. However, by that time the rulers before Bridei were beyond the purview of contemporary Irish records. Even into the historical records, there are discrepancies. When one compares the king lists with the annal obits, one sees that well into the historical period there is evidence of more than one Pictish kingship. Eliminating the obvious scribal errors and making use of the previous chapters, we have:

- Drest I reigned 100 years, Patrick arrived in his nineteenth year (SL, SB), died in 449
- Talorc II reigned four (SL) or two (SB) years
- Nechtan I reigned twenty-four (SL) or ten (SB) years, founded Abernethy in his fourth year
- Drest II reigned thirty years (SL)
- Galam I reigned twelve years (SL1)
- Drest III and Drest IV reigned five years (SL1, SB)
- Drest III reigned eight years (SB), and Drest IV five or six of those and four alone (SB)
- Drest IV reigned five years (SL)
- Gartnait III reigned seven (SL) or six (SB) years
- Cailtram reigned one (SL) or six (SB) years
- Talorc III reigned eleven years (SL)
- Drest V reigned one year (SL)
- Galam II reigned four years with Bridei (SL2), died in 578 or 580 (rect. 576x582)
- Bridei I reigned thirty (SL) or nineteen (SB) years, died in 581 or 584 (rect. 579x586), ruling when Columba comes to Scotland
- Gartnait IV reigned eleven (SL) or twenty (SB) years, dies in 590 or 598 (rect. 587x601)
- Nechtan II reigned twenty (SL) and eleven or twenty-one (SB) years

19. Chief Interactive Peoples

- Ciniod I son of Lugthréine reigned nineteen (?) years (SL), died in 629, 631, or 633 (rect. 628x634)
- Gartnait V reigned four years (SL), died in 635 (rect. 632x638)
- Bridei II son of Gwid reigned five years (SL), died in 637 or 641 (rect. 636x642)
- Talorc IV son of Gwid reigned twelve (SL) or eleven (SB) years, died in 649 or 653 (rect. 648x654)
- Talorcan I reigned four (SL) or five (SB) years, died in 653 or 657 (rect. 652x658)
- Gartnait VI son of Gwid reigned six and one-half (SL), six or five (SB) years, died in 659 or 663 (rect. 658x664)

Assigning dates and counting backwards we have:

- Gartnait VI died in 658x664 after ruling five, six, or six and one-half years
- Talorcan I died in 652x658, after ruling four or five years
- Talorc IV died in 648x654, after ruling twelve or eleven years
- Bridei II died in 637x642, after ruling five years
- Gartnait V died in 632x637, after ruling four years
- Ciniod I died in 628x634, after ruling nineteen (?) years. This is a questionable length, and is incompatible with the date ranges furnished by the Irish Annals
- Nechtan II ruled for eleven, twenty, or twenty-one years. His unknown obit just before the awkward reign of Ciniod I makes deriving his reign haphazard
- Gartnait IV died in 590x597, after ruling eleven or twenty years
- Bridei I died in 579x586, after ruling eleven or twenty years
- Drest V ruled for one year. He then died in 558x575
- Talorc III ruled for eleven years. He then died in 546x564
- Cailtram ruled for one or six years. He then died in 539x563
- Gartnait III ruled for six or seven years. He then died in 531x557
- Drest IV ruled for five years. He then died in 525x552
- Drest III ruled for four years alone. He then died in 520x548
- Galam ruled for twelve years. He then died in 507x536
- Drest II ruled for thirty years. He then died in 476x506
- Nechtan I ruled for ten or twenty-four years. He then died in 451x496
- Talorc II ruled two or four years. He then died in 446x494 and took over in 441x492
- Drest I ruled for one hundred years and Patrick arrived in his nineteenth year. It is already known that Patrick was born no earlier than 413 and died in 493, and that the annals become highly suspect before the late sixth century. If Patrick was made a bishop no earlier than 30 years of age and was in Ireland at least long enough to train a pupil from earliest childhood into the priesthood, he could have gone to the island anywhere from 443x480, and so by deduction, Drest's rule would have begun in the range 424x462. This is not altered by the other reigns postulated above. However, Talorc's reign is modified by it, he assumed the throne in 443x462.

In addition to the official king list, the following have also emerged.

- Drusticc daughter of King Drust of the Picts was contemporary to Abbot Uinniau (499x514). She was born in 506x549, her father in 468x531. It is very possible that the Drust in question is Drest III, though this has been speculated nowhere and it is in no way a certain correlation

- Caw, born 440x473
- Hueil, born 458x511
- Grugyn of Lleu, born 15x55 years before Catraeth

533, 565 Aed Brecc dies
580 Kenneth
642, Lochyne son of Finnie
662, Moyle Keith son of Scanalt and Eochie Jarlaly

The last three entries are to be found in the Irish Annals. The fourth person is named in a contemporary piece of literature and the first, second, and third derive from native British traditions which may go back to their lifetimes.[3] All are addressed as kings and seem to act independently. Given what has been seen above regarding both Germanic and British kingdoms, it seems likely that the Picts also partook in interpolating major figures into the surviving royal pedigree. However, there is no direct evidence of this. As has been seen, Miller was able to work out a perfectly reasonable chronology for those kings of the historical era. It should also be noted that there is no discrepancy between the Irish annals and the Pictish king list about any king listed in both sources. For this reason, the latter would appear to be an accurate representation of the kings of one Pictish kingdom extending back to Bridei I, at least.

To sum up the labors of the chapter above, the redated characters above have been alphabetized and amalgamated into a digestable form.

Acca 624x684
Æthelhild 592x670
Æthelhun 592x670
Agricola bishop 349x418, active 448
Agricola king 470x623
Ailbe 447x512, d. 527x542
Albinus 448x561
Ambrosius 423x476
Areon 420x623
Arthmael 431x528
Arthur 453x510
Aurelius 466x520
Bachan 445x525
Badwini 624x675
Baithene 554x604, active 634
Benedict 609x649
Berhtwald 622x673
Archbishop Berhtwald 612x634
Benlli 465x618
Beuno 513x604
Bitheus 483x568
Boisil 605x633

Bosa 624x654, active 680–704
Bothmael 376x590
Botulf 588x635
Brân 464x605
Breaca 465x636
Brioc 417x517
Brochmael 501x565
Budic 513x544
Cadell 465x529
Cadfan 540x601
Cadfan B 415x545
Cadoc 520x527
Cadvennus 394x625
Cadwallon 578x619, d. 634
Caneutu 605x655
Caradoc son of Alauc 506x651
Caradoc son of Ynyr 490x607
Carincinalis 356x521
Ceawlin 542x584
Centwine 625x655
Ceolfrith 641x642

Ceredig 407x478
Clydno of Strat Clut 519x629
Clydno Eidyn 497x620
Ceolred 654x691
Cœnred 654x655
Comedianus 440x590
Conan 375x582
Conindrus 376x475
Conocan 431x528
K Constantine 466x520
Constantine of Strat Clut 585x598
Corbanus 408x626
Corentin 463x591
Cudda 605x655
Cuneglasus 466x520
Cunomaglos 442x586
Cunomorus 513x536
Curig 448x560
Cuthbert 643x644, A 685–687
Cynan Colledauc 465x521
Cynan Garwyn 510x583
Cynan 623x693

19. Chief Interactive Peoples

Cynefrith 621x634, d. 669x670
Cynithryth 624x680
Dagan 374x607
Darerca 368x605
Dator 374x607
David 465x512
Deroch 456x543
Digwc 468x540
Dingad 528x621
Docco 464x545
Dogfael 420x560
Domnech 420x623
Dona 555x659
Drust son of Tallwch 431x550
Drust father of Drusticc 468x531
Drusticc 506x549
Drutwas 413x550
Dubricius 490x496
Dunawd 464x605
Dygynnelw 467x640
Eadberht 617x656, B 686–697
Ealdwine 592x670
Eata 608x633, B 664–688
Ebba 624x680
Elidyr Mwynfawr 497x620
Elli 490x607
Elno Hen 457x605
Elphin 480x615
Eluan 547x667
Enda 465x556
Eorpwald 590x622
Eosterwine 636x653, A 673x689–677x693
Etelic 490x607
Eunius 498x549
Findbar 527x607
Fingar 465x636
Fracan 442x586
Garmon 440x577
Gerennius 490x560
Germochus 490x651
Gildas 478x491

Godian 433x590
Goueznau 448x561
Gradlon 528x576
Guadam 490x577
Guedianus 444x590
Guimarchus 557x640
Guitolin 383x516
Gurgallonus 415x637
Guron 374x607
Gurval 420x611
Gwallog 520x580
Gwenael 495x571
Gwistlian 444x560
Gwrtheyrn 505x580
Gwynlliw 469x550
Hailoc 485x568
Hennin 468x576
Hereberht 605x656
Herefrith 605x667
Honorius 575x583, r. 601x655
Hueil 458x511
Hussa 520x580
Hwætberht 648x691
Idon 488x669
Illtud 465x477
Ismael 531x582
Iudicael 467x530
Iudwal 482x505
Iuniavus 444x590
Iwi 667x682
John of Beverley 641x658, r. 688–721
Jonas 500x543
Kebi 423x520
Kentigern 483x519
Llemineg 547x623
Macarius 483x488
MacCuil 376x475
Machan 490x607
Maelgwn 488x520
Maglorius 472x568
Malo 488x561
Matericus 523x685
Maucennus 465x550
Maudetus 431x528
Mawan 501x585

Medrawt 413x550
Melorius 549x576
Merchiaun 425x552
Meven 444x560
Modwenna 611x680
Mordaf Hael 497x620
Morgan son of Gwrgan 615x628
Morgan son of Athrwys 660x672
Morgan 497x605
Mouric son of Enhinti 490x607
Ninnoca 470x587
Nudd Hael 497x620
Osyth 629x661
Oudoceus 531x542
Paternus A 472x543
Paternus C 420x520
Paternus Ll 465x545
Paul Aurelian 458x525
B Paulinus 564x595, 635–594
Paulinus of Cynwyl 415x500
Peibio 514x515
Penarwan 484x623
Petroc 465x536
Petrus 374x607
Piro 492x558
Rhain 490x607
Rhydderch Hael 547x580
Rieinmellth 591x632
Riwal 482x542
Ronan 556x730
Ruilmus 442x586
Rumilius 367x475
Samson 512x525
Sanctanus 490x607
Sawyl 490x607
Selyf 548x601, 603x616
Senacus 420x552
Sigfrith 634x646, 685/686x689
Sona 566x616
Sosanus 573x623
Taliesin 480x575

Tallwch 413x532
Tatheus 445x525
Tegfedd 425x515
Teilo 515x520
Theodoric Arch 601/2
  658–690
Theodoric of the South
  530x586
Theodric 515x585
Tibba 624x680
Trifina 553x556
Tudwal of Strat Clut
  519x562
Tudwal son of Pompa
  448x561
Tudy 376x590
Tydecho 445x495
Tysilio 562x575
Uinniau 499x514, d.
  579x586
Unhwch 457x605
Urien 497x565
Verca 605x655
Vortipor 466x520
Waroc 535x557
Wenefred 488x631
Wethonoc 374x607
Winwaloe 463x571
Withur 456x543
Ynyr Gwent 488x669

Making use of the conglomerated information date ranges listed above, the same procedure should produce much more refined results.

Bishop Arthmael (431x528): He was a student of Carincinalis (356x521) and contemporary to Childebert (ruled 511–558), Cunomorus (513x536), Samson (512x525), Jonas (500x543), and Iudwal (482x505). He would have been born in 457x528 and his teacher Carincinalis would have been born in 382x521.

Austolus, Bishop of Guerec: He was contemporary to Meven (444x560) and Samson (512x525). Austolus was then born 457x575.

Bishop Bernacus: He was a contemporary to Maelgwn (488x520) and a monk, Thelych of Cornovia. He was thus born 423x545, and Thelych 373x607.

Bishop Beuno (513x604): He was contemporary to Tangusius and the chieftain Temic son of Eliud, Cadfan (540x601 d. by 632) and Cadwallon (578x619, died 634) of Gwynedd (490x603), Cynan Garwyn (510x583), Selyf (548x601) and his son Dona (555x659), Brochmael (501x565), Ynyr Gwent (488x669), Idon (488x669), Mawan (501x585), Wenefred (488x631), and Caradoc son of Alauc (506x651). Beuno is then modified to 513x602. Tangusius and Temic are established at 488x669. The others are unaffected.

Abbess Breaca (465x626): She was contemporary to Theodoric (530x586), Crewenna, and Germochus (490x651). This means Breaca dates to 465x611 and Crewenna to 415x673.

Abbot Brioc (417x517): He was the son of Alclud and Cerpus, and contemporary to Illtud (465x477), Conan of the South (375x582), and Riwal (482x542). He died at the age of ninety in the same year as Riwal. This means that Brioc would date to 417x507 and Conan to 392x582.

Bishop Cadfan of Bardsey (415x545): He was a contemporary of Hewyn, Paternus of Llanbadarn Fawr (465x545), Tydecho (445x495), Corentin (463x591), David (465x512), and Mael. Cadfan's birth range is unaffected, but Hewyn and Mael were born in 365x607.

Bishop Corentin (463x591): His see at Cornouailles, he was contemporary to Gradlon (528x576), Winwaloe (463x571), Malo (488x561), and Tudy (376x590). This reduces Tudy's birth range to 413x590.

Culfanawyd: His name may be the patronym for Manaw, but he is named as the father of three women associated with otherwise known kings. Yseult was lover to Drust son of Tallwch (431x550). Penarwan (484x623) married Owain son of Urien (515x603). Bun married Fflamddwyn. Yseult then has a date range of 464x570, which alters Penarwan's to 484x590, this is also the maximum range for Bun. The sisters' birth years modify Drust to 444x550 and give Fflamddwyn, whoever he might be, a birth range of 464x610. Culfanawyd was then born 446x552.

Archbishop David (465x512): Ailbe (447x512, died 527x542) baptized him, he was taught by Paulinus of Cynwyl (415x500), and Gwistlian (444x560) was a bishop in his youth. He was a contemporary of Constantine (466x520), Maucennus (465x550), Illtud (465x477), Cadoc (520x527), Uinniau (499x514, d. 579x586), Teilo (515x520), and Kebi (423x520). Guadam (490x577) died before he did. This does not affect David—however, it does affect Gwistlian. His birth range is modified to 444x524.

Abbot Enda (465x556): He was a student of Maucennus (465x550). He was contemporary to Kebi son of Saloman (423x520), Docco (464x545), Uinniau (499x514), and King Corbanus (408x626). This does not affect Enda, but it modifies Maucennus to 465x549 and Corbanus to 440x621.

King Frithuwald married Osyth (629x661) and was father to Osgytha who married Sigehere (623x663). The former would put his birth range at 609x681 while the latter would put his daughter at 603x683. Thus Osgytha was born 627x683 which means Frithuwald was born 609x665.

King Gradlon (528x576): He was a contemporary of Corentin (463x591), Winwaloe (463x571), and Gildas (478x491, d. 569x572). Cunomorus (513x536) and Trifina (553x556) were alive on his death. He is modified to 551x556, Corentin to 471x581 and Winwaloe to 471x571.

Hoernbiu: He was contemporary to Iudwal (482x505), Maian son of Harvian a musician to Childebert (ruling 511–558), Rivannon, Houaron, and Comes Helenus nephew of Urfoal. Maian's connection to Childebert would range him 418x522. Hoernbiu was then born 442x545 which in turn would establish Rivannon, Houaron, and Helenus at 422x583. Harvian and Maian would have been born 456x540 and 422x522, respectively.

King Hussa (520x580): He was a contemporary of Morgan (497x605), Urien (497x565), Rhydderch (547x580), and Gwallog (520x580). Together this means that Hussa could not have been born before 507. His son Hering was present at Degsastan in 603, meaning he was born 548x588 and further modifying Hussa to 530x570.

Abbot Illtud (465x477): He was a contemporary of Dubricius (490x496), Cadoc (520x527), Riwal (482x542), Brioc (417x517), and Merchiaun of Glywising (425x552). He taught Samson (512x525), Leonorus (507x508–561), Paul Aurelian (458x525), and Gildas (478x491). The above has no impact on Illtud, but Merchiaun is altered to 435x542 and Paul Aurelian to 472x525.

King Maelgwn (488x520): He married Digwc (468x540), and was contemporary to Vortipor (466x520), Cuneglasus (466x520), Constantine (466x520), and Aurelius Caninus (466x520), Curig (448x560), Kebi (423x520), Maucennus (465x550), Paternus of Llanbadarn (465x545), Tydecho (445x495), Cadoc (520x527), Gerennius (490x560), and Gildas (478x491, d. 569x572). This alters Maelgwn to 490x520, Digwc to 470x540, Curig to 450x557, and Kebi to 425x520.

Abbot Maucennus (465x550): The leader at Rosnat and contemporary of Maelgwn (488x520), Cadoc (520x527), David (465x512), Tydecho (445x495), Elphin son of Gwyddno (480x615), Gwistlian (444x560), and Darerca (368x605). This reduces Darerca to 410x605.

Bishop Maudetus (431x528): He was contemporary to Childebert (ruling 511–558) and Deroch of Leon (456x543). His disciples were Bothmael (376x590) and Tudy (376x590). Bothmael and Tudy are thereby reduced to 381x590.

Abbess Ninnoca (470x587): She was contemporary to Waroc (535x557), Morhed, Bishop of Vannes, Gurgallonus, Bishop of Vannes (415x637), and Elfin, Bishop of Vannes.

The above limits Ninnoca to 470x582, which means Morhed, Gurgallonus, and Elfin were born in 420x632.

Abbot Paternus (465x545): The leader at Llanbadarn Fawr was the son of Petronius and Guean, contemporary to Samson (512x525), Maelgwn (488x520), David (465x512), Teilo (515x520), Caradoc son of Ynyr (490x607), Malo (488x561), Cadfan of Bardsey (415x545), Ketinlau, Titechan, Guinnius, and Guppir. That means that Cadfan was born 485x545 and Ketinlau, Titechan, Guinnius, and Guppir were all born in 415x607.

Bishop Paul Aurelian (458x525): He was the son of Perphirius, contemporary of Childebert (ruling 511–558), Iudwal (482x505), Samson (512x525), Gildas (478x491), Cunomorus (513x536), Godian (433x590), and Withur (456x543). He was also a pupil of Illtud (465x477). This puts Paul Aurelian's birth range at 472x525, and narrows Godian to 447x590.

Abbot Petroc (465x536): He was son of Glywys (447x518), contemporary of King Theodoric (530x586), Cadoc (520x527), Samson (512x525), Wethonoc (374x607), Petrus (374x607), Dator (374x607), Dagan (374x607), and the hermit Guron (374x607). He baptized Constantine (466x520). Petroc modifies Wethonoc to 415x586 and Petrus, Dator, Dagan, and Guron to 415x598.

King Riwal (482x542): He was a contemporary of Brioc (417x517), Leonorus (507x508–561), Illtud (465x477), Winwaloe son of Fracan (463x571), Cunomorus (513x536), Cunomaglos (442x586), Ruilmus (442x586), Gwenael (495x571), and Fracan (442x586). He died in the same year as Brioc when the latter was ninety. Thus Riwal is unchanged. Winwaloe was born 463x571 and his father Fracan 442x554. Cunomaglos and Ruilmus were born 442x582.

Bishop Rochath: He was contemporary to Enda (465x556) and Kebi (423x520). He was therefore born in 415x570.

Abbot Samson (512x525): He was the son of Ammon and Anna, nephew of Umbraphel, cousin of his successor Maglorius (472x568). He was present at Council of Paris (554x560), a pupil of Illtud (465x477), and contemporary of Childebert (ruling 511–558), Maucennus (465x550), Iuniavus (444x590), Jonas (500x543), Iudwal (482x505), Kentigern (483x519), Petroc (465x536), Cunomorus (513x536), Teilo (515x520), Tysilio (562x575), Malo (488x561), Docco (464x545), comes Guedianus of Trigg (444x590), Comedianus (440x590), and Meven son of Gerascenus (444x560). Ailbe (447x512, d. 527x542) baptized him and Piro (492x558) died when Samson was an adult but still in Britain. With such a narrow birth range, Samson is unchanged. As his cousin, Maglorius' birth range must be 472x545. Piro died between 546 and 558, by which time Samson was dealing with Childebert. Piro was therefore born 492x533. Iuniavus can be limited to the range 477x590, and as Samson must have left for Gaul permanently by 558, Comedianus and Meven's birth ranges would date to 444x543, and 444x543, respectively.

Priest Sulgen: Along with Mael, he was contemporary to Cadfan (540x601). The two were then born 490x663.

Abbot Tatheus (445x525): He was contemporary to Caradoc son of Ynyr (490x607), Gwynlliw (469x550), and taught his son Cadoc (520x527). Gwynlliw must be modified to 482x509. These connections mean that Tatheus dates to 465x520. Caradoc is refined to 490x590.

Bishop Tudwal (448x561): He was present at the Council of Paris (554x560), and was a contemporary of Cunomorus (513x536), Samson (512x525), and Malo (488x561). He taught Lovenan. He was thus born in 474x530, and Lovenan in 449x605.

Bishop Tudy (376x590): He was contemporary to Corentin (463x591), and the student of Winwaloe (463x571) and Maudetus (431x528). Thus, Tudy would be modified to 413x590.

Abbot Tysilio (562x575): The son of Brochmael (501x565) was a contemporary of Samson (512x525) and Beuno (513x602), and was taught by Guimarchus (557x640). He was present at Maserfelth/Cocboy in 642. The above connections change Brochmael's birth range to 524x557 and Guimarchus to 557x630.

Abbess Winwaloe (463x571): He was contemporary to Maglos, Cunomaglos (442x586), Riwal (482x542), Corentin (463x591), Gwenael (495x571), Conocan (431x528), and Gradlon (528x576). This in no way alters Winwaloe, but does establish Maglos' birth range at 438x636.

The Battle of Ardferydd (573x579): The brothers Cadrod and Clydno (497x620), Peredur and Gwrgi, Dingad son of Cynan Garwyn (528x621), Gwenddoleu, Dreon, Dunawd (464x605), and Cynfelyn (501x564) were present and therefore were born 518x564. Dingad's birth ranges would be 528x564.

The Battle of Catraeth (576x620): Cynon son of Clydno of Aeron (537x667), Wolfstan probably of Berneich, Pobddelw, Grugyn of Gwyngwn, Tudfwlch son of Madian of Din Eidyn, Geraint of Argoed, Madawg of Elmet, and Gwanar of Pennawc were all at the battle. These were all then born 521x605. Accounting for the fall of Din Eidyn in 635x641, Wolfstan's son Yrfai and grandson Gorthen would range 539x608 and 557x626, respectively. This modifies Wolfstan to 521x590, though it does not alter the range for Catraeth and therefore has no impact on the date ranges of the other participants of the battle.

The above makes for the following birth ranges:

Acca 624x684
Æthelhild 592x670
Æthelhun 592x670
Agricola bishop 349x418, active 448
Agricola king 470x623
Ailbe 447x512, d. 527x542
Albinus 448x561
Ambrosius 423x476
Areon 420x623
Arthmael 457x528
Arthur 453x510
Aurelius Caninus 475x534
Austolus 457x575
Bachan 445x525
Badwini 624x675
Baithene 554x604, active 634
Benedict 609x649
Berhtwald 622x673
Archbishop Berhtwald 612x634

Benlli 465x618
Bernacus 423x545
Beuno 513x602
Bitheus 483x568
Boisil 605x633
Bosa 624x654, active 680–704
Bothmael 381x590
Botulf 588x635
Brân 464x605
Breaca 465x611
Brioc 417x507
Brochmael 524x557
Budic 513x544
Bun 484x590
Cadell 465x529
Cadfan 540x601
Cadfan B 485x545
Cadoc 520x527
Cadrod 518x564
Cadvennus 394x625
Cadwallon 578x619, d. 634

Caneutu 605x655
Caradoc son of Alauc 506x651
Caradoc Ynyr 490x590
Carincinalis 382x521
Ceawlin 542x584
Centwine 625x655
Ceolfrith 641x642
Ceredig 407x478
Clydno 518x564
Ceolred 654x691
Cœnred 654x655
Comedianus 440x543
Conan 392x582
Conindrus 376x475
Conocan 431x528
King Constantine 466x520
Constantine of Strat 585x598
Corbanus 440x621
Corentin 471x581

Crewenna 415x673
Culfanawyd 446x552
Cuneglasus 466x520
Cunomaglos 442x582
Cunomorus 513x536
Curig 450x557
Cuthbert 643x644, A 685–687
Cynan 623x693
Cynan Colledauc 465x521
Cynan Garwyn 510x583
Cynfelyn 501x564
Cynefrith 621x634, d. 669x670
Cynithryth 624x680
Cynon 537x605
Dagan 415x598
Darerca 410x605
Dator 415x598
David 465x512
Deroch 456x543
Digwc 470x540
Dingad 528x564
Docco 464x545
Dogfael 420x560
Domnech 420x623
Dona 555x659
Dreon 518x564
Drust son of Tallwch 444x550
Drust father of Drusticc 468x531
Drusticc 506x549
Drutwas 413x550
Dubricius 490x496
Dunawd 518x564
Dygynnelw 467x640
Eadberht 617x656, B 686–697
Ealdwine 592x670
Eata 608x633, B 664–688
Ebba 624x680
Elfin 420x632
Elidyr Mwynfawr 497x620
Elli 490x607
Elno Hen 457x605

Elphin 480x615
Eluan 547x667
Enda 501x556
Eorpwald 590x622
Eosterwine 636x653, A 673x689–677x693
Etelic 490x607
Eunius 498x549
Findbar 527x607
Fingar 465x636
Fflamddwyn 464x610
Fracan 442x554
Frithuwald 609x665
Garmon 440x577
Geraint 521x605
Gerennius 490x560
Germochus 490x651
Gildas 478x491
Godian 447x590
Gorthen 557x626
Goueznau 448x561
Gradlon 528x576
Grugyn 521x605
Guadam 490x577
Guedianus 444x543
Guimarchus 557x630
Guinnius 415x607
Guitolin 383x516
Guppir 415x607
Gurgallonus 420x632
Guron 415x598
Gurval 420x611
Gwallog 520x580
Gwanar 521x605
Gwenael 495x571
Gwenddoleu 518x564
Gwistlian 444x524
Gwrtheyrn 505x580
Gwynlliw 482x509
Hailoc 485x568
Helenus 422x583
Hennin 468x576
Hereberht 605x656
Herefrith 605x667
Hering 548x588
Hewyn 465x607
Hoernbiu 442x545

Honorius 575x583, r. 601x655
Houaron 422x583
Hueil 458x511
Hussa 530x570
Hwætberht 648x691
Idon 488x669
Illtud 465x477
Ismael 531x582
Iudicael 467x530
Iudwal 482x505
Iuniavus 477x590
Iwi 667x682
John of Beverley 641x658, r. 688–721
Jonas 500x543
Kebi 425x520
Kentigern 483x519
Ketinlau 415x607
Llemineg 547x623
Lovenan 449x605
Macarius 483x488
MacCuil 376x475
Machan 490x607
Madawg 521x605
Mael 490x607
Maelgwn 490x520
Maglorius 472x545
Maian 422x522
Mawan 501x545
Medrawt 413x550
Melorius 549x576
Merchiaun 435x542
Meven 444x543
Modwenna 611x680
Mordaf Hael 497x620
Morgan son of Gwrgan 615x628
Morgan son of Athrwys 660x672
Morgan 497x605
Morhed 420x632
Mouric son of Enhinti 490x607
Ninnoca 470x582
Nudd Hael 497x620
Osgytha 627x683

19. Chief Interactive Peoples

Osyth 629x661
Oudoceus 531x542
Paternus A 472x543
Paternus C 420x520
Paternus Ll 465x545
Paul Aurelian 472x525
B Paulinus North
   564x595, 635–594
Paulinus of Cynwyl
   415x500
Peibio 514x515
Penarwan 484x590
Petroc 465x536
Petrus 415x598
Piro 492x533
Pobddelw 521x605
Rhain 490x607
Rhydderch Hael 547x580
Rieinmellth 591x632
Rivannon 422x583
Riwal 482x542
Rochath 415x570
Ronan 556x730
Ruilmus 442x582
Rumilius 367x475
Samson 512x525
Sanctanus 490x607
Sawyl 490x607
Selyf 548x601, 603x616
Senacus 420x552
Sigfrith 634x646,
   685/686x689
Sona 566x616
Sosanus 573x623
Taliesin 480x575
Tallwch 413x532
Tangusius 488x669
Tatheus 465x520
Tegfedd 425x515
Teilo 515x520
Temic 488x669
Thelych 373x607
Theodoric Arch 601/2
   658–690
Theodoric of the South
   530x586
Theodric 515x585
Tibba 624x680
Titechan 415x607
Tudfwlch 521x605
Tudwal of Strat Clut
   519x562
Tudwal son of Pompa
   474x530
Tudy 413x590
Tydecho 445x495
Tysilio 562x575
Uinniau 499x514, d.
   579x586
Unhwch 457x605
Urien 497x565
Verca 605x655
Vortipor 466x520
Waroc 535x557
Wenefred 488x631
Wethonoc 415x586
Winwaloe 471x571
Withur 456x543
Wolfstan 521x590
Ynyr Gwent 488x669
Yrfai 539x608
Yseult 464x570

Along with this interrelated and derived information, other and more independent date-guessing is possible:

- Ailbe (447x512, died 527x542) was a contemporary of Scanlan, therefore Scanlan was born in 392x527.
- Eurgain (508x558) married Elidyr Mwynfawr (497x620), which limits Elidyr to 497x578.
- Ceredig of Elmet died in 616; he was therefore born 561x601.
- Enodoc was a bishop in the mid–sixth century, so he was born in 453x537.
- Daniel was a bishop before Comgall founded Irish Bangor in 558x564, thus he was born in the range 478x534.
- Bugi (475x584) was a contemporary of Ynyr Gwent (488x669), so Ynyr Gwent was born 488x624.
- Idon (488x669) was contemporary to Beuno (513x602) and Owain son of Urien (515x603). This would make Idon a product of 488x643.
- Meven son of Gerascenus (444x543) was contemporary to King Cadvenus of Gueroc and Iudicael (467x530). Cadvenus would have been born 427x550.
- Cadafael son of Cynfeddw ruled between Cadwallon (578x619) and Cadwaladr (596x657), and was on campaign in 655. Cadwallon died in 634, so the limits of his birth range are 600x619.
- King Godian (447x590) was contemporary to Goulven and lived after Paul Aurelian (472x525). Godian is modified to 452x590 and Goulven placed at 412x630.

- Justinian was a contemporary to Honorius king of the Thefriauci and confessor to David (465x512). He was therefore born 415x574, and Honorius in 378x639.
- Melyn son of Cynfelyn died at Chester (603x616), and so was born 548x601.
- Osyth (629x661, d. 709) was contemporary to Modwena, so Modwena was born 574x684.
- Æthelfrith (573x586) married Acha (573x584) and Bebbe. Bebbe would then date to 553x606.
- Cuthburh (651x703) married Aldfrith (650). Thus Cuthburh's birth range is restricted to 651x670.
- Æthelthryth (625x633) married Tondbert and Egfrith (645x646). Tondberht was thus born 605x653.
- Eadbald (585x596) married Ymme, who was thus born 565x616.
- Eormenred (603x634) married Oslafa, who was thus born 583x654.
- Eueilian (558x639) daughter of Cadfan married Gwydyr Drwm, and so was born 538x659.
- Gall was a contemporary of Gwenddoleu (518x564), his brother Diffydell killed Gwrgi (518x564), but was active before Bernicia and Deira united in 603x605. Gall is then dated to 478x604, and Diffydell 478x578.
- Cunomorus son of Drust died in the sixth century, and so was born in 445x584.

20

The Revised Celtic Genealogies

Cornouailles

Cybr Daniel: 475x506
Budic: 513x524
Mauricus: 531x562
Oudoceus: 531x536

Theuderic: 531x562
Meliau: 531x558
Ismael: 531x562
Melorius: 549x576

Elmet

Lleenog: 485x565
Gwallog: 523x583
Dwywei: 503x584

Cerdic: 561x601
Aneirin: 541x621

Gwynedd

Cunedda: 396x466
Einion Yrth: 434x484
Dunawd: 452x522
Owain: 452x529
Cadwallon: 472x502
Dingad: 470x560
Isaac: 470x560
Eifion: 470x560
Einion: 470x547
Cynlas: 475x547
Maelgwn: 490x520
Meurig: 488x598
Pobien: 488x587
Brochwel: 488x598
Cynlas: 488x565

Rhun: 528x558
Eurgain: 508x558
Bridei (Pictish king): 526x558
Pobddelw: 521x605
Eigion: 506x636
Iago: 506x583
Ieuanaul: 524x674
Cadfan: 544x601
Caradog: 542x712
Eueilian: 562x639
Cadwallon: 578x619
Bleiddud: 560x750
Cadwaladr: 596x657
Cuhelyn: 578x788

Lleuddinyawn

Lleudun: 427x483
Teneu: 445x501

Cynan Colledauc: 465x521
Kentigern: 483x519

Powys

Cadell: 465x529
Maig: 483x559
Cyngen: 486x539
Ieuaf: 483x559
Sanand: 504x577
Brochmael: 524x557
Mawan: 509x577
Cadell: 504x577
Tysilio: 562x575
Iago: 542x595
Cynan: 542x583
Llemineg: 547x623

Iddig: 522x615
Selyf: 560x584
Eiludd: 560x584
Tandreg: 560x584
Dingad: 560x564
Eli: 578x622
Temit: 578x622
Dona: 578x622
Gwylog: 596x660
Gwenfrewi: 596x660
Eliseg: 614x698

Tegid: 406x473
Glywys: 444x491
Petroc: 465x536
Gwynlliw: 482x509

Cadoc: 520x527
Bugi: 500x547
Beuno: 518x585

Alaogwr: 544x583
Cadfan: 562x601

Caradoc: 582x621
Cowryd: 580x639

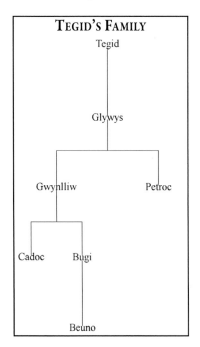
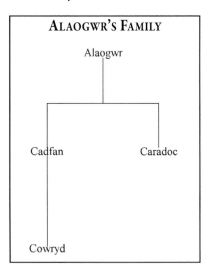

Left: The family tree of Tegid as constructed through the *vitae* as an independent house. *Right:* The descendants of Alaogwr as constructed from the source material

Rheged

Meirchion: 421x529
Cynfarch: 459x547
Elidyr: 439x567
Urien: 497x565
Efrddyl: 477x585
Llywarch: 457x605

Rhun: 524x583
Owain: 515x603
Pasgen: 515x603
Gwên: 475x643
Royth: 553x614
Rieinmellth: 591x632

Cornwall

Tudwal: 350x424
Kynwawr: 388x442
Constantine: 406x448
Drust: 426x468
Erbin: 424x466
Digain: 424x486
Cunomorus: 464x506
Dyfel: 442x504

Amlawdd 351x458
Cynyr: 389x476
Non: 427x494

Pabo Post Prydein: 499x546
Dunawd: 518x564

Geraint: 442x484
Ermid: 442x504
Saloman: 460x502
Iestyn: 460x522
Constantine: 466x520
Cyngar: 460x522
Cadwy: 460x522
Kebi: 478x520

Gwen: 407x514
David: 465x512

Sawyl: 517x584
David: 465x512

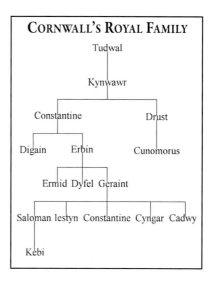

The lineage as constructable from all source materials

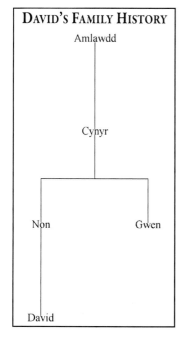

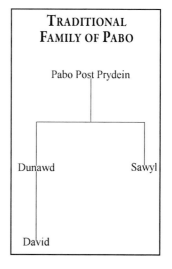

Left: The genealogical tradition for St. David. *Right:* Pabo Post Prydein's descendants independent of the greater northern tradition

The troublesome and late Pabo genealogy seems to mainly hang together with other information from primary sources. Early poems connect Dunawd to Urien's sons. The same genealogy calls Sanctanus (Sawyl) the contemporary of Matoc, grandson of Muiredach, who was an Irish king in the second quarter of the sixth century (Sanctanus rect. 517x535, Dunawd 518x555, Pabo 490x517). All this matches up nicely with the chronology adapted above. The only exception to this is David, whose birth range has been fairly well delineated in the chapter above. He will be excised from the genealogy from this point forward.

Dyfed

Eochaid Allmuir: 316x430
Corath: 334x448
Aed: 372x466
Tryffin: 410x484
Cyngar: 390x504
Agricola: 448x502
Vorteporix: 466x520
Cyngar: 484x558
Peter: 502x596
Arthur: 520x634

Nowy: 538x672
Gwlyddien: 556x688
Cathen: 589x706
Cadwgan: 627x724
Rhain: 665x742
Tewdws: 703x760
Tewdwr: 721x798
Maredudd: 741x778, d. 796
Owain: 759x797

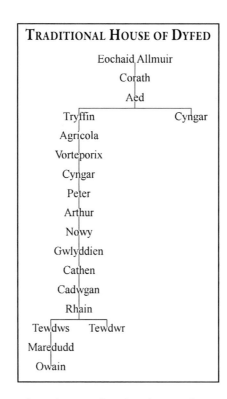

The pedigree as found in the genealogies

20. The Revised Celtic Genealogies

Triphun: 410x484
Aircol Lawhir: 448x502
Erbin: 428x522
Cynan Cylched: 428x514
Guortepir: 466x520
Triphun: 446x532
Cincar: 484x558
Drutwas: 464x550
Arthur: 502x596

Nougoy: 520x634
Cloten: 538x670
Cathen: 548x688
Catgocaun: 586x706
Petr: 624x724
Regin: 662x742
Teudas: 700x760
Margetuit: 738x778, d. 796
Owain: 756x797

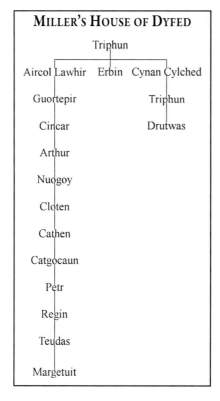

The traditional pedigree and the connecting ancestry of Drutwas

Tidlet: 316x468
Bwch Mawr: 334x506
Prawst: 374x524

Einion: 414x484
Cadwallon: 452x502
Maelgwn: 490x520

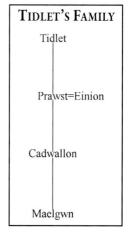

The pedigree of Maelgwn through the female line

Ceredig: 558x598
Usai: 576x636
Serwyl: 594x664
Boddw: 612x682
Arthfoddw: 630x700

Arthlwys: 648x718
Clydog: 673x756
Seissyll: 711x774
Arthen: 749x792

Father: 462x623
Gwedrog: 500x641
Nefydd: 480x661

Gwydyr the Heavy: 538x659
Braint the Tall: 498x699
St. Egryn: 556x697

Senyllt: 480x528
Nudd Hael: 498x566

Gwenddoleu: 518x546
Dreon: 536x564

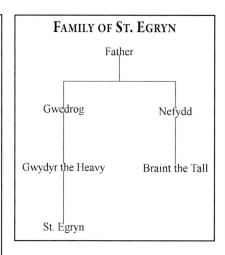

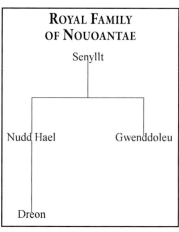

Left: The lineage of Ceredigion independent of Gwynedd. *Middle:* The date ranges of St. Egryn's family as recovered. *Right:* The lineage of Senyllt as found in the earliest sources

Meirionydd

Tybion: 346x516
Meirion: 384x534
Cadwaladr: 422x552
Gwrin Cutbeard: 460x570
Clydno: 498x588

Gwyddno: 536x606
Idris: 574x624, active 629x639
Sualda: 592x662
Brochwel: 610x700

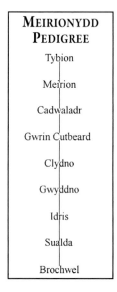

The lineage of Meirionydd independent of Gwynedd

20. The Revised Celtic Genealogies

Traditional Genealogies

Ymellyrn: 426x569
Cyngar: 459x587
Brân: 464x605
Morgan Bulc: 497x605

Pabo: 480x546
Dunawd: 518x564
Sawyl: 498x584

Eliffer: 484x543
Gwrgi: 522x561
Peredur: 522x561

Wolstan: 521x590
Yrfai: 539x608

Caradog: 482x643
Coleddog: 515x643
Morgan: 533x681

Guitcun: 516x622
Cadwallon: 534x660

Ardun: 502x581
Gwgon: 540x599
Cedwyn: 558x637

Gorthen: 557x626

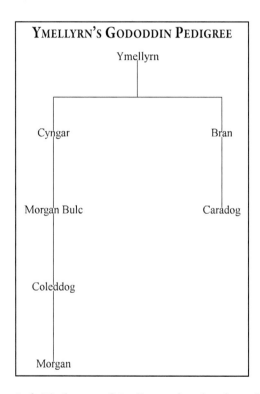

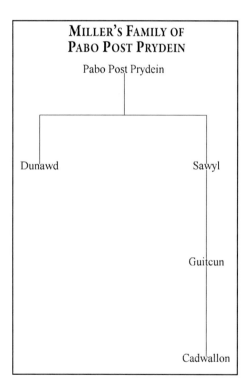

Left: The lineage of Ymellyrn as found in the traditional pedigrees. *Right:* The lineage of Pabo Post Prydein as found in the traditional pedigrees

190 Hengest, Gwrtheyrn and the Chronology of Post-Roman Britain

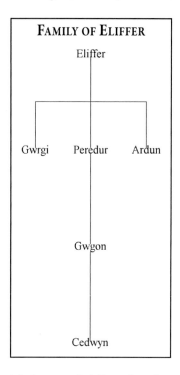

The lineage of Eliffer as found in *Trioedd Ynys Prydein*

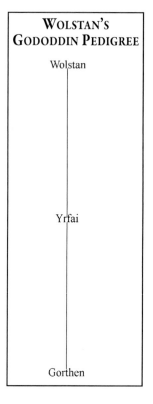

The lineage of Wolstan as found in *Y Gododdin*

Gerascenus: 406x525

Meven: 444x543

Gerascenus and Son

Geracenus
|
|
|
|
|
Meven

A royal family from the *vitae*

20. The Revised Celtic Genealogies

Gwrtheyrn: 505x580
Britu: 523x618
Pasgen: 523x618
Annan: 541x656
Briacat: 541x656

Maun: 559x694
Mepurit: 559x694
Pasgen: 577x732
Paul: 577x732

The lineage of Gwrtheyrn as found in the genealogical tradition

GWRTHEYRN'S POWYS PEDIGREE

```
                    Gwrtheyrn
                   /         \
                Britu        Pasgen
                  |            |
                Annan        Briacat
                  |            |
                 Maun        Mepurit
                  |            |
                Pasgen        Paul
```

Hussa: 530x570

Hering: 548x588

A royal Northumbrian family from the earliest sources

HUSSA AND SON

```
Hussa
  |
Hering
```

Father: 387x474   Eliwlod: 423x550
Uthr: 425x492   Amr: 471x548
Madog: 405x512   Llacheu: 471x548
Arthur: 453x510

ARTHUR'S FAMILY

```
            Father
           /      \
         Uthr    Madog
          |        |
        Arthur  Eliwlod
         / \
       Amr  Llacheu
```

The native traditions and Arthur's family

Seithuet: 402x455
Caw: 440x473
Watu: 420x493
Sinnoch: 420x493
Bedyw: 420x493
Hueil: 458x511
Gildas: 478x491

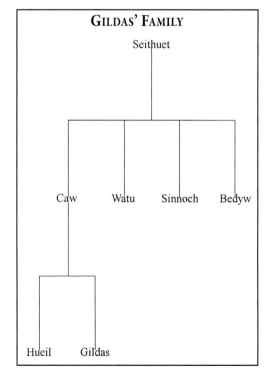

GILDAS' FAMILY

The royal family of Gildas from the *vitae* tradition

Ynyr: 452x522
Idon: 488x560

Goryon: 408x534
Culfanawyd: 446x552

Caradoc: 490x560
Digwc: 470x540

Penarwan: 484x590
Yseult: 464x570

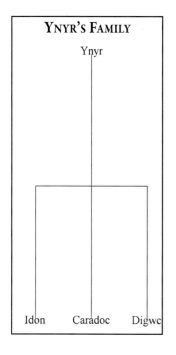

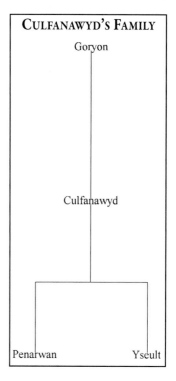

Left: The royal family of Ynyr from the *vitae* tradition. *Right:* The royal family of Culfanawyd from the *Trioedd Ynys Prydein*

Disgyfdawd: 440x560
Gall: 478x604

Ysgafnell: 458x598
Diffydell: 478x578

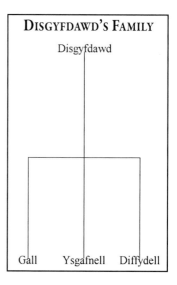

The royal family of Disgyfdawd from the *Trioedd Ynys Prydein*

Cynfelyn: 501x546
Clydno Eidyn: 518x564
Cadrod: 518x564
Cynon: 537x602
Eurneit: 536x602

Serwan: 459x602
Mordaf: 497x620

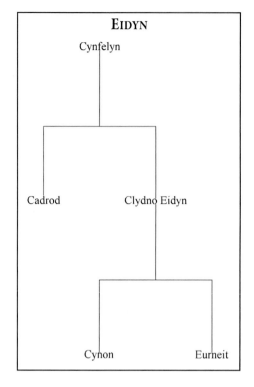
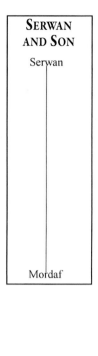

Left: The rulers of Eidyn from various sources. *Right:* A royal British family from the *vitae* tradition

Taliesin: 480x575
Afaon: 498x613

Teuyth: 524x608
Wenefred: 488x631

Drust: 468x531
Drusticc: 506x549

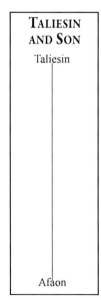
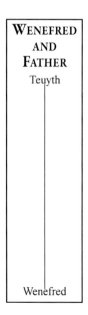
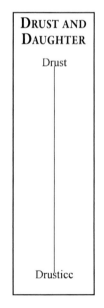

Left: A genealogical dating of the most famous British bard. *Middle:* A British saintly family from the *vitae* tradition. *Right:* A British royal family from the *vitae* tradition

20. The Revised Celtic Genealogies

Eneas Ledwic: 447x527

Clydwyn: 332x434
Clydog: 350x472
Gwledyr: 370x472
Dedyw: 350x472
Cyndwr: 368x510
Tryffin: 408x490
Cyngar: 368x510
Erbin: 386x548
Agricola: 446x508
Cynan: 426x514
Vorteporix: 466x520
Tryffin: 444x532
Cyngar: 484x558

Cadfan of Bardsey: 485x545

Drutwas: 462x550
Peter: 502x596
Arthur: 520x634
Nowy: 538x672
Gwlyddien: 556x710
Cathen: 574x748
Cadwgan: 592x586
Rhain: 627x624
Tewdws: 665x742
Tewdwr: 703x760
Maredudd: 741x778, d. 796/7
Owain: 759x796, d. 811

CADFAN AND FATHER

Eneas Ledwic
|
Cadfan of Bardsey

DYFED ROYAL FAMILY III

Clydwyn
├── Clydog ── Gwledyr ── Dedyw
├── Cyndwr ── Tryffin ── Cyngar
├── Erbin ── Agricola ── Cynan ── Cylched
│   Vorteporix ── Tryffin
              Cyngar
              Peter
              Arthur
              Nowy
              Gwlyddiien
              Cathen
              Cadwgan
              Rhain
         ┌────┴────┐
      Tewdws   Tewdwr
      Maredudd
      Owain

Left: A British saintly family from the *vitae* tradition. *Right:* Dyfed royal family with all likely branches

Father: 444x494
Riwal: 482x542

Fracan: 442x553
Wethonoc: 460x586

Romelius: 457x553

Pompa: 462x512
Tudwal: 490x530

Winwaloe: 471x571

Gwenael: 495x571

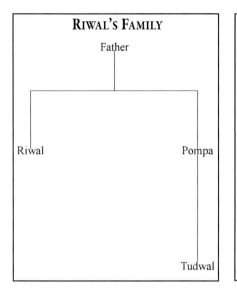
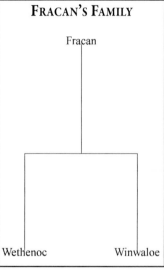

Left: Riwal's royal family as derived from the *vitae* tradition. *Middle:* Fracan's royal family as derived from the *vitae* tradition. *Right:* A Breton royal family from the *vitae* tradition

Perphirius: 434x507
Paul Aurelian: 472x525
Notolius: 452x545

Nwyfre: 445x569
Naf: 483x587

Potolius: 452x545
Sitofolla: 452x545

Gwenwynwyn: 501x625
Gwanar: 521x605

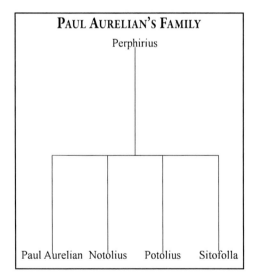
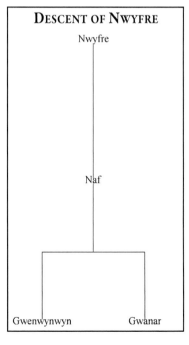

Left: A British saintly family from the *vitae* tradition. *Right:* The family of Nwyfre from the *Trioedd Ynys Prydein*

20. The Revised Celtic Genealogies 197

Medrawt: 413x550   Domnoc: 431x588

Tallwch: 413x532   Drust: 444x550

Meirchiaun: 435x542   March: 453x580

Gwyddno: 442x597   Elphin: 480x615

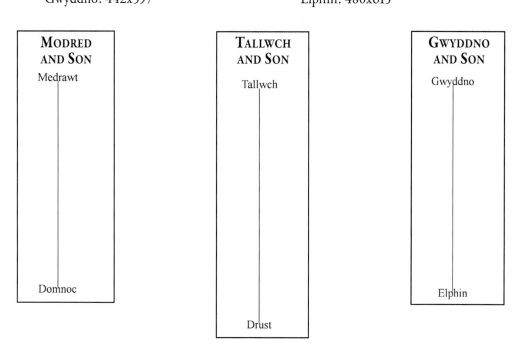

Left: Modred's birth range as derived from direct mention and local legends about his possible son. *Middle:* A British royal family from the *Trioedd Ynys Prydein*. *Right:* A British royal family from the *vitae* tradition

21

The Revised Germanic Genealogies

Frithuwald: 609x665

Father: 574x632
Æthelhild: 592x670
Æthelhun: 592x670

Osgytha: 627x683

Æthelwine: 612x650
Ealdwine: 592x670

THE REVISED GERMANIC GENAEOLOGIES FRITHUWALD AND DAUGHTER

Frithuwald
|
Osgytha

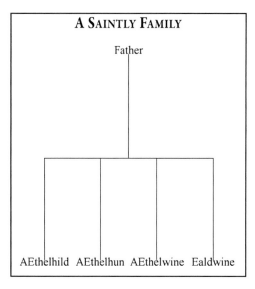

Left: A Germanic royal family from Bede and the *Historia Brittonum*. *Right:* Date-ranging several female ecclesiastics through their common father

Ida: 497x550
Æthelric: 535x568
Theodric: 515x585
Adda: 515x585
Æthelfrith: 573x586

Theodbald: 553x588
Second Generation: 553x605
Oswiu: 611x612
Æbbe: 591x622
Eanfrith: 591x604

198

21. The Revised Germanic Genealogies

Oswald: 603x604
Third Generation: 571x623
Aldfrith: 650
Ælfwine: 660x661
Ælfflæd: 654
Osthryth: 640x650
Alhfrith: 629x650

Egfrith: 645x646
Alhflæd: 629x641
Talorcan: 609x640
Œthelwald: 621x642
Fourth Generation: 589x641
Egbert: 618x659

East Anglia

Tyttla: 534x579
Rædwald: 572x604
Eni: 562x597
Ræganhere: 590x642
Eorpwald: 590x622
Sigbert: 590x628
Anna: 587x615
Æthelhere: 600x640
Æthelwald: 600x640
Æthelric: 587x620

Ricbert: 608x660
Seaxburh: 605x650
Æthelthryth: 625x633
Æthelburh: 605x653
Aldwulf: 625x658
Egbert: 631x680
Hlothere: 630x668
Eorcengota: 623x688
Eormenhild: 623x688

Mercia

Pybba: 580x605
Penda: 598x623
Eowa: 598x643
Cenwalh: 618x635
Wulfhere: 630x653
Cyneburh: 616x661
Osyth: 629x661
Æthelred: 621x641
Merewalh: 630x661
Peada: 616x641
Alweo: 616x681

Osmod: 616x681
Cundwalh: 654x691
Cenred: 656x691
Ceolred: 654x691
Ceolwald: 648x691
Mildrith: 639x699
Mildburh: 639x699
Aethelbald: 634x719
Headbert: 634x719
Eanulf: 634x719
Centwine: 672x729

Wessex

Cerdic: 397x561
Creoda: 435x579
Cynric: 473x516
Ceawlin: 519x543
Cuthulf: 511x534
Ceolwulf: 491x597
Cutha/Cuthwine: 557x561
Ceol(ric): 549x552

Ceolwulf: 549x552
Cuthgils: 509x615
Ceadda: 582x599
Cynebald: 562x599
(Cuthwulf): 575x599
Cynegils: 597x590
Cenferth: 545x619
Cenbert: 620x637

Æthelbald: 580x637
Ceolwold: 593x634
Cenwalh: 618x628
Cwichelm: 615x588
Centwine: 627x628
Cenfus: 583x637
Æscwine: 621x655
Cædwalla: 658x659

Ceawlin: 542x543
Cutha: 560x569
Cynegils: 580x602
Cuthwine: 560x598
Ceadda: 582x607
Cwichelm: 598x620
Cuthwulf: 578x616
Cynebald: 588x636
Cenberht: 620x641
Cuthred: 616x626
Ceolwold: 618x634

Cutha: 529x569
Ceolwulf: 552x592
Cuthgils: 570x615

Oswald: 598x675
Cenred: 633x652
Cuthred: 616x659
Cwoenburh: 651x690
Cuthburh: 651x670
Ine: 670x683
Ingild: 651x690

Osric: 560x674
Oswald: 560x674
Oshere: 560x674
Mul: 638x679
Cædwalla: 658x659
Cœnred: 632x652
Cwoenburh: 651x690
Cuthburh: 651x670
Ine: 671x683
Ingild: 651x690

Cenfrith: 588x633
Cenfus: 606x651
Æscwine: 624x669

22

The Ecclesiastics

The past several chapters have refined the birth ranges of many laymen and ecclesiastics as closely as is currently possible. It remains now to add in those churchmen who have more limited associations. These have been listed below, along with their associations and resulting birth ranges:

- The bishop Cynidr was a contemporary of Bishop Maedoc and Cadoc (520x527), so he was born 470x577, while Maedoc would range 420x627.
- Elwyn was a contemporary to Hia and Bishop Breaca (465x611) as they traveled to Cornwall. Elwyn and Hia were then born 433x673.
- Ethbin was a contemporary of Samson (512x525) and Winwaloe (471x571). This means Ethbin was born 457x587.
- Fingar (465x636) was contemporary to Theoderic (530x586), Hia, Findbar of Llancarfan (527x607), Breaca (465x611), and Abbot Senan. Thus Fingar and Breaca were born 477x611, giving Senan a range of 427x661 and Hia one of 415x673.
- Finian of Llancarfan was contemporary to Gildas (478x491), Gwynlliw (482x509), Cadoc (520x527), David (465x512), MacMoil, Abbot Gnouan, Elli as a youth (490x607), and Cathmael. Thus Finian was born 465x534, MacMoil and Cathmael in 410x596, Gnouan in 410x589.
- The priest Fintan was a contemporary of Docco (464x545), Kebi (425x520), and Enda (501x556). He was thus born 451x582.
- The priest Gonerus was contemporary to Bishop Tudwal (490x530) and both were contemporary to a landowner, Alvandus. Gonerus was then born 450x592 and Alvandus 429x595.
- Goulven, Bishop of Leon, was a successor of Paul Aurelian (472x525), and contemporary of Godian (452x590). He was thus born 422x575.

23

The Other Figures and a Sequence of Historical Events

The above chapters should have gone a long way towards establishing not only the individual chronologies of the period's significant persons, but in giving a better feel for the broader chronology as well. Unfortunately, there are still many people whose chronologies are incalculable to any useful degree. Among the Germanic and British peoples, this group is composed of family founders, various regional kings who were later employed into the lineages of dominant families prior to the historical horizon, and the very rare individual who was for some reason remembered in legend or literature but was never associated with any dynasty. It is the hope of the author to here address these individuals who fall into these various categories and reason through when they most logically would have been active.

To begin with, the legendary founders of certain Germanic lineages. Among the Germanic culture group, the first person of a dynasty of rulers usually named the dynasty founded. Thus Icel was the first of the Iclingas, and so on. This fact, the author believes, is well accepted. The source of conflict is the period when the founding of dynasties would have occurred. As has been seen, Germanic kingdoms began to emerge in Britain in the middle of the sixth century, and were well on their way to being absorbed into ever larger polities by 600. Thus, the most reasonable period for all the founders to have been born would be 475x600. In this, the earlier part of the range is more likely than the later. Below is a list of known founders.

Bena	Hæfer	Oisc
Bereca	Hæsta	Stæn
Brahha	Hroth	Sunna
Cumen	Icel	Wæcel
Epp	Lulla	Wæppa
Gilla	Mimmas	

The odd British chieftains are something more of a challenge. There is no guarantee they were the founders of a dynasty, and little evidence that they even existed. However, assuming the latter is true, it seems most reasonable that the men below would have been active in the first few decades of the British kingdoms, when the bardic order was reestablishing itself and the heroic age culture was first emerging. Most important, they were almost by definition active before the establishment of the dynasties that would have found it beneficial to fully integrate them into their histories. This broadly gives all the persons listed below birth years of 420x500 and activity ranges of 475x515. As was seen in the author's previous work on a study of Arthur, detailed analysis confirms the range.[1]

Uthr	Dewrarth Wledig	Garbonion	Maeswig
Soemil	and son	Ceneu	Gwrwst
Casnar Wledig	Rhufawn	Dyfnwal Moilmut	
and son Llary	Coel Hen	Meirchion	

Logically, these two groups represent the successful chieftains who attained wide fame in their own lifetimes but were unable to establish a dynasty, a stable kingdom, or a line of succession before their deaths.

It remains, then, to make some use of the secondary work done in the past thirty-five years on Dyfed and Northumbria's history as well as the British events of Ardferydd, Rhun's campaign, and Catraeth.

Molly Miller is really the only person who has attempted to reason through the materials surrounding Dyfed's history. Her treatment of Eochaid's settlement in particular is of great interest here. She dates part of Vorteporix's reign to 545x549 (her range for Gildas' famous letter). Taking the entire Dyfed lineage, she computes that the normal generation for the family was 25 years. Thus she derives a range of 400x425 for the settlement of Eochaid, his ancestor. This is roughly confirmed by correlating his migration with the departure of Constantine in 407 and the resulting and inevitable weakening of Romano-British defenses. According to legend, Aed Brosc (Eochaid's grandson) invaded Ceredigion during Carantoc's youth. Carantoc, according to the *vitae* traditions, was son to the Ceredig whom Miller clearly still assumed was the son of Cunedda.[2] Because of this, she put his reign in the third quarter of the fifth century—exactly two generations after Eochaid's period of activity. All the above agrees in putting the original Deísi invasion in the period 400x425.

However, there are a good many flaws in Miller's approximations, many of which may be seen due to her own efforts. The current author's work above has shown that the narrowest birth range among the Gildasian kings is Maelgwn at 490x520, so that Vorteporix's birth range of 466x520 is both accurate and indicates he could have been the butt of Gildas' (died 569x572) letter at any time between 521 and 535. This is at least a generation too early if the twenty-five-year generations Miller hypothesized are to be maintained.

Miller's correlations, too, look to be unlikely. Constantine did leave for the Continent in 407, but the Roman-style government at that time only controlled most of lower England. Dyfed had been lost a long time before then, and therefore any attempt to link it to contemporary events in Roman Britain is useless.

Miller herself would later show that the Ceredigion family did not derive from Cunedda, so that connection to Carantoc can no longer be used, either. It is more likely that the Carantoc named here was son to the Ceredig listed in the annals as dying in 616, and that is of no help. If the Dyfed genealogy has been tampered with, there is no reason why the Deisi could not have arrived anywhere from the early fourth to the middle fifth century. The genealogy worked out above only barely limits this to something like 325x450.

Although the Dyfed material is difficult, it cannot compare to the complications to be found in Bernician chronology before the ascent of Æthelfrith. Miller has interpreted the materials most carefully, and therefore her calculations are the most accurate.[3] She gives

Bernician reigns as Ida (555–567), Glappa (567–568), Æthelric (568–572), Theodric (572–579), Frithuwald (579–585), Hussa (585–592), and Æthelfrith (592–604). Deira has been made at Ælle (569–599) and Æthelric (599–604), which is consistent and seems reasonable with the evidence at hand. As has been seen, however, contemporary British poetry is clear that Hussa fought Urien and his allies, while his earlier contemporary Theodric was active when Urien died. A Bedan notice is just as clear that Frithuwald was active when Augustine landed in Britain in 597. As has been concluded above, the lineages of several dynasties have been consolidated into a single line of kingship.

As the British poems say that Theodric was holed up in Lindisfarne when Urien died, he was most likely a king in Lindsey. Hussa, as a clear threat to Rheged, Elmet, Strathclyde, and probably a Gododdin kingdom, was likely a king somewhere in northern Bernicia. That neither he nor his son Hering is specifically named as a descendant of the Bernician lineage is a good indication that he was not a part of the surviving dynasty. He may well have ruled in Pennawc, an historical kingdom of whom no rulers are known. It was absorbed into Bernicia within the generation before Degsastan (603).

Frithuwald's kingdom is also unknown. He could not have ruled all of Bernicia immediately before Æthelfrith and still have been ruling five years into Æthelfrith's reign, nor could he have ruled in Deira, where Ælle is known to have been active as a contemporary of Augustine. Perhaps he ruled in Pennawc or Lindsey. Alternatively, he could have controlled any number of other minor kingdoms in what would become medieval Northumbria.

With the above knowledge in place, we can be certain that Æthelfrith ruled 592–604, while all that may be reliably ventured is that Hussa reigned for seven years, Æthelric for four, Glappa for one, and Ida for twelve. Frithuwald was active for a six-year reign including 597, while Theodric was king for seven. Theodric's floruit can be further limited by his contemporaneity to Urien and Morgan.

Gwynedd has also been looked at uniquely by Dr. Miller, and will be treated here.[4] Taking note of several discrepancies in the Gwynedd foundation legend, she was able to see two flaws in the genealogy of that house. The first should be clear at the outset; nine sons by one man implies about thirty-six children. Such is an outrageous number. As Miller summized, it likely means that whomever assigned him all those sons, and then assigned those sons provinces within Gwynedd, was trying to use the official history to cover up the real history of several originally independent kingdoms with another that made them all equally invested in the contemporary kingdom.[5] This information means that none of their lines of descent may be believed without outside corroboration. Miller did her part, and the Gwynedd genealogy listed above has proven the most likely variant.

The second flaw occurs above Cunedda. In *Historia Brittonum*, Maelgwn's great-grandfather Cunedda is named as the migrant from Manau of Gododdin and as Maelgwn's *atavus*, or great-great-great-grandfather. In the genealogy, Cunedda is Maelgwn's great-grandfather. Miller has convincingly argued that the entire origin legend was written down for some political purpose, and most likely this occurred with the ascension of the Merfyn Frych dynasty. She also suggested that *atavus* is a clue that the accomplishments of two individuals, Padarn and Cunedda, were telescoped into one.[6] In this case, *atavus* indicates that Padarn, the great-great-great-grandfather in the genealogy, was the true migrant. He was either a part of the Cunedda dynasty that originally migrated, or was one of the legendary kings of Gwynedd who was attached to the predominant lineage at a later date. Cunedda, as the father of nine males, then represents the establishment of Gwynedd. This revelation in no way alters our outlook on the historical Gwynedd dynasty. It does, however, provide another pedigree for the region. Aetern father of Padarn father of Tacit would have founded a historical and separate family from that of Cunedda. Miller's researches suggested that Padarn migrated in 398x401. If all of her other conjecture is sound, he could be date-guessed with a birth range of 343x386. The family line would then go:

Aetern: 305x368
Padarn Peisrud: 343x386
Tacit: 361x424

The century following the Roman withdrawal is notoriously difficult for its chronology. However, historians have often found that individuals of the next century are often too broadly dated to be of much practical use as well. Fortunately, there are a series of events in the north at this time that appear to be interrelated—Kentigern's banishment with the conquest of Morgan and his return with the accession Rhydderch, the career of Urien, Rhun's raid North at the beginning of his reign, and the battles of Arfderydd and Catraeth. A more thorough examination of each will shed some light on both their specific chronologies and their relationships to each other. As Rhydderch (537x580) asked Kentigern (483x519, present at the council in Gaul no earlier than 554) to return on his accession to the throne, likely Kentigern returned before or at the same time as Rhydderch's alliance with Urien (497x565). Thus Kentigern could have returned at any time between 554 and 599, while the alliance belongs to the period 554x620. Incidentally, this reduces Urien's birth range to 499x565.

As Clydno (518x564) and his brother Cadrod were present at Arfderydd (573x579) and raided Rhun son of Maelgwn (528x558), while Cynon son of Clydno (537x602) and Pobddelw (521x605) were at Catraeth, likely Arfderydd occurred before Catraeth. This would mean that Catraeth took place in the range 574x620. Because Maelgwn was born 490x520 and is known to have died of a plague, he is unlikely to have lived into his fifties and less likely to have been alive at the time of Arfderydd. This means that Rhun's campaign occurred first, then Arfderydd, and finally Catraeth.

With only the documents at hand for reference, these five events cannot be much more precisely dated or more certainly ordered. However, Professor Koch has come up with an interesting theory in his linguistic study of *Y Gododdin* that is not only highly plausible, but would do much to improve the situation.

First, there is the likely and oft-repeated connection of modern Catterick with Catraeth. Second, he noted the clear chronological overlap between the "Urien" confederacy and the battle of Catraeth as spoken of in *Y Gododdin*. Third, there is the fact that one Taliesin poem in honor of Gwallog of Elmet speaks of his battle at Catterick. Fourth, there is the curious mention of a "Madawg Elmet" in *Y Gododdin*. Fifth, Urien and his alliance were likely active in and around Catterick at some point during their careers if Urien and Morgan were sieging at Lindisfarne, a site which is beyond Elmet from either Rheged and Gododdin, at the time of Urien's death. Finally, it seems reasonable that Gwallog, and likely the entire "Urien" coalition, were opposed to the Gododdin forces at Catraeth.

If the above conclusions are the correct ones, then Catraeth represented a battle fought primarily between British kingdoms. This possibility explains a curiosity of British history: it is no coincidence that the Urien history and two versions of *Y Gododdin* were only preserved through the efforts of Gwynedd. Nor is the fact that a specific enemy is not named in either case. As has often been mentioned, both the history and the elegy were a part of the nationalizing movement in Gwynedd during the ninth century. The coalition of Urien and his men served as a symbol for the power of the united British kingdoms, and Urien's assassination served as a warning about the consequences of internal bickering. The banding together of the British peoples, which is a major aspect of *Y Gododdin*, is heroic because the participants did so in order to confront a vague but Germanic-implied foe. In both cases, if the enemies they were fighting were named as British, the uniting theme being emphasized in Gwynedd would have been undermined.

If Koch's conjecture is accepted for the moment, we have Kentigern's return/Rhydderch's accession, Rhun's campaign, Arfderydd, and Urien's confederacy with Catraeth. Kentigern returned and Rhydderch succeeded to the throne in 554x574 and Rhun became king in the span 543x575 (the earliest age when Rhun would have been an adult and the last year Maelgwn could have been alive, respectively), Arfderydd occurred in 573x579, and the Urien confederacy was active in the range 574x620. Such is, again, merely speculation. However, it is speculation that seems to hang together remarkably well. If it is accurate, it limits Rhydderch to 537x559 and again further limits Urien's birth range to 519x565.

24

The Heroic Age in Britain

This book began with the purpose of using the primary sources as a foundation for establishing floruits and genealogies of as many individuals as possible, with secondary sources being utilized to tighten their date ranges. It was hoped that this method would help to construct a rough relative chronology of early Britain. This goal has been reached to some extent. What has emerged in the process, however, is thematically much more satisfying.

As was suggested decades ago in studies on African oral family histories, the official Celtic and Germanic pedigrees have been seen to be accurate only as far back as living memory. Before that, they were highly suggestive to the contemporary political climate.[1] Alliances, recent acquisitions, and changes of location are among many factors which could affect a pedigree before that point.

What happened in the oral stage of their history may only be guessed at based on what we may see in the written record, but certain pieces of evidence point towards the same conclusions Dr. Vansina posited. The names and positions of ancestors found before then have been added. For one, there are the progenitures of each line. As was noted above, lineages normally begin with gods such as Beli (Belatacudros), Woden, or Tyr. This clearly indicates that regnal records were kept while both cultures still clung to aspects of pagan worship, and therefore beginning no later than 550 among the British and 600 among the Germanic peoples.

Gildas has also given us reason to believe there were oral records kept well before our first preserved genealogies. He tells us of the shameless bards of his time, and bemoans their function of singing the praises of the kings.[2] The easiest way to extol a king might have been to tell him how powerful and successful he had been in the past and how generous he was in the present. But in praising his ancestors, or even in creating a genealogical line, a bard could do far more to heighten the stature of his patron. Doing so successfully solidified the innate royalty of his lineage, and therefore the king's right to hold his position. In short, a bard created an ideology that supported the status quo. His role as a historian would become, in time, the most important function of the bard.

However, creating a family line involved more than simply inventing names to string together before a bard's contemporary king. As may be evidenced in the earliest segments of each genealogy and where it has been possible to check, the first individuals after the founder were inevitably those of locally or regionally well-known leaders. Thus, Coel Hen and Maxen Wledig are common in genealogies of the North and in Wales, respectively, while Cunedda (Constantine) appears to have been the figure of choice in Cornwall. Adding figures of their stature to a pedigree would have done much to raise the respectability of a king and his kingship.

It has also been seen that the historical traditions of the Germanic office of *Bretwalda* were begun only a decade or so before Æthelberht's known reign begins. However, there is clear evidence of British over-kingships before that period in the mention of several individuals.

Recent thinking has concluded that Urien may not have been as important as his prominence in *Historia Brittonum* would indicate.[3] However, the most prominent bard of the period lived in his hall, and it was his family, not those of any other British chieftain, with whom the Northumbrian kings intermarried. Also at some time before 600, and possibly at the head of another coalition, was the Din Eidyn king. His allies and tributaries are to be found in *Y Gododdin*.

As we go further back in time, British over-kings become more easily seen. Gwrtheyrn clearly had powers extending well beyond the borders of his kingdom proper. Rhun, by his march against the allied northern kings, demonstrated his kingdom as superior to that of several noteworthy contemporaries. That no one dared invade his kingdom during his long absence also implies that he either took tribute from a good many smaller kingdoms dotted around his own, or that he was simply too intimidating to contend with[4]; either option shows the extent of his powers. In the generation before Rhun, Gildas says that Maelgwn took tribute from many of the contemporary kings of modern Wales.[5] Whether or not that statement is an exaggeration, his power was clear to Gildas and those who read him.

The careers of figures before Gildas' time, as has been seen, are unclear. Often the scholar is left with little more than guesswork to put the puzzle pieces together. However, even here there are indications of over-kingships. Legend suggests that Ambrosius united the British against the invaders, though whether this was on a local or a larger scale is debatable. The simple fame of Arthur suggests that his power extended well beyond his own kingdom. The earliest stories have him interacting with Gawein, Drust, and Hueil. These characters were the eponym for Galloway,[6] a possible king of the northern British[7] and a likely king in the Foirtrinn region, respectively. There are a good many earlier kings with the title *gwledig* that implies the awe they were held in by their contemporaries or those who followed them and thus suggests that they, too, were over-kings. Ceredig of Strathclyde and Coel Hen are only two examples.

However, in noting all those individuals who preceded Maelgwn, we must also keep in context the size of a typical kingdom at the time. Ceredig is only associated with one hill fort. Until well into the sixth century, the other over-kings we know of either have vaguely defined kingdoms or no land has been associated with them at all. As has been seen, kingdoms only began to take on their medieval size several decades into sixth century.

Throughout the island, among the Irish, Picts, Germanic tribesmen, and Britons, the pattern is clear. When governments began to form beyond the local level, they were small in scale. Kingdoms as we would expect them did not exist yet. But how does this new knowledge help us to better understand the period in question? We should begin by realizing that we cannot look at the early period in the same way any longer.

Instead, we should turn to other and more ancient Celtic literature for guidance. In the oldest stories, all younger warriors normally stayed in their lord's hall for years before being given enough land to be independent. This helped to forge a strong sense of loyalty and a personal sense of debt to the king. Their obligation was reinforced with gifts and bonding physical activities such as raids, the hunt, and feasts. However, living in such close proximity would have made friction inevitable, and the raids which brought fame and fortune to the king would also have served to alleviate those tensions.

In Ireland, we can see a clearer picture of what Britain was moving toward. The island contained hundreds of kingdoms. Each of them could function individually or give allegiance to a more powerful neighbor when it was necessary for its own survival. These kingdoms regularly conducted raids on each other. The attacks were not political in nature. They probably had no economical motivation beyond booty either. Instead, they helped to maintain a mutual respect between war bands.

British villages also depended on a personal interaction with the kings. However, they functioned on a system of government that was largely Roman in nature—with elected and senior members of the society functioning as elders and making the community decisions. For kings, such a preexisting organization was a godsend and made tribute and any other communications with the peasants in their kingdom simpler. That was the extent of the in-place political structure, however. The last years of Roman rule had eliminated all organization on a larger scale. Because of this fact, every village had to be dealt with individually.

In this environment, it seems unlikely that the early kings thought in terms of conquering other regions; conquest meant more work and spreading thin the few men they trusted. If a conquering king took an oath of fealty from a defeated enemy, that king could continue to function autonomously and alleviate such pressure. However, it also meant that such a man would still have all his resources intact. When the over-king weakened or died, the defeated man would have warriors at hand to reassert his independence. In an era with such personal allegiance, a third factor was also key. If a king made conquests his goal, then he would lose his men as he conquered. During the turbulent fifth century, these men would have been all but irreplaceable in the new territories and progressively more difficult in his original territories. All in all, the economic and political circumstances of the period worked against any thoughts of expansion.

The use of active date-guessing, then, has proven useful in conjunction with taking careful appraisal of primary and secondary sources and applying those appraisals to a better understanding of the events and lineages they claim to represent. It has not only allowed for the establishment of some tighter relative and absolute date ranges for individuals and events, but has provided some further evidence about the nature of the kingdoms in the fifth and sixth century, of recordkeeping, and of the process of nationalizing history which seems to have occurred throughout the island. This is only a start, however. The avenues that this study will open up are only just revealing themselves.

25

The Age of Saints

It has been seen throughout this book that *romanitas* was still alive and well even after the development of British kingships. The early kings made use of already established local governments to more efficiently collect tribute and control the villages. Roman learning eventually fell off, but the political system itself remained intact and became a basic component of the manorial system throughout Europe.

The transformation from Roman to native rule was not a smooth one, however, and certainly that aspect of *romanitas* known as Christianity represented one of the most difficult transitions. Before the departure of Constantine, it was not the dominant religion on the island. In fact, the regions which were most thoroughly Christian in 410 were overrun almost immediately by the Germanic settlers. Only those areas on the periphery of Roman rule, where Christianity was present but weak, managed to retain their independence.

Yet Christianity survived. The nature of the period was transformation. Stable civilization and structure gave way to the fluidity of heroic age society and culture. The general peace that was Rome was replaced with incessant war and raiding. All over Europe, nearly every aspect of Roman civilization disappeared as the Continent metamorphosized into a feudal system of rule. Learning was hoarded by the powerful. Long-range trade shut down almost entirely. Bureaucracy and law faded, and even Latin was extinguished as a living language.

Through all this Christianity remained and was not forced to change. It did so by not attracting attention. It did maintain a public presence; both monasteries and churches were active during the fifth century. Nonetheless, it is not associated with any conversions in Britain even though much of the island remained non–Christian in this period.

As the fifth century came to a close, Christianity revived. For a little over two centuries, beginning roughly with Patrick's mission and not slowing down til the Council of Whitby in 664, Christianity was a powerful force among the British, creating the Age of Saints.

The Age of Saints is a unique occurrence in British history, perhaps best seen as a reaction to the period. It can be defined by three peculiarities—Christianity as a counterculture to the heroic age, heightened intellectual endeavors, and migration. These ingredients occurred for generally different reasons, but together helped make the era truly unique in British history.

As a religious movement, the Age of Saints philosophically opposed the political developments of the fifth and sixth centuries. To the Romanized elements of the British population, the onset of heroic-age culture would have seemed like the transformation of their society into something primitive. They may have understood that the transformation was necessary in order to survive, but they must also have seen that they were turning their own society into a mirror image of the very barbarians who were threatening them.

Just as religion functioned as a connection to Rome, so the faith itself with all its ethics served as a touchstone to the civilization that many Britons still felt a connection to. Investing in holy orders not only served to shield oneself from the barbaric world around them, it provided a basis for how to live one's life in a civilized manner.

The Age of Saints was also a period of heightened intellectual activities which can be said to focus around the monastery at Llanilltud, although Llancarfan and later Whithorn produced its important scholars. Illtud's skill in Latin is said to have been legendary. And though we have none of his writings, his student Gildas was perhaps the greatest intellect of his age. As has been seen, his *De Excidio Britanniae* is a mark of that brilliance and a clue to both Illtud's aptitude for the dying language and his ability to teach it to the ecclesiastics in Britain and Ireland.

But Illtud's students were not the only force of the period. Mugentius, Maucennus, and Uinniau in Whithorn are all mentioned repeatedly as teachers and masters of learning. Cadoc in Llancarfan served as a king, an abbot, and as the wise old man among the Britons. Columba's efforts with Kentigern would establish a long-held peace between Dalriada and Strathclyde. Columba would also be responsible for a large repository of knowledge at Iona and, eventually, for the establishment of a set of annals there.

The plethora of intellectual activity throughout the island at this time was largely due to the makeup of "Celtic Christianity." On the Continent, authority came from those leaders who interacted with the public: the bishops and archbishops. As a result, they tended to be religious men with great faith, though not necessarily men with a great deal of education. In Britain, such offices existed and were also filled by respected individuals, but the abbots were the more important ecclesiastics. Unlike their more socially conscious counterparts, their focus was on knowledge. Their influence was why Latin remained in use among the educated, and why the Roman atmosphere of the original church was passed on.

Migration also seems to have been a key aspect of the Age of Saints. Columba came to Iona from Ireland, as did Uinniau. Patrick went to Ireland from Britain. Gildas, David, Samson, Kentigern, and Dubricius all traveled widely, and Gildas, Leonorus, and Paul Aurelian ended their careers in Breton monasteries.

Migration occurred for many reasons. Columba was banished. Patrick and Uinniau moved solely for the purpose of conversion. Kentigern ran away from a familial clash, and David, Gildas, and Dubricius served as teachers.

Two other factors appear to emerge as a result of the work on genealogies and relative dating done above. First, the migrations from Wales appear to have taken place around the middle of the sixth century. Second, and admittedly with only the House of Lleudun as an example, migrations took place for political reasons.

That the saintly migrations took place around 550 is important for two reasons. *Annales Cambriae* records that in 547 or 549 a great plague descended on Wales. Granting that the *Annales Cambriae* dates are not accurate, it does provide a rough estimate for the event. The period around 550 was one of plague, and it seems only reasonable that people would have left for Wales *en masse* at this time in order to escape it.

The date leads to the second reason why the saints' migration of around 550 is significant. The first historically known Breton kings—Cybr Daniel of Cornouailles, Iudoc and Iudicael of Dumnonie, Riwal and Pompeia of Dumnonie, Romelius and Gradlon of

Quimper, and Cunomorus were coincidentally active around mid-century as well. With new kingdoms and the influx of a significant number of Britons, there may well have been a need for ecclesiastical leadership. The most acceptable churchmen would have been those whose religious philosophy was the same as their own, one where the abbots were more powerful than the bishops. Only natives of the British Isles would have been suitable. The migrations of the great saints make perfect sense in this context.

    The presence of so many well-educated British ecclesiastics in Brittany would, in time, be of great help to continental Europe. When Roman-based Christianity began to lose its vigor in the seventh century, the Celts were able to reinfuse the rest of Europe with, not only the love of learning that was an integral part of their faith, but also the beauty that they had learned to use as an expression of that love of learning.

26

Conclusion

This chapter is in effect a conclusion not just for the present volume, but in addition for the two books the author has previously written on the subject of post–Roman Britain. It is for this reason that the previous chapters have largely dealt with summing up the various issues and topics this volume has explored.

Origins of Arthurian Romances raised the nearly outrageous question, "Would it be possible to use literary sources to understand events which occurred before historical sources were accessible?" The unexpected answer and the resulting methodology necessary to do so were then employed in a unique and more thorough look at one aspect of the Arthurian legend than has ever been managed. The process necessarily had circumstantial yet startingly consistent results. Historically, the search for the Holy Grail was a series of witch-hunts against various fertility-based groups during the century or so following 410.

The next step was taken in my second book, *Evidence of Arthur*. Analysis of all the early sources and sources with information that derived from traditional knowledge gave clear and consistent indications of what information was reliable with regard to Arthur, and where. Arthur was historical, likely was centered around Old Carlisle, and was active in the decades around 500.

With such promising results, a broader look was taken of the entire period in the first part of the present work. In this study, all sources relating to the post–Roman period up to 700 were employed. These were thoroughly analyzed and the results dictated how each source was made use of. In due course, the origin legends of Kent, Dalriada, Gwynedd, and Wessex have been laid out, and have been shown to be more the product of later historians than any historical fact.

A chronological look at the Kentish legend also led to some idea of the floruit of Gwrtheyrn and the nature of two of the Powysian houses. In addition, it gave a vague impression of Gwrtheyrn's influence beyond his own kingdom during his reign. Gwrtheyrn was active in the later sixth century. He ruled from an ill-defined area occasionally called Dubonnia, and may well have collected tribute as far east as Kent and as far north as Powys. Only after his death was his dynasty forced to migrate north into medieval Powys. In its place, one of the Wessex kingdoms was founded.

A by-product of the above research was to better understand the earliest history of the Germanic peoples in Britain, from their use as auxiliaries in Roman times to their transformation into politically and militarily independent groups. The Germanic peoples did not begin settling Britain in 449.[1] Nor were they first invited to the island by any ruler of all

Britain, for the simple fact that there were none during the entire fifth century. The Germanic peoples had been settling in Britain as independent auxiliaries of the Roman state since the last third of the fourth century. They would continue to do so until well into the fifth.

The study also led to some concept of how the British and Germanic kingdoms developed through the fifth and sixth centuries. The British retained a local and fairly Roman form of government well after the Roman withdrawal. However, the influx of foreign emigrants pushed the Germanic settlements ever westward and to the North. These emigrations would eventually force the British to develop more militarily oriented governments, which would lead to kingships and, eventually, kingdoms. In the meantime, their creation of primitive monarchies stifled the Germanic peoples' advance into British territories. The slowing progression would eventually cause overseas emigration to cease. The process would have rendered Germanic Britain more crowded than the land could support. This, the finite resources available, and the Germanic traditions of raiding and fighting in general would soon lead to kingships among them as well. These developments would set the stage for the political and cultural warfare of the next few centuries.

The most obvious result of this book is the derivation of relative dates for a significant number of figures in Britain from 400 to 700. This is interesting in and of itself. However, far more important is how the date ranges may be used to better understand the period. Rhun, or possibly even Maelgwn as an old king, was contemporary to Urien. There is no mention of this, or of which Reged ruler Rhun's army went through in his march north. Gwynedd's activities are never given in conjunction with Powys, and yet as a dominant kingdom in Maelgwn and Rhun's time, it is likely some significant interaction occurred between Cadell or possibly Gwrtheyrn. To any evidence of these connections or dozens of others, the above work should lend support.

To those who wish to better understand the development of Christianity on this island, the relative floruits of hundreds of holies and the legends surrounding them should be of aid as well. David was dealing with Irish pagans in Dyfed as late as the middle of the sixth century and Samson met with a native coven at around the same time. These instances imply that the pagan rites had become underground institutions by circa 550.

The results of date guessing are not concrete, and do not allow the scholar much precision as to birth years. The reader should be surprised and concerned if they did, for such is not the nature of the study. Instead, they suggest possibilities, and make clear that other possibilities are highly unlikely. The world of Arthur may never be more than dimly glimpsed at, but the dynamics of Maelgwn, Gwrtheyrn, and certainly Urien's lives may just be recoverable. It is hoped that this book is a good start in that direction.

Appendix

The Historia Section in Gildas

Thompson's examination of Gildas' *historia* up to Ætius is a wonderful, inventive, and possible look at the author's motivations for creating the origins of items we know to have been made centuries earlier than his time. Gildas' own comments about the holes in his sources,[1] and Sims-Williams' note that with Ambrosius he begins to flounder,[2] allow for a new look on the *superbus tyrannus* issue.

For one, it could hardly have been forgotten how the barbarians had come to the island. Gildas' accurate use of the terms surrounding the *foederati* arrangement make clear that even the details of the late Roman defense mechanism in Britain were still known in his day. However, the chronology of the early fifth century was probably not well understood, and this especially makes sense if many of the keepers of living memory had been killed or had migrated overseas in the time between the appeal to Ætius and the emergence of Ambrosius.[3]

So, not knowing that the Germanic peoples had been on the island since the first century, and not wishing to find fault with the Romans (he had other interests in dealing with them), he placed the source of the current problems just before the temporary solution of Ambrosius. This decision allowed him to make those who tried to rival the Romans in power appear foolish and cowardly. It also made his theme simpler to understand. Namely, that God punished the Britons when they went against God's commandments, but rewarded them as soon as they returned to him. To have put the *foederati* any earlier would have complicated his message and required too much explanation. In this decision, he would have known his audience to be what has already been guessed at in the pages above—without any concrete historical dates before Ambrosius with which to argue his relative dating of events.

Why did Gildas give one man, the *superbus tyrannus*, the blame for the fiasco that followed? The author has previously suggested that the scapegoat might have been intended as Arthur, and that his later fame and the coincidental linguistics between Gwrtheyrn's name and the title Gildas gave him have suggested a different possibility to later generations of scholars.[4] If Gildas had intended Arthur, he could not have named him because he was a hero of the past too well-liked to bluntly slander.

However, if Gildas did not know the timing of the events before Ambrosius, he most probably would not have known the person or mechanism responsible for the Germanic presence on the island either. And, since the Britons were the buffoons of his *historia*, not the Romans, his fool also had to be a native. Not knowing anyone with so much power in the past, and not understanding that it had been more events and groups that had allowed the Germanic onslaught than the acts of any one person, he chose a mere title, "great king," as his culprit. His qualms with specifically identifying characters in his *historia* have been well documented, and his lack of knowledge about the circumstances surrounding the letter to Ætius noted.[5] All the evidence fits together nicely if Gildas assumed one man had invited the Germanic peoples into Britain, and then went about inventing such a figure to fulfill the task which historical events and Gildas' oratorical needs required of him. In this interpretation, it is simply another irony of history that Gildas' literary device would be so easily confused with a historical figure. It is unfortunate as well, as the new creation took on a life of its own that marred the king and further confused what was already a poorly recorded era of history.

Cunedda's Migration

The date and possible purposes for Cunedda's migration have been explained in recent works, but in the context of the above discussion, perhaps the entire event can be put in a more complete perspective. Legend has it that he began his career in Manau Gododdin as a king. For some reason, he and his war band moved to Gwynedd in the middle of his career. There he founded the dynasty that would dominate Wales for the next couple of centuries. Dr. Miller's studies in date-guessing and the poetry of Claudian firmly place a major Pictish war in 398,[6] while archaeology has shown that Traprain Law, a royal hill fort of Gododdin, was no longer occupied after the mid–fifth century. Thus, two loosely connected facts could easily be used as evidence that the migration of Cunedda did take place.[7]

What has not been noted is that Traprain Law, or Dun Pelder, was not in Manau. Even with our loose knowledge of the period, it is known that Din Eidyn was the royal center of Lothian, and that this site is between Traprain Law and Manau. This flaw in Miller's theory does much to discredit her here, especially as there is no true historical context for the migration of Cunedda (only unexplained happenstance). The event need not be associated with any Pictish incursion, or any military event the Romans could have been aware of. A dynastic struggle or war with other British leaders might have forced Cunedda away from Gododdin.

It is possible that Cunedda was not a king in Manau but only the leader of a band of roving marauders. In that case, he may have found stories of the land further south appealing. As has been seen, the entire fifth century was one of very little political organization among the Britons south of Hadrian's Wall. At any time in the period, a man with a strong group of warriors behind him could have moved into Anglesey and established a small kingdom there. Once accomplished, it would have been a simple matter of hiring a bard to create a history that better suited him.

Miller's paper on Stilicho's Pictish Wars also seems to have been flawed in attempting to tie in historical fact derived from Claudian with what Gildas wrote. As has been seen, Gildas begins to lose a good deal of historical footing in speaking of Ætius in the middle of the fifth century, and certainly by the time he mentions the Roman legions in Britain after 410 he has lost access to any oral history he might have been drawing on. It is possible that in speaking of three Pictish wars Gildas drew on a written source, but this is unnecessary given the information he provides. More likely, he guessed about them based on what he knew as we know he did with the other events taking place before his mention of Ætius. To him the Picts were a greater threat than the Germanic peoples at the time, and so had been in the past. Three is such an obvious number with its religious and traditional use that it was likely nothing more than a literary device.

The Pictish Assault

That the Pictish attack Gildas speaks of was in actuality conducted by the Germanic peoples now seems extremely likely, and any of a number of factors would explain why he switched the two groups in his writings, not the least being that he did not know the culprit and made an educated guess. However, the Germanic attack in the *Gallic Chronicles* does deserve some discussion. The entry states that the island of Britain was entirely covered by the Germanic peoples in 441. This, as has been seen, is not possible. The British culture continued in most of Britain nearly to 500. As has been postulated before, the chronicler's access to British information was probably through London or Kent. Either of these regions might well have been consumed by the invaders at about 441, leaving the chronicler to believe that all of Britain had been taken with it. But what is more important here is the direction from which the attack took place, and the group or groups who were involved.

The date could not indicate a widespread Germanic immigration into Britain. As has been seen, that had been taking place for centuries by the time the event took place. Auxiliaries in Roman forts had been present since the first century, and *foederati* settlements had occupied the eastern and southern coasts since the mid–fourth century. Immigration would not have been possible if these were still functioning in Britain at this time, nor would it have been necessary if they had not. Regardless, there would already have been a strong and pervasive Germanic presence without additional migrations.

Instead, it seems far more likely that the Germanic warriors formerly under Roman supervision were the cause of concern for the Gallic chroniclers. Many of them had retained their ethnic and political identity through their service to Rome, and therefore would still have been regarded as Germanic by a man of Gaul. Because of their military use in Britain they would also have been organized enough to make an effective attack. Further, it has been seen that long-range pay and supplies had stopped coming to them by 410, and it is unlikely the isolated villages along the coast would have had the resources to compensate for the diminished supplies in the long run. Finally, it has been noted that much of London was still controlled by the British till well into the fifth century, and it was the center of continental trade. Any continental Germanic peoples would have set about first conquering it before the less developed areas of Britain simply because of the wealth of the region.

Contrary to what appears in the *Gallic Chronicles,* Germanic control in the fifth century seems to have been haphazard. Key *civitates* may well have remained British far beyond the mid–fifth century, while many of the smaller settlements seem to have been abandoned after the watershed, or may have become more Germanic in character at that point. This argues strongly for *foederati* revolts, not foreign invasions, in the fifth century.

Date-Guessing Results

Secular Date Ranges

Some of the following sections have spaces
which represent different families in that particular area.

Aeron

Cynfelyn: 501x546
Clydno Eidyn: 518x564

Cadrod: 518x564
Cynon: 537x602

Eurneit: 536x602

Aran

Corbanus: 440x621

Bernicia

Ida: 497x550
Æthelric: 535x568
Theodric: 515x585
Adda: 515x585
Æthelfrith: 573x586
Theodbald: 553x588
Second Generation: 553x605
Oswiu: 611x612

Oswald: 603x604
Eanfrith: 591x604
Æbbe: 591x622
Third Generation: 571x623
Aldfrith: 650
Ælfwine: 660x661
Ælfflæd: 654
Osthryth: 640x650

Alhfrith: 629x650
Egfrith: 645x646
Alhflæd: 629x641
Œthelwald: 621x642
Talorcan: 609x640
Fourth Generation: 589x641
Egbert: 618x659

Hussa: 530x570

Hering: 548x588

Beorhæth: 615x670

Brycheiniog

Guadam: 490x577

Ceredigion

Ceredig: 558x598
Usai: 576x636
Serwyl: 594x664

Boddw: 612x682
Arthfoddw: 630x700
Arthlwys: 648x718

Clydog: 673x756
Seissyll: 711x774
Arthen: 749x792

Cornouailles

Cybr Daniel: 495x506
Budic: 513x524
Mauricus: 531x562

Oudoceus: 531x536
Theuderic: 531x562
Meliau: 531x558

Ismael: 531x562
Melorius: 549x576

Cornwall

Tudwal: 350x424
Kynwawr: 388x442
Constantine: 406x448
Drust: 426x468

Erbin: 424x466
Digain: 424x486
Cunomorus: 464x506
Dyfel: 442x504

Geraint: 442x484
Ermid: 442x504
Saloman: 460x502
Iestyn: 460x522

Constantine: 466x520
Cyngar: 460x522
Cadwy: 460x522

Kebi: 478x520
Gerennius: 490x560
Guedianus: 444x543

Comedianus: 440x543
Germochus: 490x651
Conan: 392x582

Cyndrwynyn

Egryn: 473x573
Gwyn: 491x611
Ermid: 511x591
Cerennior: 491x611

Cyndrwyn: 549x609
Caranfael: 509x649
Cynddylan: 587x627

Heledd: 567x647
Boddug: 527x687
Eluan: 547x667

Dalriada

Nath I: 445x478
Aillil Molt: 463x496
MacEire: 501x512
Fergus Mór: 519x530
Domnall: 519x546

Baetán: 539x550
Colgu: 555x567
Eochaid: 537x564
Rónán: 576x588
Aillil: 557x588

Fiachna: 557x588
Colman Rímid: 557x574
Fergus: 557x588
Mael Duin: 575x620

Gabrán: 508x548
Áedán: 551x566
Eóganán: 526x586
Eochaid Buide: 589x604
Artúr: 564x604

Gartnait: 564x584
Conaing: 564x604
Duncath: 544x624
Connad Cerr: 607x642
Domnall Brecc: 607x630

Conall Crandomna: 607x642
Cano: 582x622
Dunchad: 596x642
Domangart: 628x661
Ferchar: 636x680

Nisse: 419x483
Domangart: 457x501
Comgall: 495x519

Conall: 533x537
Connad Cerr: 571x575

Donnchad: 551x555
Ferchar: 589x613

Deira

At this stage, deriving the historical Deiran genealogy appears to be beyond the abilities of the information at hand given the tools at our disposal. The author has therefore below listed each member of the dynasty along with the combined birth ranges of all possible combinations. As the birth range at the center of all date-guessing here, Æthelric has been italicized.

Acha: 573x584
Æbbe: 591x622
Ælfric: 558x586
Ælfwine: 660x661
Ælle: 537x578
Æthelhun: 625x633
Æthelric: 555x578
Aldwulf: 625x658

Eadfrith: 607x616
Eanflæd: 622x628
Edwin: 587x598
Egfrith: 645x646
Hereric: 558x597
Hereswith: 591x640
Hild: 613x614
Osfrith: 607x616

Osric: 578x624
Osthryth: 640x650
Oswald: 603x604
Oswine: 596x637
Oswiu: 611x612
Uscfrea: 605x636
Yffi: 521x560
Yffi: 624x654

Dubonnia

Ambrosius: 423x476

Guitolin: 383x516
Gwrtheyrn: 505x580, 560x593
Britu: 523x618

Pasgen: 523x618
Annan: 541x656
Briacat: 541x656
Maun: 559x694

Mepurit: 559x694
Pasgen: 577x732
Paul: 577x732

Dumnonie

Iudwal: 482x505

Jonas: 500x543

Iudicael 467x530

Fracan: 442x543

Durotriges

Theodoric: 530x586

Dyfed

Eochaid Allmuir: 338x444
Corath: 376x462
Aed: 414x480
Tryffin: 452x498
Cyngar: 432x518
Erbin: 470x536
Cynan Cylched: 470x536
Agricola: 490x516

Vorteporix: 508x534
Tryffin: 488x574
Cyngar: 526x572
Drutwas: 506x597
Peter: 544x610
Arthur: 562x631
Nowy: 580x649
Gwlyddien/Cloten: 598x667

Cathen: 616x685
Cadwgan: 634x703
Rhain: 665x739
Tewdws: 703x757
Tewdwr: 683x777
Maredudd: 741x775
Owain: 759x793

East Anglia

Tyttla: 534x579
Rædwald: 572x600
Eni: 562x597
Ræganhere: 590x638
Eorpwald: 590x618, 616x633
Sigbert: 590x628
Anna: 587x615

Æthelhere: 600x640
Æthelwald: 580x640
Æthelric: 587x620
Ricbert: 608x656
Seaxburh: 605x650
Æthelthryth: 625x633
Æthelburh: 605x653

Aldwulf: 625x658
Egbert: 631x680
Hlothere: 630x668
Eorcengota: 623x688
Eormenhild: 623x673

Elmet

Lleenog: 485x565
Gwallog: 523x585

Dwywei: 503x584
Cerdic: 561x601

Aneirin: 541x621

Essex

Sledd: 523x581
Sæberht: 561x599
Seaxa: 541x619

Sæward: 579x627
Seaxred: 581x635
Seaxbald: 579x637

Sigeferth: 559x657
Sigeberht: 605x645
Sæbbi: 619x653

Swithelm: 609x659
Swithfrith: 597x675
Seleferth: 577x695
Sigehere: 623x663

Swæfheard: 637x687
Sigeheard: 637x671
Swæfred: 637x671
Sigebald: 595x733

Offa: 641x701
Sigemund: 655x709
Selered: 613x771

Eteliciaun

Etelic: 490x607

Foirtrinn

Seithuet: 402x455
Caw: 440x473
Watu: 420x493

Sinnoch: 420x493
Bedyw: 420x493
Hueil: 458x511

Gildas: 478x491

Glywising

Tegid: 406x473
Glywys: 444x491
Petroc: 465x536

Gwynlliw: 482x509
Cadoc: 520x527
Bugi: 500x547

Beuno: 518x585

Rhain: 490x607

Merchiaun: 435x542

Arthmail: 490x607

Gododdin

Wolstan: 521x590

Yrfai: 539x608

Gorthen: 557x626

Ymellyrn: 426x569
Cyngar: 459x587
Brân: 464x605

Morgan Bulc: 497x605
Caradog: 482x643
Coleddog: 515x643

Morgan: 533x681

Gwynedd

Tacit: 305x368

Padarn Peisrud: 343x386

Aetern: 361x424

Cunedda: 396x466
Einion Yrth: 434x484
Dunawd: 452x522
Owain: 452x529
Cadwallon: 472x502
Dingad: 470x560
Isaac: 470x560
Eifion: 470x560
Einion: 470x547
Cynlas: 475x547

Maelgwn: 490x520
Meurig: 488x598
Pobien: 488x587
Brochwel: 488x598
Cynlas: 488x565
Rhun: 528x558
Eurgain: 508x558
Bridei (Pictish king): 526x546[8]
Pobddelw: 521x605
Eigion: 506x636

Iago: 506x583
Ieuanaul: 524x674
Cadfan: 544x601
Caradog: 542x712
Eueilian: 562x639
Cadwallon: 578x619
Bleiddud: 560x750
Cadwaladr: 596x657
Cuhelyn: 578x788

Dogfael: 420x560

Kent

Eormenric: 523x560
Æthelberht: 561x578
Ricula: 541x581
Eadbald: 585x596
Æthelwald: 579x596
Æthelburh: 587x596
Sæberht: 561x599
Eormenred: 603x634
Eanswith: 579x634
Eorcenberht: 597x634

Æthelthryth: 625x633
Æthelhun: 605x653
Uscfrea: 605x633
Eanswith: 597x658
Æthelred: 621x672
St. Æthelberht: 621x672
Æbbe: 621x672
Eormenburh: 621x672
Egbert: 631x663
Hlothere: 630x668

Eorcengota: 615x672
Eormenhild: 615x672
Mildfrith: 639x710
Merchelm: 639x710
Mildfrith: 639x710
Mildburh: 639x710
Eadric: 649x701
Wihtred: 649x701
Werburh: 633x721

Leon

Father: 444x494
Riwal: 482x542

Godian: 452x590

Ruilmus: 482x582

Pompeia: 462x532
Tudwal: 490x530

Deroch: 456x543

Lleuddinyawn

Lleudun: 427x483
Teneu: 445x501

Cynan Colledauc: 465x521

Kentigern: 483x519

Mercia

Cearl: 571x580
Cwœnburh: 589x598

Penda: 598x623
Eowa: 598x643
Cenwalh: 618x635
Wulfhere: 630x653
Cyneburh: 616x661
Osyth: 629x661
Æthelred: 621x641

Osfrith: 607x616
Eadfrith: 607x616

Merewalh: 630x661
Peada: 616x641
Alweo: 616x681
Osmod: 616x681
Cundwalh: 654x691
Cenred: 656x691
Ceolred: 654x691

Pybba: 580x605

Ceolwald: 648x691
Mildrith: 639x699
Mildburh: 639x699
Aethelbald: 634x719
Headbert: 634x719
Eanulf: 634x719
Centwine: 672x729

Merioneth

Tybion: 346x516
Meirion: 384x534
Cadwaladr: 422x552

Gwrin Cutbeard: 460x570
Clydno: 498x588
Gwyddno: 536x606

Idris: 574x624, active 629x639
Sualda: 592x662
Brochwel: 610x700

Picts[9]

Mailcon: 490x520
Female: 488x538
Bridei: 526x546

Female: 506x546
Domelch: 485x576
Gwyddno: 543x564

Female: 543x584
Gartnait: 543x574
Uerb: 543x572

Appendix

Lutrin: 523x572
Nectu: 562x602
Cinioch: 573x600, 609x615–628x634
Female: 561x590
Uiud: 541x590
Garnard: 582x618
Breidei: 583x622, 632x638–637x642

Talorc: 594x628, 636x644–648x654
Female: 579x608
Eanfrith: 591x604
Male: 589x646
Female: 609x626
Donuel: 589x646
Talorcen: 609x636, 642x651–647x655

Bile: 594x690
Female: 627x664
Gartnait: 627x644, 646x656–651x660
Drest: 627x650
Female: 627x646
Derelei: 607x666

Aed Brecc: 478x550

Kenneth: 525x565

Finnie: 549x609

Lochyne: 587x627

Scanalt: 569x532

Moyle Keith: 607x647

Eochie Jarlaly: 607x647

Powys

Cadell: 465x529
Maig: 483x559
Cyngen: 486x539
Ieuaf: 483x559
Sanand: 504x577
Brochmael: 524x557
Mawan: 509x577
Cadell: 504x577

Tysilio: 562x575
Iago: 542x595
Cynan: 542x583
Llemineg: 547x623
Iddig: 522x615
Selyf: 560x584
Eiludd: 560x584
Tandreg: 560x584

Dingad: 560x564
Eli: 578x622
Temit: 578x622
Dona: 578x622
Gwylog: 596x660
Gwenfrewi: 596x660
Eliseg: 614x698

Alaogwr: 544x583
Cadfan: 562x601

Caradoc: 582x621

Cowryd: 580x639

Eliud: 450x651

Temic: 488x669

Tangusius: 488x669

Quimper

Gradlon: 528x576

Romelius: 457x553

Gwenael: 495x571

Rheged

Meirchion: 443x529
Cynfarch: 481x547
Elidyr: 461x567
Urien: 519x565

Efrddyl: 499x585
Llywarch: 479x605
Rhun: 537x583
Owain: 537x603

Pasgen: 537x603
Gwên: 497x643
Royth: 555x614
Rieinmellth: 591x632

Uther's Father: 387x474
Uthr: 425x492
Madog: 405x512

Arthur: 453x510
Eliwlod: 423x550

Amr: 471x548
Llacheu: 471x548

Selgouia

Senyllt: 480x528
Nudd Hael: 498x546

Gwenddoleu: 518x564

Dreon: 536x564

Strathclyde

Cynllwb: 369x451
Ceredig: 407x469
Cynwyd: 445x487
Dyfnwal: 483x505
Gwyddno: 521x543
Cynfelyn: 501x543

Tudwal: 519x541
Neithon: 559x581
Clydno: 519x581
Beli: 597x609
Rhydderch: 537x559
Cynon: 537x619

Bruide: 635x645
Owain: 615x627
Constantine: 555x597
Elffin: 633x665
Beli: 651x703

Vannes

Father: 467x502
Chanao: 505x536, x-560
Macliau: 497x520

Waroc: 535x538
Jacob: 531x558

Canao: 553x576
Trifina: 553x556

Vidimael: 532x573

Alvandus: 429x595

Wessex

Ceawlin: 542x543
Cutha: 560x569
Cynegils: 580x602
Cuthwine: 560x598
Ceadda: 582x607
Cwichelm: 598x620
Cuthwulf: 578x616

Cynebald: 588x636
Cenberht: 620x641
Cuthred: 616x626
Ceolwold: 618x634
Osric: 560x674
Oswald: 560x674
Oshere: 560x674

Mul: 638x679
Cædwalla: 658x659
Cœnred: 632x652
Cwoenburh: 651x690
Cuthburh: 651x670
Ine: 671x683
Ingild: 651x690

Cutha: 529x569
Ceolwulf: 552x592

Cuthgils: 570x615
Cenfrith: 588x633

Cenfus: 606x651
Æscwine: 624x669

Unattached Royal Families

Pabo: 480x546
Dunawd: 518x564

Sawyl: 498x584
Guitcun: 516x622

Cadwallon: 534x660

Gerascenus: 406x425

Meven: 444x543

Ynyr: 452x522
Idon: 488x560

Caradoc: 490x560

Digwc: 470x540

Eneas Ledwic: 447x527

Cadfan of Bardsey: 485x545

Gwyddno: 442x597

Elphin: 480x615

Tallwch: 413x532

Drust: 444x550

Medrawt: 413x550

Enhinti: 452x589

Serwan: 459x602

Urfoal: 364x585

Domnoc: 431x588

Mouric: 490x607

Mordaf: 497x620

Father: 384x565

Helenus: 422x583

Et cetera

Elidyr Mwynfawr: 497x578
Hennin: 468x576
Cunomorus: 513x536
Sanctanus: 490x607
Withur: 456x543

Hailoc: 485x568
Domnech: 420x623
Cadvennus: 394x625
Dygynnelw: 467x640
Tegfedd: 425x515

Hoernbiu: 442x545
Harvian: 456x540
Maian: 422x518
Rivannon: 422x583
Houaron: 422x583

Maglos: 404x564

Cunomaglos: 442x582

Ecclesiastical Date Ranges

Archbishops
Berhtwald: 621x634, 692

Aran

Bishop
Enda: 501x556

Monks
Rochath: 415x570

Berneich

Bishops
Felix: 567x600, 630–647
Eata: 608x633, 664–688
Æthelwine: 612x650, 680–692

Eadberht: 617x656, 686–697
Acca: 624x684

John of Beverley: 641x658, 688x721

Abbots
Hwætberht: 648x686, 716x720+
Botulf: 588x635, +674
Sigfrith: 634x646, 685x686–689
Eosterwine: 636x653, 681x683–685x686

Ceolfrith: 641/2, 680x681–717
Benedict: 609x649, 673–689
Cuthbert: 643x644, 685–687
Ealdwine: 592x670
Cudda: 605x655, 685
Verca: 605x655, 685

Hereberht: 605x656, 685x686
Cynefrith: 621x634, 669x670
Tibba: 624x680
Ebba: 624x680
Cynithryth: 624x680

Priests
Herefrith: 605x667, 685

Monks
Iwi: 667x682

Brycheiniog
Bishops
Dubricius: 490x496 Teilo: 515x520

Ceredigion
Abbot
Paternus of Llanbadarn: 465x545

Monks
Ketinlau: 415x607 Guinnius: 415x607 Guppir: 415x607
Titechan: 415x607

Cornwall
Abbots
Fingar: 477x611 Docco: 464x545 Elwyn: 433x673
Breaca: 477x611 Iuniavus: 477x590 Hia: 433x673
Cynan Colledauc: 465x521

Monks
Crewenna: 415x673

Dalriada
Abbots
Columba: 521, 563–597 Baithene: 554x604, 634

Deira
Bishops
Aedan: 571x605, 635–651 Paulinus: 564x595, 625–644 Bosa: 624x654, 680–704
Boisil: 605x633

Abbots
Badwini: 624x675 Sigfrith: 634x646, 685/686–689

Dubonnia
Bishop
Garmon: 440x577

Dumnonie
Bishops
Paternus Av: 472x543 Gwenael: 495x571 Tudy: 413x590
Albinus: 448x561 Gerennius: 490x560 Bothmael: 381x578
Winwaloe: 471x571 Malo: 488x561

Abbots
Brioc: 417x507 Samson: 512x525 Maudetus: 431x528
Leonorus: 507x508, 561 Maglorius: 472x545

Monks
Ethbin: 457x587
Areon: 420x623

Dyfed

Bishops
Gwistlian: 444x524 David: 465x512, 586x592 Paternus of Cynwyl: 420x520

Abbots
Bitheus: 483x568 Paulinus of Cynwyl: 415x520

Ercing

Bishops
Samson: 512x525, 2 years

Abbots
Piro: 492x533 Samson: 512x525

Glywising

Abbots
Bachan: 445x525 Carincinalis: 382x521 Petroc: 470x536
Gnouan: 410x589 Elli: 490x607 Tatheus: 465x520
Cadoc: 520x527 Illtud: 465x477
Finian of Llancarfan: 465x534 Machan: 490x607

Priests
Petrus: 415x598 Dator: 415x598 Dagan: 415x598

Monks
Guron: 415x598 MacMoil: 410x596 Cathmael: 410x596
Findbar of Llancarfan: 527x617

Gueroc

Bishops
Austolus: 457x575

Gwlad

Abbots
Cynidr: 470x577 Maedoc: 420x627

Gwynedd

Bishops

Kebi: 451x513　　　Curig: 450x557　　　Bernacus: 423x545

Abbots

Cadfan: 485x545　　　Guimarchus: 557x630　　　Tysilio: 566x575
Beuno: 518x585

Monks

Hewyn: 465x607　　　Mael: 465x607　　　Sulgen: 490x663

Manau

Bishops

Conindrus: 376x475　　　Rumilius: 367x475　　　MacCuil: 376x475

Nouant

Abbots

Uinniau: 499x514, 579x586　　　Maucennus: 465x549

Powys

Bishops

Tydecho: 445x495

Abbots

Wenefred: 488x631

Quimper

Bishops

Corentin: 471x581　　　Conocan: 431x528

Strathclyde

Bishops

Kentigern: 483x519　　　Macarius: 483x488

Vannes

Bishops

Paul Aurelian: 472x525　　　Goulven: 422x575　　　Gurgallonus: 420x632
Houaron: 422x583　　　Tudwal: 490x530　　　Elfin: 420x632
Goueznau: 448x561　　　Morhed: 420x632　　　Eunius: 498x549, 578x579

Abbots

Arthmael: 457x528

Monks

Lovenan: 449x605
Gonerus: 450x592

Et cetera

Agricola: 349x418
Gildas: 478x491
Modwenna: 611x680

Ronan: 556x730
Sona: 566x616

Sosanus: 573x623
Matericus: 523x685

Irish

Darerca: 410x605
Ninnoca: 470x582

Patrick: 413x443
Senan: 427x661

Ailbe: 447x512
Fintan: 451x582

Major Events

Honorian Rescript: 410
Germanus' first visit: 429
Germanus' second (?) visit: 437x446
Dyfed's Irish dynasty founded: 353x499
Rome falls: 476
Patrick's writings: 456x493
Cunedda's dynasty begins: 411x521
Illtud's school: 495x500–546x558
Riothamus' campaign: 458x460
Badon: 478x491
Patrick's floruit 443x493
Ceredig's floruit: 422x493
Ambrosius' floruit: 438x521
Arthur's floruit: 468x565
Camlann: 478x565

Maelgwn's rule: 505x540–535x572
De Excidio written: 521x535
Samson meets Childebert: 546x558
Gwrtheyrn's floruit: 560x593
Migration of Columba: 563
Bridei's rule: 559x576–579x586
Rhun's campaign: 543x572
Ardferydd: 573x579
Dubonnia's conquest: 560x595
Budic's death: 567x573
Urien's floruit: 574x620
Northern Memoranda: 664x671
Catraeth: 576x620
Dalriada united: 563x575
Æthelberht's *Bretwalda*: 593x596–616

Augustine's arrival: 597
Kentish source: 593x616
Æthelfrith's *Bretwalda*: 605–617
Circenn: 598
Degsastan: 603
Chester: 616
Rædwald's *Bretwalda*: 616–626
Edwin's *Bretwalda*: 626–632
Cadwallon in Northumbria: 632–633
Penda's rule: 633x655
Winwæd: 655
Council of Whitby: 664
Trent: 678x679
Nechtanesmere: 685
Bede's *Historia Ecclesiastica*: 732
Anglo-Saxon genealogies: 787+

Chapter Notes

Introduction

1. Piggott, "The Sources of Geoffrey of Monmouth I: The Pre-Roman King List," A 15 (Gloucester, 1941), 269–286.
2. Tatlock, *The Legendary History of Britain* (Berkeley: University of California Press, 1950), 7–115.
3. Dumville, "Sub-Roman Britain: History and Legend," *History* 62 (London, 1977a), 173–192.
4. It is assumed that he made use of the records kept for centuries in Egypt and now gone, but there is no proof of this.
5. Pharaoh Ptolemy II Philadelphus commissioned the work to cater to the new ruling class of Greeks that had recently assumed power. These descendants of Alexander's soldiers were unknowledgeable about Egypt and wanted an easily accessible and readily digestible version of Egyptian history.
6. Jordan, *Riddles of the Sphinx* (New York: New York University Press, 1998), 35–37.
7. Contra Dumville. The noted scholar is a well-respected paleographic expert, but his writings have spanned broadly Irish and British history, Patrick's chronology, Gildas, English geneaologies and king-lists, *Y Gododdin*, and *Historia Brittonum*.

Chapter 1

1. Prosper, year 429.
2. Morris, "Pelagian Literature," *JTS* 16 (1965), 36.
3. Lot, "De la valeur historique du *De Excidio* ... de Gildas," *Medieval Studies in Memory of Gertrude S. Loomis*, ed. Roger S. Loomis (New York: Columbia University Press, 1927), 235; Thompson, "Gildas and the history of Britain," *Brit* 10 (Stroud, 1979), 211; Wright, "Gildas' Prose Style and its Origins," *Gildas: New Approaches*, eds. David N. Dumville and Michael Lapidge (Woodbridge: Boydell Press, 1984), 107–128. This point is disputed by Myres and H. Williams, who have seen indirect references in Gildas' phraseology. However, in light of Gildas' Pelagian values, this seems unlikely. Myres, "The *Adventus Saxonum*," *Aspects of Archaeology in Britain and beyond*, ed. William F. Grimes (London: H.W. Edwards, 1951), 227; H. Williams, *Gildae De Excidio Britanniae* (London: Published for the Honourable Society of Cymmrodorion, 1899), 18.
4. Higham, *Rome, Britain and the Anglo-Saxons* (London: Seaby, 1992), 52.
5. Patrick was the most famed slave of the fourth and fifth centuries.
6. Alcock, *Arthur's Britain* (London: Allen Lane, 1971).
7. Myres, *The English Settlements* (Oxford: Clarendon Press, 1986). The document also seems to counter the arguments against Alcock's positions quite well.
8. Carver, "Kingship and Material Culture in Early Anglo-Saxon East Anglia," *The Origins of the Anglo-Saxon Kingdoms*, ed. Stephen Bassett (Leicester: Leicester University Press, 1989), 156.
9. Miller, "The Foundation Legend of Gwynedd in the Latin Texts," *BBCS* 27 (Cardiff, 1978a), 515–532.
10. Miller suggested the connective genealogy may have been formed as late as the writing of the *Historia Brittonum*.
11. It is widely accepted that Gildas wrote between 500 and 570, and the kings he decries are the sons and grandsons of kings.
12. Bassett, "In Search of the Origins of the Anglo-Saxon Kingdoms," *The Origins of the Anglo-Saxon Kingdoms*, ed. Steven Bassett (Leicester: Leicester University Press, 1989), 23; Wood, "Kings, Kingdoms and Consent," *Early Medieval Kingship*, eds. Peter H. Sawyer and Ian N. Wood (Leeds: University of Leeds, 1977), 18–20; Dumville, "Kingship, Genealogies and Regnal Lists," *Early Medieval Kingship*, eds. Peter H. Sawyer and Ian N. Wood (Leeds: University of Leeds, 1977b), 91–92; Yorke, "The Kingdom of the East Saxons," *ASE* 14 (London, 1985), 1–30; Arnold, *An Archaeology of the Early Anglo-Saxon Kingdoms* (New York: Routledge, 1988), 197–199.

13. Lapidge, "Gildas' Education and the Latin Culture of Sub-Roman Britain," *Gildas: New Approaches*, ed. David N. Dumville and Michael Lapidge. (Woodbridge: Boydell Press, 1984), 27–50.

14. Riché, *Education and Culture in the Barbarian West, Sixth through Eighth Centuries* (Columbia: University of South Carolina Press, 1976), 17–51.

15. Lapidge, "Gildas' Education and the Latin Culture of Sub-Roman Britain," *Gildas: New Approaches* (Woodbridge: Boydell Press, 1984), 27–50; Higham, *Rome, Britain and the Anglo-Saxons* (London: Seaby, 1992), 84, 164, 219.

16. Davies, *Wales in the Early Middle Ages* (Leicester: Leicester University Press, 1982), 132–133. Davies sites several examples of town elders acting in a local context, with and without the king's presence but always with his approval. Preserved documents of the meetings were, of course, kept in Latin. Such is the essence of the Roman local government and the activities of the *ordines*.

17. *De Excidio Britanniae*, 23.5–24.4.

18. Miller, "Date-Guessing and Dyfed," *SC* 13 (Cardiff, 1978c), 33–61.

Chapter 2

1. *Historia Brittonum*, preface.

2. Faulkner, *The Decline and Fall of Roman Britain* (Stroud: Tempus, 2000), 158.

3. Cameron, *Claudian: Poetry and Propaganda at the Court of Hadrian* (Oxford: Clarendon, 1970).

4. Thomas, *Christianity Up to About A.D. 500* (London, 1981).

5. Dark, "St. Patrick's *Uillula* and the Fifth-Century Occupation of Romano-British Villas," *Saint Patrick: A.D. 493–1993*, ed. David N. Dumville (Woodbridge: Boydell Press, 1993), 19–24.

6. Thompson, "St. Patrick and Coroticus," *JTS* 31 (1980), 12–27.

7. Mohrmann, *The Latin of St. Patrick: Four Lectures* (Dublin: Dublin Institute for Advanced Studies, 1961).

8. Jones and Casey, "The Gallic Chronicle Restored: A Chronology for the Anglo-Saxon Invasions and the End of Roman Britain," *B* 19 (Stroud, 1988), 367; Miller, "The Last British Entry in the *Gallic Chronicles*," *B* 19 (Stroud, 1978), 317.

9. Miller, "The Last British Entry in the 'Gallic Chronicles,'" *B* 9 (Stroud, 1978), 315–318.

10. *Chronica Minora I* (Berlin, 1886), 515–660, ed. Theodor Mommsen; Miller, "The Last British Entry in the 'Gallic Chronicles,'" *Brit* 9 (Stroud, 1978b), 315–318; Jones and Casey, "The Gallic Chronicle Restored: A Chronology for the Anglo-Saxon Invasions and the End of Roman Britain," *Brit* 19 (Stroud, 1978), 367–398; Burgess, "The Dark Ages Return to Fifth-Century Britain: The 'Restored' Gallic Chronicle Exploded," *Brit* 21 (Stroud, 1990), 185–195.

11. Mendelssohn compiled a complete list of discrepancies. Mendelssohn, *Zosimi comitis et exadvocati fisci historia nova* (Lipsiae, rep. 1963).

12. On the relevant passage alone, 6.10.2, see Thompson; Thompson, "Zosimus 6.10.2 and the Letters of Honorius," *CQ* 32 (London, 1977), 449–452.

13. Thompson, *St. Germanus of Auxerre and the end of Roman Britain* (Woodbridge: Boydell Press, 1984), 47–54.

14. Levison, "Bischof Germanus von Auxerre und die Quellen zu seiner Geschichte," *Neus Archiv der Gesellschaft für ältere deutsche Geschichtskunde* 29 (1903–04), 112; Bardy, "Constance de Lyon, biographe de saint Germain d'Auxerre," *Saint Germain d'Auxerre* (Auxerre, 1950), 96–97; Thompson, *St. Germanus of Auxerre and the End of Roman Britain* (Woodbridge: Boydell Press, 1984), 26.

15. Prosper of Aquitaine, *Chronicle*, 429.

16. The details of the incident are unimportant, though the personal bias shown through his editing in this and other instances is significant.

17. Bardy, "Constance de Lyon, biographe de saint Germain d'Auxerre," *Saint Germain d'Auxerre* (Auxerre, 1950), 107; Thompson, *St. Germanus of Auxerre and the end of Roman Britain* (Woodbridge: Boydell Press, 1984), 8–14. Incidentally, Thompson did pick up that the "tribunicionary power" associated with one of the British characters was just a descriptor, and not intended as a title.

18. Wacher, *The Towns of Roman Britain* (London: B.T. Batsford, 1974), 220–223, 238, 276, 312–315, 389; Todd, *Roman Britain, 55 B.C.–A.D. 400, The Province Beyond Ocean* (Brighton: Harvester Press, 1981), 241–242.

19. Thompson, *St. Germanus of Auxerre and the End of Roman Britain* (Woodbridge: Boydell Press, 1984), 13–14.

20. Kerlouégan, "Les destinées de la culture latina dans l'île de Bretagne au VI ème siècle. Recherches sur le *De Excidio Britanniae* de Gildas," unpublished Ph.D. thesis (Paris, 1977).

21. Lapidge, "Gildas' Education and the Latin Culture of Sub-Roman Britain," *Gildas: New Approaches*, ed. David N. Dumville and Michael Lapidge (Woodbridge: Boydell Press, 1984), 41–47. Lapidge was able to use the essays of Cicero as a guideline and systematically show Gildas' parallel use of the Roman style of legal argumentation.

22. Radzsher, *L'enseignement des lettres classiques d'Ausone à Alcuin* (Paris: Alphonse Picard et Fils, 1905), 161–169.

23. Lapidge, "Gildas' Education and the Latin Culture of Sub-Roman Britain," *Gildas: New Approaches*, ed. David N. Dumville and Michael Lapidge (Woodbridge: Boydell Press, 1984), 30–31.

24. A case could be made that Gildas was educated in a secular setting, but there is no indication in any of the secondary readings that this is so. It also seems a rather extreme conclusion to draw.

25. Ibid., 32–35.

26. Ibid., 35–39.
27. Ibid., 39–41; Wright, "Gildas's Prose Style and Its Origins," *Gildas: New Approaches*, ed. David N. Dumville and Michael Lapidge (Woodbridge: Boydell Press, 1984), 107–114.
28. Wright, "Gildas's Prose Style and Its Origins," *Gildas: New Approaches*, ed. David N. Dumville and Michael Lapidge (Woodbridge: Boydell Press, 1984), 107–128.
29. Schaffner, "Britain's Iudices," *Gildas: New Approaches*, ed. David N. Dumville and Michael Lapidge (Woodbridge: Boydell Press, 1984), 151–155.
30. *De Excidio Britanniae*, 15.3, 18.2, 18.3.
31. Thompson, "Gildas and the History of Britain," *Brit* 10 (Stroud, 1979), 206.
32. The century mark is a common apparatus in the determination of credibility in oral sources. Here, however, it would represent the remembrances of the oldest people in his society during his youth. If he was forty-three, then he is unlikely to have remembered anything before perhaps five years of age. Beyond that, it is a matter of chance. If there was firsthand experience dating back another sixty-five years before his birth, then 550 is a strong possibility for his year of publication. If his teachers were as young as forty, he would have had access to little beyond seventy years before his time of writing.
33. Sims-Williams, "Gildas and the Anglo-Saxons," *CMCS* 6 (Cambridge, 1983a), 22–24; Brooks, "The Creation and Early Structure of the Kingdom of Kent," *The Origins of the Anglo-Saxon Kingdoms*. ed. Stephen Bassett (Leicester: Leicester University Press, 1989), 58–64.
34. Dumville, "The Chronology of *De Excidio Britanniae*, Book I," *Gildas: New Approaches*, ed. David N. Dumville and Michael Lapidge (Woodbridge: Boydell Press, 1984), 82.
35. Lapidge, "Gildas' Education and the Latin Culture of Sub-Roman Britain," *Gildas: New Approaches*. eds. David N. Dumville and Michael Lapidge (Woodbridge: Boydell Press, 1984), 27–50.
36. Wright, "Gildas's Geographical Perspective: Some Problems," *Gildas: New Approaches*, ed. David N. Dumville and Michael Lapidge (Woodbridge: Boydell Press, 1984), 85–105.
37. Gregory of Tours, *The History of the Franks*, ed. Lewis Thorpe (Harmondsworth: Penguin, 1974), 34.
38. Ibid., 31.
39. Ibid., 26.
40. Rowland agreed on their early composition, and suggested that their entire lack of romance might be another indication that they belonged to the earliest stratum of traditions. Rowland, *Early Welsh Saga Poetry* (Cambridge: D.S. Brewer, 1990), 95.
41. Haycock, " 'Preiddeu Annwn' and the Figure of Taliesin," *SC* 14/15 (Cardiff, 1984), 52–77.
42. I. Williams' writing goes through the specific paleographic considerations in *Canu Taliesin* (Cardiff: Gwasg Prifysgol Cymru, 1960).
43. *The Gododdin: The Oldest Scottish Poem*, ed. Kenneth H. Jackson (Edinburgh: Edinburgh University Press, 1969), 51–3.
44. Sir Ifor Williams and Kenneth H. Jackson have edited the most widely accepted versions: Williams's *Canu Aneirin* (Cardiff: Gwasg Prifysgol Cymru, 1938) and Jackson's *The Gododdin: The Oldest Scottish Poem* (Edinburgh: Edinburgh University Press, 1969).
45. Charles-Edwards, "The Authenticity of the *Gododdin*: An Historian's View," *Astudiaethau ar yr Hengerdd*, eds. Rachel Bromwich and R. Brinley Jones (Cardiff: Gwasg Prifysgol Cymru, 1978), 50–51.
46. Jackson, "Edinburgh and the Anglian Occupation of Lothian," *The Anglo-Saxons: Studies Presented to Bruce Dickens*, ed. Peter Clemoes (London: Bowes and Bowes, 1959), 35–42; "The Britons of Southern Scotland," *Antiquity* 29 (Gloucester, 1955), 77–88; Charles-Edwards, "The Authenticity of the *Gododdin*: An Historian's View," *Astudiaethau ar yr Hengerdd*, eds. Rachel Bromwich and R. Brinley Jones (Cardiff: Gwasg Prifysgol Cymru, 1978), 64; Dumville, "Early Welsh Poetry: Problems of Historicity," *Early Welsh Poetry: Studies in the Book of Aneirin* (Aberystwyth: National Library of Wales, 1988), 2.
47. *The Gododdin of Aneirin*, ed. and trans. John T. Koch (Cardiff: University of Wales Press, 1997).
48. Miller, "Historicity and the Pedigrees of the Northcountrymen," *BBCS* 26 (Cardiff, 1975b), 260–265, 273–280.
49. *The Gododdin of Aneirin*, ed. and trans. John T. Koch (Cardiff: University of Wales Press, 1997), lxvi–lxx, lxxxix–cx. He was building off of Jarman, Jackson, and Charles-Edwards. *Aneirin: Y Gododdin—Britain's Oldest Heroic Poem*, ed. Alfred O.H. Jarman (Llandysul: Gomer Press, 1988), lxi–lxiii, lxx–lxxv; *The Gododdin: The Oldest Scottish Poem*, Kenneth H. Jackson (Edinburgh: Edinburgh University Press, 1969), 63–67; Charles-Edwards, "The Authenticity of the *Gododdin*: An Historian's View," eds. Rachel Bromwich and R. Brinley Jones. *Astudiaethau ar yr Hengerdd*. (Cardiff: Gwasg Prifysgol Cymru, 1978), 44–66.
50. Rowland, *Early Welsh Saga Poetry* (Cambridge: D.S. Brewer, 1990), 42.
51. Ibid., 46–47.
52. Ibid., 43.
53. Rowland believes that the beheader had control of the field, while Sir Ifor Williams believed the act was performed to save the king from disgrace; Rowland, *Early Welsh Saga Poetry* (Cambridge: D.S. Brewer, 1990), 78; I. Williams, "The Poems of Llywarch Hen," *The Beginnings of Welsh Poetry*, ed. Rachel Bromwich (Cardiff: University of Wales Press, 1972), 143; *Canu Llywarch Hen*, ed. Sir Ifor Williams (Cardiff: Gwasg Prifysgol Cymru, 1935), liv).
54. Rowland, *Early Welsh Saga Poetry* (Cambridge: D.S. Brewer, 1990), 367–389.
55. N.J.A. Williams, "Canu Llywarch Hen and

the Finn Cycle," *Astudiaethau ar yr Hengerdd*, ed. Rachel Bromwich and R. Brinley Jones (Cardiff: Gwasg Prifysgol Cymru, 1978), 234–265.

56. Rowland, *Early Welsh Saga Poetry* (Cambridge: D.S. Brewer, 1990), 82.

57. Ibid., 87–88.

58. Sims-Williams, *Religion and Literature in Western England, 600–800* (Cambridge: Cambridge University Press, 1990), 80; Poulin, "Hagiographie et Politique. La première de S. Samson de Dol," *Francia* 5 (Paris, 1977), 1–26. The reasoning behind this stance appears to be simply that the other Breton lives were written then, so that if Samson's was made in the seventh century it would stand in isolation.

59. *The Life of Samson of Dol*, trans. Thomas Taylor (Felinfach: Llanerch, 1991), xxxix; "Gildas's Geographical Perspective: Some Problems," *Gildas: New Approaches*, eds. David N. Dumville and Michael Lapidge. (Woodbridge: Boydell Press, 1984), 199 fn. 25; Davies, "Property Rights and Property Claims in Welsh 'Vitae' of the Eleventh Century," *Hagiographie, cultures, et sociétés ive-xiie siécles*, ed. Evelyne Patlagean and Pierre Riché (Paris: Etudes augustiniennes, 1981), 515; Duine, "La vie de S. Samson, à propos d'un ouvrage récent," *Annales de Bretagne* 28 (Paris, 1912–13), 332–56 ; Sharpe, "Gildas as Father of the Church," *Gildas: New Approaches*, ed. David N. Dumville and Michael Lapidge (Woodbridge: Boydell Press, 1984), 193 fn. 25..

60. *Vita Samsoni*, Books 26 and 27.

61. Johnson, *Origins of Arthurian Romances* (McFarland, 2012), 145–148.

62. Ibid., 152–153.

63. Dumville, "Tribal Hidage," *The Origins of the Anglo-Saxon Kingdoms*, ed. Stephen Bassett (Leicester: Leicester University Press, 1989), 225–230.

64. Stenton, *Anglo-Saxon England* (Oxford: Clarendon, 1971), 43, 296–297; Hart, "The Tribal Hidage," *TRHS* 21 (London, 1971), 133; Davies and Vierck, "The Contexts of the Tribal Hidage: Social Aggregates and Settlement Patterns," *Frümittlealterliche Studien* 8 (Berlin, 1974), 225; Hill, *Atlas of Anglo-Saxon England* (Oxford: Blackwell, 1982), 77; Sims-Williams, *Religion and Literature in Western England 600–800* (Cambridge: Cambridge University Press, 1990), 17.

65. Campbell, "Bede's *Reges* and *Principes*," (Jarrow Lecture, 1979), 5–8; Bassett, "In Search of the Origins of the Anglo-Saxon Kingdoms," *The Origins of the Anglo-Saxon Kingdoms*, ed. Stephen Bassett (Leicester: Leicester University Press, 1989), 24.

66. Brooks, "The Formation of the Mercian Kingdom," *The Origins of the Anglo-Saxon Kingdoms*, ed. Stephen Bassett (Leicester: Leicester University Press, 1989), 159.

67. Higham, *An English Empire* (Manchester: Manchester University Press, 1995), 76–77.

68. I. Williams, "Marwnad Cynddylan," *BBCS* 6 (Cardiff, 1932), 134–135.

69. The following scholars have generated opposing but unsupported theses regarding the dating and context for the poem; Finberg, *Lucerna* (London: St. Martin's Press, 1964); Richards, "The 'Lichfield' Gospels," *JNLW* 18 (Aberystwyth, 1973–74), 135–145; Gruffydd, "Marwnad Cynddylan," *Bardos*, ed. R. Geraint Gruffydd (Cardiff: Gwasg Prifysgol Cymru, 1982), 10–28.

70. "Marwnad Cynddylan," trans. John T. Koch. *The Celtic Heroic Age: Literary Sources for Ancient Celtic Europe and Early Ireland and Wales*, eds. John T. Koch and John Carey (Malden, MA: Celtic Studies Publications, 1994), ll. 28 and 48, respectively.

71. Dumville, "On the North British Section of the *Historia Brittonum*," *WHR* 8 (Cardiff, 1977c), 348.

72. Jackson, "On the Northern British Section in Nennius," *Celt and Saxon: Studies in the Early British Border*, ed. Nora K. Chadwick (Cambridge: University Press, 1963), 30, 38, 47.

73. Ibid., 45.

74. Sisam was the first to suggest that the genealogies were added around 800: "Anglo-Saxon Royal Genealogies," *PBA* 39 (London, 1953), 294, 328.

75. Dumville, "On the North British Section of the *Historia Brittonum*," *WHR* 8 (Cardiff, 1977c), 348.

76. Ibid., 348–349.

77. Ibid., 349.

78. Chadwick and Chadwick, *The Growth of Literature* (Cambridge: Cambridge University Press, 1932), 155.

79. Davies, "The Orthography of the Personal Names in the Charters of Liber Landevensis," *BBCS* 28 (Cardiff, 1980), 553–557; Koch, "When Was Welsh Literature First Written Down?," *SC* 20/21 (Cardiff, 1985–86), 43–66; Sims-Williams, "The Emergence of Old Welsh, Cornish, and Breton Orthography," 600–800: The Evidence of Archaic Old Welsh," *BBCS* 38 (Cardiff, 1991), 20–86.

80. *The Gododdin of Aneirin*, ed. and trans. John T. Koch (Cardiff: University of Wales Press, 1997), cxxi–cxxii.

81. Ibid, cxxiii.

82. As Chadwick long ago noted, Rhydderch is known as "Hael," generous, in the genaeologies while he is "Hen," old, in *Historia Brittonum*; Chadwick, "Early Culture and Learning in North Wales," *Studies in the Early British Church* (Cambridge: Cambridge University Press, 1958), 67.

83. Kirby, "Strathclyde and Cumbria: A Survey of Historical Development to 1092," *TCWAAS* 62 (Kendall, 1962), 71–92.

84. Bede, *Historia Ecclesiastica*, 1.36–37.

85. Ibid., 3.14.

86. Bede, *Historia Ecclesiastica*, 4.26.

87. Jackson, "The Sources for the Life of St. Kentigern," *Studies in the Early British Church*, ed. Nora K. Chadwick (Cambridge: Cambridge University Press, 1958), 286–293.

88. MacQueen, "Yvain, Ewen, and Owein ap Urien," *TDGNHAS* 33 (Dumfries, 1956), 107–131; Carney, *Studies in Irish Literature and History*

(Dublin, 1950), 79; *The Gododdin of Aneirin*, ed. and trans. John T. Koch (Cardiff: University of Wales Press, 1997), lxxvi–lxxix.

89. Ibid., lxxviii–lxxix.

90. Ibid., lxxix.

91. *The Gododdin of Aneirin*, ed. and trans. John T. Koch (Cardiff: University of Wales Press, 1997), lxxix.

92. *Symeonis Monachi Opera Omnia*, ed. Thomas Arnold, vol. 1 (London: Longman, 1882–1885), 48.

93. MacQueen, "Yvain, Ewen, and Owein ap Urien," *TDGNAHS* 33 (Dumfries, 1956), 107–131; "A Reply to Professor Jackson," *TDGNAHS* 36 (Dumfries, 1959), 175–83.

94. Jackson, "The Sources for the Life of St. Kentigern," *Studies in the Early British Church*, ed. Nora K. Chadwick (Cambridge: Cambridge University Press, 1958), 314–315.

95. Davies, *An Early Welsh Microcosm* (London: Royal Historical Society, 1978), 4.

96. Ibid., 5.

97. Davies, "*Liber Landavensis*: Its Construction and Credibility," *EHR* 88 (London, 1973), 337–342.

98. *Llandaff Charters*, ed. Wendy Davies (Aberystwyth: National Library of Wales, 1979), 21. This method consists of an editor's formula, a witness list, and a feasible chronology for the persons in that list.

99. Davies, *An Early Welsh Microcosm* (London: Royal Historical Society, 1978), 14–15.

100. Richmond and Crawford, "The British Section of the Ravenna Cosmography," *Archaeologia Cambrensis* 93 (1949), 1.

101. Richmond and Crawford also followed Haverfield in using the details regarding the Roman political structure in coming to the same conclusion. However, the Romans had the attitude that all old Roman territories were not lost and would be recovered. Because of their outlook, it might have seemed perfectly rational to continue recording the region with its Roman administration well into the seventh century. The perception of Anglo-Saxons as newcomers to Britain, however, would not have persisted so long.

102. We shall see reason for dating this "new" development to the late fourth century, and pushing back the date of the source of the British section to perhaps a century earlier than 500.

103. So old, in fact, that Garmon's context was forgotten by the time the information about him was transferred to Gwynedd.

104. Dumville, "Sub-Roman Britain: History and Legend," *History* 62 (London, 1977), 186.

105. Ibid., 186.

106. Chadwick, "Early Culture and Learning in North Wales," *Studies in the Early British Church*, ed. Nora K. Chadwick (Cambridge: Cambridge University Press, 1958), 110–118.

107. Although Judith McClure has written a convincing argument that Bede may have penned the *vita*, such a connection would create no serious differences in the work's interpretation. At worst, it would indicate that Bede matured as an historian; McClure, "Bede and the *Life of Ceolfrith*," *Peritia* 3 (Galway, 1984), 71–84.

108. *The Age of Bede*, trans. and ed. David H. Farmer (Harmondsworth: Penguin, 1965), 36–37.

109. Kirby, "Northumbria in the Time of Bede," *St. Wilfrid at Hexham*, ed. David Kirby (Newcastle-upon-Tyne, 1974), 2–4; Bonner, "Bede and His Teachers and Friends," *Famulus Christi: Essays in Commemoration of the Thirteenth Centenary of the Birth of the Venerable Bede*, ed. Gerald Bonner (London: S.P.C.K., 1976), 20, 22; Mayvaert, "Bede the Scholar," *Famulus Christi: Essays in Commemoration of the Thirteenth Centenary of the Birth of the Venerable Bede*, ed. Gerald Bonner (London: S.P.C.K., 1976), 56, 62; Mackay, "Bede's Hagiographical Method: His Knowledge and Use of Paulinus of Nola," *Famulus Christi: Essays in Commemoration of the Thirteenth Centenary of the Birth of the Venerable Bede*, ed. Gerald Bonner (London: S.P.C.K., 1976), 91, 120; Wormald, "Bede and Benedict Biscop," *Famulus Christi: Essays in Commemoration of the Thirteenth Centenary of the Birth of the Venerable Bede*, ed. Gerald Bonner (London: S.P.C.K., 1976), 55; Blair, *An Introduction to Anglo-Saxon England* (Cambridge: Cambridge University Press, 1977), 325–326; Campbell, *The Anglo-Saxons* (London: Penguin, 1982), 84; Lapidge, "The Anglo-Latin Background," *A New Critical History of Old English Literature*, eds. Stanley B. Greenfield and Daniel G. Calder (New York: New York University Press, 1986), 16–22.

110. Laistner, *Thought and Letters in Western Europe A.D. 500–900* (Ithaca: Cornell University Press, 1957), 162; Kirby, "Bede's Native Sources for the *Historia Ecclesiastica*," *Bulletin of the John Rylands Library* 48 (London, 1965–1966), 341–371; Lapidge, *The Anglo-Saxon Library* (Oxford: Oxford University Press, 2006), 60; Brown, *A Companion to Bede* (Woodbridge: Boydell Press, 2009), 3–8. Lapidge has claimed a library of roughly 250 books in addition to biblical and liturgical materials, while Laistner estimated nearly 200 books.

111. Miller, "Bede's Use of Gildas," *EHR* 90 (London, 1975a), 241–261.

112. Kirby, "Bede and Northumbrian Chronology," *EHR* 78 (London, 1963), 514–527.

113. The argument has often been made that the entire book was composed to negate Wilfrid's power by counterposing him with John of Hexham, Aidan, and especially Cuthbert: Goffart, *Narrators of Barbarian History* (Princeton: Princeton University Press, 1988), 235–328; Goffart, "The *Historia Ecclesiastica*: Bede's Agenda and Ours," *Haskins Society Journal* 12 (Woodbridge, 1990), 29–45; DeGregorio, "Bede's History in a Harsher Climate," *Venerable Bede*, ed. Scott De Gregorio (Morgantown, 2006), 203–226.

114. Kirby, "King Ceolwulf of Northumbria and the *Historia Ecclesiastica*," *SC* 14/15 (Cardiff, 1980), 168–173; Higham, *An English Empire* (Manchester: Manchester University Press, 1995), 9–13.

115. Wormald went so far as to say that the primary purpose of the book was to show that his people were God's chosen; Wormald, "Engla Land: The Making of an Allegiance," *Journal of Sociology* 7:1 (London, 1994), 1–24.

116. Take "black earth," for example. Post-Roman scholars have long taken it to mean a settlement's disuse, whereas archaeologists focusing on other periods have often seen it as an indication of heavy use.

Chapter 3

1. *Crith Gablach*, ed. David Binchy (Oxford, 1970), preface.

2. *The Laws of the Earliest English Kings*, ed. and trans. F.L. Attenborough (Cambridge: The University Press, 1922), 34.

3. Mulchrone, "Die Abfassungszeit und Überlieferung der Vita Tripartita," *ZCP* 16 (Berlin, 1926), 411–452; Stokes, *The Saltair na Rann*; Strachan, "The Verbal System of Saltair na Rann," *Transactions of the Philological Society* (Oxford, 1895), 1–76.

4. Bannerman, *Studies in the History of Dalriada* (Edinburgh: Scottish Academic Press, 1974), 118–132.

5. Hector Chadwick saw certain genealogical discrepancies which indicated a date of about 750: Chadwick, *Early Scotland. The Picts, the Scots, and the Welsh of Southern Scotland* (Cambridge: Cambridge University Press, 1949), 35–37.

6. *Vita Columbae*, 3.5.

7. *Historia Ecclesiastica*, 3.6.

8. Ibid., 1.1.

9. Chadwick, *Early Scotland*, 122.

10. These are the *Fland*, the *Duan*, and *The Chronicle of the Kings of Scotland*.

11. Bannerman, *Studies in the History of Dalriada* (Edinburgh: Scottish Academic Press, 1974), 122.

12. *Book of Leinster*, A List, 190b.

13. *Yellow Book of Lecan*, ed. Lambert A.J. McKenna; *Leabhar Breac*, ed. Robert Atkinson (Dublin, 1887).

14. Pp. 593 and 46.

15. *Historia Ecclesiastica*, 1.1.

16. O'Rahilly, *Early Irish History and Mythology* (Dublin: Dublin Institute for Advanced Studies, 1946a), 222; MacNiocaill, *Ireland Before the Vikings* (Dublin: Gill and Macmillan, 1972), 9–14.

17. Miller, "The Foundation Legend of Gwynedd in the Latin Texts," *BBCS* 27 (Cardiff, 1978a), 515–532.

18. Hughes, *Early Christian Ireland: Introduction to the Sources* (Ithaca, NY: Cornell University Press, 1972), 121–123.

19. Ibid., 118–119.

20. Ibid., 141.

21. Grosjean, "Sur quelques exégetes irlandáis du viie siècle," *Sacris Erudiri* 7 (Steenbrugge, 1955), 67–98.

22. Hughes, *Early Christian Ireland: Introduction to the Sources* (Ithaca, NY: Cornell University Press, 1972), 138.

23. MacNeill, "The Authorship of the *Annals of Tigernach*," *Ériu* 7 (Dublin, 1914), 30–114.

24. Hughes, *Early Christian Ireland: Introduction to the Sources* (Ithaca, NY: Cornell University Press, 1972), 106.

25. Ibid., 124.

26. Though it has been well established on internal evidence that the *Annals of Ulster* is consistently one year behind on true dates; Walsh, "The Dating of the Irish Annals," *HIS* 2 (Dublin, 1940–1941), 365–369; O'Rahilly, *Early Irish History and Mythology* (Dublin: Dublin Institute for Advanced Studies, 1946a), 242–243.

27. Ó Máille, *The Language of the Annals of Ulster* (Manchester: Manchester University Press, 1910), 9.

28. Hughes, *Early Christian Ireland: Introduction to the Sources* (Ithaca, NY: Cornell University Press, 1972), 142.

29. The *Welsh Annals* are to be found in four manuscripts. The best is *Harleian 3859*, written around 1100. It is also to be found in the Exeter Cathedral Library 3514 of the thirteenth century, and recorded under *Cotton Domitian A* and the flyleaves of the *Breviate Domesday Manuscript*, both of the late thirteenth century.

30. Phillimore, "The *Annales Cambriae* and Old-Welsh Genealogies from Harleian Ms. 3859," *Y Cymmrodor* 8 (Cardiff, 1888), 144.

31. Hughes, "The Welsh Latin Chronicles: *Annales Cambriae* and Related Texts," *PBA* 59 (London, 1975), 235.

32. Ibid., 235–236.

33. The Gildan mention of Badon and the overwhelming references to Camlann indicate these were both battles of importance well beyond the regions in which they were fought, wherever they may have been located.

34. Hughes, "The Welsh Latin Chronicles: *Annales Cambriae* and Related Texts," *PBA* 59 (London, 1975), 237.

35. Rowland has noted that, while Urien and his allies are entirely absent from the secular records, several of his literary enemies—Gwrgi and Peredur, Dunawt, and Cerdic son of Gwallawg are present. This has some very interesting implications. However, they are not relevant to the present discussion.

36. Hughes, "The Welsh Latin Chronicles: *Annales Cambriae* and Related Texts," *PBA* 59 (London, 1975), 233–258.

37. Ibid., 367–389; I. Williams, "The Poems of Llywarch Hen." *PBA* 18 (London, 1931), 269–302.

38. Rowland, *Early Welsh Saga Poetry* (Cambridge: D. S. Brewer, 1990), 120–141.

39. Ibid., 141–145.
40. O'Rahilly, "On the Origins of the Names *Érainn* and *Ériu*," *Ériu* 14 (Dublin, 1946), 7–28; MacCana, "Aspects of the Theme of the King and Goddess," *EC* 6 (Paris, 1955), 356–413.
41. Dumville, " 'Nennius' and the *Historia Brittonum*," *SC* 11 (Cardiff, 1976), 78–95. More recently, Higham has suggested that the author may have been an outsider of the Welsh culture, as was the case with Alcuin and Asser in creating Anglo-Saxon histories; Gruffydd, "From Gododdin to Gwynedd: reflection on the story of Cunedda" *SC* 24/25 (Cardiff, 1989/1990), 1–14.
42. Chadwick, "Early Culture and Learning in North Wales," *Studies in the Early British Church*, ed. Nora K. Chadwick (Cambridge: Cambridge University Press, 1958), 29–34.
43. Ibid., 120.
44. Higham, *King Arthur: Mythmaking and History* (New York: Routledge, 2002), 117. In a matter of four years, three Mercian kings died attempting to maintain their position of dominance.
45. Chadwick, "Early Culture and Learning in North Wales," *Studies in the Early British Church*, ed. Nora K. Chadwick (Cambridge: Cambridge University Press, 1958), 34–36.
46. Ibid., 74–79.
47. Dumville, "*Historia Brittonum*: An Insular History from the Carolingian Age," *Historiographie im frühen Mittelalter*, Scharer and Scheibelreitr (eds.), Munich, 1994), 406–434.
48. Chadwick, "Early Culture and Learning in North Wales," *Studies in the Early British Church*, ed. Nora K. Chadwick (Cambridge: Cambridge University Press, 1958), 47.
49. *The Historia Brittonum: 3.The Vatican Recension*, ed. David N. Dumville (Cambridge: D. S. Brewer, 1985), 4–8.
50. Dumville continues to believe that the ninth-century rivalry between Gwynedd and Powys was the cause for the development of the Vortigern legend in *Historia Brittonum*, and Higham concurs. Whether the animosity of Gwynedd or Dyfed was the case, two facts remain. First is that both Dyfed and Gwynedd influenced our modern version of *Historia Brittonum*. Second, it is plain that the additional information to be found on Vortigern there is political mudslinging and nothing more; Dumville, "*Historia Brittonum*: An Insular History from the Carolingian Age," *Historiographie im frühen Mittelalter*, eds. A. Scharer and G Scheibelreiter (Munich, 1994), 411; Higham, *King Arthur: Mythmaking and History* (New York: Routledge, 2002), 130.
51. Ford, *The Poetry of Llywarch Hen* (Berkeley: University of California Press, 1974), 24–32.
52. Rowland, "A Study of the Saga Englynion," Unpublished Ph.D. thesis (Cardiff, 1982), 82–90. There is no englyn for Dwg.
53. Rowland, *Early Welsh Saga Poetry* (Cambridge: D. S. Brewer, 1990), 8–10.
54. I. Williams, *Canu Llywarch Hen* (Cardiff: Gwasg Prifysgol Cymru, 1935), xxiv; "Llywarch Hen and the Finn Cycle," *Astudiaethau ar yr Hengerdd*, ed. Rachel Bromwich and R. Brinley Jones (Cardiff: Gwasg Prifysgol Cymru, 1978), 234–265.
55. Rowland, *Early Welsh Saga Poetry* (Cambridge: D.S. Brewer, 1990), 11–39.
56. Ibid., 367–389.
57. TYP, lxxx–lxxxiii.
58. Ibid., xx–xxi, xxvi.
59. Ibid., cx–cxi.
60. Ibid., cxi–cxv.
61. Hodgkin, *A History of the Anglo-Saxons* (Oxford: Clarendon Press, 1935); Plummer, *Two of the Saxon Chronicles Parallel*, vol. 2 (Oxford: Clarendon Press, 1892–1899), civ.
62. Stenton, "The South-Western Element in the Old English Chronicle," *Essays in Medieval History Presented to Thomas Frederick Tout* (Manchester, 1925), 15–24.
63. Stenton, *Anglo-Saxon England* (Oxford: Clarendon, 1959), 22–23.
64. Dumville, "The West Saxon Genealogical Regnal List and the Chronology of Early Wessex," *Peritia* 4 (Galway, 1985), 21–66.
65. Kirby, "Problems of Early West Saxon History," *EHR* 80 (London, 1965), 10–29.
66. Chadwick, *Origins of the English Nation* (Cambridge: The University Press, 1907), 25–35.
67. Stenton, "The Foundations of English History," *TRHS* 9 (London, 1926), 163–164.
68. As has been seen, the Powysian genaeologies are the most notorious example.
69. The study of Glastonbury's literature is far and away the most complete on the subject; Lesley Abrams and James P. Carley (eds.) *The Archaeology and History of Glastonbury Abbey: Essays in Honour of the Ninetieth Birthday of C. A. Ralegh Radford* (Woodbridge: Boydell, 1991).
70. Lejeune, "The Troubadours," *Arthurian Literature in the Middle Ages*, ed. Roger S. Loomis (Oxford: Clarendon Press, 1959), 393–399.
71. Johnson, *Origins of Arthurian Romances* (McFarland, 2012).
72. The present author has no further plans in that arena. However, Gawain's obvious and ancient ties to Galloway (Galweiya) and Carlisle would be the best subjects.

Chapter 4

1. Wells, *Bones, Bodies, and Disease* (London: Thames and Hudson, 1964).
2. Ibid., 179.
3. Miller, *Sicilian Colony Dates* (Albany: State University of New York Press, 1970), 122–123.
4. Angel, "The Length of Life in Ancient Greece," *Journal of Gerontology* 2 (St. Louis, 1947), 18–24.
5. To find this one, add the odds of living fifteen years to itself (x), and subtract that total from x2.

6. MacNeill, "The Irish Law of Dynastic Succession," *Studies* 8 (Dublin, 1919), 367–382, 640–653; Charles-Edwards, *Early Irish and Welsh Kinship* (Oxford: Clarendon Press, 1993).

7. Byrne, *Irish Kings and High-Kings* (London: St. Martin's, 1973), 281–284.

8. *The Law of Hywel Dda*, trans. and ed. Dafydd Jenkins (Llandysul: Gomer Press, 1986); Kelly, *A Guide to Early Irish Law* (Dublin: Dublin Institute for Advanced Studies, 1988); Gagarin, *Early Greek Law* (Berkeley: University of California Press, 1986).

Chapter 5

1. His sister's name was Æthelberga, and names tended to run consistent in the English royal families.

Chapter 6

1. An excellent example of this is Thompson's paper. However, Zosimus has seemingly been quite deliberate in dating the Honorian rescript, and the scholar takes pains to show that he was quite accurate here. "Zosimus 6.10.2 and the Letters of Honorius," *CQ* 32 (1982), 445–462.

2. Thompson, "Britain, A.D. 406–410," *Brit* 8 (Stroud, 1977), 303–318; Stevens, "Marcus, Gratian, Constantine" *Athenaeum* 35 (New Haven, 1957), 316–347.

3. Thompson has done a wonderful job of taking the most likely chronology for the above series of events, and if the sources being used were proven to be accurate, his is the most likely to relay historical fact.

4. Based on Zosimus, who said that barbarians from across the Rhine threatened Britain and forced them to take up a new government in order to fight them off.

5. Thompson, "Britain, A.D. 406–410," *Britannia* 8 (Stroud, 1977), 318.

6. Ibid., 306–315.

7. Zosimus, *Zosimus: New History*, trans. Ronald T. Ridley (Canberra: Canberra Central Printing, 1982), 6.5.2

8. Faulkner has recently stated that the idea of continuity is based entirely on the evidence of Verulanium and the *Vita Germani*. However, he gives no specific evidence to support his theory. Further, the aspect of Roman culture that the author believes survived would not have been easily recoverable in the archaeological record; Faulkner, *The Decline and Fall of Roman Britain* (Stroud: Tempus, 2000), 174–7.

9. Myres has written an interesting paper hypothesizing that Pelagius' theories may have been given a political application focusing on the upper class. If this is so, it may help to explain the movement toward independence by Britain around 410. The subsequent loss of the wealthy portion of the British population in the years following the Hadrianic rescript would then explain the anarchy Germanus found on his first visit. Myres, "Pelagius and the end of Roman Britain," *The Journal of Roman Studies* 50 (London, 1960), 21–36.

10. The author would like to emphasize that Constantius is careful not to call Elafius a tribune. It appears clear that he had some idea what this person's responsibilities were, and they could most easily be equated with that of a tribune.

11. It is possible that a king might have been intentionally erased from the *vita*. However, Constantius appears to have no issues with rulers, and seems to be almost disinterested in the trips to Britain. It has been noted that they are lacking in detail.

12. Prosper of Aquitaine, *Prosperi Aquitaini opera*, eds. P. Callens and M. Gastaldo (Turnhout: Brepols, 1972), year 429.

13. The debate is largely settled in favor of 493, though for the purpose of the following discussion such a differentiation is unnecessary.

14. Mohrmann, *The Latin of St. Patrick. Four Lectures* (Dublin: Dublin Institute for Advanced Studies, 1961), 50.

15. That Patrick's ancestors could also be in religious orders would not have raised an eyebrow in the fifth century. Up to that point, it was not against church canon for a priest to be married and involved in conjugal relations.

16. Dumville has raised objection to the assumption, but has produced no evidence that the connection might be invalid; Dumville, "Coroticus," *St. Patrick: A.D. 1993*, ed. David N. Dumville (Woodbridge: Boydell Press, 1993), 114–115.

17. Johnson, *Evidence of Arthur: Fixing the Legendary King in Place and Time* (McFarland, 2014).

18. Ibid.

19. *De Excidio Britanniae*, 25.2–26.1

20. Wright, "Gildas's Prose Style and Its Origins," *Gildas: New Approaches*, eds. David N. Dumville and Michael Lapidge (Woodbridge: Boydell Press, 1984), 107–128.

21. Taliesin, *Book of Taliesin*, trans. John T. Koch and John Carey, *The Celtic Heroic Age*, eds. John T. Koch and John Carey (Malden, MA: Celtic Studies Publications, 1995), 341-3.

22. *De Excidio Britanniae*, 27.

23. Mac Cana, "Aspects of the Theme of the King and Goddess," *EC* 6 (Paris, 1955), 356–413.

24. O'Rahilly, "On the Origin of the Names *Érain* and *Ériu*," *Ériu* 35 (Dublin, 1946b), 7–28.

25. Campbell, "The End of Roman Britain," *The Anglo-Saxons*, ed. James Campbell (London: Penguin, 1982), 8–19.

26. Thompson, *St. Germanus of Auxerre and the end of Roman Britain* (Woodbridge: Boydell and Brewer, 1984), 37.

Chapter 7

1. Tacitus, *The Complete Works of Tacitus*, trans. Alfred J. Church and William J. Brodribb, ed. Moses

Hadas (New York: Modern Library, 1942), 1.59, 2.66.

2. Dio Cassius, *Dio's Roman History*, trans. Earnest Cary (London: W. Heinemann, 1914), 71.16.

3. Zosimus, *Zosimus: New History*, trans. Ronald T. Ridley (Canberra: Canberra Central Printing, 1982), 1.68.

4. Frere, *Britannia: A History of Roman Britain*. (London: Routledge and Kegan Paul, 1967), 186.

5. Sextus Aurelius Victor, *Liber de Caesaribus*, trans. H.W. Bird (Liverpool: Liverpool University Press, 1994), 39.41-2.

6. Ammianus Marcellinus, ed. John C. Rolfe (Cambridge: Harvard University Press, 1971-72), 29.4.

7. Goffart, *Barbarians and Romans 418-584: The Techniques of Accommodation* (Princeton: Princeton University Press, 1980).

8. Salway, *Roman Britain* (Oxford: Oxford University Press, 1984), 228.

9. Ibid., 232.

10. Frere, *Britannia: A History of Roman Britain*. (London: Routledge and Kegan Paul, 1967), 184, 188.

11. Ibid., 348; Cunliffe, *Rome and the Barbarians* (London: Bodley Head, 1975), 430.

12. Myres, "Romano-Saxon Pottery," *Dark-Age Britain: Studies Presented to E.T. Leeds*, ed. Donald B. Harden (London: Methuen, 1956), 16-39. Contra Gillam, "Romano-Saxon Pottery: An Alternative Explanation," *The End of Roman Britain*, ed. P. John Casey (London: B.A.R., 1979), 103-118; Roberts, *Romano-Saxon Pottery* (Oxford: B.A.R., 1982). Even if the pottery may not be considered proof of a Germanic presence, the fact forces any scholar to admit it is good evidence for such a presence.

13. Evison, "Distribution Map of England in the First Two Phases," *Angles, Jutes and Saxons*, ed. Vera I. Evison (Oxford: Clarendon Press, 1981), 126-167.

14. Roberts, *Romano-Saxon Pottery* (Oxford: B.A.R., 1982).

15. Bede, *Historia Ecclesiastica*, 1.15. Incidentally, as the *Anglo-Saxon Chronicle* may have used one of several dating systems, what was listed there as 449 may have meant the year 449x450 beginning March 25 or September 24; *The Anglo Saxon Chronicle*, trans. George N. Garmonsway (London: Dent, 1953), xxvii.

16. Härke, *Angelsächsische Waffengräber des 5. bis 7. Jarhhunderts* (Cologne, 1992).

17. Arnold, *An Archaeology of the Early Anglo-Saxon Kingdoms* (New York: Routledge, 1988), 189.

18. Ibid., 188-210.

19. Certainly *skops* and metalworkers, as prized members of society, were not slaves.

20. Arnold, *An Archaeology of the Early Anglo-Saxon Kingdoms* (New York: Routledge, 1988), 199.

21. Miller, "The Dates of Deira," *ASE* 8 (London, 1979), 61; Dumville, "Kingship, Genealogies and Regnal Lists," *Early Medieval Kingship*, eds. Peter H. Sawyer and Ian N. Wood (Leeds: University of Leeds, 1977b), 78.

22. Chaney, *The Cult of Kingship in Anglo-Saxon England* (Manchester: University Press, 1970), 12-17. De Vries argued that the roles of war leader and sacral kingship were originally separated and distinguished by Woden and Tiw, respectively. De Vries, "Das Königtum bei den Germanen," *Saeculum* 7 (Munich, 1956), 290, 296-300.

23. Gildas, *De Excidio Brittaniae*, 26.2.

Chapter 8

1. Used loosely by John Morris, though more recently by Brooks and Yorke; Morris, *The Age of Arthur* (London: Weidenfeld and Nicolson, 1973); Brooks, "The Creation and Early Structure of the Kingdom of Kent," *The Origins of the Anglo-Saxon Kingdoms*, ed. Stephen Bassett (Leicester: Leicester University Press, 1989), 58-64; Yorke, *Kings and Kingdoms of Early Anglo-Saxon England* (London: Routledge, 1990), 26.

2. Bede, *Historia Ecclesiasticae*, preface.

3. A.D. 735-739.

4. Bede, *Historia Ecclesiastica*, 1.25.

5. Sims-Williams, "The Settlement of England in Bede and the *Chronicle*," *ASE* 12 (London, 1983), 22 fn. 90.

6. Bede, *Historia Ecclesiastica*, 1.15

7. Dumville, "Kingship, Genealogies and Regnal Lists," *Early Medieval Kingship*, eds. Peter H. Sawyer and Ian N. Wood (Leeds: University of Leeds, 1977b), 72-104.

8. Sims-Williams, "The settlement of England in Bede and the *Chronicle*," *ASE* 12 (London, 1983), 25.

9. Bede, *Historia Ecclesiasticae*, 4.16; Chadwick, *Origins of the English Nation* (Cambridge: The University Press, 1907), 3-5, 26-28, 84, and 97.

10. Bede, *Historia Ecclesiasticae*, 2.5.

11. Wheeler, "Gildas' de Excidio Britanniae, Chapter 26," *EHR* 41 (London, 1926), 501-502; Brooks, "The Creation and Early Structure of the Kingdom of Kent," *The Origins of the Anglo-Saxon Kingdoms*, ed. Stephen Bassett (Leicester: Leicester University Press, 1989), 67.

12. Higham, *King Arthur: Mythmaking and History* (New York: Routledge, 2002), 130-31.

13. Undermining the established history of a native kingdom would have sent a message of division. Conversely, the editor's purpose was to unify the Anglo-Saxons.

14. Harrison, *The Framework of Anglo-Saxon England to 900 A.D.* (Cambridge: Cambridge University Press, 1976), 121-123.

15. This is the only reference to Æthelberht before 593.

16. Jackson, *Language and History in Early Britain* (Edinburgh: University Press, 1953), 464-466 and 677.

17. Ibid., 616-617. Sims-Williams, however, has expressed concerns with this conclusion: Sims-

Williams, "The Settlement of England in Bede and the *Chronicle*," *ASE* 12 (London, 1983b), 33–34.

18. Turville-Petre, "Hengest and Horsa," *Saga-Book of the Viking Society* 14 (London, 1953–1957), 287. Turville-Petre called Æsc a Wessex substitute for Oisc, without explaining the linguistics. Whether or not there was originally such a connection, they hold the same position in the sources and the Kentish lineage.

19. Sims-Williams, "The Settlement of England in Bede and the *Chronicle*," *ASE* 12 (London, 1983b), 1–5, 26–41.

20. There will be a great deal more to be said of these characters in the next chapter.

21. Sims-Williams, "The Settlement of England in Bede and the *Chronicle*," *ASE* 12 (London, 1983b), 19–20.

22. A good number of scholars have demonstrated the need of the Germanic peoples to continue their continental traditions: Enright, "The Sutton Hoo Whetstone Sceptre: A Study in Iconography and Cultural Milieu," *ASE* 11 (1983), 119–134; Mitchell, "The Whetstone as Symbol of Authority in Old English and Old Norse," *Scandinavian Studies* 57 (Cambridge, 1985), 1–31; Nicholson, "*Beowulf* and the Pagan Cult of the Stag," *Studi Medievali* 27 (Spoleto, 1986), 637–669; Neuman de Vegvar, "The Iconography of Kingship in Anglo-Saxon Archaeological Finds," *Kings and Kingship, Acta 11*, ed. J. Rosenthal (Binghamton: Center for Medieval and Early Renaissance Studies, State University of New York at Binghamton, 1984), 1–15; Webster, "Death's Diplomacy: Sutton in the Light of Other Male Princely Burials," *Sutton Hoo: Fifty Years After*, ed. R. Farrell and C. Neuman de Vegvar (Oxford, OH: American Early Medieval Studies, Miami University, Department of Art, 1992), 75–82; Carver, "The future of Sutton Hoo," *A Voyage to the Other World: The Legacy of Sutton Hoo*, eds. C.B. Kendall and P.S. Wells (Minneapolis: University of Minnesota Press, 1992b), 183–200.

23. Northumbria was a special case because of its place in history. Northumbria was the origin point for much of the material in Bede and *Historia Brittonum*, and because it had recorded and retained an early history of its own, Kent could not maintain any claim that it had converted Northumbria.

24. Leslie Abrams and James P. Carley (eds.) *The Archaeology and History of Glastonbury Abbey. Essays in Honour of the Nineteeth Birthday of C. A. Ralegh Radford* (Woodbridge: Boydell Press, 1991).

25. Harrison, *The Framework of Anglo-Saxon History* (Cambridge: Cambridge University Press, 1976), 122–123.

26. Wallace-Hadrill, *Early Germanic Kingship in England and on the Continent* (Oxford: Clarendon Press, 1971), 45.

27. Brooks, "The Creation and Early Study of the Kingdom of Kent," *The Origins of the Anglo-Saxon Kingdoms*, ed. Stephen Bassett (Leicester: Leicester University Press, 1989), 55–74.

28. Bede, *Historia Ecclesiasticae*, 4.26.

29. The alternatives to this line of reasoning are to suggest a Wessex source dating from that period, which seems much less likely. Alternatively, one could believe that somehow a British annal was found by the makers of the *Anglo-Saxon Chronicle* and employed here alone. This annal would have remained entirely hidden from historians except for this one instance. This possibility seems even less feasible.

30. Dumville, "Kingship, Genealogies and Regnal Lists," *Early Medieval Kingship*, eds. Peter H. Sawyer and Ian N. Wood (Leeds: University of Leeds, 1977b), 72–104.

31. The royal family was known as the Oiscingas, and Æsc Oisc is named as Iurminric's father.

32. Sims-Williams believed that this could have been done as late as the eighth century, whereas the present scholar would simply say that whenever the Kentish Source was created, Gildas' relative chronology suited the needs of the writer and his patrons. "The Settlement of England in Bede and the *Chronicle*," *ASE* 12 (London, 1983b), 22.

Chapter 9

1. Myres, *Anglo-Saxon Pottery and the Settlement of England* (Oxford: Clarendon Press, 1969), 95–99; Dumville, "Sub-Roman Britain: History and Legend," *History* 62 (London, 1977), 185.

2. Turville-Petre, "Hengest and Horsa," *Saga-Book of the Viking Society* 14 (London, 1953–1957), 287; Sims-Williams, "The Settlement of England in Bede and the *Chronicle*," *ASE* 12 (London, 1983b), 22.

3. Turville-Petre, "Hengest and Horsa," *Saga-Book of the Viking Society* 14 (London, 1953–1957), 274–277.

4. Dumville, "Kingship, Genealogies and Regnal Lists," *Early Medieval Kingship*, eds. Peter H. Sawyer and Ian N. Wood (Leeds: University of Leeds, 1977b), 72–104; Vansina, *Oral Tradition as History* (Madison: University of Wisconsin Press, 1985), 178–185.

5. Bede, *Historia Ecclesiastica*, 2.5.

6. Turville-Petre, "Hengest and Horsa," *Saga-Book of the Viking Saga* 14 (London, 1953–1957), 273–290; de Vries, "Die Ursprungssage der Sachsen," *Niedersächen Jarhbuch für Landesgeschichte* 31 (Berlin, 1959), 30–32; Olrik, "Epic Laws of Folk Narrative," *International Folkloristics: Classic Contributions by the Founders of Folklore*, ed. Alan Dundes (Lanham, MD: Rowman and Littlefield, 1999), 104.

7. *Skjoldungasaga*.

Chapter 10

1. *Historia Brittonum*, Chapters 32–49.

2. Contra Dumville, *History* 62 "Sub-Roman

Britain: History and Legend" (London, 1977a), 185–187.

3. Kirby, "Vortigern," *BBCS* 23 (Cambridge, 1970), 49–50.

4. Ironically, Germanus is said to have condemned Vortigern in the name of God and watched him die. It has now been shown that Germanus died no later than 448, a year before Bede or any other Insular source places the *adventus*.

5. Kirby has elaborated on much the same arguments; Kirby, "Vortigern," *BBCS* 23 (Cardiff, 1970), 40–41, 44, 54–59.

6. Chadwick, "Early Culture and Learning in North Wales," *Studies in the Early British Church*, ed. Nora K. Chadwick (Cambridge: Cambridge University Press, 1958), 47.

7. Miller, "Bede's Use of Gildas," *EHR* 90 (London, 1975), 241–261; Dumville, "Sub-Roman Britain: History and Legend," *History* 62 (London, 1977a), 187.

8. Kirby, "British Dynastic History in the Pre-Viking Period," *BBCS* 27 (Cardiff, 1976), 101–110.

9. Rowland, *Early Welsh Saga Poetry* (Cambridge: D. S. Brewer, 1990), 141–145.

10. Miller, "Forms and Uses of Pedigrees," *THSC* (London, 1978d), 195–206.

11. Miller, "The Disputed Historical Horizon of the Pictish King-Lists," *BBCS* 28 (Cardiff, 1978e), 1–34.

12. Miller, "The Foundation Legend of Gwynedd in the Latin Texts," *BBCS* 27 (Cardiff, 1978a), 515–532.

13. Kirby, "British Dynastic History in the Pre-Viking Period," *BBCS* 27 (Cardiff, 1976), 105–110.

14. *Historia Brittonum*, chapter 61. He is listed as an ancestor of Coel Hen, though this is clearly an example of an artificial genealogy.

15. *A Guide to Early Welsh Literature*, eds. Alfred O.H. Jarman and Gwilym R. Jones (Cardiff: University of Wales Press, 1976), 3.

16. Sims-Williams, "The Settlement of England in Bede and the *Chronicle*," *ASE* 12 (London, 1983b), 16.

17. Brodeur, "Arthur *Dux Bellorum*," *University of California Publications in English* 3 (Berkeley, 1939), 237–284; Higham, *King Arthur: Mythmaking and History* (New York: Routledge, 2002), 134–5.

18. Brooks, "The Creation and Early Structure of the Kingdom of Kent," *The Origins of the Anglo-Saxon Kingdoms*, ed. Stephen Bassett (Leicester: Leicester University Press, 1989), 67.

Chapter 11

1. Treated as a fact by John Morris in *The Age of Arthur* (London: Weidenfeld and Nicolson, 1976), 48.

2. To reuse an old theory, somewhere the battle could have been listed as happening twenty-seven years after the Romans. As Wheeler showed, it is possible the British believed that 473 was the last year there were Roman consuls, so that 500 could have been the intended date. A later writer, assuming 410 as the last date of the Romans, would then have altered the date to 437. Such is an extremely hypothetical possibility, but points out the flexibility of such an early date and the overwhelming significance of antiquarian date-guessing; "Gildas' De Excidio, Chapter 26," *EHR* 41 (London, 1926), 499–500.

3. Johnson, *Evidence of Arthur* (McFarland, 2014). The simple fact that there is such an overwhelming amount of information about Camlann, and that all of it involves Arthur, while apart from *Annales Cambriae* and *Historia Brittonum* there is no mention of Badon with Arthur in all of British literature, points against Arthur's participation.

4. Alcock, *Arthur's Britain* (London: Allen Lane, 1971), 68–71.

5. Having said that, but being aware of historical documents' potential political influences throughout the fifth through the tenth centuries, the Battle of Gueleph may mark a contemporary political alliance or rivalry between the houses that was given some tradition with the addition of Ambrosius and Guitolin to the historical record at Gueleph. This possibility is nowhere evidenced in the studies of the period or the sources, but is nowhere countered either.

Chapter 13

1. Johnson, *Origins of Arthurian Romances* (McFarland, 2012).

Chapter 15

1. *Vita Columbae*, 1.33
2. Bede, *Historia Ecclesiastica*, 1.25
3. Despite the centrality of Rhun to the *Northern History*, it must be kept in mind that he is only remembered in a single ecclesiastical and British source; the question of his very historicity is an unanswered one; Higham, "Britons in Northern England in the Early Middle Ages: through a thick glass darkly," *Northern History* 38 (Leeds, 2001), 5–25.

4. The later and generally less reliable *Anglo-Saxon Chronicle* claims that Brochmael's grandson Selyf was at Chester. This is highly improbable given the generational margins set out above. Generally, historians have gone with the *Annales Cambriae* absolute chronology here, as will the present author, because the Welsh were more knowledgeable about Powysian history than the Northumbrians could have been.

5. Kirby, "Bede and Northumbrian Chronology," *EHR* 78 (London, 1963), 514–527; Miller, "The Dates of Deira," *ASE* 8 (London, 1979), 35–61.

6. Aldhelm was also a student of Hadrian, whose term included the range 588x643.

Chapter 16

1. One note to the genealogical chapters: individuals for whom known and accepted date-ranges cannot be rationalized with other date-ranges and the given genealogy have been assigned bolded birth-ranges.
2. He could not be a figure in the Glywising genaeology and the saintly figure who appears in the *vita*, especially in the primary source *Vita Samsoni*.
3. Bannerman, *Studies in the History of Dalriada* (Edinburgh: Scottish Academic Press, 1974), 124–125.
4. I have here used the likely British form of the name simply for the sake of making a connection between the two date-ranges easier for the reader.
5. As Professor Sims-Williams observed some time ago, there is no direct evidence to date Urien; Sims-Williams, "The Death of Urien," *CMCS* 32 (Cardiff, 1996), 25–26.

Chapter 18

1. The given birth-year for David is unsupported by the evidence. Miller, "Date-Guessing and Dyfed," *SC* 13 (Cardiff, 1978c), 48.
2. The date is a fabrication designed to highlight the importance of the bishoprics of Wales over Canterbury; Miller, "Date-Guessing and Dyfed," *SC* 13 (Cardiff, 1978c), 33–61
3. As was demonstrated in the first half of the book, Hengest's association and at least several connectors are fabrications of the seventh century. They are only included here for the sake of completeness.

Chapter 19

1. Miller, "Date-Guessing and Dyfed," *SC* 13 (Cardiff, 1978c), 48.
2. In the first half of this book, it was determined that the limits of Gildas' birth-year are 478x491.
3. The foundations for such a claim have been laid out in the author's previous work, *Origins of Arthurian Romances* (McFarland, 2012).

Chapter 23

1. Johnson, *Evidence of Arthur* (McFarland, 2014).
2. Miller, "Date-Guessing and Dyfed," *SC* 13 (Cardiff, 1978c), 36–37.
3. Miller, "Bede's Use of Gildas," *EHR* 90 (London, 1975a), 241–261.
4. Miller, "The Foundation Legend of Gwynedd in the Latin Texts," *BBCS* 27 (Cardiff, 1978a), 515–32.

5. Ibid. 531–32.
6. Ibid., 515–527.

Chapter 24

1. Vansina, *Oral Tradition as History* (Madison: University of Wisconsin Press, 1985).
2. Gildas, *De Excidio Britanniae*, 34.6.
3. *The Gododdin of Aneirin*, ed. and trans. John T. Koch (Cardiff: University of Wales Press, 1997), cxv.
4. Legend has it that the wives of the warriors who left had to bear the children of their servants in order to continue their households.
5. Gildas, *De Excidio Britanniae*, 33.2.
6. Newell, "Arthurian Notes," *MLN* 17 (Baltimore, 1902), 277–278.
7. *Trioedd Ynys Prydein*, ed. and trans. Rachel Bromwich (Cardiff: University of Wales Press, 1978), 329–333.

Chapter 26

1. Miller, "Bede's Use of Gildas," *EHR* 90 (London, 1975a), 252–58; Dumville, "The Chronology of *De Excidio Britanniae*, Book I," *Gildas: New Approaches*, eds. David N. Dumville and Michael Lapidge (Woodbridge: Boydell Press, 1984b), 61–84; Johnson, *Evidence of Arthur* (McFarland, 2014).

Appendix

1. *De Excidio Britanniae*, 4.4.
2. Sims-Williams, "Gildas and the Anglo-Saxons," *CMCS* 6 (Cambridge, 1983a), 15–25.
3. *De Excidio Britanniae*, 25.1.
4. Johnson, *Evidence of Arthur* (McFarland, 2014).
5. Sims-Williams, "Gildas and the Anglo-Saxons," *CMCS* 6 (Cambridge, 1983a), 1–18.
6. Miller, "Stilicho's Pictish War," *Brit* 6 (Stroud, 1975d), 141–145.
7. Ibid., 141–145; "The Foundation Legend of Gwynedd in the Latin Texts," *BBCS* 27 (Cardiff, 1978a), 398–453; Alcock, *Arthur's Britain* (London: Allen Lane, 1971), 181.
8. 546 derived from the Pictish genaeology below.
9. Initial range is derived via genealogy, secondarily by way of reign length and obits in the older annals. The generation following Bile Gartnait and Drest is unimportant to the present author's purposes. The unnamed males and females in this genealogy represent persons that scholarship has determined did exist, but of whom there are no direct records.

Bibliography

Primary Sources

Adamnan. *Life of Saint Columba, Founder of Hy (Iona)*. trans. and ed. William Reeves (Lampter: Llanerch, 1988).

Alcuin. "De Pontificibus et Sanctis Ecclesiae Eboracensis Carmen," *The Historians of the Church of York*. ed. James Raine (London: University of London Press, 1879–1894).

Ammianus Marcellinus. trans. John C. Rolfe (Cambridge: Harvard University Press, 1971–72).

Aneirin. *Aneirin: Y Gododdin—Britain's Oldest Heroic Poem*. ed. Alfred Owen Hughes Jarman (Llandysul: Gomer Press, 1988).

_____. *Canu Aneirin*. ed. Sir Ifor Williams (Cardiff: Gwasg Prifysgol Cymru, 1938).

_____. *The Gododdin of Aneirin*. trans. and ed. John T. Koch (Cardiff: University of Wales Press, 1997).

_____. *The Gododdin: The Oldest Scottish Poem*. ed. Kenneth H. Jackson (Edinburgh: Edinburgh University Press, 1969).

The Anglo-Saxon Chronicle. trans. George Norman Garmonsway (London: Dent, 1953).

"Annales Cambriae," ed. and trans. John Morris. *Nennius: British History and the Welsh Annals* (London: Phillimore, 1980).

Annals of Clonmacnoise, Being Annals of Ireland from the Earliest Period to A.D. 1408, Translated into English A.D. 1627 by Conell Mageoghagan. ed. Denis Murphy (Dublin: University College Dublin Press, 1896).

Annals of Inisfallen (MS. Rawlinson B.503). ed. and trans. Seán MacAirt (Dublin: Institute for Advanced Studies, 1951).

Annals of Tigernach. ed. Whitley Stokes. *Revue Celtique* 16 (Paris, 1895), 374–419.

_____. *Revue Celtique* 17 (Paris, 1896), 6–33, 119–263, 337–420, 458.

_____. *Revue Celtique* 18 (Paris, 1897), 9–59, 150–198, 267–303, 390–391.

Annals of Ulster. ed. Seán Mac Airt and Gearóid Mac Niocaill (Dublin: Institute for Advanced Studies, 1983).

The Anonymous History of Abbot Ceolfrith. ed. and trans. David H. Farmer. *The Age of Bede* (Harmondsworth: Penguin, 1983), 211–230.

Bede. *The Age of Bede*. ed. David H. Farmer (Harmondsworth: Penguin, 1983), 185–210.

_____. *Bede: A History of the English Church and People*. trans. Leo Sherley-Price (Baltimore: Penguin Books, 1955).

_____. *Bede: Life of Cuthbert*. trans. James Francis Webb. *The Age of Bede*. ed. David H. Farmer (Harmondsworth: Penguin, 1983), 41–104.

_____. *Bede: Lives of the Abbots of Wearmouth and Jarrow*. trans. David H. Farmer.

The Book of Leinster formerly Lebar na Núachongbála. ed. Richard Irvine Best et al. 6 vols. (Dublin: Dublin Institute for Advanced Studies, 1954–1983).

Canu Llywarch Hen. ed. Sir Ifor Williams (Cardiff: Gwasg Prifysgol Cymru, 1935).

Chronica Minora I. ed. Theodor Mommsen (Berlin: Berolini APVD Weidmannos, 1886), 515–660.

Columbanus. *Sancti Columbanus Opera*. trans. G.S.M. Walker (Dublin: Dublin Institute for Advanced Studies, 1957).

_____. *Le Pénitential de saint Columban*. ed. Jean Laporte (Dublin: University College Dublin Press, 1958).

Constantius. "Vitae Germani," *Bibliotheca Hagiographica Latina* (Brussels: Société de Bollandistses, 1898–1901).

Culhwch ac Olwen: An Edition and Study of the Oldest Arthurian Tale. ed. Rachel Bromwich and D. Simon Evans (Cardiff: University of Wales Press, 1992).

Dio Cassius. *Dio's Roman History*. trans. Earnest Cary. 9 vols. (London: W. Heinemann, 1914).

Early Welsh Genealogical Tracts. ed. Peter C. Bartrum (Cardiff: Wales University Press [sic], 1966).

Gildas. *De Excidio Britanniae*. trans. Michael Winterbottom (Chichester, 1978).

Gregory of Tours. *Gregory of Tours: The History of the Franks*. trans. and ed. Lewis Thorpe (Harmondsworth: Penguin, 1974).

The Law of Hywel Dda. trans. and ed. Dafydd Jenkins (Llandysul: Gomer Press, 1986).
"The Laws of Æthelberht," *The Laws of the Earliest English Kings.* ed. and trans. F.L. Attenborough (Cambridge: The University Press, 1922), 4–17.
"The Laws of Hlothere and Eadric," *The Laws of the Earliest English Kings.* ed. and trans. F.L. Attenborough (Cambridge: The University Press, 1922), 18–23.
"The Laws of Ine," *The Laws of the Earliest English Kings.* ed. and trans. F.L. Attenborough (Cambridge: The University Press, 1922), 36–61.
"The Laws of Wihtred," *The Laws of the Earliest English Kings.* ed. and trans. F.L. Attenborough (Cambridge: The University Press, 1922), 24–32.
Leabhar Breac. ed. and trans. Robert Atkinson (Dublin: Royal Irish Academy, 1887).
The Life of Samson of Dol. trans. Thomas Taylor (Felinfach: Llanerch, 1991).
The Lives of St. Ninian and St. Kentigern. ed. and trans. Alexander Penrose Forbes (Edinburgh: Edmonston and Douglas, 1874).
The Llandaff Charters. ed. Wendy Davies (Aberystwyth: National Library of Wales, 1979).
The Mabinogion. trans. Gwyn Jones and Thomas Jones (London: Dent, 1974).
"Marwnad Cadwallon ap Cadfan," trans. John T. Koch. *The Celtic Heroic Age: Literary Sources for Ancient Celtic Europe and Early Ireland and Wales.* eds. John T. Koch and John Carey (Malden, MA: Celtic Studies Publications, 1994), 351–53.
"Marwnad Cynddylan," trans. John T. Koch. *The Celtic Heroic Age: Literary Sources for Ancient Celtic Europe and Early Ireland and Wales.* eds. John T. Koch and John Carey (Malden, MA: Celtic Studies Publications, 1994), 360–362.
"Moliant Cadwallon," trans. John T. Koch. *The Celtic Heroic Age: Literary Sources for Ancient Celtic Europe and Early Ireland and Wales.* eds. John T. Koch and John Carey (Malden, MA: Celtic Studies Publications, 1994), 353–56.
Patrick. *The Works of St. Patrick.* ed. Ludwig Bieler (Westminster, MD: Newman Press, 1953).
"The Poems of Llywarch Hen," trans. Sir Ifor Williams. *PBA* 18 (London, 1931), 269–302.
"The Poetry of Llywarch Hen," trans. Patrick K. Ford. *The Celtic Heroic Age: Literary Sources for Ancient Celtic Europe and Early Ireland and Wales.* eds. John T. Koch and John Carey (Malden, MA: Celtic Studies Publications, 1994), 363–384.
Prosper of Aquitaine. *Prosperi Aquitani opera.* eds. P. Callens and M. Gastaldo (Turnhout: Brepols, 1972).
The Psaltair na Rann. ed. Whitley Stokes (New York: AMS Press, 1989).
Simeon of Durham. *Symeonis Monachi Opera Omnia.* ed. Thomas Arnold. 2 vols. (London: Longman, 1882–1885).
Skene, William F., ed. *The Four Ancient Books of Wales.* 4 vols. (Edinburgh, 1868).
Stephanus, Eddius. *Eddius Stephanus: Life of Wilfrid.* trans. James Francis Webb, ed. David H. Farmer. *The Age of Bede* (Harmondsworth: Penguin, 1983), 105–184.
Tacitus, Cornelius. *The Complete Works of Tacitus.* trans. Alfred J. Church and William J. Brodribb, ed. Moses Hadas (New York: Modern Library, 1942).
Taliesin. *Canu Taliesin.* ed. Sir Ifor Williams (Cardiff: Gwasg Prifysgol Cymru, 1960).
_____. *Book of Taliesin.* trans. John T. Koch and John Carey. *The Celtic Heroic Age* (Malden, MA: Celtic Studies Publications, 1995).
Trioedd Ynys Prydein: The Welsh Triads. ed. and trans. Rachel Bromwich (Cardiff: University of Wales Press, 1978).
Two of the Saxon Chronicles Parallel. trans. and ed. Charles Plummer. 2 vols. (Oxford: Clarendon Press, 1892–1899).
Victor, Sextus Aurelius. *Liber de Caesaribus.* trans. H.W. Bird (Liverpool: Liverpool University Press, 1994).
Vita St. Hilarii Arelatensis. ed. Jacques-Paul Migne. *Patrologia cursus completus.* 221 vols. (Paris: Excudebat Migne, etc. [sic], 1844–1864).
Yellow Book of Lecan. Duanaire. ed. Lambert Andrew Joseph McKenna (Dublin: Irish Texts Society, 1939–40).
Zosimus. *Zosimus. New History.* trans. Ronald T. Ridley (Canberra: Canberra Central Printing, 1982).

Secondary Sources

Abrams, Leslie and James P. Carley, eds. *The Archaeology and History of Glastonbury Abbey: Essays in Honour of the Nineitieth Birthday of C.A. Ralegh Radford* (Woodbridge: Boydell, 1991).
Alcock, Leslie. *Arthur's Britain* (London: Allen Lane, 1971).
Anderson, Marjorie Ogilvie. *Kings and Kingship in Early Scotland* (Edinburgh: Scottish Academic Press, 1980).
Angel, John Lawrence. "The Length of Life in Ancient Greece," *Journal of Gerontology* 2 (St. Louis, 1947), 18–24.
Arnold, Christopher J. *An Archaeology of the Early Anglo-Saxon Kingdoms* (New York: Routledge, 1988).
Attenborough, F.L., ed. and trans. *The Laws of the Earliest English Kings* (Cambridge: The University Press, 1922).
Bannerman, John. "Notes on the Scottish Entries in the Early Irish Annals," *Scottish Gaelic Studies* 11 (Edinburgh, 1968), 149–170.
_____. *Studies in the History of Dalriada* (Edinburgh: Scottish Academic Press, 1974).
Bardy, Gustave. "Constance de Lyon, Biographe de Saint Germain d'Auxerre," *Saint Germain* (Auxerre, 1950), 89–108.
Bartholomew, P. "Fifth-Century Facts," *B* 13 (Stroud, 1987), 261–270.

Bartrum, Peter C. "Some Studies in Early Welsh History," *TSC* (London, 1949), 279–302.

———. *A Welsh Classical Dictionary: People in History and Legend Up to About 1000 A.D* (Cardiff: National Library of Wales, 1993).

Bassett, Stephen. "In Search of the Origins of Anglo-Saxon Kingdoms," *The Origins of the Anglo-Saxon Kingdoms*. ed. Stephen Bassett (Leicester: Leicester University Press, 1989), 3–27.

Bassett, Stephen, ed. *The Origins of the Anglo-Saxon Kingdoms* (Leicester: Leicester University Press, 1989).

Benedikt, Kolon, ed. *Die Vita S. Hilarii Arelatensis. Eine eidographische Studie* (Paderborn: Schöningh, 1925).

Bieler, Ludwig, and David A. Binchy, eds. and trans. *The Irish Penitentials* (Dublin: Dublin Institute for Advanced Studies, 1963).

Blair, John. "Frithuwold's Kingdom and the Origins of Surrey," *The Origins of the Anglo-Saxon Kingdoms*. ed. Stephen Bassett (Leicester: Leicester University Press, 1989), 97–107.

Blair, Peter Hunter. *An Introduction to Anglo-Saxon England* (Cambridge: Cambridge University Press, 1977).

Bonner, Gerald. "Bede and His Teachers and Friends," *Famulus Christi: Essays in Commemoration of the Thirteenth Centenary of the Birth of the Venerable Bede*. ed. Gerald Bonner (London: S.P.C.K., 1976), 19–39.

Bonner, Gerald, ed. *Famulus Christi: Essays in Commemoration of the Thirteenth Centenary of the Birth of the Venerable Bede* (London: S.P.C.K., 1976).

Brodeur, Arthur G. "Arthur Dux Bellorum," *University of California Publications in English* 3 (Berkeley, 1939), 237–284.

Bromwich, Rachel, and R. Brinley Jones, eds. *Astudiaethau ar yr Hengerdd* (Cardiff: Gwasg Prifysgol Cymru, 1978).

Brooks, Nicholas. "The Creation and Early Structure of the Kingdom of Kent," *The Origins of the Anglo-Saxon Kingdoms*. ed. Stephen Bassett (Leicester: Leicester University Press, 1989), 55–74.

———. "The Formation of the Mercian Kingdom," *The Origins of the Anglo-Saxon Kingdoms*. ed. Stephen Bassett (Leicester: Leicester University Press, 1989), 159–170.

Brown, George Hardin. *A Companion to Bede* (Woodbridge: Boydell Press, 2009).

Burgess, Richard W. "The Dark Ages Return to Fifth-Century Britain: The 'Restored' Gallic Chronicle Exploded," *Brit* 21 (Stroud, 1990), 185–195.

Byrne, Francis John. *Irish Kings and High-Kings* (London: St. Martin's Press, 1973).

———. "A Poem on the Airgialla," *Ériu* 19 (Dublin, 1962), 179–188.

Cameron, Alan. *Claudian: Poetry and Propaganda at the Court of Hadrian* (Oxford: Clarendon, 1970).

Campbell, James. "Bede's *Reges* and *Principes*," (Jarrow Lecture, 1979).

———. "The End of Roman Britain," *The Anglo-Saxons*. ed. James Campbell (London: Penguin, 1982).

Campbell, James, ed. *The Anglo-Saxons* (London: Penguin, 1982).

Carney, J. *Studies in Irish Literature and History* (Dublin: Institute for Advanced Studies, 1955).

Carver, Martin O.H. "The Future of Sutton Hoo," *A Voyage to the Other World: The Legacy of Sutton Hoo*. eds. Calvin B. Kendall and Peter S. Wells (Minneapolis: University of Minnesota Press, 1992), 183–200.

Casey, P. John, ed. *The End of Roman Britain* (Oxford: B.A.R., 1979).

Chadwick, Hector Munroe. *Early Scotland. The Picts, the Scots, and the Welsh of Southern Scotland* (Cambridge: Cambridge University Press, 1949).

———. *Origin of the English Nation* (Cambridge: The University Press, 1907).

Chadwick, Hector M., and Nora K. Chadwick. *The Growth of Literature*. 3 vols. (Cambridge: Cambridge University Press, 1932–1940).

Chadwick, Nora Kershaw. "Early Culture and Learning in North Wales," *Studies in the Early British Church*. ed. Nora K. Chadwick (Cambridge: Cambridge University Press, 1958), 29–120.

———. *Poetry and Letters in Early Christian Gaul* (London: Bowes and Bowes, 1955).

Chadwick, Nora Kershaw, ed. *Celt and Saxon: Studies in the Early British Border* (Cambridge: University Press, 1963).

———. *Studies in Early British History* (Cambridge: University Press, 1954).

———. *Studies in the Early British Church* (Cambridge: Cambridge University Press, 1958).

Chaney, William A. *The Cult of Kingship in Anglo-Saxon England: The Transition from Paganism to Christianity* (Manchester: University Press, 1970).

Charles-Edwards, Thomas Mawbray. "The Authenticity of the *Gododdin*: An Historian's View," eds. Rachel Bromwich and R. Brinley Jones. *Astudiaethau ar yr Hengerdd* (Cardiff: Gwasg Prifysgol Cymru, 1978), 44–71.

———. *Early Irish and Welsh Kinship* (Oxford: Clarendon Press, 1993).

Clemoes, Peter, ed. *The Anglo-Saxons: Studies in Some Aspects of Their History and Culture Presented to Bruce Dickens* (London: Bowes and Bowes, 1959).

Cunliffe, Barry. *Rome and the Barbarians* (London: Bodley Head, 1975).

Dark, Kenneth Rainsbury. *Civitas to Kingdom: British Political Continuity 300–800* (Leicester: Leicester University Press, 1994).

———. "St. Patrick's *Uillula* and the Fifth-Century Occupation of Romano-British Villas," *Saint Patrick: A.D. 493–1993*. ed. David N. Dumville (Woodbridge: Boydell Press, 1993), 19–24.

_____. "A Sub-Roman Defense of Hadrian's Wall?," *Brit* 18 (Stroud, 1992), 111–120.

Davies, Wendy. "Annals and the Origins of Mercia," *Mercian Studies*. ed. Ann Dornier (Leicester: Leicester University Press, 1977), 17–29.

_____. *An Early Welsh Microcosm: Studies in the Llandaff Charters* (London: Royal Historical Society, 1978).

_____. "*Liber Landavensis*: Its Construction and Credibility," *EHR* 88 (London, 1973), 335–342.

_____. *The Llandaff Charters*. Aberystwyth: National Library of Wales, 1979.

_____. "The Orthography of the Personal Names in the Charters of Liber Landevensis," *BBCS* 28 (Cardiff, 1980), 553–557.

_____. "Property Rights and Property Claims in Welsh 'Vitae' of the Eleventh Century," *Hagiographie, cultures, et sociétés ive–xiie siécles*. ed. Evelyne Patlagean and Pierre Riché (Paris: Etudes augustiniennes, 1981), 515–533.

_____. *Wales in the Early Middle Ages*. Leicester: Leicester University Press, 1982.

_____, and H. Vierck. "The Contexts of the Tribal Hidage: Social Aggregates and Settlement Patterns," *Frümittlealterliche Studien* 8 (Berlin, 1974), 224–292.

DeGregorio, Scott. "Bede's History in a Harsher Climate," *Venerable Bede*. ed. Scott DeGregorio (Morgantown, 2006), 203–226.

DeGregorio, Scott, ed. *Innovation and Tradition in the Writings of the Venerable Bede* (Morgantown: West Virginia University Press, 2006).

Dornier, Ann, ed. *Mercian Studies* (Leicester: Leicester University Press, 1977).

Drijvers, John Willem, and David Hunt. *The Late Roman World and Its Historians* (New York: Routledge, 1999).

Drinkwater, J. "Patronage in Roman Gaul and the Problem of the Bagaudae," *Patronage in Ancient Society*. ed. A. Wallace-Hadrill (London: Routledge, 1989), 189–203.

Duine, François. "La vie de S. Samson, à propos d'un ouvrage récent," *Annales de Bretagne* 28 (Paris, 1912–13), 332–56.

Dumville, David N. "The Chronology of *De Excidio Britanniae*, Book I," *Gildas: New Approaches*. eds. David N. Dumville and Michael Lapidge (Woodbridge: Boydell Press, 1984b), 61–84.

_____. "Early Welsh Poetry: Problems of Historicity," *Early Welsh Poetry: Studies in the Book of Aneirin*. ed. Brynley F. Roberts (Aberystwyth: National Library of Wales, 1988), 1–16.

_____. "Gildas and Maelgwn: Problems of Dating," *Gildas: New Approaches*. eds. David N. Dumville and Michael Lapidge (Woodbridge: Boydell Press, 1984a), 51–59.

_____. "Gildas and Uinniau," *Gildas: New Approaches*. eds. David N. Dumville and Michael Lapidge (Woodbridge: Boydell Press, 1984c), 207–214.

_____. "*Historia Brittonum*: An Insular History from the Carolingian Age," *Historiographie im frühen Mittelalter*. eds. A. Scharer and G. Scheibelreiter (Munich: Oldenbourg, 1994), 406–434.

_____. "Kingship, Genealogies and Regnal Lists," *Early Medieval Kingship*. eds. Peter H. Sawyer and Ian N. Wood (Leeds: University of Leeds, 1977b), 72–104.

_____. "'Nennius' and the *Historia Brittonum*," *SC* 11 (Cardiff, 1976), 78–95.

_____. "On the North British Section of the *Historia Brittonum*," *WHR* 8 (Cardiff, 1977c), 345–354.

_____. "Some Aspects of the Chronology of the *Historia Brittonum*," *BBCS* 25 (Cardiff, 1974), 439–445.

_____. "Sub-Roman Britain: History and Legend," *History* 62 (London, 1977a), 173–192.

_____. "The Tribal Hidage: An Introduction to Its Texts and Their Historicity," *The Origins of the Anglo-Saxon Kingdoms*. ed. Stephen Bassett (Leicester: Leicester University Press, 1989), 225–230.

_____. "The West Saxon Genealogical Regnal List and the Chronology of Early Wessex," *Peritia* 4 (Galway, 1985), 21–66.

Dumville, David N., ed. *The Historia Brittonum: 3. The "Vatican" Recension* (Cambridge: D.S. Brewer, 1985).

_____. *Saint Patrick: A.D. 493–1993* (Woodbridge: Boydell Press, 1993).

Dumville, David N., and Michael Lapidge, eds. *Gildas: New Approaches* (Woodbridge: Boydell Press, 1984).

Ekwall, Eilert. *The Concise Oxford Dictionary of English Place-Names* (Oxford: Clarendon Press, 1960).

Enright, Michael J. "The Sutton Hoo Whetstone Sceptre: A Study in Iconography and Cultural Milieu," *ASE* 11 (London, 1983), 119–134.

Evison, Vera I., ed. *Angles, Jutes and Saxons* (Oxford: Clarendon Press, 1981).

Evison, Vera Ivy. "Distribution Map of England in the First Two Phases," *Angles, Jutes and Saxons*. ed. Vera I. Evison (Oxford: Clarendon Press, 1981), 126–167.

Farrell, Robert T., and Carol L. Neuman de Vegvar, eds. *Sutton Hoo: Fifty Years After* (Oxford, OH: American Early Medieval Studies, Miami University, Department of Art, 1992).

Faulkner, Neil. *The Decline and Fall of Roman Britain* (Stroud: Tempus, 2000).

Finberg, Herbert Patrick Reginald. *Lucerna: Studies in Some Problems in the Early History of England* (London: St. Martin's Press, 1964).

Fleuriot, Léon. "Varia I: Le 'saint' Breton *Winniau* et le Pénitentiel dit 'de Finnian' " *ÉC* 15 (Paris, 1976–8), 607–614.

Ford, Patrick K. *The Poetry of Llywarch Hen* (Berkeley: University of California Press, 1974).

Förstemann, Ernst Wilhelm. *Altdeutches Namenbuch, i, Personnamen* (Nordhausen, 1856).

Frere, Sheppard S. *Britannia. A History of Roman Britain* (London: Routledge and Kegan Paul, 1967).

Gagarin, Michael. *Early Greek Law* (Berkeley: University of California Press, 1986).

Gelling, Margaret. "Latin Loan-Words in Old English Place Names," *ASE* 6 (London, 1977), 10–11.

Gillam, John P. "Romano-Saxon Pottery: An Alternative Explanation," ed. P. John Casey. *The End of Roman Britain* (Oxford: B.A.R., 1979), 103–118.

Goffart, Walter. *Barbarians and Romans 418–584: The Techniques of Accommodation* (Princeton: Princeton University Press, 1980).

_____. "The *Historia Ecclesiastica*: Bede's Agenda and Ours," *Haskins Society Journal* 12 (Woodbridge, 1990), 29–45.

_____. *Narrators of Barbarian History* (Princeton; Princeton University Press, 1988), 235–328.

Greenfield, Stanley Brian, and Daniel Gilmore Calder, eds. *A New Critical History of Old English Literature* (New York: New York University Press, 1986).

Grimes, William Francis, ed. *Aspects of Archaeology in Britain and Beyond* (London: H.W. Edwards, 1951).

Grosjean, Père. "Sur quelques exégètes irlandáis du viie siècle," *Sacris Erudiri* 7 (Steenbrugge, 1955), 67–98.

Gruffydd, R. Geraint. "From Gododdin to Gwynedd: Reflections on the Story of Cunedda," *SC* 24/25 (Cardiff, 1989–1990), 1–14.

_____. "Marwnad Cynddylan," *Bardos*. ed. R. Geraint Gruffydd (Cardiff: Gwasg Prif. Cymru, 1982), 10–28.

Harden, Donald Benjamin, ed. *Dark-Age Britain: Studies Presented to E.T. Leeds* (London: Methuen, 1956).

Härke, Heinrich G.H. *Angelsächsische Waffengräber des 5. bis 7. Jarhhunderts* (Cologne: Rheinland-Verlag and Habelt, 1992).

Harrison, Kenneth. *The Framework of Anglo-Saxon History to 900 A.D* (Cambridge: Cambridge University Press, 1976).

Hart, Cyril Roy. "The Tribal Hidage," *TRHS* 21 (London, 1971), 138–157.

Haycock, Marged. "'Preiddeu Annwn' and the figure of Taliesin," *SC* 14/15 (Cardiff, 1984), 52–77.

Higham, Nicholas J. "Britons in Northern England in the Early Middle Ages: Through a Thick Glass Darkly," *Northern History* 38 (Leeds, 2001), 5–25.

_____. *An English Empire* (Manchester: Manchester University Press, 1995).

_____. *King Arthur: Mythmaking and History* (New York: Routledge, 2002).

_____. *The Kingdom of Northumbria, A.D. 350–1100* (Stroud: Alan Sutton, 1993).

_____. "Medieval 'Overlordship' in Wales: The Earliest Evidence," *WHR* 16 (London, 1992a), 145–159.

_____. *Rome, Britain and the Anglo-Saxons* (London: Seaby, 1992b).

Hill, David Henry. *Atlas of Anglo-Saxon England* (Oxford: Blackwell, 1982).

Hills, Catherine. "The Archaeology of Anglo-Saxon England in the Pagan Period: A Review," *ASE* 8 (London, 1976), 297–329.

Hodgkin, Robert Howard. *A History of the Anglo-Saxons* (Oxford: Clarendon Press, 1935).

Hope-Taylor, Brian. *Yeavering: An Anglo-British Centre of Early Northumbria* (London: HMSO, 1977).

Hughes, Kathleen. *Early Christian Ireland: Introduction to the Sources* (Ithaca, NY: Cornell University Press, 1972).

_____. "The Welsh Latin Chronicles: *Annales Cambriae* and Related Texts," *PBA* 59 (London, 1975), 233–258.

Jackson, Kenneth Hurlstone. "The British Language during the Period of English Settlements," ed. Nora K. Chadwick. *Studies in Early British History* (Cambridge: Cambridge University Press, 1954), 61–82.

_____. "The British Languages and Their Evolution," *Literature and Western Civilization II, The Medieval World*. eds. David Daiches and Anthony Thorlby (London: Aldus, 1973), 113–126.

_____. "The Britons of Southern Scotland," *Antiquity* 29 (Gloucester, 1955), 77–88.

_____. "Edinburgh and the Anglian Occupation of Lothian," *The Anglo-Saxons: Studies in Some Aspects of Their History and Culture Presented to Bruce Dickens*. ed. Peter Clemoes (London: Bowes and Bowes, 1959), 35–42.

_____. *Language and History in Early Britain: A Chronological Survey of the Brittonic Languages 1st to 12th c. A.D.* (Edinburgh: University Press, 1953).

_____. "On the Northern British Section in Nennius," *Celt and Saxon: Studies in the Early British Border*. ed. Nora K. Chadwick (Cambridge: University Press, 1963), 20–62.

_____. "The Sources for the Life of St. Kentigern," *Studies in the Early British Church*. ed. Nora K. Chadwick (Cambridge: Cambridge University Press, 1958), 273–357.

_____. "Varia II: Gildas and the Names of the British Princes," *CMCS* 3 (Cambridge, 1982), 30–40.

Jarman, Alfred Owen Hughes, and Gwilym Rees Hughes, eds. *A Guide to Early Welsh Literature*. 3 vols. (Cardiff: University of Wales Press, 1976).

Johnson, Flint. *Evidence of Arthur: Fixing the Legendary King in Factual Time and Place* (McFarland, 2014).

_____. *Origins of Arthurian Romances: Early Sources for the Legends of Tristan, the Grail and the Abduction of the Queen* (McFarland, 2012).

Jones, Michael E., and John Casey. "The Gallic Chronicle Restored: A Chronology for the Anglo-Saxon Invasions and the End of Roman Britain," *Britannia* 19 (Stroud, 1978), 367–398.

Jordan, Paul. *Riddles of the Sphinx* (New York: New York University Press, 1998).

Kelly, Fergus. *A Guide to Early Irish Law* (Dublin: Dublin Institute for Advanced Studies, 1988).

Kendall, Calvin B., and Peter S. Wells, eds. *A Voyage to the Other World: The Legacy of Sutton Hoo*

(Minneapolis: University of Minnesota Press, 1992).

Kerlouégan, François. "Les destinées de la culture Latina dans l'île de Bretagne au VI ème siècle. Recherches sur le *De Excidio Britanniae* de Gildas," unpublished Ph.D. thesis, Paris, 1977.

Kirby, David. "Bede and Northumbrian Chronology," *EHR* 78 (London, 1963), 514–527.

———. "Bede's Native Sources for the *Historia Ecclesiastica*," *Bulletin of the John Rylands Library* 48 (London, 1965–1966), 341–371.

———. "British Dynastic History in the Pre-Viking Period," *BBCS* 27 (Cardiff, 1976), 81–114.

———. "King Ceolwulf of Northumbria and the Historia Ecclesiastica," *SC* 14/15 (Cardiff, 1980), 168–173.

———. "Northumbria in the Time of Bede," *St. Wilfrid at Hexham*, ed. David P. Kirby (Newcastle-upon-Tyne: Oriel Press, 1974), 1–8.

———. "Problems of Early West Saxon History," *EHR* 80 (London, 1965), 10–29.

———. "Strathclyde and Cumbria: A Survey of Historical Development to 1092," *TCWAAS* 62 (Kendall, 1962), 71–92.

———. "Vortigern," *BBCS* 23 (Cardiff, 1970), 37–59.

Kirby, David P., ed. *St. Wilfrid at Hexham* (Newcastle-upon-Tyne, 1974).

Koch, John T. "When Was Welsh Literature First Written Down?," *SC* 20/21 (Cardiff, 1985–86), 43–66.

Laistner, M.L.W. *Thought and Letters in Western Europe A.D. 500–900* (Ithaca: Cornell University Press, 1957).

Lapidge, Michael. "The Anglo-Latin Background," *A New Critical History of Old English Literature*. eds. Stanley Brian Greenfield and Daniel Gilmore Calder (New York: New York University Press, 1986), 16–22.

———. *The Anglo-Saxon Library* (Oxford: Oxford University Press, 2006).

———. *Columbanus; Studies on the Latin Writings* (Woodbridge: Boydell Press, 1997).

———. "Gildas' Education and the Latin Culture of Sub-Roman Britain," *Gildas: New Approaches*. eds. David N. Dumville and Michael Lapidge (Woodbridge: Boydell Press, 1984), 27–50.

Lejeune, Rita. "The Troubadours," *Arthurian Literature in the Middle Ages*. ed. Roger S. Loomis (Oxford: Clarendon Press, 1959), 393–399.

Levison, Wilhelm. "Bischof Germanus von Auxerre und die Quellen zu seine Geschichte," *Neues Archiv der Gesellschaft für ältere deutsche Geschichteskunde* 29 (Paris, 1903–1904), 95–175.

Lloyd-Jones, John. *The Court Poets of the Welsh Princes* (London: Geoffrey Cumberlege Amen House, 1948).

Lot, Ferdinand. "De la valeur historique du *De Excidio ... de Gildas*," *Medieval Studies in Memory of Gertrude S. Loomis*. ed. Roger S. Loomis (New York: Columbia University Press, 1927), 229–264.

Mac Cana, Proinsias. "Aspects of the Theme of the King and Goddess," *EC* 6 (Paris, 1955), 356–413.

Mackay, Thomas W. "Bede's Hagiographical Method: His Knowledge and Use of Paulinus of Nola," *Famulus Christi: Essays in Commemoration of the Thirteenth Centenary of the Birth of the Venerable Bede*. ed. Gerald Bonner (London: S.P.C.K., 1976), 77–92.

MacNeill, Eoin. "The Authorship and Structure of the *Annals of Tigernach*," *Ériu* 7 (Dublin, 1914), 30–114.

———. "The Irish Law of Dynastic Succession," *Studies* 8 (Dublin, 1919), 367–382, 640–653.

———. "Mocu, Maccu," *Ériu* 3 (Dublin, 1907), 42–49.

MacNiocaill, Gearóid. *Ireland before the Vikings* (Dublin: Gill and Macmillan, 1972).

MacQueen, John. "A Reply to Professor Jackson," *TDGNAHS* 3rd series 36 (Dumfries, 1959), 175–83.

———. "Yvain, Ewen, and Owein ap Urien," *TDGNAHS* 33 (Dumfries, 1956), 107–131.

Mayvaert, Paul. "Bede the Scholar," *Famulus Christi: Essays in Commemoration of the Thirteenth Centenary of the Birth of the Venerable Bede*. ed. Gerald Bonner (London: S.P.C.K., 1976), 40–69.

McClure, Judith. "Bede and the *Life of Ceolfrith*," *Peritia* 3 (Galway, 1984), 71–84.

Mendelssohn, Ludwig. *Zosimi comitis et exadvocati fisci historia nova* (Lipsiae, rep. 1963).

Miles, Dillon, ed. *The Romano-British Countryside* (Oxford: B.A.R., 1982).

Miller, Molly. "Bede's Use of Gildas," *EHR* 90 (London, 1975), 241–261.

———. "The Commanders of Arthuret," *TCWAAS* 75 (Kendall, 1975c), 96–117.

———. "Date-Guessing and Dyfed," *SC* 13 (Cardiff, 1978c), 33–61.

———. "Date-Guessing and Pedigrees," *SC* 11 (Cardiff, 1976), 96–109.

———. "The Dates of Deira," *ASE* 8 (London, 1979), 35–61.

———. "The Disputed Historical Horizon of the Pictish King-Lists," *BBCS* 28 (Cardiff, 1978), 1–34.

———. "Forms and uses of pedigrees," *THSC* (London, 1978d), 195–206.

———. "The Foundation Legend of Gwynedd in the Latin Texts," *BBCS* 27 (Cardiff, 1978a), 515–532.

———. "Historicity and the Pedigrees of the Northcountrymen," *BBCS* 26 (Cardiff, 1975b), 255–280.

———. "The Last British Entry in the 'Gallic Chronicles,'" *Brit* 9 (Stroud, 1978b), 315–318.

———. *Sicilian Colony Dates* (Albany: State University of New York Press, 1970).

———. "Stilicho's Pictish War," *Brit* 6 (Stroud, 1975d), 141–145.

Mitchell, Samuel Alfred. "The Whetstone as Symbol of Authority in Old English and Old Norse," *Scandinavian Studies* 57 (Cambridge, 1985), 1–31.

Mohrmann, Christine. *The Latin of St. Patrick: Four Lectures* (Dublin: Dublin Institute for Advanced Studies, 1961).

Moisl, Herman. "The Bernician Royal Dynasty and the Irish in the Seventh Century," *Peritia* 2 (Galway, 1983), 103-126.

Morlet, Marie Thérèse. *Es nams de personne sur la territoire de l'ancienne Gaule dès vi au xii siècle*, I (Paris: Centre National de la recherche scientifique, 1968).

Morris, John. *The Age of Arthur* (London: Weidenfeld and Nicolson, 1973).

_____. *Arthurian Period Sources, Vol. 3: Persons* (Chichester: Phillimore, 1995).

_____. *Londinium: London in the Roman Empire*. rev. Sarah Macready (London: Weidenfeld and Nicolson, 1982).

_____. "Pelagian Literature," *JTS* 16 (London, 1965), 26-80.

Morris-Jones, Sir John. "Taliesin," *Y Cymmrodor* 28 (Cardiff, 1918), 1-290.

Mulchrone, Kathleen. "Die Abfassungszeit und Überlieferung der Vita Tripartita," *ZCP* 16 (Berlin, 1926), 411-452.

Myres, John Nowell Linton. "The *Adventus Saxonum*," *Aspects of Archaeology in Britain and Beyond*. ed. William Francis Grimes (London: H.W. Edwards, 1951), 221-241.

_____. *Anglo-Saxon Pottery and the Settlement of England* (Oxford: Clarendon Press, 1969).

_____. *The English Settlements* (Oxford: Clarendon Press, 1986).

_____. "Pelagius and the End of Roman Britain," *The Journal of Roman Studies* 50 (London, 1960), 21-36.

_____. "Romano-Saxon Pottery," *Dark-Age Britain: Studies Presented to E.T. Leeds*. ed. Donald B. Harden (London: Methuen, 1956), 16-39.

Neuman de Vegvar, Carol L. "The Iconography of Kingship in Anglo-Saxon Archaeological Finds," *Kings and Kingship, Acta 11*. ed. Joel T. Rosenthal (Binghamton: Center for Medieval and Early Renaissance Studies, State University of New York at Binghamton, 1986), 1-15.

Newell, William W. "Arthurian Notes," *MLN* 17 (Baltimore, 1902), 277-278.

Nicholson, Lewis E. "*Beowulf* and the Pagan Cult of the Stag," *Studi Medievali* 27 (Spoleto, 1986), 637-669.

Olrik, Axel. "Epic Laws of Folk Narrative," *International Folkloristics: Classic Contributions by the Founders of Folklore*. ed. Alan Dundes (Lanham, MD: Rowman and Littlefield, 1999), 83-105.

Ó Máille, Thomas. *The Language of the Annals of Ulster* (Manchester: University Press, 1910).

O'Rahilly, Thomas F. *Early Irish History and Mythology* (Dublin: Dublin Institute for Advanced Studies, 1946a).

_____. "On the Origin of the Names *Érain* and *Ériu*," *Ériu* 35 (Dublin, 1946b), 7-28.

Ó Riain, Pádraig. "St. Findbarr: A Study in a Cult," *Journal of the Cork Historical and Archaeological Society* 82 (Cork, 1977), 63-82.

Phillimore, Egerton. "The *Annales Cambriae* and Old-Welsh Genealogies from Harleian Ms. 3859," *Y Cymmrodor* 8 (Cardiff, 1888), 141-183.

Piggott, Stuart. "The Sources of Geoffrey of Monmouth I: The Pre-Roman King List," *A* 15 (Gloucester, 1941), 269-286.

_____. "The Sources of Geoffrey of Monmouth II: The Stonehenge Story," *A* 15 (Gloucester, 1941), 305-319.

Poulin, Jean-Claude. "Hagiographie et Politique. La première de S. Samson de Dol," *Francia* 5 (Paris, 1977), 1-26.

Radzsher, Marius. *L'enseignement des lettres classiques d'Ausone à Alcuin* (Paris: Alphonse Picard et Fils, 1905).

Rhys, Sir John. *Celtic Britain* (London: Society for Promoting Christian Knowledge, 1884).

Richards, Melville. "The 'Lichfield' Gospels," *JNLW* 18 (Aberstwyth, 1973-74), 135-145.

Riché, Pierre. *Education and Culture in the Barbarian West, Sixth through Eighth Centuries* (Columbia: University of South Carolina Press, 1976).

_____. "La survivance des écoles publiques en Gaulau Ve siècle," *Le moyen âge* 63 (Brussels, 1957), 421-436.

Richmond, Sir Ian Archibald. *Roman and Native in North Britain* (Edinburgh: Nelson, 1958).

_____, and Osberht Guy Stanhope Crawford, "The British Section of the Ravenna Cosmography," *Archaeologia Cambrensis* 93 (Cardiff, 1949), 1-50.

Roberts, Brynley F., ed. "*Culhwch ac Olwen*, The Triads, Saints' Lives," *The Arthur of the Welsh*. eds. Rachel Bromwich, Alfred O.H. Jarman, and Brynley F. Roberts (Cardiff: University of Wales Press, 1991), 73-95.

_____. *Early Welsh Poetry: Studies in the Book of Aneirin* (Aberystwyth: National Library of Wales, 1988).

Roberts, William I. *Romano-Saxon Pottery* (Oxford: B.A.R., 1982).

Rosenthal, Joel Thomas, ed. *Kings and Kingship, Acta 11* (Binghamton: Center for Medieval and Early Renaissance Studies, State University of New York at Binghamton, 1986).

Rowland, Jenny. *Early Welsh Saga Poetry* (Cambridge: D.S. Brewer, 1990).

_____. "A Study of the Saga Englynion," unpublished Ph.D. thesis, Aberystwyth, 1982.

Salway, Peter. *Roman Britain* (Oxford: Oxford University Press, 1984).

Sawyer, Peter H., and Ian N. Wood, eds. *Early Medieval Kingship* (Leeds: University of Leeds, 1977).

Schaffner, Paul. "Britain's Iudices," *Gildas: New approaches*. eds. David N. Dumville and Michael Lapidge (Woodbridge: Boydell Press, 1984), 151-155.

Sharpe, Richard. "Gildas as the Father of the Church," *Gildas: New Approaches*. eds. David N.

Dumville and Michael Lapidge (Woodbridge: Boydell Press, 1984), 193–205.

Sims-Williams, Patrick. "The Death of Urien," *CMCS* 32 (Cardiff, 1996), 25–26.

———. "The Emergence of Old Welsh, Cornish, and Breton Orthography, 600–800: The Evidence of Archaic Old Welsh," *BBCS* 38 (Cardiff, 1991), 20–86.

———. "Gildas and the Anglo-Saxons," *CMCS* 6 (Cambridge, 1983a), 1–30.

———. *Religion and Literature in Western England, 600–800* (Cambridge: Cambridge University Press, 1990).

———. "The Settlement of England in Bede and the *Chronicle*," *ASE* 12 (London, 1983b), 1–41.

Sisam, Kenneth. "Anglo-Saxon Royal Genealogies," *PBA* 39 (London, 1953), 287–348.

Stenton, Frank Merry. *Anglo-Saxon England* (Oxford: Clarendon, 1947).

———. "The Foundations of English History," *TRHS* 9 (London, 1926), 163–164.

———. "The South-Western Element in the Old English Chronicle," *Essays in Medieval History Presented to Thomas Frederick Tout* (Manchester: University of Manchester Press, 1925), 15–24.

Stevens, Courtenay Edward. "Gildas sapiens," *EHR* 56 (London, 1941), 353–373.

———. "Marcus, Gratian, Constantine" *Athenaeum* 35 (New Haven, 1957), 316–347.

Strachan, John. "The Verbal System of Psaltair na Rann," *Transactions of the Philological Society* (Oxford, 1895), 1–76.

Sweet, Henry. "Some of the Sources of the *Anglo-Saxon Chronicle*," *Englische Studien* 2 (Leipzig, 1879), 310–312.

Tatlock, John Strong Perry. *The Legendary History of Britain: Geoffrey of Monmouth's Historia Regum Britanniae and Its Vernacular Versions* (Berkeley: University of California Press, 1950).

Taylor, C.C. "The Nature of Romano-British Countryside." *The End of Roman Britain*. ed. Dillon Miles (London, 1983), 1–15.

Thomas, Charles. *Christianity in Roman Britain to A.D. 500* (Berkeley: University of California Press, 1981).

Thompson, Edward A. "Britain, A.D. 406–410," *Brit* 8 (Stroud, 1977), 303–318.

———. "Gildas and the History of Britain," *Brit* 10 (Stroud, 1979), 203–226.

———. *The Historical Work of Ammianus Marcellinus* (Cambridge: University Press, 1947).

———. *St. Germanus of Auxerre and the End of Roman Britain* (Woodbridge: Boydell and Brewer, 1984).

———. "St. Patrick and Coroticus," *JTS* 31 (London, 1980), 12–27.

———. "Zosimus 6.10.2 and the Letters of Honorius," *CQ* 32 (London, 1982), 445–462.

Thurneysen, Rudolf. *A Grammar of Old Irish* (Dublin: Dublin Institute for Advanced Studies, 1946).

———. "Wann sind die Germanen nach England gekommen?"

Todd, Malcom. *Roman Britain, 55 B.C.–A.D. 400. The Province Beyond Ocean* (Brighton, UK: Harvester Press, 1981).

Turville-Petre, Joan E. "Hengest and Horsa," *Saga-Book of the Viking Society* 14 (London, 1953–1957), 273–290.

Vansina, Jan. *Oral Tradition as History* (Madison: University of Wisconsin Press, 1985).

Vries, Jan de. "Das Königtum bei den Germanen," *Saeculum* 7 (Munich, 1956), 289–309.

———. "Die Ursprungssage der Sachsen," *Niedersächen Jarhbuch für Landesgeschichte* 31 (Berlin, 1959), 20–37.

Wacher, John. *The Towns of Roman Britain* (London: B.T. Batsford, 1974).

Wade-Evans, Arthur W. "The Origin of Cornwall," *Notes and Queries* 193 (London, 1948), 289–292.

———. *Welsh Christian Origins* (Oxford: The Alden Press, 1934).

Wallace-Hadrill, A., ed. *Patronage in Ancient Society* (London: Routledge, 1989).

Wallace-Hadrill, John Michael. *Early Germanic Kingship in England and on the Continent* (Oxford: Clarendon Press, 1971).

Walsh, Paul. "The Dating of the Irish Annals," *IHS* 2 (Dublin, 1940–1941), 355–375.

Webster, Leslie. "Death's Diplomacy: Sutton in the Light of Other Male Princely Burials," *Sutton Hoo: Fifty Years After*. ed. Robert T. Farrell and Carol L. Neuman de Vegvar (Oxford, OH: American Early Medieval Studies, Miami University, Department of Art, 1992), 75–82.

Welch, Martin. "The Kingdom of the South Saxons: The Origins," *The Origins of the Anglo-Saxon Kingdoms*. ed. Stephen Bassett (Leicester: Leicester University Press, 1989), 75–83.

Wells, Calvin. *Bones, Bodies and Disease* (London: Thames and Hudson, 1964).

Wheeler, G. Henry. "Gildas' *De Excidio* Chapter 26," *EHR* 41 (London, 1926), 497–503.

Williams, Griffith John, and Evan John Jones. *Gramadegau'r Penceirddiaid* (Cardiff: Gwasg Prifysgol Cymru, 1934).

Williams, Hugh. *Gildae De Excidio Britanniae* (London: Published for the Honourable Society of Cymmrodorion, 1899).

Williams, Sir Ifor. *The Beginnings of Welsh Poetry*. ed. Rachel Bromwich. Cardiff: University of Wales Press, 1972.

———. "Marwnad Cynddylan," *BBCS* 6 (Cardiff, 1932), 134–141.

———. *Wales and the North* (S.l.: Kendall, 1952).

Williams, N.J.A. "Llywarch Hen and the Finn Cycle," *Astudiaethau ar yr Hengerdd*. ed. Rachel Bromwich and R. Brinley Jones (Cardiff: Gwasg Prifysgol Cymru, 1978), 234–265.

Wood, Ian N. "The End of Roman Britain: Continental Evidence and Parallels," *Gildas: New Approaches*. eds. David N. Dumville and Michael

Lapidge (Woodbridge: Boydell Press, 1984), 1–25.

———. "Kings, Kingdoms and Consent," *Early Medieval Kingship*. eds. Peter H. Sawyer and Ian N. Wood (Leeds: University of Leeds Press, 1977), 1–30.

Wormald, Patrick. "Bede and Benedict Biscop," *Famulus Christi: Essays in Commemoration of the Thirteenth Centenary of the Birth of the Venerable Bede*. ed. Gerald Bonner (London: S.P.C.K., 1976), 141–169.

———. "Engla Land: The Making of an Allegiance," *Journal of Sociology* 7:1 (London, 1994), 1–24.

Wright, Neil. "Gildas's Geographical Perspective: Some Problems," *Gildas: New Approaches*. eds. David N. Dumville and Michael Lapidge (Woodbridge: Boydell Press, 1984), 85–105.

———. "Gildas's Prose Style and Its Origins," *Gildas: New Approaches*. eds. David N. Dumville and Michael Lapidge (Woodbridge: Boydell Press, 1984), 107–128.

Yorke, Barbara. "The Jutes of Hampshire and Wight and the Origins of Wessex," *The Origins of the Anglo-Saxon Kingdoms*. ed. Stephen Bassett (Leicester: Leicester University Press, 1989), 84–96.

———. "The Kingdom of the East Saxons," *ASE* 14 (London, 1985), 1–30.

———. *Kings and Kingdoms of Early Anglo-Saxon England* (London: Routledge, 1990).

Index

Aed Slane 38, 122–5, 127
Aedan, Bishop 54, 114, 166, 226
Aedán son of Gabrán 110, 114, 118, 122, 124–8, 132, 135, 155–6, 163, 170, 219
Ælfwine 115, 117, 120, 125, 145–6, 154, 199, 218–9
Ælle 113, 117, 129, 146–7, 155, 204, 219
Aeneid 80
Æsc 78, 83, 240
Æscwine 150, 152, 164, 200, 224
Æthelberht 35–6, 54, 76–80, 82–5, 91, 112–3, 117, 149, 159, 208, 222, 229, 239
Æthelfrith son of Æthelric 105, 113, 117, 128, 144–5, 154, 157, 182, 198, 203–4, 218, 229
Æthelfrith son of Oswiu 115, 117, 129
Æthelred, King of Mercia 115, 117, 150, 161, 171, 199, 222
Æthelwalh 115, 117, 120, 171
Ætius 11–12, 19, 62, 70, 79, 98, 101, 215–7
Agricola, Bishop 55, 61, 166, 174, 179, 229
Ailbe 122–3, 126, 153, 155, 157, 164, 165, 170, 174, 177–9, 181, 229
Aillil Molt 122–3, 127–8, 134, 219
Ainmire 110, 122–8
Albinus 57, 74–5, 156, 167, 174, 179, 226
Alcock, Leslie 12, 231, 241, 242
Aldfrith 26, 119–21, 145, 154, 156, 166, 169, 182, 199, 218
Aldhelm 55, 116, 118, 241
Alfred 42–3

Alhflæd 114, 145, 199, 218
Ambrosius 10–12, 70, 88, 93–95, 105, 107, 166, 174, 179, 208, 215, 219, 229, 241
Ammianus Marcellinus 16–17
Aneirin 21–2, 24–6, 63, 112–3, 135, 183, 220
Anglo-Saxon Chronicle 13, 42–3, 69, 71, 77–79, 82–3, 86, 90, 100–1, 154–61, 163–4, 239, 240, 241
Annales Cambriae 24, 38–9, 93–4, 101, 137, 154–8, 161, 211, 241
Annals of Innisfallen 38
Annals of Tigernach 38, 126, 153
Annals of Ulster 38, 123, 236
Ansehis 68, 82–5, 100
Arfderydd, Battle of 157, 159, 162–3, 205–6
Arthmael 57, 166, 174, 176, 179, 228
Arthur 12, 42, 73, 93, 157, 162, 165–6, 174, 179, 192, 203, 208, 213–4, 215, 223, 241
Athrwys 108–9, 132, 175, 180
Augustine, Archbishop 33, 113, 118, 127, 144, 204
Aurelius Caninus 107, 165–6, 168, 174, 177, 179
Austolus, Bishop 57, 169, 176, 179, 227

Badon, Battle of 12–13, 93–5, 107, 166, 229, 236, 241
Bangor 27, 37–8, 101, 122, 123, 125, 127, 128, 129, 159, 181
Battle of Finnsburg 13, 84
Bede 6, 14, 16, 27, 32–3, 37, 43, 54–7, 65, 69, 74–7, 79–80, 82–3, 85–7, 91, 100, 102, 113, 116–7, 119–20, 137, 144, 152, 198, 229, 235, 240, 241
Benedict Biscop 55, 115, 116, 118, 121–2, 166, 167, 174, 179, 225
Benlli 31, 107, 168, 174, 179
Berhtwald 55, 116, 118, 120–1, 171, 174, 179, 225
Bernacus 57, 176, 179, 228
Bertha 79–80, 112
Beuno 57, 139, 159, 162, 163, 166–8, 171, 174, 176, 179, 181, 184, 221, 228
Black Book of Carmarthen 42
Book of Llandaff 26
Bosa 55, 115, 118, 120, 171, 174, 179, 226
Breaca 155, 170–1, 174, 176, 179, 201, 226
Brendan 126–8, 155, 164
Brennych 144, 153, 179, 225
Bretwalda 113, 208, 229
Bridei son of Maelchu 110, 126–8, 136–7, 154, 162, 167, 172–4, 183, 221–2
Brioc 57, 156, 158, 165, 167, 170, 174, 176–9, 227
Brochmael 136–7, 162, 167, 171, 174, 176, 179, 184, 223
Budic 111–2, 132, 154, 162–3, 170, 174, 179, 183, 218
Bugi 139, 159, 181, 184, 221

Cadell 31, 87–8, 107, 138–9, 168, 174, 179, 184, 214, 223
Cadfan 57, 136, 139, 159, 162–3, 166–7, 171, 174, 176, 179, 182–3, 221, 228
Cadoc, St. 57, 139, 153, 155, 157–9, 165, 167–71, 174, 177–9, 184, 201, 211, 221, 227
Cadwaladr son of Cadwallon

253

39, 136, 154, 159, 181, 183, 188, 221
Cadwallon son of Cadfan 26, 39, 91, 114, 117, 124, 136, 154, 156, 159, 162, 166–8, 174, 176, 179, 181, 183, 221, 229
Cadwallon son of Einion 29, 136, 183, 187, 221
Cædwalla 33, 115–7, 120, 150, 164, 200, 224
Cainnech 124, 126, 128, 158, 167
Canterbury 74–5, 79, 81, 82, 242
Canu Heledd 40, 88
Canu Llywarch Hen 22, 41
Canu Taliesin 22, 233
Caradoc son of Ynyr 158, 167, 169, 174, 178
Carantoc 57, 203
Catraeth 105, 112–3, 174, 179, 203, 205–6, 229
Caw 164, 172, 174, 192, 221
Ceadda 55, 115, 118, 150, 199–200, 224
Ceawlin 77, 113, 150, 163–4, 174, 179, 199–200, 224
Ceneu 142, 203
Cenwalh of Wessex 114–5, 117, 150, 164, 200
Ceolfrith 32, 55–6, 121
Ceolwulf of Wessex 150, 152, 164, 199–200, 224
Cerdic 39, 43, 112–3, 117, 135, 183, 220, 236
Ceredig of Strathclyde 17, 62–3, 93, 140, 169, 171, 174, 179, 181, 208, 224
Ceredigion 154, 188, 203, 218, 226
Chanao 111–2, 141, 167, 224
Chester, Battle of 39, 119, 122, 137, 154, 160, 162, 182, 229, 241
Chronicle of Ireland 37–8
Claudian 17, 216
Clydno 113, 140, 153, 159, 163–4, 170, 174, 179, 194, 205, 218
Coel 142–3, 203, 207–8, 241
Cœnred 120, 150, 156, 161, 174, 179, 200
Cœnwalh 119–21, 171
Colgu 122–4, 127, 134, 219
Colman, Bishop 55, 115, 118, 120, 123–4, 127–9, 134
Columba 55, 57, 87, 110–1, 113, 116, 118, 124, 126–8, 155, 163, 167–9, 171–2, 211, 226, 229
Columbanus 20, 27, 55, 114, 118

Comgall 37, 110, 122–4, 126–8, 130, 132, 135, 219
Conall Crandomna 37, 123, 125, 132, 135, 219
Conall son of Comgall 110, 122–4, 127–8, 132, 135, 219
Confessio 17, 56
Constantine, Emperor 10, 59–60, 96–7, 203, 210
Constantine of Cornwall 57, 62, 107, 155, 157, 165–6, 168, 170, 174, 177–9, 185, 207, 218–9
Corentin 57, 154–5, 157, 160, 168, 174, 176–7, 179, 228
Cornouailles 132, 154, 176, 183, 211, 218
Council of Austerfield 120–1
Council of Orleans 111
Council of Paris 110–1, 157, 169–70, 178
Council of Toledo 56, 170
Crith Gablach 35
Cuichelm 115, 118
Cunedda 13, 41, 88, 136, 159, 183, 203–5, 207, 216, 221, 229
Cuneglasus 107, 165–6, 168, 174, 177, 180
Cunomorus 110–1, 155–7, 163–8, 170, 174, 176–8, 180, 182, 185, 212, 218
Cutha 77, 150, 152, 163–4, 199–200, 224
Cuthbert 55, 116, 118–9, 166–7, 174, 180, 225, 235
Cybr Daniel 132, 163, 183, 211, 218
Cynan Garwyn 21, 112, 139, 157, 162, 167, 170–1, 174, 176, 179, 180
Cynddylan 24, 78, 141, 162, 167, 219
Cyndrwynyn 24, 141, 219
Cynegils 114, 117, 150, 164, 199–200, 224
Cynon son of Clydno 113, 140, 179–80, 194, 205, 218, 224
Cynric 43, 150, 199

Dalriada 36–7, 40, 43, 105, 124–6, 129–30, 132–4, 155, 211, 213, 219, 226, 229
Daniel of Gwynedd 159, 181
Daniel of West Saxons 32, 116, 118
David 20, 30, 44, 55, 142–3, 153, 155, 157–60, 164–5, 167–71, 175–8, 180, 182, 185–6, 201, 211, 214, 227, 242

De Excidio Britanniae 14, 19, 27, 56, 63, 81, 86, 107, 211
Degsastan, Battle of 113, 154, 177, 204, 229
Deira 24, 33, 76–7, 114, 145–7, 154–6, 182, 204, 219, 226
Din Eidyn 28, 113, 179, 208, 216
Docco 57, 110, 155, 158, 163, 168, 170, 175, 177–8, 180, 201, 226
Domangart 110, 122–9, 132, 135, 155, 219
Domnall Brecc 123–5, 129, 132–3, 135, 219
Domnall son of Erc 110–1, 122–7, 134, 219
Drest I 161, 172–3
Druim Cett 110, 124
Dubonnia 78, 88–9, 94, 157, 213, 219, 226, 229
Dubricius 55, 107, 109–10, 157–8, 165, 175, 177, 180, 211, 226
Dumnonie 135, 211, 220, 226
Dumville, David N. 23–25, 31, 71, 76, 231, 237, 238, 240
Durham 78, 157, 163
Dwg 41, 162, 237
Dwywei 113, 135, 183, 220
Dyfed 36, 38, 41, 76–77, 87, 91–2, 94, 101–2, 143, 157, 186–7, 195, 203, 214, 220, 227, 229, 237

Eadbald 113–4, 117, 149, 159, 168, 182, 222
Eadric 36, 149, 222
Eanflæd 26, 114–5, 117, 119–20, 146, 154, 156, 219
Earconwald 55, 115, 118, 161
East Anglia 11, 13, 114–5, 147, 157, 199, 220
Eata 55, 115–6, 118–9, 154, 166, 175, 180, 225
Ecgfrith 25–6, 119–21, 156, 166, 168
Edwin 24–6, 37, 39, 112–4, 117–8, 122, 129–30, 146, 154–6, 159, 168, 170, 219, 229
Elafius 19, 61, 63, 238
Eliseg 30, 87–9, 92, 138, 184, 223
Elmet 24, 39, 112–3, 135, 158, 179, 181, 183, 204–5, 220
Enda 153, 155, 163, 167–8, 171, 175, 177–8, 180, 201, 225
Enodoc 57, 155, 181
Eochaid Allmuir 186, 203, 220
Eochaid Buide 122, 132, 134–5

Index

Eochaid son of Domnall 110–1, 122, 126, 219
Eoganan 110, 124–5, 128, 132, 135, 219
Eorpwald 114, 118, 147, 158, 168, 175, 180, 199, 220
Eosterwine 56, 121–2, 166, 175, 180, 225
Epistola ad Coroticum 56, 62, 106
Essex 11, 70, 75, 148, 158, 161, 220
Eurgain 136, 159, 181, 183, 221

Fergus 37, 110–1, 123–8, 132, 134, 219
Fintan 122, 127, 201, 229
foederati 68–70, 74, 82, 84, 87, 96–8, 100, 215, 217
Frithuwald 144, 161, 177, 180, 198, 204

Gabran 37, 110, 122–4, 126–8, 130, 132, 134–5, 155, 219
Gallic Chronicles 17, 69, 217
Garmon 30–2, 86–9, 107, 110, 168–9, 175, 180, 226
Germanus 9, 11, 17–19, 30–2, 44, 60–1, 70, 86, 110, 186, 229, 238, 241
Gildas 1, 3, 6, 9, 13–14, 16, 19–20, 27, 32–3, 41, 56–7, 62–4, 66, 70, 72, 76, 79, 81–2, 84, 86–7, 91, 93–4, 100–1, 107, 122–3, 139, 155–8, 162–8, 170–1, 175, 177–8, 180, 192, 203, 207–8, 211, 215–7, 221, 229, 231, 232, 240, 242
Glywising 78, 138–9, 158, 165, 177, 221, 227, 242
Godian 160, 170, 175, 178, 180–1, 201, 222
Gododdin 21–2, 25–6, 28–9, 41, 111–3, 159, 189–90, 204–5, 216, 221
Gorthen 112, 179–80, 189, 221
Gradlon 154, 156, 164, 167–8, 175–7, 179–80, 211, 223
Gregory of Tours 20, 24, 57, 79, 111
Gregory the Great 20, 113
Grugyn 113, 174, 179–80
Guitolin 93–5, 100, 166, 175, 180, 220, 241
Gwallog 21, 112, 135, 142, 154, 158, 162, 168–71, 175, 177, 180, 183, 205, 220
Gwrtheyrn 1, 6–7, 30, 41, 75–7, 86–94, 100–1, 107, 168, 175, 180, 191, 208, 213–4, 220

Gwynlliw 139, 157–8, 166, 171, 175, 178, 180, 184, 201, 221

Hadrian 17, 60–1, 65, 96–7, 115, 118
Hadrian's Wall 10, 13, 17, 75, 143, 216
Harleian 3859 38, 41, 236
Heathfield, Synod of 115, 117, 119
Heledd 40, 141, 219
Hengest 6–7, 11–14, 33, 74–9, 81–4, 86, 90, 100, 102, 159
Hereric 113, 117–8, 146, 219
Herodotus 12, 14, 47
Hilda 56, 113, 115, 118, 120
Historia Brittonum 3, 7, 16, 23–5, 30–2, 36, 39–41, 74, 76–9, 82, 86–7, 89–91, 94, 100–2, 130, 144, 153–61, 172, 198, 204, 208, 231, 234, 237, 240, 241
Historia Ecclesiastica 41, 43, 74, 77–8, 82, 86, 130, 229
Hlothere 36, 147, 149, 159–60, 199, 220
Hoernbiu 177, 180, 225
Honorius 114, 118, 175, 180, 182
Horsa 6, 11, 33, 74–6, 78, 81–4, 86, 90, 102
Hueil 164, 166, 172, 174–5, 180, 192, 208, 221
Hussa 112, 144, 154, 162, 169, 171, 175, 177, 180, 191, 204, 218
Hwaetberht 56, 167, 175, 180, 225

Idon 107–9, 158, 167, 175–6, 180–1, 193, 224
Illtud 56, 109–10, 156–8, 164–7, 170, 175–8, 180, 211, 227, 229
Ine 116, 118, 150, 164, 200, 224
Irish Annals 37–9, 51, 101, 105, 116, 129–30, 172–4
Iurminric 78, 84–5, 91–2

Jackson, Kenneth H. 24–5, 28–9
Jocelyn 28
John of Beverley 120, 171, 175, 180, 225

Kebi 57, 155, 157–9, 163, 165, 168–9, 175, 177–8, 180, 185, 201, 219, 228
Kentigern 28–9, 56, 89, 102, 110–1, 136, 155, 157, 163, 168–70, 175, 178, 180, 184, 205–6, 211, 222, 228
Koch, John T. 26–8, 205

Leon 160, 169, 177, 201, 222
Leonorus 57, 156, 158, 164–7, 170, 177–8, 211, 227
Lleu 113, 160, 174
Llywarch Hen 22–3, 41
Lupus 18–19

MacErc 122, 126
Macliau 111–2, 141, 167, 224
Madawg 113, 179–80, 205
Maelgwn 62, 89, 107, 113, 136, 153, 155, 157–9, 161, 163–71, 175–8, 180, 183, 187, 203, 205–6, 208, 214, 221
Maglorius 56–7, 109, 157, 170, 175, 178, 180, 227
Malo 56, 154, 156–7, 163, 167–70, 175–6, 178, 226
Manau 63, 160, 176, 204, 216, 228
Marwnad Cynddylan 22, 24, 40
Maucennus 56–7, 109, 153, 165, 167–70, 175, 177–8, 211, 228
Maudetus 169, 175, 177, 179, 227
Meirchion 139, 142, 185, 223
Mercia 11, 23–4, 33, 39–40, 114–6, 120, 149, 160–1, 171, 199, 222
Merfyn Frych 40–1, 204
Merovingian 52, 80
Meurig 107–9, 131–2, 136, 183
Meven 57, 156–7, 163, 169–70, 175–6, 178, 180–1, 190, 224
Miller, Molly 13, 18, 32, 47–52, 88, 109, 174, 203–4
Morgan of Gododdin 89, 111, 142, 168, 171, 175, 177, 180, 189, 204–5, 221
Muirchertach 123–4, 126–7

Nath I 122–3, 133–4, 219
Nechtan II 162, 172–3
Nechtanesmere, Battle of 26–7, 229
Niall Noígiallach 37, 87, 126, 128
Ninnoca 58, 163, 169, 171, 175, 177–8, 180, 229
Northern History 24–5, 27, 56, 89, 241
Northern Memorandum 26, 77, 101

Osthryth 115, 118, 145–6, 156, 161, 199, 218–9

Oswald 37, 56, 91, 114, 117–8, 123–4, 129, 145–6, 150, 153–4, 156, 161, 164, 199–200, 218–9, 224
Oswiu 24–7, 37, 39, 112, 119–21, 145–6, 170, 198, 218–9
Outigern 56, 86–91
Owain son of Hywel Dda 38, 41, 157, 186–7, 195, 220
Owain son of Urien 24–6, 112, 139, 142, 157, 160, 162, 169, 171, 176, 181, 185, 223

Padarn Peisrud 40, 204–5, 221
Paternus of Llanbadarn 58, 154, 157, 159–60, 168–70, 175–8, 181, 226
Paternus of Vannes 58, 154, 169, 175, 181, 226
Patrick 17, 41, 56, 61–2, 66, 106, 126, 161–2, 169, 172–3, 211, 229, 231
Paul Aurelian 58, 156, 158, 160, 164–6, 169–70, 175, 177–8, 181, 196, 201, 211, 228
Paulinus 114, 118, 159, 168, 175, 181, 226
Pelagius 9, 17, 31, 60–1, 231, 238
Penda 24, 26, 39, 114, 118, 125, 129, 150, 154, 158, 160–1, 167–8, 199, 222, 229
Petroc 56, 58, 110, 155, 157–8, 167, 170–1, 175, 178, 181, 184, 221, 227
Pillar of Eliseg 30, 87–9
Pobddelw 112–3, 136, 179, 181, 183, 205, 221
Powys 30–1, 40–1, 77, 86–9, 94, 101, 137, 139, 152, 162, 184, 191, 213–4, 223, 228, 237

Rædwald 113–4, 118, 147, 157, 199, 220
Rhodri Mawr 40–1, 101
Rhun son of Urien 24–6, 56, 58, 89, 112–3, 139, 142, 168, 170–1, 185, 223, 241
Rhydderch 26, 29, 89, 109–12, 140, 153–4, 159, 162–4, 168–71, 175, 177, 181, 205–6, 224, 234

Ricula 113, 149, 158, 222
Rieinmellth 24–6, 112, 139, 170–1, 175, 181, 185, 223
Riwal 155–6, 158, 165–7, 170, 175–9, 181, 195–6, 211, 222
romanitas 6, 60–1, 66, 74, 210
Run son of Maelgwn 136, 153, 158–9, 163–4, 167, 170, 183, 205–6, 208, 214, 221

Sæbbi 115, 117–8, 148, 220
Sæberht 118, 148–9, 158, 220, 222
Samson 20, 23, 56, 109–10, 155–8, 162–71, 175–9, 181, 201, 211, 214, 227, 229
Saxon Shore 10, 19, 68–70, 75, 101
Senchus fer n'Alban 36–7, 101, 105, 133–4
Sims-Williams, Patrick 78, 84, 215, 239, 240, 242
Soemil 155, 203
Strathclyde 21–2, 26, 28–9, 62, 111, 125, 140, 163, 204, 208, 211, 224, 228
superbus tyrannus 16, 79, 86, 91, 215
Synod of Whitby 27, 115–6

Taliesin 21–2, 26, 63–4, 112, 168, 170, 175, 181, 194, 205
Talorc IV 127, 129, 137, 162, 173, 223
Talorcan I 127, 129, 145, 162, 173, 199, 218
Tatheus 158, 167, 176, 178, 181, 227
Teilo 58, 107, 109, 154–5, 157, 162–3, 165, 169–70, 176–8, 181, 226
Theodoric, Archbishop 116, 118, 176, 181
Theodoric of the South 155, 159–60, 170–1, 176, 178, 181
Theodric 112, 144–5, 153–4, 162–3, 169–71, 176, 181, 198, 204, 218
Third Council of Paris 110, 157, 169–70, 178
Trent, Battle of 115, 117, 119, 229

Trioedd ynys Prydein 42, 190, 193, 196–7
Tudfwlch 58, 112, 140, 179, 181
Tudy 58, 154, 169, 176–7, 179, 181, 227
Tydecho 58, 157, 159–60, 162, 167–9, 171, 176–7, 181, 228
Tysilio 138–9, 157, 162, 167, 170–1, 176, 178–9, 181, 184, 228

Uinniau 27, 57, 107, 110, 127–8, 163, 165–8, 171, 173, 176–7, 181, 211, 228
Urien 21–7, 39, 41, 63, 89, 101, 105, 112–3, 139, 142, 144, 154, 159–60, 162, 164, 168–71, 176–7, 181, 185–6, 204–6, 208, 214, 223, 229, 236, 242

Vita Ceolfrith 32, 121
Vita Columbae 55, 101
Vita Cuthberti 27, 54–5, 57
Vita Garmoni 30–2, 102
Vita Germani 18, 60, 66, 238
Vita Kentigerni 28, 55–6
Vita Samsoni 23, 55–7, 242
Vortigern 10–12, 16, 74, 76, 79, 81–2, 86–7, 89, 91, 93–4, 102, 237, 241

Waroc 111–2, 141, 155, 163, 169, 171, 176–7, 181, 224
Wenefred 163, 167, 171, 176, 181, 194, 228
Wight, Isle of 76, 98, 115, 164
Wilfrid 32–3, 55–7, 115–6, 119–21, 171, 235
Winnoc 57, 111–2, 135, 156
Winwæd, Battle of 114, 119, 158, 161, 229
Winwaloe 58, 154–6, 158, 168, 170, 176–9, 181, 195, 201, 226
Woden 13, 71, 78, 84, 207, 239

Y Gododdin 21–2, 25–6, 28, 42, 63, 112–3, 172, 190, 205–6, 208, 231
Yrfai 112, 179, 181, 189, 221

Zosimus 18, 59–60, 69–70, 238